C0-AUB-773

PLATE I

Panoramic view of the excavation and the Jordan valley, from the dump north of the tell at the end of the 1964 season.

a) From n. to e. In the valley, tell Mazar. Foreground n.e. the mediaeval tell. E. the Zerqa valley

b) From e. to s.w. Foreground the ruins of the L.B. sanctuary, last phase. The stone wall to the left belongs to an earlier phase

DOCUMENTA ET MONUMENTA ORIENTIS ANTIQUI

VOLUMEN SEXTUM DECIMUM

EXCAVATIONS AT TELL DEIR ʿALLĀ

I

VT MEMORIA SERVETVR ILLORVM QVI DE HAC SERIE CONSTITVENDA ET PROPAGANDA BENE MERITI SINT

A. DE BUCK, A. FALKENSTEIN, S. R. K. GRANVILLE, B. HROZNÝ, J. KÖHLER, J. SIMONS, E. A. SPEISER

EXCAVATIONS AT TELL DEIR ʿALLĀ

I

A STRATIGRAPHICAL AND ANALYTICAL STUDY OF THE EARLY IRON AGE POTTERY

BY

H. J. FRANKEN

WITH CONTRIBUTIONS BY

J. KALSBEEK

With 82 Figures and 15 Plates

LEIDEN
E. J. BRILL
1969

PRINTED IN THE NETHERLANDS

CONTENTS

Page

List of Plates IX
List of Figures XI
Bibliography XIII
Preface XV

Introduction. 1
The aims of the expedition 1
The choice of the site. 1
Position and physical features of the tell. 2
Difficulties concerning the identification of the site 4
Administration and organization 8
Strategy and methods of excavation 11
Method of recording 15
The history of the site 19

PART ONE

THE STRATIGRAPHY OF THE IRON AGE DEPOSITS

I. The stratigraphy of Tell Deir ʿAllā (Iron Age) 25
Stratigraphy and phases 25
Terminology 26
Clay deposits and bricks 26
Walls. 27
Floors, streets and courtyards 27
Pits 29
Bread-ovens 29
Wind-blown material 30
Erosion. 30
Water 30
The earthquake cracks 31
Colours. 32
Sections 32

II. Phases A-M 33
The first period. Phases A-D 33
Phase A 33

Phase B . . . 36
Phase C . . . 40
Phase D . . . 42
The second period. Phases E-M . . . 44
Phase E . . . 44
Phase F . . . 46
Phase G . . . 48
Phase H . . . 50
Phase J . . . 53
Phase K . . . 56
Phase L . . . 59
Phase M . . . 61

PART TWO

STUDY OF THE POTTERY

III. Preliminary remarks . . . 67

IV. A systematic approach to the study of the Iron Age pottery, by J. KALSBEEK 73
The raw material . . . 73
Methods of improving the clay . . . 74
Temper . . . 75
Shrinkage . . . 77
Tiny holes in the fabric of the pot . . . 78
Break lines and flaws from shrinking . . . 79
Tools used for building and throwing pottery . . . 80

V. Survey of manufacturing different parts of a pot, by J. KALSBEEK . . . 81
Rims . . . 81
The neck . . . 83
The shoulder . . . 84
The body . . . 85
Bases . . . 86
Handles . . . 86

VI. General survey of the techniques of pot building found at Deir ʿAllā . . . 88
The use of the mould . . . 88
Coiling . . . 89
Turning without coiling . . . 91
The wheel as used in Deir ʿAllā . . . 92

The potter's kiln 94
Hand built E.I.A. pottery in Palestine. 97
Rims made of non plastic clays and the type series 99

VII. Description of the pottery and typology 102
The bases 102
Cooking pots 118
Deep bowls 133
Thin walled bowls 140
Bowls 145
Large shallow bowls 157
Jars 161
Handles. 170
Painted decoration on pottery 172

VIII. The pottery according to the phases 175
Phase A 177
Phase B. 182
Phase C. 192
Phase D 198
Phase E. 202
Phase F. 208
Phase G 212
Phase H 218
Phase J 224
Phase K 228
Phase L. 234

IX. Dating and dates 240
The evidence for dating 244
Evidence from imported material 245
Evidence from local Palestinian and Trans-Jordanian wares 246

Appendix. Some potter's terms 248

Plates II-XV . . . . at the End of the Book

LIST OF PLATES

Pl. I Panoramic view of the excavation and the Jordan valley, from the dump north of the tell at the end of the 1964 season.

a From n. to e. In the valley, tell Mazar. Foreground n.e. the mediaeval tell. E. the Zerqa valley.

b From e. to s.w. Foreground the ruins of the L.B. sanctuary, last phase. The stone wall to the left belongs to an earlier phase.

Pl. II a Tell Deir ʿAllā, looking n.

b Tell Deir ʿAllā, looking w.

Pl. III a Tell Deir ʿAllā, looking s. (1960)

b Tell Deir ʿAllā, looking e.

Pl. IV a Photograph of section 5.50/15.50-20, with earthquake crack, dated to phase C.

b Section drawing of the same.

Pl. V a A typical section through phases A-D courtyard deposits. Section to the left cf. fig. 3. The black burnt deposit clearly shows the disruptions by the shifting of the earth. In the centre: collapsed sides of a pit. Looking s.

b Trench D, looking s. Foreground phase A courtyards. Burnt floor of B 1 furnace. Top left the round tower, (wall K 13), cut through wall F (G) 8. Below the round tower remains of wall E 7 and phase D courtyards.

Pl. VI a Phase A stone pavement (E 619), immediately on top of the ruins of the unfinished rebuilding of the L.B. sanctuary, looking s.e. To the left ash deposits from D 908, sunken into a pit.

b Phase A accumulation over the red burnt L.B. ruins. Thick ash deposit (D 908), interrupted by pits and cracks.

Pl. VII a Phase B furnaces and walls B 5 and 4, looking s.e. Three furnace floors run up against wall B 5.

b Phase F bread ovens in section, with thick ash deposits on the right. Cf. fig. 82, 0.50/16-18.

Pl. VIII a Phase G bread ovens between walls G 3 and 4, looking s.

b Foreground wall F (G) 8 and walls F 7-6, looking w. N. of wall F 6 the stone fill. Wall G 9 is seen in section built over the stone fill of the phase F building.

Pl. IX a Wall F 8 in section, showing the reed 'foundation' and cracks running through it.

b Wall J 3 and wooden beam underneath. On the left wall J 1.

Pl. X a Phase J road levels, looking s., and stone pavement running along wall J 1.

b Phase K, wall K 13, the round tower dug into the ruins of wall F 8.

Pl. XI a Phase M, wall M 5.

b Phase M cistern, showing the circular pattern of the compressed fill in horizontal section.

Pl. XII Fill of phase M cistern near the surface. In the centre, a wall of a house built on a clay deposit over the cistern with stone floor. In the burnt debris of this house, a mediaeval grave.

Pl. XIII Bases.

Pl. XIV Iron Age pottery.

Pl. XV Iron Age pottery.

LIST OF FIGURES

1 Contour map of Tell Deir ʿAllā, showing the position of the area 11
2 Plan of squares and sections in the excavated area 13
3 Example of section drawing with description of the deposits 31
4 Plan of phase A 33
5 Plan of phase B 36
6 Plan of two furnaces 37
7 Section through furnaces 38
8 Plan of phase C 41
9 Plan of phase D 42
10 Plan of phase E 44
11 Plan of phase F 47
12 Plan of phase G 48
13 Plan of phase H 51
14 Plan of phase J 54
15 Wall J 4 in section 55
16 Plan of phase K 56
17 Schematic drawing of the process of accumulation and denudation between periods II and III 57
18 Plan of phase L 59
19 Plan of phase M 62
20 Bases of jars, construction drawing 103
21 Bases of small bowls and lamps, construction drawing 105
22 Juglets, construction drawing 106
23 'Industry' pot, construction drawing 107
24 Ring bases, construction drawing 113
25a Bases, types 2 to 7, statistical chart 110
25b Bases, types 8 to 11, ring bases, statistical chart 118
26 Late Bronze Age cooking pot type 2, construction drawing 118
27 Cooking pot type 1, construction drawing 120
28 Cooking pot type 2, construction drawing 123
29 Cooking pot type 2, the variants 125
30 Cooking pot type 3, construction drawing 128
31 Cooking pots types 1 to 3, statistical chart 132
32 Deep bowls types 1 to 3, construction drawing 133
33 Deep bowls types 1 to 3, statistical chart 140
34 Bowls type 4, rim variants 141

35 Bowls type 4, statistical chart . . . 141
36 Bowls types 5 to 16, rim shapes . . . 147
37 Bowls types 5 to 16, statistical chart . . . 148
38 Bowls types 5 to 16, wall shapes, statistical chart . . . 149
39 Bowls types 4 to 16, burnishing, statistical chart . . . 150
40 Bowls types 17 to 18, construction drawing . . . 158
41 Bowls types 17 to 18, statistical chart . . . 159
42 Jars type 1, construction drawing . . . 161
43 Jars type 1, statistical chart . . . 163
44 Jars type 2, statistical chart . . . 168
45-47 Phase A . . . 177-181
48-52 Phase B . . . 182-191
53-55 Phase C . . . 192-197
56-57 Phase D . . . 198-201
58-60 Phase E . . . 202-207
61-62 Phase F . . . 208-211
63-65 Phase G . . . 212-217
66-68 Phase H . . . 218-223
69-70 Phase J . . . 224-227
71-73 Phase K . . . 228-233
74-76 Phase L . . . 234-238
77 Deep bowls phases H, J and K . . . 239
78 Chart illustrating the percentages of the main types through phases B-L . . 241
79 Statistical chart of the main types of phases A-L . . . 242
80 East section of the excavated area . . . } Following the Plates
81 South section of the excavated area . . . } Following the Plates
82 West section of the excavated area . . . } Following the Plates

The figures are drawn by J. Kalsbeek, B. C. Dekker and A. J. Cool.

BIBLIOGRAPHY

Albright, W. F.	1932	Annual of the American Schools of Oriental Research. Tell Beit Mirsim Vol. xii
	1940	Bulletin of the American Schools of Oriental Research no. 90
Amiran, R.	1963	The Ancient Pottery of Eretz Yisrael. Jerusalem
Dothan, M.	1955	Atiqot Vol. i
Franken, H. J.	1962	Vetus Testamentum Vol. xii
	1964	Vetus Testamentum Vol. xiv
	1965	Antiquity Vol. 39
Glueck, N.	1945-'49	AASOR Vol. xxv-xxviii Explorations in Eastern Palestine iv
Hamilton, R. W.	1934	Quarterly of the Department of Antiquities of Palestine Vol. iv
Kelso, J. L. and Thorley, J. P.	1943	AASOR Vol. xxi-xxii
Leach, B.	1951	A Potter's Book. London
Matson, F. R.	1966	Ceramics and Man. London
Noth, M.	1938	Das Buch Josua. Tübingen
Rieth, A.	1960	5000 Jahre Töpferscheibe. Konstanz
Rothenberg, B.	1965	Excavations at Timna. Museum Haaretz Telaviv, Bulletin no. 7
Shepard, A. O.	1961	Ceramics for the Archaeologist. Washington
Tufnell, O.	1940	Lachish Vol. ii. The Fosse Temple. London
	1958	Lachish Vol. iv. The Bronze Age. London
Yadin, Y c.s.	1958	Hazor Vol. i. Jerusalem

PREFACE

It was originally intended that this volume should contain a full report of four seasons' excavation of the Iron Age strata at Deir 'Allā. While working on the pottery of this site in the last few years it became increasingly clear, however, that the first volume should rather be confined to ceramic studies. The new light thrown on the methods of pot-making in the Early Iron Age resulting from this study, and the consequent new approach to the study of hand-made pottery as published here, seem to me to be of a much wider archaeological and anthropological interest than a mere catalogue of the Trans-Jordanian-village ceramic repertoire would be in itself.

The first part of the general introduction is followed by a stratigraphical study of the Iron Age levels, as this is necessary for the understanding of the division into phases used in the pottery study. The second part of the ceramic study is based on lines of inquiry suggested or followed up by *J. Kalsbeek*, a member of the team since 1961, who is a potter and sculptor. It was a very great advantage to have someone working with me who was an experienced craftsman, capable and willing to experiment and put any number of theories to the test and whose eyes are trained to see even the tiniest clues to his methods of work that the ancient potter may unwittingly have left in his finished product.

The initiative in beginning the study of Palestinian "antiquities" within the Theological Faculty at Leiden was taken by Prof. P. A. H. de Boer after we had travelled together through several countries in the Near East in 1953. The Dutch Organization for Pure Scientific Research at The Hague first made it financially possible for me to be trained in Palestinian field work at Jericho, where I worked under Miss K. M. Kenyon, and then stimulated the plan for a Dutch excavation in the Jordan valley in 1959 by offering to finance the enterprise. The object of the excavation was to collect material for a detailed stratigraphical study of the chronology of the end of the Late Bronze Age and the Early Iron Age.

In the summer of 1959 the first contacts were made with the Department of Antiquities of the Hashemite Kingdom of Jordan, and the expedition was able to start work in December 1959. We excavated for three months during the winter seasons of 1960, 1961, 1962 and 1964. In 1961 I was given a grant to study material in the Palestine Archaeological Museum in Jerusalem during that summer.

It is a pleasure to be able to acknowledge my indebtedness to all those who have contributed in many ways to the accomplishment of this piece of research, both in Jordan and Holland. At the head of any list of acknowledgements must first come Dr. A. Dajani and the staff of the Department of Antiquities in the Hashemite Kingdom of Jordan, who warmly welcomed the expedition and provided us with every facility and practical help. Representatives of the department were: S. Rashid (1960), A. Ajash (1961), M. Darwish (1962), M. Obeid and M. Jamra (1964).

Saleh Mouasher Bey, the owner of the tell, kindly gave us his permission to excavate there, to make soundings in his lands in search for the ancient cemeteries, and to use a large open space west of the village as a camp site. In 1960 and 1961 use was made of some village rooms belonging to him and during our absence all the camp equipment was stored on his farm at Deir ʿAllā.

The mukhtar of the village, Sheik Abu Feisal, treated the team as his guests and protégés, and in so doing truly represented the whole village community. We are also most grateful for the cordial relationship we enjoyed with the staff of the Agricultural Research Station, and in particular with the ungrudging practical help of Alexander Corbrusli.

We not infrequently had to ask for material help in the form of camp equipment, the loan of books, etc. and this was most generously given at various times by the Palestine Museum, the Arab Legion, the British School of Archaeology, the American School of Oriental Research and the École Biblique. Due to Mrs. C. M. Bennett's hospitality and enthusiasm, many of the team profited from the facilities of the British School of Archaeology in Jerusalem. Our photographer was also able to make use of the dark room there.

Visitors to the site who helped us greatly by discussing the archaeological problems were: Dr. A. Dajani, Miss K. M. Kenyon, Prof. P. W. Lapp, Mr. Y. Sa'ad, R. de Vaux, O.P. and Prof. H. T. Waterbolk.

In Holland technical help and advice on statistical method was given by Dr. W. R. van Zwet.

The thin slides used in the second part of this study were prepared and analysed by J. van Leeuwen and G. D. Ave Lallemand, Geological Dept., Leiden University. The carbon 14 datings were provided by Dr. J. C. Vogel, University of Groningen.

Mrs T. Mulder and Miss Y. Kerkhof typed and re-typed the MSS and my wife crossed the t's and dotted the i's of my English.

The team members were as follows

Site supervisor

1960 – Prof. Dr. H. Brunsting, Miss R. Lahr, E. Schroten, L. Veenendaal
1961 – W. Ettema, S. Koopmans, J. F. van Regteren Altena, H. H. van Regteren Altena
1962 – J. P. Eggink, Miss V. I. Kerkhof, S. Runia, Miss M. J. Versteeg
1964 – J. A. Bakker, J. Berry (English), Miss M. J. Versteeg

Draughtsman

1960–64 W. Ball (English)
1962 – B. Jonk
1964 – O. Cosijn

Photographer

1960 – L. Grollenberg, OP
1961–64 S. Scholten

Surveyor

1960 – N. W. Schmidt
1961 – P. Koetsier

Repair and conservation

1960-64 Mrs. C. A. Franken-Battershill
1962-64 Miss V. I. Kerkhof

Ceramic analysis

1961 and 1964 J. Kalsbeek

Registration

1960-64 Mrs. C. A. Franken-Battershill

Housekeeper

1960 – Mrs. C. A. Schmidt-Flürscheim
1961 – Miss L. Schouten
1962-64 Miss C. G. Hänisch ten Cate (Mrs. Bakker)

Field director

1960-64 Dr. H. J. Franken

Miss Diana Kirkbride (Mrs H. Helbaek) (English) was a member of the team during the 1960 and 1961 seasons. She was in charge of reconnaisance work and the search for cemeteries. It was largely due to her that such good relationships were established between the expedition and local authorities. In 1961 H. Wiersma was her assistant.

Other members of the team for a shorter spell were

Americans

Dr. P. W. Lapp
Dr. A. van Röhr Sauer
Mr. and Mrs. N. Totten

English

Miss C. Pickard (Mrs. Norton)

French

Mlle. D. Auscher

Netherlands

Dr. J. H. Bannier
J. B. H. Otker
Dr. W. G. N. v. d. Sleen
Prof. Dr. H. T. Waterbolk
Father Willemse

It is with very deep regret that I have to record the death of Egbert Schroten, student of Arabic and a valuable member of the team in 1960.

INTRODUCTION

The Aims of the Expedition

When, in 1960, the author was given the opportunity of excavating a site in Palestine or Trans-Jordan,[1] it was decided that research should be made into the cultural development of the transition from the Late Bronze Age into and including the Early Iron Age. This research was to be, first and foremost, of a chronological nature. That is to say, it was not the intention of the expedition to excavate a site for its historical potential nor yet even for its social or anthropological interest, though, of course, neither of these aspects could be ignored. At the time that the expedition was being prepared extremely little accurate chronological material for this period was available. The need for a closely detailed chronological sequence of pottery and other artifacts was urgent. A considerable corpus of material of this period was available in museums and published in typologies based on stylistic criteria. These typologies fitted into a rather broadly differentiated and loosely fixed time scale, which could only be drawn tighter if a large-scale excavation could provide a typology based on stratigraphical rather than stylistic criteria.

A secondary aim of the expedition was to train Dutch archaeologists in the techniques of excavation in the Middle East. This excavation was the first in which Dutch archaeologists had turned their attention to a Middle Eastern tell, and the limited aims of the expedition were ideal for putting new archaeological techniques into practice and evolving others. With a team largely inexperienced in excavating outside Europe this research programme, which demanded slow and patient excavation in a comparatively compact area of space and within a limited time range, proved very satisfactory from a didactic point of view.

The Choice of Site

The period of transition between the Late Bronze and Iron Ages is an exceptionally interesting, important and confused period of Canaanite and Hebrew history, and has attracted archaeologists no less than Old Testament scholars since the days of Petrie. Yet the centuries covering this period can still be called the Dark Ages of Palestinian history. As the transition from the one culture to the other appears from Biblical evidence to be largely bound up with population movements and the infiltration of non-Canaanite tribes into Palestine, with at least some of these thrusts coming from

[1] The use of Palestine and Trans-Jordan rather than Israel and Jordan is made throughout this volume because a geographical and not a political designation is required. By Palestine is meant all the land west of the Jordan river, by Trans-Jordan, all that east of the river. Whenever the word Israel occurs it denotes the ancient Biblical state.

the east, it seemed desirable to choose a site in Trans-Jordan, not too far from the border between the desert and the sown, which might be expected to reveal the two cultures living side by side, before they became archaeologically indistinguishably fused.

A site in the Jordan valley was attractive for three reasons. The first was that Jericho had disappointingly not provided any information about this period. Another site in the same region might provide stratified material which would fill the gap in the Jericho typologies. The second reason was linked to the negative L.B. evidence from Jericho. If the main Hebrew entry into Palestine was not evident at Tell es-Sultân, it was worth choosing a site not far from the Wâdī Far'ah on the route west to Shechem.

The third reason was that the author's field training in the Middle East had been exclusively on a mud-brick site, nor had any of the Dutch archaeologists on the team any experience of a stone-built site. Furthermore a mud-brick site offers a much greater depth of finely stratified deposits than does a stone-built site.

A further impulse towards an East Bank site in the Jordan valley came from the fact that this whole area was in a phase of rapid transformation. Everywhere new buildings, new agricultural installations, new roads, new irrigation schemes were bringing with them more chance archaeological finds, requiring more rescue digs. It was clear that Trans-Jordanian pottery should be dove-tailed into a general Palestinian chronology as soon as possible.

With all these considerations came the usual practical ones of an excavation permit, availability of labour, camping conditions and so forth, including the most important condition of all: that the site chosen should not be overlaid with deep deposits of a later date than the period in question.

Tell Deir 'Allā appeared to fit all these requirements best.

Position and Physical Features of the Tell

The main Shûneh-Irbid road cuts the lowest contours of the eastern foot of the tell,[1] which lies four kms. north of the bridge over the River Zerqā (Biblical Jabboq). From the crest several other tells both large and small can be discerned: Tell el-Mazâr, Tell el-Fukhâr, Tell el-Khṣâṣ, Tell 'Adlîyeh, Tell Qu'adân and Tell Abū Ṣarbûṭ.[2] Farther north the great bulk of Tell es-Sa'īdiyeh is clearly visible.

In his admirable description of this region, Nelson Glueck writes: "It is one of the most prominent tells in the entire Jordan valley, and only Tell el-Huṣn (Beth-shan) and Tell es-Sultân (Jericho) can compare favourably in importance and position with it. It is visible for many km. round about, completely dominating one of the richest, widest, and best watered expanses of the entire Jordan valley, namely the Ghôr Abu 'Obeideh, located between the Wâdī Râjeb and the Wadi Zerqa.... To the e. of it, however, there is

---

[1] Map ref. 209178.

[2] Glueck 1945-'49 (fig. 101, p. 306)

only a small, fertile plain, which soon runs into the broken qattârah hills overlooking the w.side of the rich little Zôr of the Wâdī Zerqā .... After leaving its canyon in the e.hills, the Wâdī Zerqā wanders sedately in its own little Zôr, which cuts through its own valley or Ghôr till it reaches the Jordan .... The strategically located Tell Deir ʿAllā, guarding the approaches to and from the Wâdī Zerqā, and benefiting naturally from the general agricultural and economic advantages of the rich country side around Tell Deir ʿAllā, was bound to become the seat of rich settlements that throve on agriculture and trade, and to a degree ... also on industry."[1]

The tell in its present state has an approximately square base measuring 200 m. on all sides. The foot of the tell is on all sides lower than the surrounding fields. Although if looked at from a distance the tell seems to have a higher and lower terrace, in fact it slopes continuously from east to west across the top. The highest point of the tell is ±200 m. below sea level.

The climate has in the course of many centuries done most of the damage to the tell, though man has also played his part (see below). The Jordan valley is subject to a long, extremely hot and completely dry summer; the latest rains fall in May and do not fall again until October or even November. When the rains do at last come, they fall in short, extremely heavy showers upon a parched land. Any sloping area which has not been irrigated for cultivation during the summer months becomes so dry that a hard crust of earth forms, in which it is hard work to make an impression with a pick.

These slopes, and in particular the slopes of the tell, form an excellent catchment area, as the rain water can scarcely penetrate the earth; however, should the surface of the slope be broken (rabbit holes and shallow hollows scratched out by bitches as nests for their pups are the most normal disturbances now that there is a settled population living round the tell), the rain water swiftly forms a stream-bed below the surface and cuts deep gashes down the slope. This must have caused the southern slope to wear comparatively quickly. Here, as the contour map indicates (fig. 1), a large fan-shaped area has been eroded away by rain water. How much is hard to estimate, but more than half of the tell may have been washed away.

Wind erosion has on the whole altered the face of the tell less drastically, and yet it has none the less affected the tell on all sides. There is a prevailing mild, north wind which blows constantly through the summer months and through the greater part of the winter, when it is extremely cold because it is snow-chilled from Mt. Hermon. It is this wind that slightly changed the axis of the tell, which now runs practically due east-west, but which must have been aligned slightly more n.w.-s.e., to judge from excavated walls that now run out of the tell surface on the n.w.-side.

On the west end of the tell, however, it is clear that the area has been enlarged rather than reduced by the action of the wind. The very fierce eastern gales, the Sherqia, which funnel down through the Zerqā gap and rage at regular intervals during the winter months, must be responsible for this shift of material onto the west end of the

[1] *Op. cit.*, p. 308-9.

tell and for the denudation of the east end, which at present forms a very steep slope.

The chief of the man-made alterations to the ancient tell is the mediaeval Arabic cemetery which covers almost the entire surface. The graves on the highest part of the tell have been eroded away to the lowest part of the burial, which can be traced in outline on the surface. This is of interest because it can now be deduced that the surface of the tell must have lain at least 1 m. higher in the 14-15th centuries A.D. Farther to the west the graves still penetrate 0.50 m. to nearly 1 m. below the surface. Down the slopes of the tell they lie shallower, but they have almost entirely destroyed the upper levels within the excavation area, and most of the levels of every earlier phase along the northern slope. The graveyard belongs to the mediaeval Arab settlement which is still unexcavated. It forms a low tell directly east of Deir ʿAllā across the main road. The cutting and widening of the main road has obliterated the foot of the eastern slope, and further damage to this part has been done by farmers digging away the decayed mud-brick debris to use as fertilizer and top dressing for their fields. The modern village graveyard is situated on the foot of the s.e. slope, and is only advancing very slowly up the southern slope. One farmstead has been built on the lower s.w. slope.

Difficulties Concerning the Identification of the Site

The first nineteenth century explorer to visit Tell Deir-ʿAllā seems to have been Merrill, who in his volume, *East of the Jordan*, p. 388, describes the site briefly and identifies it with Biblical Succoth.

Nelson Glueck, in his *Explorations*, includes a lucid summary of opinions about this identification, which is worth quoting extensively:

> "What then is the evidence for the location of Succoth? The Biblical evidence is very clear to the effect that it was located in the east Jordan Valley, (Gen. 33:17 Ps. 60:8; 108:7; Josh. 13:27; Judges 8:5, 6,14; I Kings 7:46) close to the point where the Jabbok emerges from the eastern hills into the valley. It can be seen all the way from Tell ed-Damieh. Its association with the Jacob and Gideon stories makes it likely that this site was important both in the Bronze and Iron Ages. The actual examination of the great mound of Tell Deir-ʿAllā, which is about 12.5 kms. n.n.e.-n.e. of Tell ed-Damieh, and which, as commonly and correctly agreed, is to be identified with Biblical Succoth, revealed the presence of some M.B. II and L.B. II sherds, and great quantities of Iron Age I-II sherds .... The Biblical, topographical and archaeological evidence thus all substantiate the equation of Tell Deir-ʿAllā with Biblical Succoth. Albright summed up the previous consensus of opinion with regard to the relationship of Tell Deir-ʿAllā and Succoth when he said: The identification of Succoth with Tell Deir-ʿAllā agrees so well with the indications of the Jacob and Gideon stories that it is generally accepted and cannot be far wrong. *(A.A.S.O. R.* VI, p. 46) This identification was already made in the Talmud, according to which as Dar ʿalah or Tar ʿalah is to be identified as Succoth. (Talmud Yerushalumi, Shebiʾith IX, 2, 38 d) .... There have been some, however, who wanted to identify or who considered the possibility of identifying Biblical Succoth not with Tell Deir-ʿAllā, but rather with Tell el-Ekhsas, about 2.6 kms. w.s.w. of Tell Deir-ʿAllā .... Its L.B. II and Iron Age I-II sherds were contemporary with those of Tell Deir-ʿAllā. The primary attraction of Tell el-Ekhsas to those who would identify it with Succoth, lies in its name, which means

"Mound of Booths". This is, as Père Abel has suggested (*Geographie* II, p. 470), a direct translation of Succoth, which means "Booths". And that, aside from its pottery and the general geographical position it occupies in the proximity of Tell Deir ʿAllā, is its particular claim to recognition as the original site of Biblical Succoth .... One site which would merit more serious consideration than Tell el-Ekhsas ... is Tell Qa'adan. It is about half a km. n.e. of Tell Deir ʿAllā. In addition to L.B. II and Iron Age I-II sherds, and some Byzantine and mediaeval Arabic ones, there were some Chalcolithic sherds there .... If ,however, we had to choose only between the two sites of Tell el-Ekhsas and Tell Qa'adan for the one to be identified with Biblical Succoth, we would select the latter, as being nearer to the Jabbok and being occupied during a longer range of history.... There is, we believe, only one other possibility for identification with Succoth, which needs to be considered, and that is the great double site of Tell Umm Hamad. It is about 5.7 kms. n.e.-n.n.e. of Tell ed-Damieh, and a little less than 7 kms. s.s.w.-s.w. of Tell Deir ʿAllā. It is perhaps the most extensive site in the entire Jordan valley, and one of the most important. The e. part of the great double site overlooks the Jabbok. While this e. part ... had an Iron Age I-II occupation ... nevertheless, its Iron Age settlement could not compare in density with that on Tell Deir ʿAllā. ... Furthermore, being, as compared with Tell Deir ʿAllā, a considerable distance from the point where the Jabbok stream emerges from the e. hills ... Tell Umm Hamad does not fit as well into the Jacob-Esau story as Tell Deir ʿAllā does."[1]

This quotation gives the general trend of Glueck's argument in favour of identifying Tell Deir ʿAllā with Succoth. His thesis is built up from first hand topographical knowledge of the Jordan valley and its tells, but this was limited archaeologically to a surface survey. This topographical and archaeological information is closely linked to a comparatively orthodox acceptance of the Biblical traditions. He did not have the advantage of excavating any of his four candidates for the title of ancient Succoth, and he naturally assumed that Deir ʿAllā was the site of a settlement, a city, during the periods represented by surface sherds, just as other tells of its size are.

In the light of four season's excavation at Deir ʿAllā, some of Glueck's observations now have to be re-adjusted or even corrected, and this leads to evidence against the equation Tell Deir ʿAllā=Succoth.

1. There is now physical evidence that the Zerqā (Jabbok) river bed once ran to the north of the tell. The lowest part of Trench D showed that periodic flooding of the river had deposited wash along the northern foot of the tell. Almost 2 metres had accumulated even later than the early Islamic period, and the stratification of this deep deposit clearly shows that the present bed of the river Zerqa is a comparatively recent development. The part of the old bed where it emerged from the mountains can still be traced; cultivated land has otherwise obliterated all other evidence.

This fact still leaves Tell Deir ʿAllā "a striking landmark and a boundary point,"[2] but now on the wrong side of the river for those who identify it with Succoth in Gad.

2. The site was not inhabited by a settled folk at the beginning of the Early Iron Age, and for the greater part of the Late Bronze Age the whole site was reserved for a

---

[1] *Op. cit.*, p. 347-350.
[2] *Op. cit.*, p. 350.

sanctuary with no ordinary settlement of any kind (cf. History, below). Of the M.B. Age there is no trace: the tell did not exist in that period. No sherds of this period were found by the expedition.

This makes it impossible to associate either the Jacob or Gideon stories with it, unless Succoth was not an ordinary village.

3. The presence of a metal industry during the Iron I period, combined with semi-nomadic living conditions on the tell (cf. History, below) tends rather to weaken than strengthen the equation Deir ʿAllā = Succoth.

It seems quite unnecessary to juggle the text, as does Albright,[1] in order to make sense of I Kings 7:46, and Glueck's translation of the unaltered text—"in the earthern foundries (or, in the thickened earth moulds) between Succoth and Zarethan"[2]—is much to be preferred. Glueck reports that he picked up fragments of slag at Deir ʿAllā, but did not use this evidence in connection with his reading of the O.T. text to draw the following logical deduction: that if foundries were situated *between* Succoth and Zarethan, then a tell exhibiting signs of metal workings in the Iron Age was most likely not to be either of these sites but belong to the industrial area in between.

The excavations have already confirmed Glueck's suggestion of copper casting at Deir ʿAllā, though as yet in far too small an area for any far reaching conclusions to be drawn. The question of why Solomon had the copper vessels for the Temple in Jerusalem cast in this region at all, should, if satisfactorily answered, provide the key to a better understanding of the whole problem. Glueck asks just this question with regard to a reading of the I Kings text which places the foundries "at the crossing of Adamah between Succoth and Zarethan": "Why should the copper be cast in the ford of Adamah or at the ford of Adamah?"[3] Without formulating the difficulties, he had already offered a partial answer on p. 345: "...the copper was poured in the foundries or moulds which existed in the Jordan valley, where there was good clay for the purpose...." In other words the Jordan valley provided the material for the foundries which the Jerusalem area could not. But intimately attached to this material need was the necessity of hiring skilled labourers; otherwise the raw clay could have been transported to Jerusalem as it is for potters' workshops to-day; this would have been far easier than the transport of many extremely large, bronze vessels up through the mountains to Jerusalem. The raw metal was most probably taken up from the Arabah to be smelted in this part of the Jordan valley. The chief difficulty surely lay in the fact that until well on in the Davidic period the Philistines had the monopoly of metal working in their hands. They not only controlled this vital industry, but it is also explicitly stated in the O.T. that the Israelites were ignorant of this skill. In the short space of time between David's defeat of the Philistines and Solomon's plans for the Temple, it is highly unlikely that a skilled group of metal workers could have been recruited from Israelite ranks; hence the

---

[1] Albright 1940 (p. 14)

[2] *Op. cit.*, p. 347.

[3] *Op. cit.*, p. 346.

necessity of having the work done in an area where this industry was well developed, even though it lay so far from Jerusalem, the religious and political centre of the land.

It was not one of the aims of the expedition to identify Succoth, but it was surely within its scope to attempt an identification of Deir ʿAllā. With so small a fraction of the tell yet excavated, it is perhaps premature to make such an attempt here; nevertheless the three points made above seem to be of a sufficiently positive quality to disqualify Deir ʿAllā as a candidate for the site of ancient Succoth. The sites mentioned in the O.T. as being situated in the east side of the northern half of the Jordan valley are listed by Glueck as: Adamah, Succoth, Zarethan, Zaphon and Jabesh Gilead. As he also discovered seventeen Iron Age sites between Tell ed-Dâmieh and Tell es-Saʾīdīyeh, it is not surprising that the fitting together of site and place name in this region causes difficulty. Bearing in mind his description of Tell Deir ʿAllā as an archaeological site of the first importance and the paucity of Biblical place names in this region, the following tentative suggestion is offered for an identification of Tell Deir ʿAllā.

There is one site mentioned in the O.T. which must lie in this region though it does not feature in Glueck's list, and that is the Gilgal to which the people of Jabesh Gilead went to proclaim Saul king after he had delivered them from the Ammonites (I Sam. 11 :15). This is not to suggest that Saul should be pushed back to a date which coincides in time with the L.B. Deir ʿAllā sanctuary in its original size and lay-out, but rather that there is a possibility that the tradition of a holy place went on into the Early Iron Age, though it does not seem likely that the tribes to which this sanctuary belonged chose another site for the rebuilding of the sanctuary after the earthquake disaster (although the earthquake may have been taken as a sign that the location was not the right one). It is likely that it was rebuilt on a much smaller scale than the original lay-out, and that erection must have cost tremendous effort. It is therefore possible that a sanctuary will be found to the east of the excavated area. Whether this will prove to be so, the fact still remains that until just after 1200 B.C. there was a very large sanctuary in full use.

As will be demonstrated in a subsequent Vol. of the Deir ʿAllā publication, the pottery from the last occupation level of the sanctuary differs in many ways from that of the preceding level, and the two repertoires are separated by a fire, which destroyed at least the buildings west of the cella. The two repertoires represent different traditions, and it is likely that the last users of the sanctuary were new occupants of the region.

This suggests the possibility that the archaeological evidence may provide some substantial background to the story of how the tribes of Reuben, Gad and half Manasseh built "an altar over against the land of Canaan, in the borders of the Jordan" Josh. 22 :11. In this obscure story there is much self-contradiction. For instance in v. 10 the altar appears to have been built west of the river, though in v. 11 it clearly happened to the east. M. Noth remarks: גְּלִילוֹת הַיַּרְדֵּן (10) ist ein term. techn. der nach den folgenden Angaben eine Stelle unmittelbar am Jordan auf der W Seite bezeichnet, aber nur hier vorkommt und nicht mehr genau festgelegt werden kann; (11, wo an eine Stelle auf dem Ostufer gedacht zu sein scheint, ist ein Zusatz...)"[1] The "geliloth" (circles) in v. 11 could be taken literally if one remembers that there are dolmens – huge stone tables, each standing on top of a circular stone platform – situated no distance from Deir 'Allā in the hills above. Noth traces the hand of P in the redaction of this text. "Der sachliche Inhalt von 9-34 weist nun aber deutlich darauf hin, dasz es sich hier von Hause aus um eine ortsätiologische Ueberlieferung handelte, die offenbar auf die Erklärung eines Namens oder einer Bezeignung hinauslief (cf. v. 34). Der ursprüngliche Sinn dieser Ueberlieferung ist deswegen kaum noch zu ermitteln, weil nicht nur das Ganze von P sehr stark umgestaltet worden zu sein scheint im Interesse einer ernsten Warnung vor illegitimen Kulten und Kultstätten, vielleicht auch eines Hinweises auf die Jahwe-Treue der im Ostjordanland wohnenden Glieder der nach-exilischen Gemeinde...." This story, in which the wrathful Israelites are appeased by the explanation of the altar's having been set up as a reminder for future generations of the kinship between the Trans-Jordanian tribes and the Israelites, may reflect a far older and much less innocent (from the later point of view) reason for its erection. In this case the name Deir 'Allā may stem from the original name (which was replaced in the story by the name "Ed", a witness), and date from the L.B. Age.

Administration and Organization

Each season began on Jan. 1 and ended in the first week of April, with a full week's holiday in the seventh week. The team travelled out together by ship to Beirut and overland to Deir 'Allā. The director, his wife and the housekeeper went out a little in advance so as to make the necessary preparations, so that the work could start the day after the team arrived.

The total number of the team never exceeded 14 and this was composed mainly of Netherlanders, although there were always a representative of the Dept. of Antiquities from 'Amman, and either part- or full-time foreign guest-archaeologists.[2]

Dutch members of the team were chosen in the first instance from the three Dutch archaeological institutes on a recommendation from their professors and because of their general suitability and enthusiasm. When there were not enough candidates from these institutes, theological students were chosen in preference to history or semitic language students. These students became the site supervisors and their numbers varied from 4 to 6. The rest of the team consisted of a photographer, a draughtsman, one or more technical staff who dealt with the registration, restoration and conservation of finds, and a housekeeper. For two of the four seasons a potter worked on the study of ancient pottery techniques, and in the first season there was in addition an administrator-book keeper and a surveyor, and in the second year a full time surveyor.

The work was so arranged that each member of the team was individually directly

[1] Noth 1938 (p. 105)

[2] See Preface.

responsible for his or her piece of work to the director. The director was in the field whenever excavation was taking place and was alone responsible for the strategy and methods of excavation employed. He drew all the sections in the field, sometimes with the site supervisors, sometimes with the foreman. His wife was responsible for the co-ordination and of the technical staff in camp.

The following is a sketch of the duties of the various people involved:

a) The site supervisors: Their work on the tell is described in detail below, and so it is sufficient to say here that the site supervisors were responsible for the work that went on in their own squares; they were expected to see that the labourers carried out the work that they and the director had planned for the day, that sherds were put into the right baskets, and that all finds were labelled. If an archaeological situation came up which the site supervisor could not solve himself, he was expected to shift his men to another part of his square immediately or, if that was impracticable, to stop work on that section until the director could come and discuss the problem and give further advice. They were also expected to keep an eye on the welfare of the men who worked under them.

b) The draughtsman: He was responsible for drawing all the registered objects, any sherds indicated to him by the director, and, if necessary, objects in situ on the tell. He also helped the site supervisors plan their areas in the years that a surveyor was not part of the team.

c) The photographer: He had to organize his own time so that he was free to work on the tell when sent for, and yet could develop his photographs quickly in order not to hold up the work on the tell. He also photographed the registered finds and the drawing sheets. On the tell the director indicated to him the salient points of the situation to be photographed, and it was then his duty to see the site was sufficiently well prepared and cleaned before he took the photograph.

d) The technical staff: The work here was extremely varied and has been described in greater detail below.

e) The potter's study: This study, which has formed the basis for much of this publication, was begun in the field and continued in Holland. Various local experiments were made, e.g. clay from various find spots in the hills above Deir ʿAllā was collected, slibbed and tested. Visits to a local potter at the refugee township of Kereimeh were regularly made so that Near-Eastern methods of pot making could be observed.

f) The housekeeper: She was in charge of the camp as a whole. She was responsible for the general hygiene of the camp, for wholesome meals arriving on time, for the marketing and buying of stores. She stocked and ran a small canteen, and took a great deal of the social duties off the director's shoulders by receiving guests.

The labour force of the expedition consisted of three groups: the pick-men, hoe-men and basket boys recruited from Deir ʿAllā district, the six very experienced and well-trained Jerichoans who worked as pick-men-foremen, and the camp personnel.

1. The labour force on the tell: The village of Deir ʿAllā consisted partly of refugees and partly of settled Beduin. In spite of the East Ghôr Canal Project and other agri-

cultural schemes and in spite of widespread emigration to West Germany, there was always a surplus of unemployed. In order that the economic structure of the various communities should not be disturbed, men and boys were recruited via the three most powerful landowner sheikhs of the district. The maximum number employed in any one season was 70. Each pick-man had 1 hoe-man and 6-8 basket boys. Their wages were settled by arbitration of the Dept. of Antiquities before each season began. No baksheesh was ever given, but instead bonus wages were awarded at the end of each month to all labourers who had come regularly. There was also an extra hand-out at the end of Ramadan for the Aiyid. Where possible, old men were employed rather than boys. If they worked slowly, they also worked steadily and reliably and were a stabilizing influence over the whole group. There was a foreman whose job it was to keep the attendance sheets, to recruit new men when necessary, and to arbitrate when quarrels arose. He could recommend that a man be dismissed, but the director had the last say. On the whole there was very little quarrelling on the tell and almost no disputes about working hours or wages.

2. The Jerichoans: This group of men has been working together on excavations since their initial training under Miss Kenyon at Jericho. They are employed almost all the year round on one excavation or another, and formed an elite corps among the workmen. They are exceptionally good at fine trowel work, and if well directed combine skill and observation to a very high degree. Most of them speak English and it is from them that the trainee site supervisor can learn a great deal. One of them was in charge of the pot-washing. They had a fixed daily rate of pay, and lived in a tent on the camp complex. They cooked for themselves and were otherwise independent.

3. Camp personnel: The camp cook was the only member of the camp personnel not recruited from the village. He has cooked for very many tented expeditions and was an invaluable member of the team. There were also a second cook, a house boy, a washer-woman, and a boy and his donkey who were hired to carry water all day to the camp. There was also a night-watchman who acted as caretaker of the equipment during the time that the expedition was away in Holland.

The camp site was lent to us by the courtesy of Saleh Mouasher Bey. It was a large level area directly between the irrigated fields and the westernmost limits of the village. The tell lay a stone's throw to the north, and the Government Agricultural Research Station with its fine cypresses and pepper trees, lawns and flower beds bordered the camp to the south. The expedition built a high brick wall along the eastern side of the site as a wind-break against the worst of the Sherqia. Part of it collasped in a gale one season. It also served the useful purpose of screening the camp site from the waste space which formed the village rubbish dump and communal latrine.

The camp was entirely under canvas for the first two seasons with the exception of the photographer's dark room, which was situated in a village house close enough to the pumpstation for its electric light to be tapped. A three roomed village-type house was constructed on the camp site, in which the kitchen, store room-cum-sick bay and registration room were accommodated.

The working day began with tea and sandwiches at 6.45 a.m. Work started at 7 a.m. and continued until 9.30 a.m., when there was a half an hour's break for breakfast. Work continued then until 0.30 p.m., when there was a pause of an hour for a light lunch. Work on the tell finished at 4.30 p.m. with a substantial tea. Members of the expedition were then free, and towards the end of the season when the evenings were longer the more energetic members of the team would go swimming in the Zerqā or walk down to the Jordan. It was during this period of the day that the director selected the sherds from the mats, and any student who was interested was encouraged to join in these pottery sessions. Supper was at 7 p.m., and after supper site supervisors were expected to help with the numbering of sherds, to discuss their sections with the director and to check their field notebooks. Everyone was encouraged to get to bed reasonably early and after 9.30 p.m. a rule of silence was imposed in the interests of sleep and study alike.

This timetable was somewhat modified during Ramadan in order to make this rigorous month less trying for the workmen. There was no work on Fridays and trips to other archaeological sites on foot or in the expedition's car were frequently arranged. During the week's holiday everyone except the director and his wife was expected to leave the camp, and members were encouraged not to stick together but to take the opportunity to see new places and different people. As most of the team were urban in origin, it was often a greater strain than they realized to live in such a small community out of reach of city lights. This week's break paid handsomely in terms of renewed enthusiasm for the work and renewed tolerance for other men's idiosyncrasies.

Strategy and Methods of Excavation

Once the aim of the excavation had been established and a site chosen, the next problem was how to confine work to an area that would yield sufficient material for the chronological study without getting involved in costly investigation of aspects of archaeology only remotely related to the object of the expedition; moreover it was important that little damage be done to the site as a whole in view of a possible full-scale excavation there in the future. As the aim of the expedition was to collect a representative collection of pottery shapes in strict stratigraphical sequence, the possibility of getting involved in a series of aristocratic or military structures where the artifacts could be expected either to be rare, imported or for a specific purpose, had, if possible, to be avoided. This line of thought led to the rejection of the higher eastern end of the tell as a suitable site for the trenches as it appeared from a surface examination to contain either a citadel or the better-class quarter of the town.

Through consideration of the physical characteristics of the tell in combination with these other factors and the problem of where best to place the dump, the question of where best to position the excavation area resolved itself: only the north side of the tell answered all the requirements.

Trench D was therefore pegged out on the saddle of the tell, approximately 30 m.

west of the highest point of the tell, running down the northern slope. The dump lay to the north in a small strip of uncultivated ground.

That the best laid plans go astray is well illustrated here. That portion of the tell which, had the aims of the expedition been different, would almost certainly have been selected for excavation was avoided. As a result an area which superficially looked of only average importance and interest but which, as it turned out, concealed the main cella of the L. B. sanctuary was selected. The very situation, which such pains had been taken to avoid, occurred.

All considerations of historical and religious interest aside, this situation offered the excavators exactly what they did not seek—pottery of a specialized and limited use. On the other hand, it offered possibilities which any expedition with a different aim would rejoice to find. To push on ruthlessly with the expedition's purpose in the face of such a discovery would have been to lose sight of the wood for the trees, and therefore during the last season the area was widened in order to get a better idea of the L.B. structures as a whole.

The object of a sounding in an archaeological site is generally to ascertain the main periods represented and to give the excavators an idea of the structures lying beneath the surface. For this reason small deep pits are often dug in different parts of the tell with an eye to the discovery of the whereabouts of town walls, gates or citadels. It is not the place here to discuss whether soundings are a responsible way of obtaining archaeological evidence, but rather to explain that the work at Deir ʿAllā, while perhaps superficially bearing some resemblances with a sondage, was in fact of a very different nature.

A square was laid out along a datum line of 30 m. divided into three parts of ten metres square each. Excavation then proceeded in terraces, stepped down the northern slope of the tell. The advantages of this method over any other for an accurate and economical realization of the expedition's aims should become clear after reading the following description of how it was carried out:

The first step or trial cut was dug down until the ground area measured 5 m. square. Immediately two keys for the further excavation of the area were formed: the southern or back "wall" where the east-west axis of the tell was depicted in section, and the east and west sides which were the main line of the trench. The next 5 m. square was then driven down in steps from the top-soil directly west of the first cut. By studying both the western and southern sections, the archaeologist has the advantage of knowing what sort of archaeological situation to expect as he cuts the next step. He is not restricted to digging down only from the top, for after the first staircase is cut, he can cut back any one of the steps, even starting on the bottom tread, should the occasion demand. In this way a "walking baulk" is created, moving, in this case, westward and southward, providing a constant control for the stratigraphy of the area. (fig. 2)

Before a staircase west of any area could be dug, the whole west section of the existing stepped trench had to be drawn in detail, as it was this wall of earth which would disappear as the new staircase bit into it. As each step went down, sections had to be drawn of

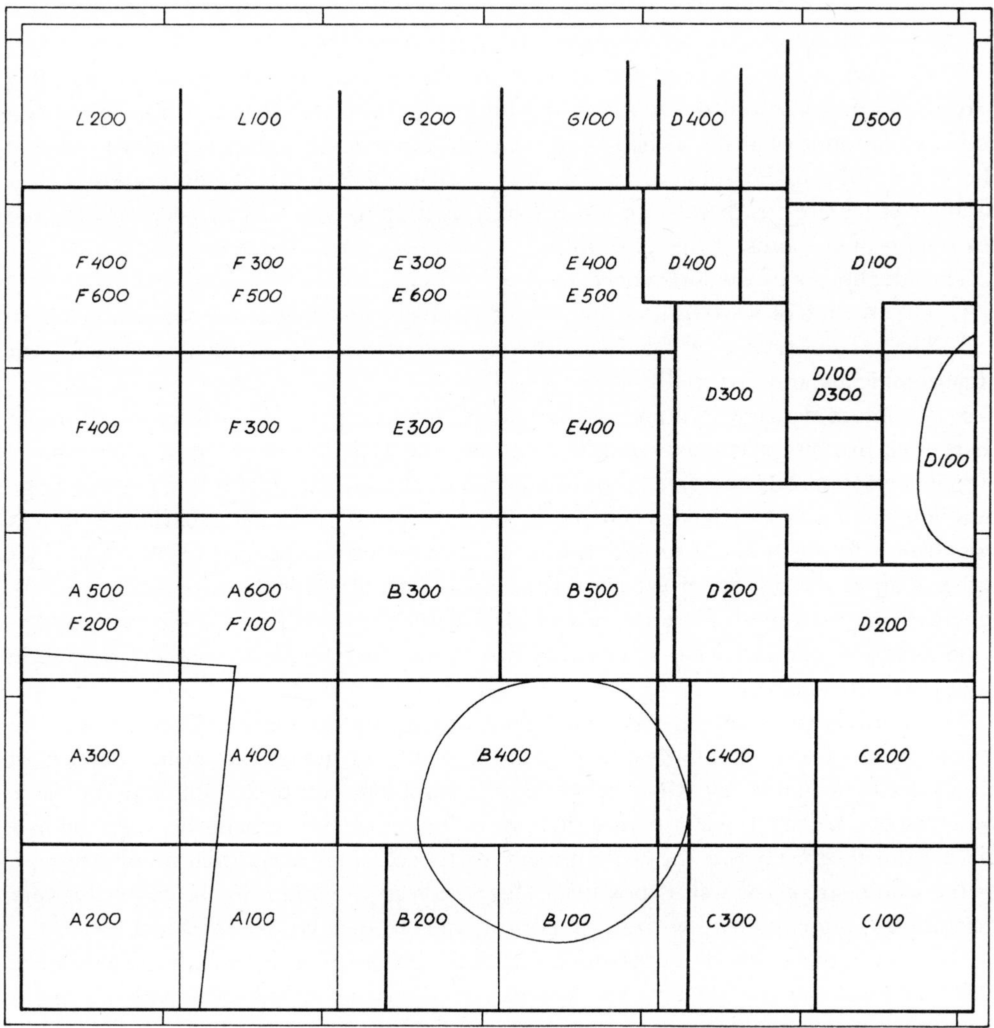

Fig. 2. Plan of squares and sections in the excavated area.
This chart shows the exact position of the squares and of all the sections that have been drawn. Three major features of the stratigraphy have been drawn in outline (the large building – left, the 'cistern' – middle, and the round tower – right), to show why certain sections have not been drawn entirely.

its south and west walls. By working in this way baulks did not appear as free-standing earth walls between areas, and therefore no deep pits were created. The necessity of cutting stairs and gangways in the side of the area to make access possible was thus eliminated. Instead each terrace had an open, northern end, from which earth could be carried directly to the dump without the basket boys having to climb in and out of an ever deepening area.

There were some conventional baulks left standing in each area until the full extension had been reached, or they no longer served a useful purpose.

While work was in progress and excavation extended down the slope of the tell, this way of digging allowed the work in the higher levels to be abandoned as soon as a sufficient amount of material had been collected from undisturbed deposits to enable the chronology to be studied. In this way the finished trench finally appeared as a number of terraces, each cut into the tell only as deep as was strictly necessary for the realization of the aims of the expedition.

The advantages of this procedure are:

1. The creation of a maximum number of controls and checks on the stratigraphy.

2. The possibility of a very economical way of obtaining the material required, both archaeologically and financially.

3. Minimum damage is done to the site. Whenever part of a structure of more than usual promise was uncovered, it could be, and was, left intact until such time as it could be completely excavated. For instance, the round tower in phase K and the large building in phases E-J have been preserved for a later full-scale excavation. It was possible to do this without undue trouble as both features happened to lie at the sides rather than in the middle of the excavation area. This was not the case when the L.B. sanctuary came to light. Here the terraces lay directly over the whole complex, and as soon as it was realized what it was that was being uncovered, a complete change in policy was imperative.

The disadvantages are obvious and of an organizational nature. They are not intrinsic faults. The chief disadvantage is the difficulty of getting an overall picture of structures as a whole and their relation to a complete complex. One and the same wall may be excavated over a period of years in longer or shorter lengths, with the first pieces gone months before the last fragment is exposed. This means that no photograph of the whole stretch of wall is possible. This handicap can and must be off-set by very careful planning combined with many photographs of details. (see below, p. 17)

To sum up, this method of excavation suited the purposes of the expedition extremely well. With another aim in view, another way of obtaining the material evidence might well be found more suitable. As it was, the earthquake cracks running through the tell, (cf. p. 31) had in places dislocated large portions of the stratigraphy, which could only be sorted out in vertical cuts in closely spaced steps, both sideways and downwards. With these conditions the sequence of the rebuilding of the walls could also best be studied this way. (There are no stone foundations, and the original position of a wall can only be seen in section.)

As every wall was planned as soon as it appeared, these remaining highest courses of bricks would have very frequently provided false evidence had there not been enough sections to check on the total remaining depth of the wall. These top courses had sometimes sunk into an earthquake crack, or were leaning far off their true courses or had even sprung off their lower courses to stand beside them, thus giving the false impression of a wall of double thickness. Plans therefore did on occasion have to be corrected with the help of the sections.

Method of Recording

Although only one area of the tell was to be opened up, it seemed wise to fit it into a grid system which covered the whole tell. Similarly the numbering system was kept as simple as possible so that it was capable of being integrated into a large scale excavation should this prove worth doing. Fig. 1 shows the position of the excavated area on the tell, and fig. 2 shows the 1 m. grid system of the excavated area, the position of the sections drawn during excavation and the position of the squares. The main datum line runs east-west across the summit of the mound where a Jordanian Government survey triangulation point is sited. This gives the exact position of the tell itself and its height. The 1 m. grid system was laid out with wooden pegs (later replaced by long iron pins) at the west, south and east sides. The west-east co-ordinate, from which all subsequent measurements were taken and the plans drawn, runs 0.50 m. south of the excavated area, and the south-north co-ordinate runs 0.50 m. west of the same.

The position of deposits referred to in the text is given first by the distance east of the south-north line, and then by the distance north of the west-east line; therefore 23/25 indicates a point 23 m. to the east and 25 m. to the north.

The exact position of each square is:

square A:0.50 – 10.50 / 0.50 – 10.50
square B:10.50 – 20.50 / 0.50 – 10.50
square C:20.50 – 30.50 / 0.50 – 10.50
square D:24.50 – 30.50 / 14 – 60 began as a trench down the eastern side of the slope of the tell intended to locate the L.B. levels and the depth of the archaeological deposits. This 6 m. wide trench was later enlarged. For the Iron Age levels its position is: 20.50 – 30.50 / 10.50 – 30.
square E:10.50 – 20.50 / 10.50 – 25.50
square F: 0.50 – 10.50 / 10.50 – 25.50
(these two squares are where 5 m. extensions to the north of squares A and B were made in the 1961 season)
square G:10.50 – 20.50 / 25.50 – 30.50
square H:30.50 – 40.50 / 0.50 – 3.50
square K:40.50 – 50.50 / 0.50 – 3.50
(these two squares are an eastward extension, made in the 1962 season).

The positions of the various plans published in Chapter 1 are fixed in the same way, as are the exact positions of the sections in the section drawings, to which we have added the absolute height below sea level. These heights are taken from the triangulation point, which formed a fixed point for the co-ordination of the many section drawings. In no case have find-spots been given in terms of height but always in relation to an archaeological deposit, the position of which can be assessed from the section drawings.

Neither have heights of wall stumps etc. been given as their attribution to a certain level is independent of such measurements.

Sections and plans were drawn in the field at a scale of 1:25. The sections published here are at a scale of 1:50, and plans have been redrawn to a scale of 1:200, unless stated otherwise.

On the section drawings the heights have been normally given with the triangulation point on the top of the tell fixed as — 200 m.

Each square (A, B, C etc.) was subdivided into four 5m² sub-squares and given a series number: 100, 200, 300, 400. The top-soil of a sub-square, therefore, would be numbered A 100, and the first archaeological feature found would be labelled A (or B or C etc.) 101. A new number dit not necessarily signify a new stratigraphical level, as every element of the stratigraphy was treated as a deposit—including walls, pits, ovens ect.—needing definition and identification and therefore a number. As excavation in the sub-squares was often taking place at different absolute heights because of the method of stepping or terracing, some features, and in particular walls, obtained more than one number. A wall that ran through two sub-sections but which was excavated in two or even three portions might therefore be numbered thus A 123 and A 209. It might also extend into another square altogether in which case it also bore the letter of that square followed by the sub-square number. The advantage of this system was that a different tempo of excavation could be used in the different sub-squares without work being held up in one or dangerously speeded up in another. When semi- or wholly untrained site supervisors were used, as was occasionally the case at Deir ʿAllā, this system allowed for an easy correction of slips in recording made in the field. For instance, a site supervisor might think he could distinguish two phases in a wall, and so award them different numbers. This also meant that the pottery, small finds, etc., if any, were kept separate under the same numbers. If, as the work continued, he realized that he had made a division when in fact there was none, no harm was done. The numbers did not have to be changed on the plans, or on the sherds; only a note had to be added in the field book that the two numbers equalled each other. If a certain number of finds were made in one deposit, e.g. bangles, ear-rings and beads in an Arabic grave, then they were all given the number of the deposit with a lower register letter following it. C 307 a, b, c, etc. would indicate that C 307 was the grave, and that there was a certain group of grave goods associated with the burial.

Each site supervisor had a field notebook of graph-paper interleaved with writing-paper. In this notebook each new feature of the stratification was numbered, described and where necessary sketched on a plan on the graph-paper. The site supervisor was expected to study it in relation to its surrounding deposits, and he supervised its excavation and made sure that all the objects belonging together were marked with the same number.

In some parts of the excavation, and particularly in the first phase of the Iron Age, occupation and floor levels were so finely layered that it was virtually impossible to remove one after the other separately.

There was little sense in trying to do so as several of these layers together only constituted the thickness of an ordinary sherd, and therefore one layer alone could not contain a sherd; therefore a collective number was given to such a deposit, and when the letter S is added after a sub-square number, it indicates the topmost layer of such a deposit.

Although the general work of laying out the squares and making the contour map of the tell was carried out by a surveyor, the site supervisors, sometimes with the help of the draughtsman, usually planned the various architectural remains found in their own squares. It was absolutely impracticable to have fixed points inside the squares. Even fixed points set in baulks were of little use as they were cut down too often to serve any long term purpose. So four fixed points were made in each sub-square: two in the south section and two in the east. Once these points had been related to the grid system and the absolute height established, they were sufficient for all the measurements in a 5 m^2 square, and while digging went on they could be lowered with the simple aid of a plumb bob. Thus a three dimensional recording of each archaeological deposit was obtained.

Photography

As soon as a feature of interest was uncovered, as well as being planned and described in the field notebooks, it was also photographed. In most cases these were taken with a Linhof 13 $\times$ 18 plate-camera. No further excavation was done in the area where the photograph had been made until the photographer had developed the negatives and the director had passed them as satisfactory. During most of the first season there was no plate-camera and as it was not possible to hold up the work until a whole reel had been taken on the "Miranda" camera, some unsatisfactory photographs were undetected until it was too late to retake them.

A certain amount of colour photography was also done, both of the objects and of the tell. As these were chiefly for teaching purposes only, slides were made. In general Ferrania colour film proved more satisfactory than any other make. A number of detail studies of the sections were very satisfactory. Photos of "local colour" were made only when it seemed that a record of scenes or buildings or household installations was of such a nature that it could have a valuable bearing upon similar archaeological situations. For instance the collapse and swift disintegration of a single-roomed, mudbrick house after the first rains was put on record photographically because it was of considerable interest to see the stages in which this occurred.

The Stichting Nederlandse Onderwijs Film (The Netherlands Educational Film Corporation) co-operated in making a short film of the excavations for use in Dutch elementary schools.

Registration of finds

Small finds were given a field number on the site and brought down to the registration room in camp by the site supervisors at the end of the day. These small finds included flints, bones, shells, charcoal and grain, as well as all artifacts apart from potsherds or large stone objects. These were placed in separate receiving boxes and dealt with the following day by the registrars.

Charcoal and grain was lifted and packed directly into plastic bags which were stapled shut with their field number on the outside. In this way there was little chance of contamination for potential C 14 tests. Animal bones were scraped and brushed clean of dirt and incrustation, immersed in boiling paraffin wax for strengthening and wrapped in soft paper before being packed in plastic bags in groups in the same way as the charcoal. The air trapped in the bags cushioned the objects and breakage en route to Holland was minimal. Human bones from the Arabic graveyard were re-interred in a large communal pit near the camp site. Shells were washed and packed in cigarette boxes. Flints were treated similarly except that their field number was written on them in Indian ink. The number was protected from washing or rubbing off by a very thin solution of celluloid and acetone smeared over it.

Only artifacts such as beads, arrowheads, seals, complete or half-complete pottery vessels, stone querns etc. were entered in the registration book. These finds obtained a serial number written inside a circle, as well as the field number. Both these numbers were written onto or attached to the object. The register contained a brief description of the object including its measurements, its field number, its photograph or the reduced photograph of its drawing, the number of the negative or drawing sheet and a space for its ultimate destination to be filled in after the division of finds with the Dept. of Antiquities. The register was kept in duplicate, one copy of which was given to the Dept. at the end of each season. Furthermore a duplicate card system was also filed on which comparative material could be added with notes of a more technical nature.

Any object needing repair or restoration was treated before registration except in the case of metal objects. Before being handed on to the camp laboratory these were always drawn and sometimes photographed first in case of accident.

Once an object was restored and registered it was passed on to the draughtsman who drew it life size, if it were a piece of pottery or a stone object. Tiny objects such as beads were drawn twice life size. A selection of drawn objects was then made and these were photographed singly and where necessary also in groups. The drawing sheets were also photographed, reduced to 1:5 their size. Positives made from these negatives were then cut up and pasted into the registration books and the card system.

Potsherds

These were kept apart in baskets according to the deposit being excayated, and at the end of the day were brought into camp for washing. After washing they were laid out on mats to dry in their respective stratified groups. They were sorted daily by the director and all diagnostic pieces—rims, bases, handles and decorated fragments were kept, as well as any pieces which could be built up to form at least a section of a vessel. The diagnostic pieces were all marked with their field number and if more than one fragment came from a given area a serial number was added thus: DA/B 467.12 (Deir

'Allā/Square B, sub-square and deposit 467, the 12th piece kept). This meant that when the material was worked over later and certain sherds were selected for drawing, there would be no muddle between, for example three cooking-pot rims all from B 467, each of which needed a closer identification.

Sherds which made up into a recognizable vessel were not numbered like this but treated as a small find and entered in the register.

A small camp laboratory dealt with the preliminary cleaning of bronzes, elementary soil analysis and the restoration and strengthening of objects and structures found. In the last season successful experiments were made in the lifting of sections by pull-offs.[1]

The History of the Site

The history of the inhabitants of Deir 'Allā and their place in the whole development of the area can only be written after a large-scale excavation of the tell has taken place and several specialist studies have been completed. The sketch which follows here is only intended as a framework on which to hang the study of the stratigraphy of the site. The deepest soundings revealed that the tell had grown up on a spur of the "bad lands" or sterile foot hills of the eastern range of mountains. This site was first chosen for building on in the early L.B. Age when it was further artificially heightened to form a temple mound on which a sanctuary was built. The materials used for this raised platform included many Chalcolithic sherds, presumeably from one of the typical Chalcolithic villages which straggled along wadi beds in this area. The sanctuary had an active life from the 16th century to the beginning of the 12th century B.C. The earliest levels are still almost entirely unexcavated and the chief information available about the sanctuary comes from its last phase which was destroyed by earthquake followed by a wholesale conflagration.

A C 14 test of one of the burnt roof beams gives a date of 1180 $\pm$ 60 B.C. (Groningen no. 4553). A check of this date is provided by the discovery in the last phase of the cella of an imported Egyptian faience vase bearing the cartouche of Queen Taousert who reigned from 1205 B.C. to 1194 B.C.[2]

The whole sanctuary complex stretches for over 70 m. along the northern slope of the tell, and only its northern limits have been reached. A cella, presumed to be the main one, lies on a raised podium with store rooms to the west and, separated by a small courtyard, a "treasury" to the east, where clay tablets of a hitherto unknown script were found.[3] These rooms are at a lower absolute level than the cella.

Still farther east is a complex of rooms the contents of which make it possible to deduce that they formed living quarters for one or more of the sanctuary servers.

---

[1] Franken 1965
[2] Franken 1962
[3] Franken 1964

There is no trace of any defence system whatsoever. The absence of a city wall in this particularly uneasy period of history, coupled with the extent of the sanctuary and the absence of ordinary dwellings makes it almost certain that during this phase there was no regular settlement here. The whole character of the remains so far excavated indicates that this was a holy place, the generally recognized sanctity of which was sufficient security against the troubled times. It must have been a central sanctuary for the tribes of this part of the Jordan valley.

The survivors of the earthquake disaster immediately attempted to rebuild but failed because of another outbreak of fire. Many pits were dug down into the debris of the destroyed sanctuary either in an attempt to salvage cult treasures or to loot them. Traces of two more attempts at rebuilding have been found on the western tip of the excavated area.

Although it is possible that the site remained a holy place into the Early Iron Age, it is clear that if it did so it was under very different circumstances. The hypothesis of a continuation of a sanctuary is based on the many fragments of ritual vessels (in particular, incense burners) in these deposits, and on the discovery of part of a large building in a phase characterized by the absence of any buildings whatsoever.

The circumstances are different because it is clear that the Early Iron Age occupants of the site were a different group from the people who used the sanctuary throughout the L.B. Age. These new settlers came before the stumps of the ruined L.B. walls had been completely levelled off by erosion, and this evidence points to their having arrived almost immediately after the final destruction. Their work in levelling off the site can be seen in phase A. There is no evidence that they were the cause of the original population abandoning their sanctuary.

Some of the characteristics of the newcomers are listed here:

1. Their pottery traditions, while certainly derived from L.B. traditions, do not show an immediate continuation of these traditions as exhibited at Deir ʿAllā. Both the pottery repertoire and the shapes of certain types differ somewhat. As far as technique is concerned, there seem to be signs of degeneration in comparison with the L.B. Age. The fast wheel was not used, and it is possible that the origins of this pottery are to be sought in the Trans-Jordanian mountains rather than in the valley. Their trade relations or the spheres of influence under which they fell are reflected in the fragments of Philistine type pottery found.

2. The newcomers were not a group of farmers who settled permanently at the site. No houses have been found in this phase. Occasionally a small post-hole was observed, 5 cms. in diameter and about 25 cms. deep, which may have been caused by tent pegs. Owing to the disturbed condition of these levels (cf. p. 31) no coherent plan can be reconstructed from these holes.

3. The few walls of this period belong either to furnaces or to courtyards. These large yards, and the many pits together with the furnaces all indicate an industrial use for the site. The furnaces were used for smelting bronze, and very many tiny metal drops were found—waste from the casting of metal objects. The very many thin layers

of burnt clay cannot be attributed to ordinary destruction levels, but indicate an annual series of industrial activities.

4. The site was inhabited during the winter months and for the rest of the year abandoned (cf. p. 33). Many flint sickle-blades come from this period indicating that a crop was raised, and the animal bones point both to domestic livestock and hunting activities. Bread ovens were also found.

All these characteristics give a picture of a seminomadic folk who were itinerant metal workers and came to live in the Jordan valley during the winter months where they could grow a crop, and graze their animals in favourable climatic conditions at a time of year when the animals were bearing their young. Here they worked their furnaces until the weather became too hot, whereupon they moved back up into the hills to sell their produce and collect the raw materials for further smelting the following year.

This period of semi-nomadic occupation is called in this publication the first Iron Age period. This is not meant to replace the current divisions of the Iron Age in Palestine but is strictly confined to the history of Deir ʿAllā. This tribe of semi-nomads was eventually driven away from the site or prevented from returning to it, when new settlers started to build a small walled town. It seems that the transition falls between phases D and E. There is nothing to suggest violent destruction by new invaders. Nor are there any indications that a time lag separates the two cultures. The material remains characterize a different way of life from the semi-nomads.

1. Right from the beginning there are heavy walls and substantial buildings arranged along streets.

2. The pottery tradition, while stemming from the same general Early Iron Age stream, is not derived from the semi-nomads but is developed differently from theirs. This type of pottery is not typically Palestinian, but rather points to a homeland farther east.

3. No wheel-burnished pottery has been found in these levels. This settlement must be provisionally dated as lasting from the 11th to the 10th century B.C. This second group of settlers is referred to in the publication as belonging to the second Iron Age period.

From the evidence available it can be concluded that after the end of the second period the tell was abandoned for an unknown length of time. Erosion took place and in square A erosion tip lines run over the remains of the large buildings of phase J (cf. fig. 81). The material contained in these erosion deposits came from higher parts of the eastern part of the tell. It proved extremely difficult to isolate the latest period from the previous one as it is so near the surface of the tell and is so disturbed by the Arabic graves. For clarification an extension was made to the east (squares H and K) and the following characteristic features were revealed:

1. a fully developed 7th century Palestinian pottery repertoire with wheel-made (thrown) pottery emerges right from the start.

2. the typical Trans-Jordanian pottery types of the second period have completely disappeared.

3. refuse pits are a common feature of the courtyards.

Although it is possible that this occupation reflects a migration or infiltration from the east, it is equally possible that these settlers came across the Jordan from the west.

This settlement lasted well into the Persian period. After that the tell was abandoned only to be used as a graveyard during the Middle Ages by villagers who lived just to the east of it.

PART ONE

THE STRATIGRAPHY OF THE IRON AGE DEPOSITS

CHAPTER ONE

THE STRATIGRAPHY OF TELL DEIR 'ALLĀ (IRON AGE)

Stratigraphy and Phases

The study of the stratigraphy of a Near Eastern tell is the study of how the mound was formed. This is not an aim in itself but serves the purpose of elucidating the sequence of events in the history of the people who lived on the various surfaces which make up the strata found there. The complete history of the occupants of a site can only be derived from the interpretation of the finds (including, as well as artifacts and buildings, specialist reports on the techniques in which these were made and analyses of organic and inorganic material) in relationship to the strata in which they were found.

This chapter contains an archaeological analysis of the deposits which form the mound, with a short indication of the evidence it contains for human history. It is primarily the history of the sequence of events on the tell. Every element of the stratigraphy has been termed a deposit, and numbered as such. For quick reference, on the plans and sections, walls have been given a sequence number in each phase, and the field numbers are listed in the description of each deposit.

This division into phases is not based on a typology of the finds found in them but on the successive building phases or soil deposits in the order in which they lay in the excavation area. While being accurate for the area excavated, this picture is not necessarily complete for the site as a whole, where there may be a greater number of levels. In the following study each phase has been sub-divided according to successive deposits within each phase and the interpretation has been made from a study of the bed lines.

An extension of the excavated area may show that some phases are not at all, or only slightly represented (cf. the introduction to phase A). It may then become clear that certain deposits are more important than has been deduced from the evidence available at present. The finer division of the deposits into sub-phases serves the purpose of accurately locating objects found and of providing co-ordination in case excavation is continued; so it should be stressed that this division into phases is not an absolute or final one.

The criterion for the division into phases was any alteration in building plans. This sometimes gave an unbalanced picture, as, for example, in phase B which was certainly of a longer duration than D. Likewise phase A was a comparatively short period. There is a major break distinguishing phase D from E (cf. p. 44), and another after phase M and the following phases (cf. p. 61). The latter are not included in this volume but will be published after the conclusion of the excavation of these levels.

The first period (semi-nomadic) covers phases A-D (Early Iron I), the village phases E-M (Early Iron II). (In order to prevent any confusion with the Roman number I, the letter I has not been used.)

Terminology

Before turning to the description of the various phases, some explanatory remarks are necessary concerning the terminology used.

Clay deposits and bricks

The tell is almost entirely built up from clay deposits. The clay was quarried near the tell or even from the slopes of the tell itself, and then carried up to the level where the people who used it lived and worked. In this age-long process of quarrying, carrying and building, a great number of sherds that had fallen down the slopes and had been buried under the surface accumulation of later times were transported back to the top of the mound; therefore it was discovered that the walls of the large building (phase H, walls 1-6) had been made of bricks manufactured from clay taken from Late Bronze erosion levels, containing exclusively L.B. sherds. Except in phase N and apart from the remains of walls, no intentionally laid clay deposits were found. Most of the deposits came from collapsed walls and roofs, and the finer strata were made up of clay washed by rainwater from the houses. In many cases, especially in phases A-D, but also later, these clay deposits contained particles of burnt earth. Bricks from the same wall often showed many different colours from the natural grey to brick red, and clay wash also showed some colour differentiation.

The archaeological analysis of the stratigraphy is not concerned with tracing the origins of deposits back beyond the stage where human interference with the materials occurred; therefore what is termed "clay" here, may not be pure clay in the geological sense of the word. Where possible the description "clay" has been replaced by some more definite term such as "wash from roofs", "debris of wall" etc. Clay, in the technical sense of the word, is found in the natural and undisturbed, banded clay beds on which the tell is situated. It is also found on the rising ground immediately to the east of the mound.

When this substance has been used, well mixed and badly mixed clays can be distinguished. When well mixed, this banded clay has obviously been well soaked in basins before being made into bricks. Often, however, bricks are found in which lumps of the banded clay are clearly visible.

The average size of the bricks in the Iron Age is 60 × 40 × 10/12 cms. This is not their original size. Bricks were higher when freshly made and dry. The bricks from the thoroughly burnt L.B. ruins (where temperatures of up to 1100° centigrade were reached) are indeed thicker. The reason for this is that in the L.B. burnt bricks, the original holes from the "tibbin" or straw mixed with the clay are preserved showing exactly how much straw was used and leaving impressions of all the organic bodies, such as fruit stones or grain, which had been mixed in. In the ruins of the Iron Age which were not destroyed by fire, not only has all the vegetable matter decomposed but the rain-water seeping through the tell combined with the pressure of later deposits has joined forces to compress the bricks. If the I.A. brick makers used as much straw as the builders of the 13th century L.B. temple did, it can be deducted that bricks lost between one sixth and one third of their original height. The amount of straw used is likely to be variable, as it probably depended on the quality of the harvest as it still does to-day. In years of drought and bad harvests tibbin is scarce and bricks are dear and of a poorer quality.

Walls

Walls were made of sun-dried, unbaked bricks. Stone foundations have nowhere been found. Walls were built directy onto the ground without either foundation trenches or stones. Some phase H walls were laid on wooden beams, and phase F wall 8 was erected on a layer of reeds. (Pl. IX, a)

The bricks were occasionally made from clay taken from the undisturbed beds near the tell, but more often from the slopes of the tell itself. Sometimes bricks of both kinds appear in the same wall. There were even cases where it seemed probable that bricks had been re-used. In a few cases, (cf. phases K and M) light grey to near white walls were found. Very often walls, especially when these were only one brick wide, were in a very bad state of preservation. Walls near the present surface of the tell, often largely destroyed by the Arabic graves dug into them, were hardly recognizable. These brick walls after falling into ruin tend to decompose in their own rubble, and often only a vertical cut will reveal the lowest courses of bricks in their original position; unless the colour of individual bricks varies. Indirect light on a vertical cut was often needed where bricks were the same colour to ascertain whether there was a wall at all. Similarly, re-building of a wall could often be detected only in a vertical cut through the width of the wall. As soon as a wall was found, it was drawn on a plan. These plans do not always show the original stance of the wall as many walls lean to one side or the other. In this case the plans have been corrected with the aid of the section drawings where the walls are drawn exactly as they were found.

Floors, streets and courtyards

Inside the houses the floors were usually marked by a dirty surface on which the house was built. Dry clay became very hard and walking on it crushed the surface to a fine powdery dust. In no case was the effect of regular sweeping within the houses observed. Where such regular sweeping did occur, very hard floor levels, giving the appearance of slight burnishing, resulted; moreover the floor, unless re-laid, tended to become lower than the base of the walls. No attempts to improve floors were noticed except in one case (cf. phase G) where a floor of bricks had been laid.

Floors were, however, sometimes re-laid in an accidental manner. The street level outside the houses tended to rise constantly from the rubbish thrown out of them and the silt washed off roofs and walls in the rainy season. After a while one stepped down into a house. A brick doorsill would prevent the muddy stream that flowed between the houses after a heavy shower from pouring into the house. As the process went on, however, the entrance to the house became too low and the step into the house too deep. In phase H, a house wall H16 (cf. fig. 13) actually collapsed when a stream of mud poured over the kitchen floor burying the cooking equipment under a thick layer of silt.

As the added height of the streets was never dug away, it sometimes happened that the owner of a house had to dismantle the roof of his house, letting the clay roof fall inside the walls and if necessary adding more earth until the house floor was once more flush with the street outside; then the walls had to be raised, the door renewed and a window, if there was one, replaced. (Fig. 81 shows a cut lengthwise through a wall where a door is blocked and another reconstructed on a higher level, east of the old one.) How often and over how great a period of time this would have had to be done can only be estimated from a study of the sherds associated with the many road levels, the earliest of which belong to phase E. The latest preserved level of this road is 3 m. above the earliest one and belongs to phase J. Fig. 81 shows the many re-buildings of a group of houses during this period.

In some of the houses of the second period, round stone platforms were found which are not floors, as they covered only part of the floor space. The roughly rounded form of these platforms suggested rather a special industrial or household use.

The courtyards of the first period and the streets of the second period had one thing in common. They were paved and the paving was regularly renewed. A thick layer of reed was laid down over the whole area, both where a surface sloped and where it was practically level. This reed paving was found mixed with clay and covered under thin clay layers. This puzzling feature of paving or top-dressing the streets and courtyards of two different periods may perhaps be explained in the following way. Currently, during the rainy season at Deir ʿAllā, open areas swiftly turn into thick and very slippery quagmires. After a heavy shower it is almost impossible to walk up even a slightly sloping surface. Walking with a load on one's head or back (a full water jar, for example) up the tell itself is in these conditions impossible for some hours after the rain has ceased. Clearly a surfaced route of some sort was desirable to the inhabitants of the tell at all periods. A road paved with stones involved greater effort and cost, and would, moreover, eventually be buried under the rising street level. This indeed happened in phase J where the western half of the road running along wall J1 was paved with stones. It was much easier to collect enough reed growing close at hand along the banks of the Zerqa and to spread it out when the first rains came. These reed layers would at least partly drain off the rain water and allow traffic to continue. After a while, the reed too became buried in the mud and had to be relaid, although it may well have lasted a whole season.

These reed layers were already found in abundance over wide stretches of ground in the first period. As these open areas were used as yards yet were not the usual courtyards, they are here termed "occupation levels". On the section drawings the lines separating these occupation levels indicate clay deposits separating two sets of reed layers. One occupation level therefore consisted of a great number of reed layers (the traces of the reeds are thinner than cigarette paper.) The reed has survived as silver-coloured dust.

In the second period the same type of surface treatment is called a street level rather than an occupation level because the purpose of the areas so treated is clear. Courtyards of the second period however, were not treated in this way. They followed the rise of the street levels and from time to time were covered by brick debris, collapsed walls etc.

Pits

Pits, like walls, are registered as deposits. These deposits belong chronologically to the surface from which the pit was dug. During excavation pits are usually discovered after the top surface to which they belong has been dug away. This is indeed the case with pits belonging to the first period, where the upper part of the pit is filled with the same sort of material as that from which the pit is dug; therefore the accurate attribution of a pit to its stratum in this period can only be made where a baulk runs through the top of a pit. As there are so many pits, some even intersecting each other, it is necessary to dig in vertical slices in order to attribute pits to the deposits from which they are dug (cf. the Introduction). For the fill of these pits, see the paragraph below on wind-blown material, p. 30.

There were no large pits in the second period, with the exception of one in phase M. The pits of the third period were clearly refuse pits with a soft fill dug into very hard, compact clay. Along with the Arabic graves these pits caused great disturbance in the remains of the highest phases.

Bread-ovens

Bread-ovens were sited in open courtyards, and were made of thick coils of clay, spiralling upwards from a broad base. The walls of these ovens break very easily where the coils have been fitted onto each other. The height of the coil is usually less than its thickness. It is square in section and fragments often bear finger impressions showing how the coils were bonded together. No complete oven was found as the top was always missing. A few fragments of the curved top found lying inside various ovens indicate that the ovens were roughly the shape of a bee-hive, with a round opening at the top, much smaller in diameter than the base. The walls were fired hard by the heat of the fire within them.

The base of the oven naturally indicates the stratum on which it was built. But in almost all cases the bottom of the oven is considerably deeper than the lowest course of the coils. On the inside of these coils there were usually traces of burnishing, due to the regular action of a tool used to scrape the ashes out of the oven. This daily scraping of the brittle bottom of the oven is also sufficient reason for the gradual deepening of the interior. In some cases stones were found imbedded in the walls of the oven showing that the original floor was above the stones. Ovens were frequently re-built keeping pace with the gradual rise of the courtyard. Thick deposits of ash were often found near the ovens.

In the earliest period, the outside of the oven was sometimes lined with sherds over which a thick coat of clay was packed, presumeably for better insulation.

Wind-blown material

This term does not indicate loess or aeolian material, but material consisting of all kinds of particles light enough to be blown or rolled over the surface of the tell by the seasonal eastern gales. It comprised clay dust, burnt clay particles, bits of charcoal, small pebbles and vegetable matter.

This is the material found on the surface in the first period. It accumulated against irregularities on the surface and filled the open pits. These deposits were only found in the first period, in the main in the pits, and during the transition to the second period when it accumulated against the newly built walls.

Erosion

The process of erosion was constantly at work on the site.

The effect of it as a whole on the tell has already been described in the Introduction. Occasionally a strong element of erosion which had occurred during occupation was discovered in a limited area, and there seems to have been much erosion between the second and third period, following phase M. The evidence for this is mainly to be found above the large building J 1, 2, 3 in square A, phase J.

Water

Rain-water did a great deal of damage to the tell as a whole once the final occupation had come to an end. Rain-water coursing down the unbroken slope of the tell does not carry away much earth with it. But once the hard surface crust has been broken damage is swift and formidable. A ditch dug round the excavation area in an attempt to lead rain-water away from the digging activities was cut down to a depth of almost a metre after one heavy shower.

At various places underground water-channels were found running down and through the tell to emerge somewhere down the slopes. Some of these natural courses may have existed early on in the history of the tell. Usually they became blocked by the silt brought down by the water, so that over the ages the courses became shorter. Tiny particles from the roof of the water courses fell down, often in recognizable layers (presumably shaken loose by earth tremors) and piled up on the floors of the channels. In section this formed an elongated pear-shape, instead of the roughly rounded section of the original channel.

The height of these channels could be anything up to a metre and they ran snakewise through all the deposits, diverted only by bodies of compact clay such as a brick wall. None of the channels excavated was still active.

Apart from this disturbance of the strata caused by rain-water, another confusing feature must be mentioned here. This is the secondary stratification caused by water seeping slowly through the tell. It was particularly clear in the Arabic graves, where the fill of the grave often showed a strikingly colourful stratification, with pinkish lines alternating with grey dust. Another aspect of this could be seen where material dissolved in water was deposited in tiny pores in bricks or on any hard clay body. These layers of white particles could at first sight easily be mistaken for floors, tip lines or even wall plaster. Whether any time estimates can be made from the change of the chemical substance of the clay deposits through the constant influence of rain water has not yet been decided.

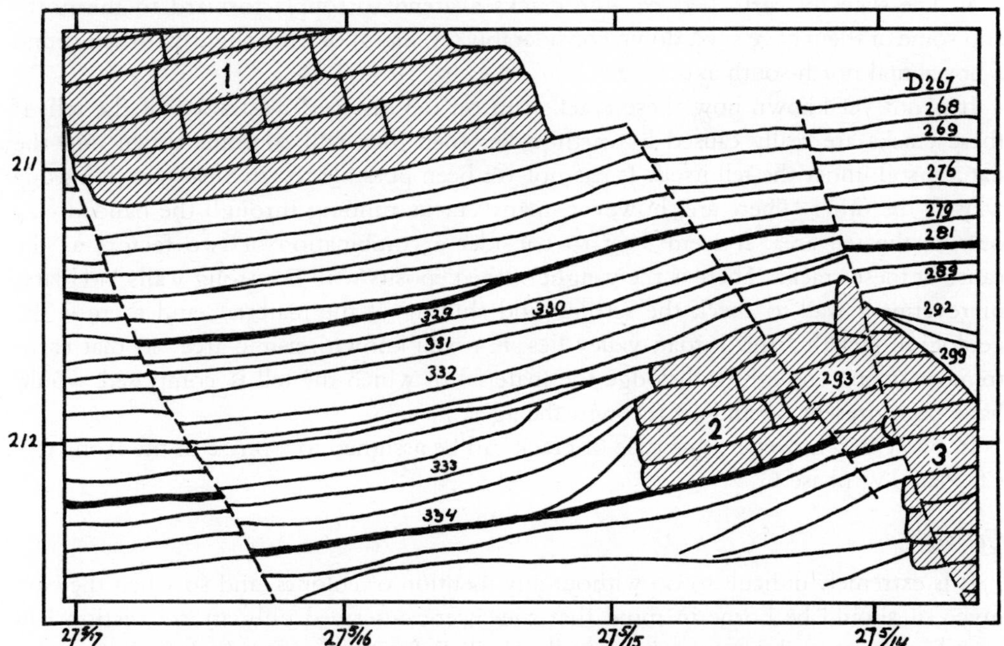

Fig. 3. Example of section drawing with description of the deposits.
Wall 1, phase F wall 8. Wall 2, phase C wall 5. Wall 3, phase B wall 10. D 267: Clay wash from wall 1. D 268: Gritty deposit (from building period of wall 1). D 269; D 276: pink coloured layers of organic material and fine clay deposits. D 279: clay wash. D 281: burnt surface, down to a depth of c. 10 cms. Organic material and ash, overlaid by thin levels of organic material. D 282, 329, 330: pink coloured organic material and clay. D 289: clay rubble from wall. D 292: clay wash from wall. D 299: partly red, burnt rubble from wall. D 331: gritty rubble from wall. D 332: rubble and wash from wall. D 333: Organic material and clay. D 334: Organic material and clay wash, overlaying a burnt surface. This surface runs under wall 2 and heat discoloured the earth to a depth of c. 5 cms. This burnt surface runs over levels of clay debris and wash from wall 3. Note the shift of slices of deposits, showing that usually the material sinks down on the north side. Cracks running through wall 1 did not cause a shift of material and have not been drawn. The crack just north of wall 1 caused a difference of height of the deposits of c. 25 cms., as can be seen on the burnt surfaces, drawn with a thick black line.

The earthquake cracks

Something has already been said, in connection with the methods of excavating, about the earthquake cracks that run through the tell.

Four observations on these cracks have to be taken into consideration before an attempt to explain them can be made.

1. The excavated area in which the cracks occur is sited alongside and in the middle of the northern slope of the mound.

2. All the cracks run more or less parallel to the line of the northern slope, or, to be more exact, to what is supposedly its original direction: i.e. slightly more to the north-west. There are no cracks running north-south.

3. The frequency of these cracks becomes denser and the cracks deeper the farther they lie to the north.

4. The slices of earth between the cracks all tend to topple forward to the north and some of them have sunk down considerably (cf. fig. 3) or even slightly turned round a horizontal north-south axis.

It is not yet known how these cracks run on the east and west sides of the tell. If these cracks are really caused by earthquakes then they will continue down into the natural soil under the tell itself. It has not yet been possible to establish this point one way or the other. There are, however, many cracks running through the banded clay outside the tell area. It seems best to consider a combination of two factors as the cause of these cracks. There is the weight of the deposits with no strong walls, no glacis or revetment wall to check the settling and shifting of the material; and there is the geological fact that the Jordan valley lies in a well-known seismic area; so that earth tremors strong enough to dislodge the material of which the tell is composed would have been present on and off through the ages.

In two cases, however, this type of crack can be assigned to a phase in the Iron Age. Cf. Plate IV, phase C.

Colours

It is extremely difficult to do without any mention of colours, and so when they are given, it should be borne in mind that they were described only after a section had been freshly scraped down, and was in the shade lighted by indirect (reflected) sunlight. Spraying a section did not as a rule give better contrasts between deposits. After a fairly long exposure to the air, a brick wall will show up in section much better than when it is freshly excavated, as the bricks tend to shrink somewhat. Material other than clay deposits, i.e. ash levels, silt deposits or sandy soils present no problems as far as colour description is concerned. When sprayed with water they usually show up very clearly.

Sections

An example of a section is published here on which each deposit is described, cf. fig. 3. All the other sections published in this volume show all the bed lines drawn in the field but, for clarity's sake, the description is limited to distinguishing factors between phases. The field numbers on these drawings are listed in the written description of the phases.

CHAPTER TWO

PHASES A - M

The First Period

Phases A - D

Phase A.

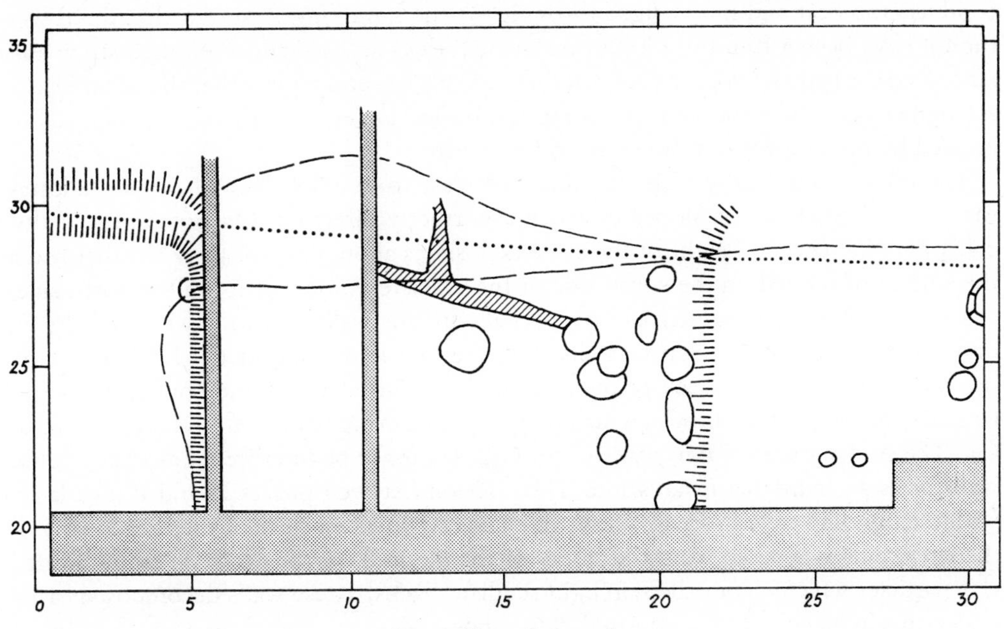

Fig. 4. Plan of phase A.

The plan of phase A shows a depression between the ruins of the L.B. cella, which was built on a brick platform, on the east side and the ruins of what seem to have been two towers on the west. The northern tower belonged to the second re-building period of the sanctuary after its total destruction and the southern tower is the third and last attempt to rebuild. From the stratigraphic evidence which is available it is clear that the attempts to rebuild did not last for more than a few years at the most.

Between these ruins lay a depression of c. two metres depth, which was filled with the earliest I.A. deposits, consisting of occupation levels with thick deposits and streaks of burnt material washed from the ruined L.B. buildings. These wash deposits penetrate like wedges between the occupation levels and partly make up these levels. Besides this, there is all the earth excavated from the phase A pits made by the new occupants. Practically all the lower deposits of phase A consist, therefore, of L.B. material. This changed after the L.B. ruins were completely levelled off.

At an early stage the depression was used to store brushwood, obviously fuel for ovens or furnaces, which caught fire leaving a deposit of white and pink coloured ash in places as much as 20 cms. thick. (Pl. VI.b) Similar fires occured in later phases, burning over the whole width of the excavated area. As a result of this fire the ruins of the latest L.B. tower caught fire and burned from the level on which the fuel had been piled up. Though the heat did not penetrate much below the ground level, the remaining bricks above the surface were all thoroughly burned red. This caused a new series of streaks of burnt L.B. clay to wash down over the I.A. deposits. This observation confirms that once a certain degree of heat is generated in a mud brick wall, the wall itself conducts the heat and burns right through. At the same time it shows that the tower cannot have been a ruin for a long time, as its bricks still contained enough straw and air to feed the flames. From the section through this tower it is clear that the burnt bricks are higher than the unburned bricks already buried under the surface, and since compressed by the influence of moisture and pressure.

The dotted line on the map, running east-west from 30.50/28 to 0.50/30 indicates the top of a crack which slopes down in a northerly direction. On both sides of this crack the difference in height of the same deposits is about 0.60 m. Deposits that reach the surface of the tell on the south side of the crack continue again on the north side.

Structures. A stone pavement not connected with any walls was found in sq. E (619), immediately on the top of burnt walls from the first rebuilding of the L.B. sanctuary. (Pl. VIa) It was probably part of the metal-industry installations and contained several large fragments of stone bowls, which may have originally belonged to the L.B. sanctuary. The scanty traces of two walls in sq. G(204) cannot be interpreted as either house walls or as an industrial installation. The division between phases A and B falls later, with the building of the furnaces in sq. D. The clay for the bricks of these and many of the later walls was taken from the slopes of the mound, for they contain many burned clay particles which colour them in light reddish shades. These walls decomposed easily under the influence of the rain and the winds and they sometimes form an almost indistinguishable part of the debris in which they are buried. Here right from the beginning is the typical feature that nowhere in the I.A. were walls built on stone foundations. They were always built on top of the existing surface.

From a sounding in 1964 (not published here) east of the excavated area, brick constructions exist with heavy walls. They could either form part of the industrial works oft he new occupants of the mound or may belong to a structure similar to the sanctuary but on a much smaller scale; thus carrying on the tradition of a holy place.

A puzzling feature are the many pits that were dug in this period. Apart from a few pits that may have been dug for treasure hunting in the area of the ruined cella, these pits usually have a typical "pear" shape in section, and their depth is sometimes over 2 m. One pit is brick lined and not pear-shaped. There must be some connection with the industry. On the plan only those pits that could be certainly attributed to phase A are drawn. Because of their depth a great number of pits near the northern limit (the slope) cannot be stratigraphically distributed over the phases. Further, the phase A deposits have been badly disturbed by many phase B pits penetrating into the earlier levels. These disturbances have not been indicated on the plan.

It is clear that a good deal of the pottery found in phase A must come from the earlier structures. Although the earliest I.A. pottery is distinguishable from the latest pottery from the sanctuary, the phase A pottery has not been used for our statistical studies. Pottery from sq. D. dates from the time after the complete levelling off of the L.B. ruins and is therefore more reliable. By the end of phase A the surface slopes from east to west, but the accumulation in sq. D. does not seem to begin before the great fire in phase A. The sq. D. deposits have been divided in 5 so that when excavation can be extended to the east and south, the new stratigraphic evidence can be properly fitted into the present picture.

List of deposits

Sub-phase	*Description*	*Field numbers*
A 1	Before the fire:	
	L.B. wash and I.A. occupation	(D 918, 919, 925)
		E 520, 521
		E 609, 610
	Pits	D 925, E 531, G 112
	Stone pavement	E 619
	L.B. wash and I.A. occupation	F 508, G 105, G 214
		G 221
		L 111, L 117, L 204
	Pit	L 217
	Thick ash level	D 908, E 517, E 601
		F 511, F 611s, G 104
		G 218, L 112, L 204
A 2	Accumulation after the fire L.B. wash and I.A. occupation	D 906, 907, E 515, 516
		E 600, 608, G 104
		G 203, 220, 213
		L 108, 116
	Pit	G 117
	Wall A 1 and clay wash	G 204, G 208
	Burnt clay deposit	D 168
A 3	Pit, lined with mud bricks	D 514
	Burnt clay and occupation levels	D 164
	Clay deposit	D 508
A 4	Burnt clay and occupation levels	D 405, 425, D 507
		D 162, 166
A 5	Clay debris and occupation levels	D 161, 167, D 404, 424
	Pit	D 167
A 6	Burnt clay and occupation levels	D 158, D 403, 423
		D 506

Phase B

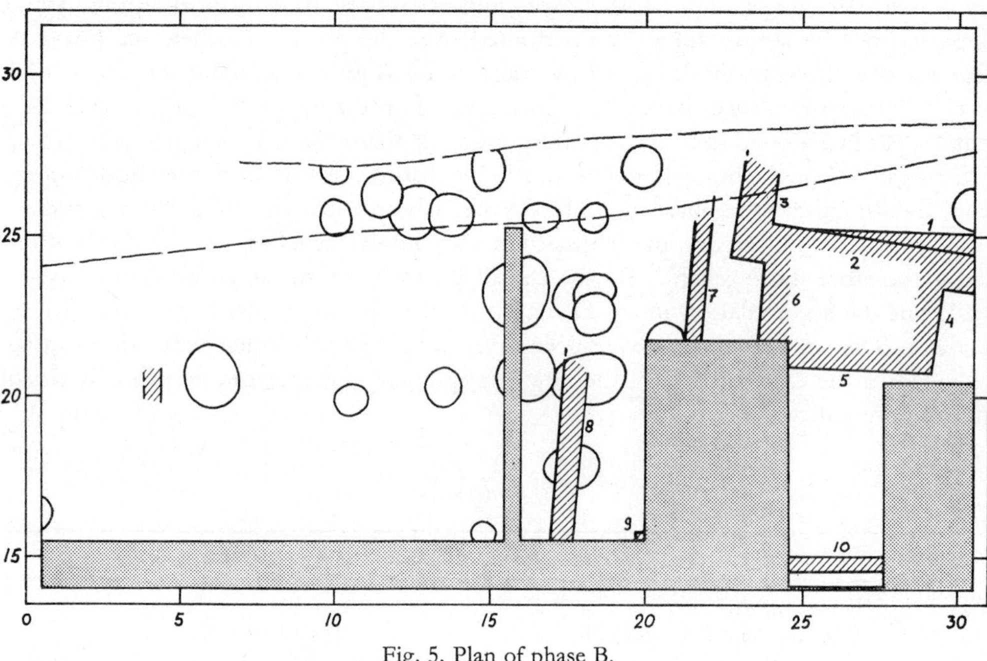

Fig. 5. Plan of phase B.

Phase B is the most important phase for the evidence of the activities of the semi-nomads. It comprises the entire period in which the furnaces were in use. One furnace was destroyed when the heavy furnace walls of phase B were built. Wall B 1 belongs to this earlier furnace, which should be attributed to the end of phase A. From the remains of wall B 1 it is not clear how this furnace was situated, but when wall B 2 was built, it was not sited on the ruined walls but cut down into them, even below the surface on which wall B 1 was erected. Part of two fire channels, lined with bricks all round and heavily burned inside, still existed (fig. 7; 29-30/12.75). They resemble the niches found in the furnace (fig. 6) but are narrower and had been exposed to higher temperatures. Walls B 2, 4, 5 and 6 form the chamber in which three furnace floors were found, two of which are shown on plans fig. 6. (Pl. VIIa) The third floor was badly damaged and did not show any special features. There is a wide opening at the north side, which in the case of the first furnace seems to have been blocked, apart from two channels on either side of the opening. Stones were incorporated in the walls of the chamber, but only in the first structure. These stones were coloured a dark red because of the heat and split in many fragments. The floors were fairly hard and burnt black to a depth of about 5 cms. beneath the surface. The original width of the four walls could only be established in a cross section, as the shape of the chamber was determined by a clay fill inside the walls. The remains of the second and third floors were each farther north than those of the previous one. The fill between the floors and inside the walls consisted of burnt

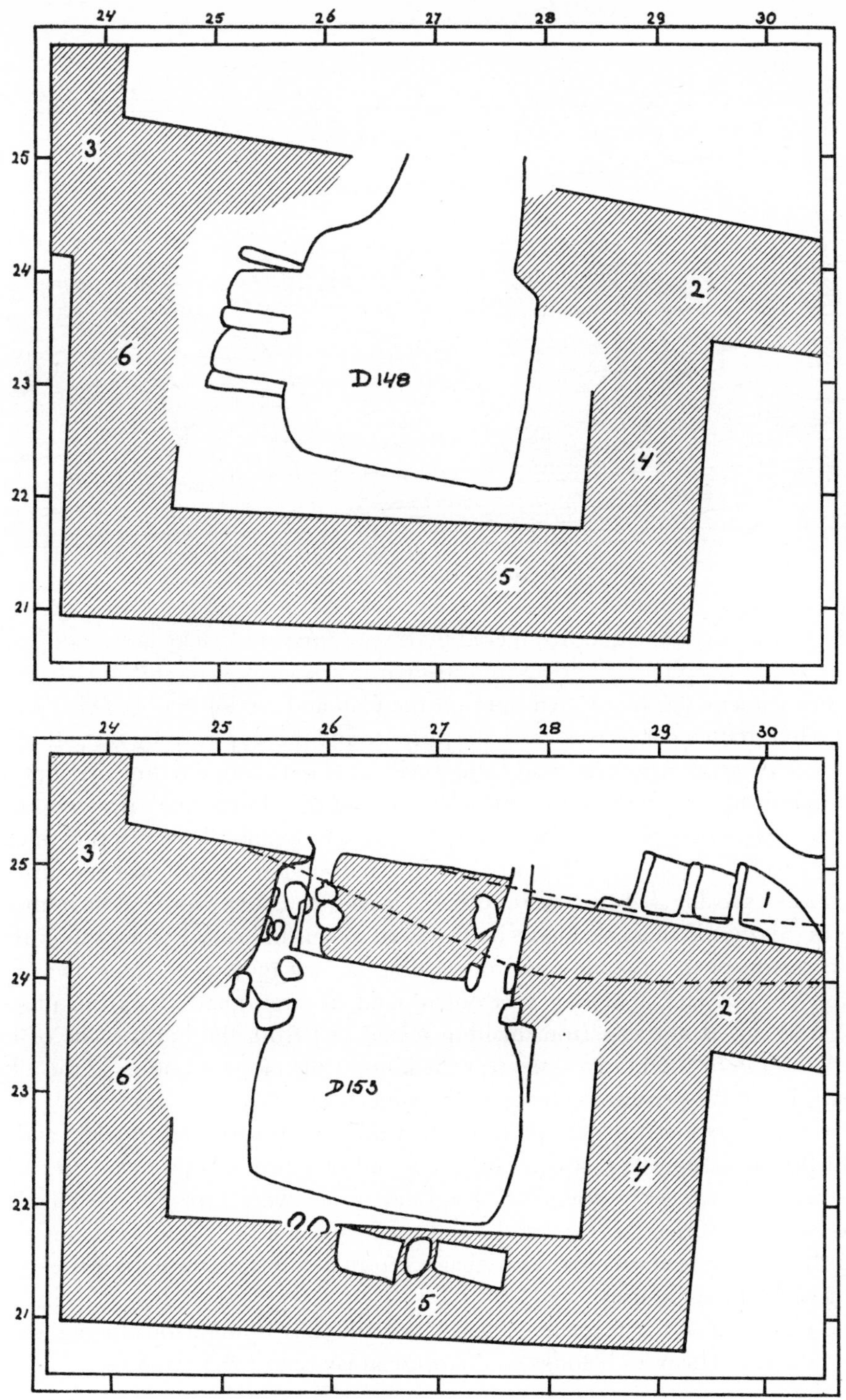

Fig. 6. Plan of two furnaces.

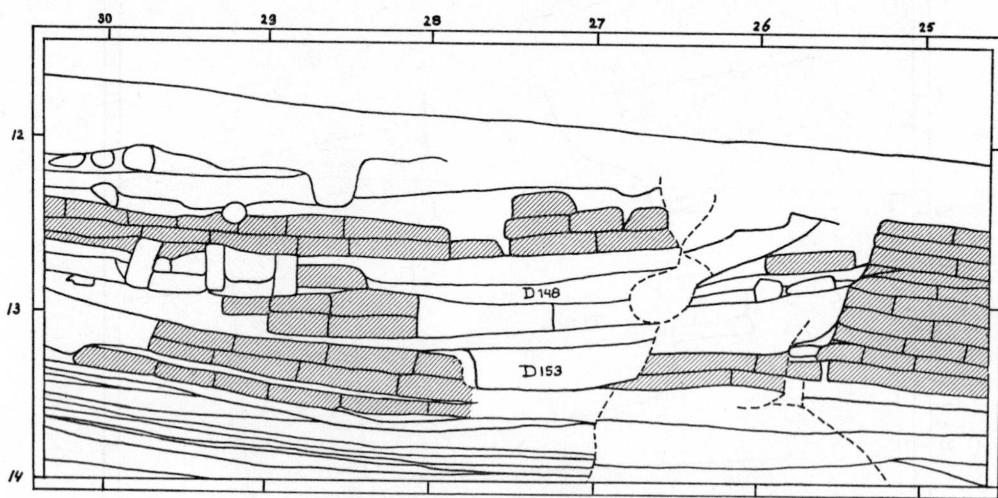

Fig. 7. Section through furnaces.

clay. The excavation was rather hampered by three enormous cracks in the soil, which widened quickly when the soil dried out during excavation, and the shifting of slices of earth between them. (cf. the dotted lines on the plan and section fig. 7). (Pl. VIIa)

There is uncertainty concerning both the purpose and the way of using these furnaces. Had they been potters' kilns one would almost certainly have found fragments of pottery spoilt during firing, but none was found. The clay end of a 'blow pipe' of a well-known shape with a drop of copper still attached to the inside of the nozzle, was found immediately east of wall B4. Many tiny drops of metal were found in the soil near the furnaces. Thus it seems probable that they were furnaces used for casting bronze. The numerous pits dug in this period must also have been related to this industry.[1] One cannot expect to find fragments of the moulds used for casting, as clay moulds crumble away. It is however a curious fact, that slag was only found in large quantities from phase E onward. And this is not slag from melting metals but from the burnt walls of kilns or furnaces. It can be found in masses near the kilns of the modern potters at the village of Kerami. From the present evidence the accumulation of deposits on the tell in this period has to be explained mainly by the destruction of furnaces and moulds, and this is possible as these deposits contain a large amount of burnt clay particles, and ash in patches or large stretches is abundant. Slag and stones were probably systematically removed from the surface by the smiths and thrown down the slope so as not to get mixed in the clay used for moulds. The villagers from phase E on brought it back while quarrying clay for their houses.

On the west side of the furnaces a wall was built (B3) running out in the present surface of the tell. This wall belongs to the original lay-out of the furnaces.

[1] It was certainly not a refinery such as described by Dr. B. Rothenberg. Cf. Rothenberg 1965. Refineries would naturally be situated near the mines.

Walls B7, 8, 9 and 10 belong to later sub-phases, in which the furnaces were still in actual use. In square F (3.80-4.40/20.50) a wall, B11, was discovered which showed up in section only after many weeks of exposure. The bricks were practically dissolved. The many pits of phase B belong to various sub-phases. Only those pits that can with certainty be attributed to phase B have been drawn in here. There were many more, running out into the surface. To these disturbances have to be added the pits dug from phase C levels that penetrated into the phase B deposits. The area south of the furnaces, square D, was the least affected by these pits. Here was found a regular sequence of occupation levels with thin deposits of burnt clay. These surfaces were used to store fuel for the fires. The same pattern is found in the whole area of phase B. To the west the deposits become thinner, showing that activities were concentrated on the east side.

Although the stratigraphy looked extremely complicated during excavation, the pattern is simple. The deposits in square D have been divided into 5 sub-phases. As in all the other squares the bedlines are constantly broken by the pits, the deposits there have been divided into three groups only.

List of deposits

Sub-phase	*Description*	*Field numbers*
B 1	Furnace walls 2-6, built on a surface which was burnt black	D 155, 429, 157
	Clay debris against the walls	D 145, 505, 506
	Occupation levels	D 159, 160
	Red-burnt surface and occupation levels covered with clay debris	D 354, 403, 422
	(Sherds from the following levels, excavated in 1964 are not included in the pottery study.) Occupation levels interleaved with clay wash and burnt clay deposits	E 507, 508, 509, 514
		E 602, 605, 606, 607
		F 507, 510, 512
		G 110, 115, 116
		G 210, 211
		L 106, 107, 110
		L 202
	Pits	E 603, 604, F 500, 501
		F 502, 503, 504
		F 600, 601, 603
		G 118, 126, G 212
		L 101, 110, 113, 114
		L 210, 216
B 2	Clay debris in front of 2nd furnace	D 153, 503
	Occupation levels covered by burnt debris	D 152, 154, 156, 348
	West of walls 3 and 6 burnt clay	D 402, 421
	Debris inside furnace	D 146
	Accumulation in square E (south)	427, 428, 436, 441, 446, 447, 450
	Pits	432, 433, 434
	Square E 300	331, 332, 340, 341, 344, 382
	Pit	379
	Square F	372, 376, 390, 392, 475, 465, 484

List of deposits (continued)

Sub-phase	*Description*	*Field numbers*
B 3	West of furnace walls, clay debris	D 502, 503
	Occupation levels	D 418
	Wall B 7	D 415
	Pit, west of wall B 7	D 419, 420
	South of furnace walls, occupation levels covered by burnt debris	D 151, 345, 348, 346
	Furnace debris	D 148
	Pit	G 103
	Square E accumulation (north)	E 427, 435, 440, 445, 448
		E 329, 330, 376
	Pit	E 375
	Accumulation (south)	E 338, 339, 343, 351, 381
	Square F 300 (north)	F 361, 371, 373, 374
		F 375, 376
	Square F 300 (south)	F 340, 341, 342, 387
	Square F 400 (south)	F 463, 464
B 4	Clay debris east of wall B 4	D 149
	Clay debris with ash and black-burnt surface	D 150, 335, 352, 360
	4 large stones on this surface	D 428
	Wall B 8	
	West of wall B 6 clay debris	D 417
	Clay debris covering pit D 420, (destruction of wall B 7)	D 416
	Pit	D 355
	Accumulation square E 400 (north) Wall 439 (B 8)	
	East of wall B 8	E 426
	West of wall B 8	E 425
	E 400 (south) Wall B 8	E 420
	Pit	E 423
	Accumulation	E 431, 449
	E 300 (north)	E 328
	E 300 (south)	336, 337, 342, 347, 349, 350
	F 300 (north)	F 331, 334, 335, 336, 359
		F 389
	F 300 (south)	F 330, 343, 344, 385, 386, 388
	F 400 (north)	F 450, 471, 473, 475
	F 400 (south)	F 455, 457, 458, 461, 462, 468
	Earthquake crack	F 466
B 5	Series of occupation levels	D 413, 414
	Pit	D 357

Phase C

Phase C shows walls built after the final destruction of the furnace walls. The stumps of walls B 5 and B 6 were still visible above the surface when a new wall, C 1, was built on top of the remains of wall B 2, running in the same direction. This is a comparatively heavy wall, of which very little survived in the excavated area. Wall C 2 runs right across the ruined furnace.

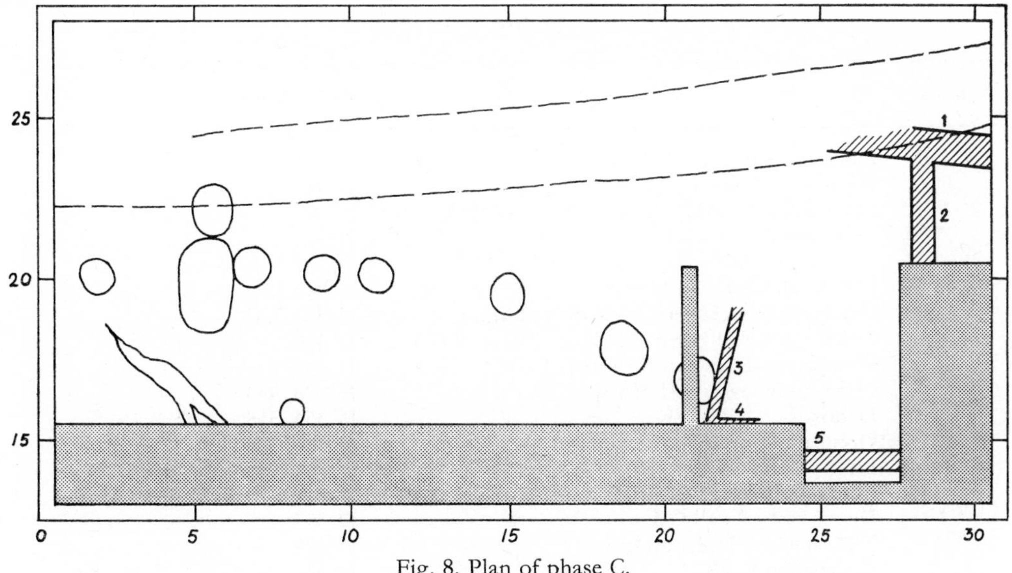

Fig. 8. Plan of phase C.

The only other walls in this phase are walls C 3 and C 4. In none of these cases has sufficient evidence been uncovered to interpret these walls. The end of phase B is marked by a great fire on the surface which burnt over a large area and scorched the surface to a depth of 5-10 cms. in places. In phase C this is followed again by long stretches of occupation levels alternating with deposits of partly burnt clay and interrupted by pits. A curious oblong pit was discovered in sq.F. (F 449) It belongs to the end of the period. Its depth is c. 1.25 m. It was originally lined with bricks, and on the north side a brick pillar, still 7 courses high was found.

The end of phase C is marked by an earthquake. Here we find one of the very few cracks that can be dated to a phase. A deep, wide crack was discovered in sq.F 400. In it were found the scattered remains of a human skeleton. These are the only human bones found in the I.A. occupation.

Phase C deposits have been divided into three sub-phases.

List of deposits

Sub-phase	*Description*	*Field numbers*
C 1	Walls C 1, 2	D 150a, 150b
	Walls C 3, 4, 5 (C 5 largely destroyed by later pit)	D 338, (C 4 in section only, no fieldnumber), D 293
	Debris from wall B 10	D 334
	Occupation levels	D 342, 412
	Clay deposits	D 343, 344, 351, 502
	Occupation levels and wash from wall B 8	E 424

List of deposits (continued)

Sub-phase	*Description*	*Field numbers*
	Occupation levels	F 329
	Pit, partly filled with bricks	F 357, E 326
C 2	Clay wash covering some stones, probably a platform	D 501
	Clay debris south of wall C 1	D 147
	Clay wash west of wall C 2	D 411
	Occupation levels between walls C 1 and C 2	D 332, 333
	Thick deposit of burnt rubble west of wall C 3	D 340
	Occupation levels east of wall C 3	D 349
	Occupation levels and debris	E 328, 430
	Debris	F 356, 358
	Occupation levels and clay debris	F 347, 338
	Pit	F 339
C 3	Clay rubble over D 411	D 410
	Debris east of wall C 3	D 347
	The same south of wall C 5	D 298
	Occupation levels	D 331
	Pit	D 339
	Occupation levels and debris	E 317, 318, 322, 327, 346, 418
	Occupation levels and debris	F 337, 346, 452, 472, 482, 483
	Pits	F 355, 485, 486, 487
	Brick lined pit	F 449
	Earthquake crack	F 466

Phase D

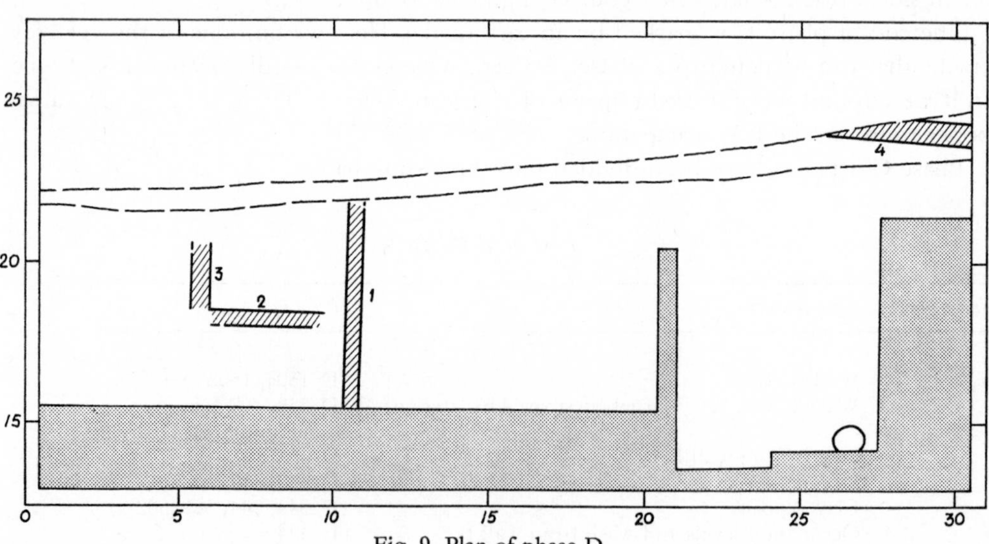

Fig. 9. Plan of phase D.

Phase D, like phase C, does not add much for the interpretation of the kind of occupation and activities that went on in this time. Its main characteristic is that none of the earlier structures have survived and only the stump of wall C 1 was still standing (wall D 4). The deposits belonging to phase D are not thicker than 60 to 70 cms, and they are thinner on the south side. To the west of wall D 1 they consist mainly of wind-blown material, whereas east of this wall we find occupation levels and clay deposits. The wind-blown material consists of an accumulation of dust, sand, burnt clay particles, charcoal and tiny pebbles, all thoroughly mixed. It was not transported by the air as is aeolian material, such as loess, but pushed by the strong east winds over the surface, piling up against and behind abandoned walls and filling up the pits. There are no occupation levels running through these deposits, but under special light conditions (low sunlight reflected from a nearby vertical section) some surfaces could be detected. It seems that human activities went on mainly east of wall D 3. It is possible that walls D 1, 2 and 3 formed part of a house. From the pottery evidence and from the general stratigraphic picture it can be concluded that phase D still belongs to the first I.A. period and not to the village. The walls were ruined by the end of phase D, apart from wall D 1 which was either rebuilt or still standing in phase E. In phase D this wall stops abruptly at 10.50 / 15.50 and is not to be seen in the baulk. To the east of wall D 1 the end of the phase is marked by a thick layer of ashes practically covering the whole surface. Phase D begins after an earthquake and ends with a huge (accidental?) fire of stored fuel. Apart from some shallow pits, no pits of the ordinary type were found east of wall D 1. A stone platform was found in a sounding between walls E 1 and 2, which precedes this building. The platform was covered by ash. A bread oven was found in square E.

Phase D has been divided into 2 sub-phases.

List of deposits

Sub-phase	*Description*	*Field numbers*
D 1	Walls D 1, 2, 3 and 4	F 349, F 455,
	Occupation levels	D 145, 330, 409
	Thick ash level	D 281, 297, 325
	Bread oven	E 444
	Occupation levels and debris	E 419, 335, 443
D 2	Thick clay deposit and occupation levels	D 144, 282, 329
	Burnt occupation level	D 323, 408
	Pit	D 290
	Occupation levels	E 321, 325
	Wind-blown material	F 345, 353, 354, 437, 459, 467, 469
	Stone platform	A 426

The Second Period

Phases E-M

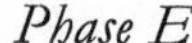

Phase E

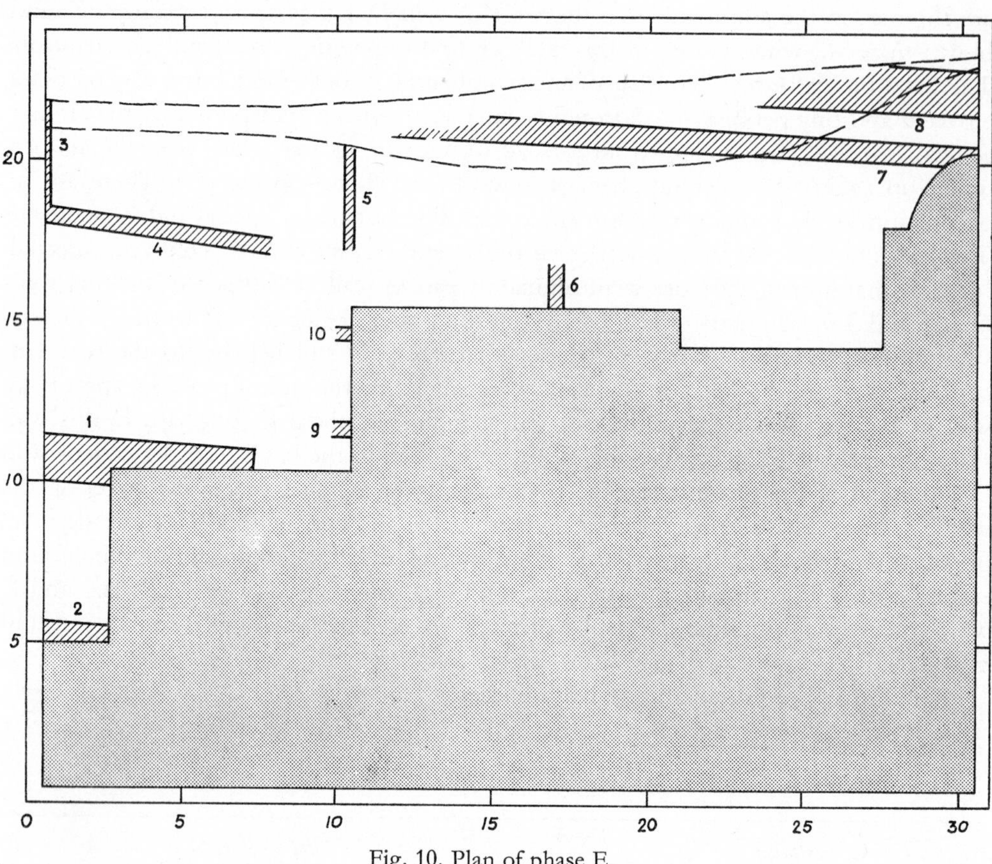

Fig. 10. Plan of phase E.

A considerable amount of building started in phase E. A substantial building (walls E 1 and E 2) appears, only a small portion of which was traced in phase E (cf. phase H). The width of wall E 1 is 1.40 m. This building had a long history and was rebuilt in phase H. The original floor consisted of clay. A curious structure was found between the two walls, looking as if a wall had been folded double. A large amount of organic material (straw?) was found in the fill, but no pottery. North of wall E 1 an accumulation of wind-blown material was found, which also piled up against wall E 4. Walls E 3 and 4 and probably E 5 form another building. Wall E 4 was in a very bad state of preservation in square E 300. Wall E 5 was built on the remains of wall D 1. In this wall a doorway was found, which was blocked with bricks. A later pit had destroyed part of the remains of this wall. Wall E 4 is slightly later than wall E 3. Two walls, E 9 and

E 10 became visible in the east section of square A but have not been further excavated. They appear to be buried in their own clay and slope down to the west. South of wall E 9 street levels appear. Between walls E 5 and E 6 a series of street levels, covered by a thick deposit of clay and wind-blown material was found. Wall E 6 survived only in a few traces. No connection between this wall and wall E 7 could be found. East of wall E 6 there was again a series of street levels or occupation levels, alternating with ashy, burnt and unburnt clay deposits. These deposits also stretch right along the south side of wall E 7. This wall was found in an almost completely decayed state, reduced to a heap of clay with bricks in a regular position recognizable only in square D. The wall seems to have run parallel to a very substantial wall E 8, which was so near the surface that the bricks had decomposed. There was no evidence that walls E 7 and 8 formed a casemate wall. They were however certainly built on the same surface. The space between these walls was filled with clay rubble. From the present evidence they cannot be interpreted as town walls. They lasted only through phase E. The position of these walls illustrates what has been said in the introduction about the wind erosion working on the north west corner of the tell.

Both from the pottery evidence and from the structural remains of this phase it becomes clear that a new type of occupation of the mound begins with phase E. Too little is known yet about the nature of the large building on the west side to ascertain its purpose, but a store house is possible. That progress was slow and that there were still large open spaces is shown by the fact that wind-blown material still accumulated in this period against the walls, a process discussed in phase D.

We have found no indications that the tell was actually abandoned for any length of time between phases D and E. Brick wall D 1 was still partly standing when the new building activities started. Wind-blown material, especially of the kind found all over the surface of the tell in the semi-nomadic period, accumulates quickly. (A basket boy emptying his basket on the top of the dump during an eastern storm could see the contents of his basket being blown as a dust cloud to the west). There is no evidence that a later phase of the "nomadic" period was eroded away from the excavated area before the new building activities started. (For the pottery evidence, see Part II.)

We assume, therefore, that a group of villagers took possession of the mound for a new settlement. This must have happened about the middle of the 12th century B.C. or slightly later. Their pottery tradition was certainly related to that of the "semi-nomads" but there are some characteristic differences. It is certainly possible that the semi-nomads continued their activities in the vicinity, leaving the mound to the villagers. There are no indications of any hostilities having taken place between the two groups.

List of deposits

Sub-phase	*Description*	*Field numbers*
E 1	Walls E 1 and 2	A 412, 403
	Walls E 3, 4, 5	no numbers
	Walls E 9, 10	no numbers
	Walls 6, 7, 8	D 317
	Burnt surface	D 143
	Occupation levels south of wall 7	D 329, 279, 316, 320
	Brick debris	E 413, 416, 417, 418
		F 381, 384
	Wind-blown material	F 237, 448, 476
	Floor between walls 1 and 2	A 424
	Fill between the walls	A 417, 427
	Brick structure	A 425a
E 2	South of wall E 7 occupation	D 141, 142, 269, 276, 291
		D 296, 315, 326, 337
	Wind-blown material	D 267, 315, E 303, 314, 315
		E 316, 415
	Brick debris	E 311, 312, F 325, 327, 383
	Wind-blown deposit	F 433, 455
	Clay debris from walls 9 and 10	F 111
	Debris between walls 1 and 2	A 417
	In this debris were found the remains of wooden beams, probably from a collapsed roof.	

Phase F

Phase F shows a rather puzzling development after phase E. Walls E 1, 2 still exist (F 1 and 2) and it is certain that walls E 3 and 4 were also still used in this phase (F 3 and 4). Owing to the rise of the surface outside, building F 1-2 got a new floor level. Wall F 5 was discovered during the last days of the 1961 season and was not further excavated. The base of this wall slopes down towards the west as do all the deposits north of wall F 1.

Wall F 8 (Pl. IXa and VIIIb) was already partly discovered in the 1960 season and was then thought to have been a town wall and related to a round tower. This wall lasted until phase J, and the round tower can only belong to phase K. In order to build the tower on level ground a cut was made into the slope of the mound, and so the part of the tower underground fitted neatly into the buried remains of wall F 8. Wall F 8 stops abruptly at 25 cms. from wall F 7, which runs in a northerly direction and is on the south side connected with wall F 6. (Pl. VIIIb) Wall F 9 runs parallel to wall F 7. Building 7, 6, 9 had a floor covered with at least one layer of large river stones. Although it is tempting to interpret this structure as a defence wall with square tower, it is difficult to see how the contemporary building F 3, 4 could fit into a defence system. It is possible that only the open spaces along the edge of the built-up area were closed by defence structures, as a protection against irregular attacks from nomads.

Only occasionally does one find pits in the village. Some deep pits were found in

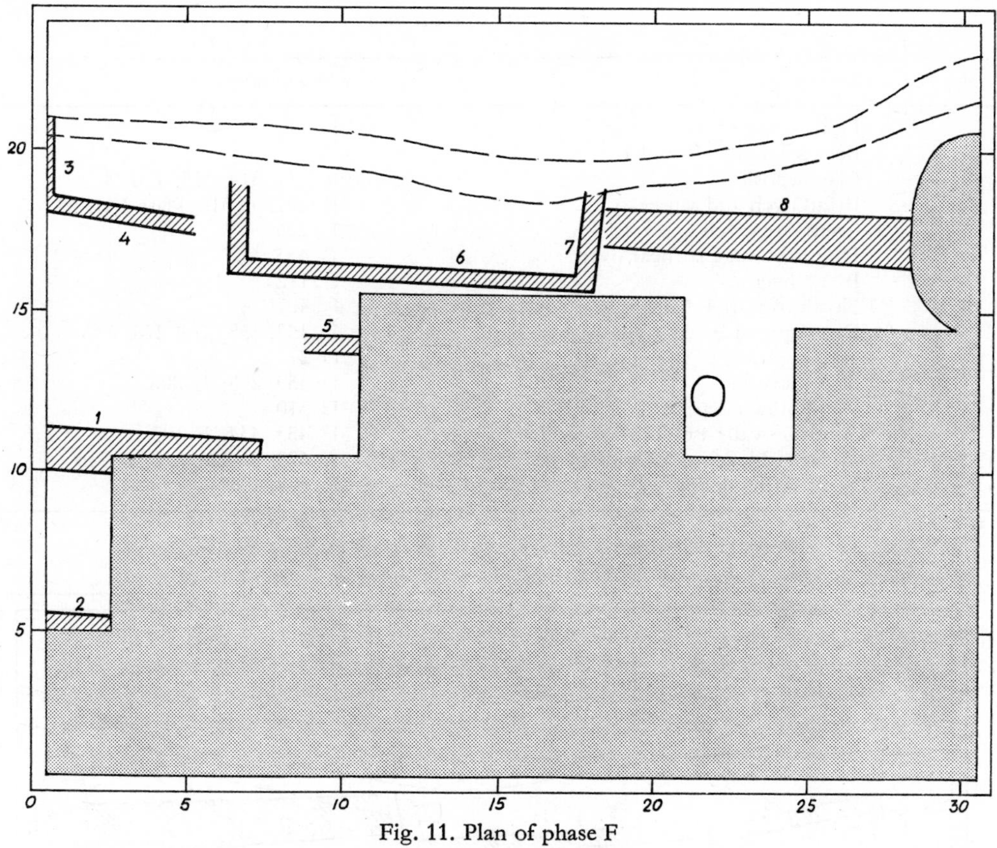

Fig. 11. Plan of phase F

square F 300 which penetrated down into phase F but could not be attributed to a phase as the upper parts began on the tell surface.

The phase F deposits have been divided into two groups.

List of deposits

Sub-phase	*Description*	*Field numbers*
F 1	Wall 8	D 336
	Walls 9,6 and 7	
	Wall 5	E 105
	Walls 3 and 4	
	Walls 1 and 2	A 412, 403
	Clay north of wall 8	D 313
	South of wall 8 occupation levels	D 267, 268, 269
	Clay east of wall 7	E 315
	Floor and stone pavement building 9-6-7	E 412, 324, F 379, 351, 352
	Decomposed bricks s. of wall 5	F 102

List of deposits (continued)

Sub-phase	*Description*	*Field numbers*
	Floor south of wall 5	F 110
	Between walls 4-6 and 1	
	Clay deposits	F 311, 314, 315, F 228
	Bread oven and ash heap	F 227, F 316 (Plate VII, b)
	Courtyard levels and ash heap	F 226
	Dug in storage jar near oven	F 453
	Bread oven	F 112
	North of wall 4 debris	F 407
F 2	Decomposed bricks south of wall 8	D 133, 358, 274, 278, 287
	Pit	D 277
	Street levels	D 359, 295, E 208
	Wind-blown deposit n. of wall 6	E 310
	South of walls 4-6 decomposed bricks	F 433, 434, F 305
	Courtyard levels n. of wall 1	A 623, F 226, 222, F 310
	N. of wall 4 debris	F 405, 406

Phase G

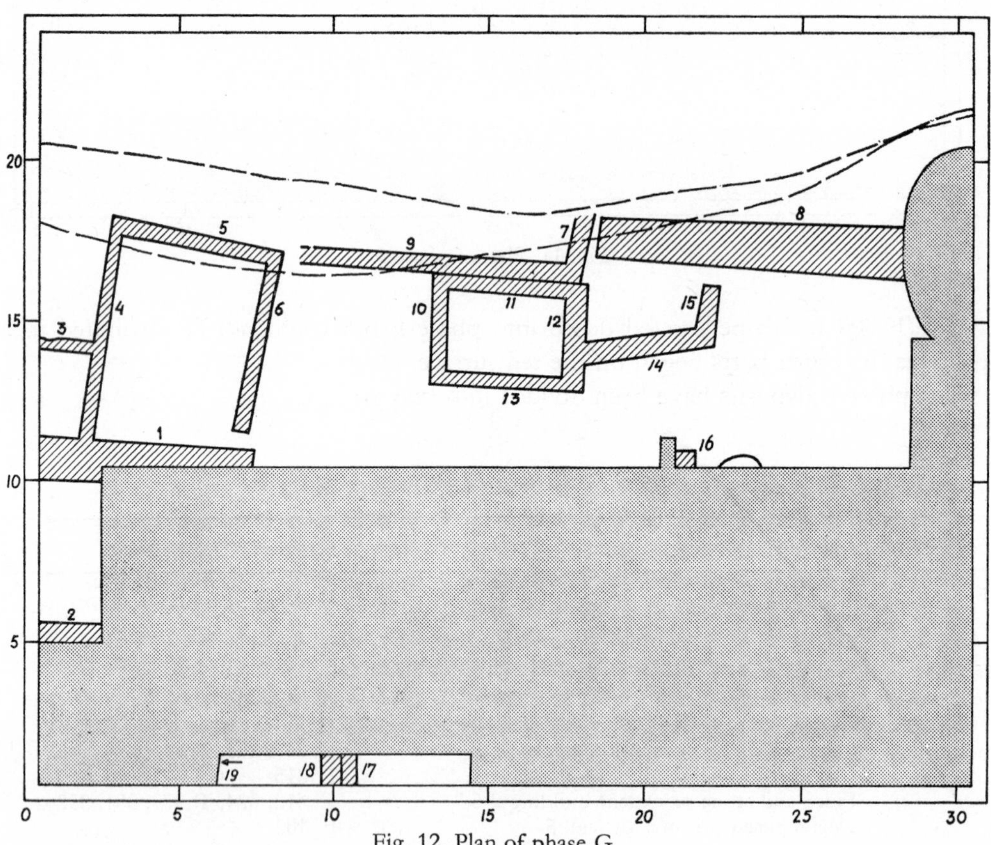

Fig. 12. Plan of phase G

Walls G 1, 2, 7 and 8 correspond with walls F 1, 2, 7 and 8 respectively. Wall G 11 is built on the ruined wall F 6, and wall G 9 (Pl. VIIIb), the wall that replaced wall F 6, runs on a line farther north. This new wall was erected on top of the layer of large stones in the previous phase, and the second layer was presumably added together with wall 9. There was no indication of a wall parallel to wall 7 on the west end of wall G 9. A road runs between walls G 18 and 19 (square A 100) to the north into a "square", formed by walls G 6, 9, 10, and turns east along walls G 13, 14, 15, 8. This street plan had a long history. The surface was regularly renewed with reed. It lasted until phase K, when the level had risen c 2 m. above the original level.

Two practically complete house plans were discovered. The house formed by walls G 4,5 and 6 shows two phases. 1) Walls 4,5 and 6a, of which few traces were discovered. To this sub-phase also belongs wall G 3. 2) Walls 4, 5b which is 20 cms. wider than wall 5 and further south, and wall 6b further east. The entrance was at the south end of wall 6. West of wall 4 a succession of bread ovens was found, buried in thick ash levels. (Pl. VIIIa)

The second house was formed by the walls G 10,11,12 and 13, with an additional room formed by walls G 14 and 15. The room was paved with bricks, the only example of this kind of paving so far found. Only a few traces of wall 10 were found.

Room G 12, 14 and 15 was used as a store room. It contained a mass of broken storage jars. This indicates a sudden collapse of walls and roof.

Wall G 16 was found standing to a height of 10 courses of bricks, and may already have existed in phase F. It protrudes into the excavated area without any traces of a doorway or an adjacent wall.

In a small sounding along the southern section of the excavated area, east of wall G 19, which is connected with walls G 2 and 1, the lowest road levels have not been reached. Wall 18 belongs to the series of rebuildings of houses, that dates from before phase G and continues until phase L, like the street. Wall G 17 is a phase G rebuilding of wall 18, which is itself a rebuilding of an earlier wall.

List of deposits

Sub-phase	*Description*	*Field numbers*
	Walls 1, 2	A 412, 403
	Walls 4, 5, 6, 3	F 429, F 303 (= 324, 423, 478) F 108, F 455
	Walls 7, 9. Wall 8	E 105, D 312 (= 336)
	Walls 10, 11, 12, 13	E 104, 103 (= 205), 204, B 519
	Walls 14, 15, 16	E 204a, D 283, D 318 (= 319)
	Walls 17, 18	A 155d, 155e
G 1	Wall G 17 (4 bricks high) is built on clay rubble accumulated against G 18	B 247
G 1	Road between walls 18 and 19	A 177
G 2	The same	A 176
G 3	Destruction wall 17	A 175

List of deposits (continued)

Sub-phase	*Description*	*Field numbers*
	Collapse of roof walls 1 and 2 with wooden beams stretching e.-w.	A 418
G 1	Ash and courtyard levels n. of wall 3	F 215, 224, 225, 236, 447
	Ash and some large stones	F 230, 232
	Bread oven	F 231
G 2	W. of wall 4; thick deposits from bread ovens	F 216, 229, F 417, 418, 419, 439, 440, 451, 478
	Bread ovens (some built on top of each other)	F 214, 217, 218, 221, 223, 421, 451
G 3	Clay debris	F 213, 427
	Road levels and clay debris	F 212, 422, 425, 447
G 1	First floor walls 1, 4, 5a, 6a	F 430
G 2	Rebuilding of this room clay debris	F 428
	Floors	F 209, 212, 107, 424
G 3	Destruction, overlaid by courtyard	F 234, 106
G 1	Street, e. of wall 6	A 176, 618, F 309, E 100
G 2	The same	A 175, 617, F 308, B 314, 511 E 201, 206
G 3	The same	A 177, 621, 622, F 307, 308, 309, B 513, E 101, 311, 312
G 1	E. of wall 16, burnt debris	D 263, 272, 273, 285
G 2	Floors or courtyard	D 262, 265, 266, 270
	Clay debris over yard	D 280, 284
	Accumulation against wall 8	D 135, 136, 137
	Wind-blown material	D 132, 307
G 3	Destruction wall 16, clay	D 261, 264, 275
	Pit, partly filled with organic matter	D 286, 294
G 1	Inside walls 7, 9: stones	E 323
	Inside walls 12, 14, 15	E 207, 409, 410
G 3	Destruction of these walls	E 203, 408, 411
G 1	Room walls 10-13, floor	E 102, 315
G 3	Destruction	B 518

Phase H

The large building in the s.w. corner is a completely new building in phase H. The e. wall, H 1, forming the e. front of the building, is a restoration of the phase G wall, which is, at this stage, already buried under nearly 2 m. of accumulated street levels on the e. and n. side. Wall H 3 corresponds with wall G 2 and may still date from that phase. No cut through these walls has yet been made in order to study their history. Nor have we yet investigated whether walls H 2 and 5 are one wall in phase G. If this should be the case, the excavated part of the original lay-out of the building suggests that here is the "hilani" type of building. The other walls are new.

In the section it was found that "sleeper beams" were used as foundations for walls H 4 and 6. The thickness of these walls remained the same, indicating that they are not ordinary house walls, but originally built for the same unknown purpose. On this level, inside walls H 4,5 and 6, wooden floor beams (?) were found (cf. below). Wall H 2 was

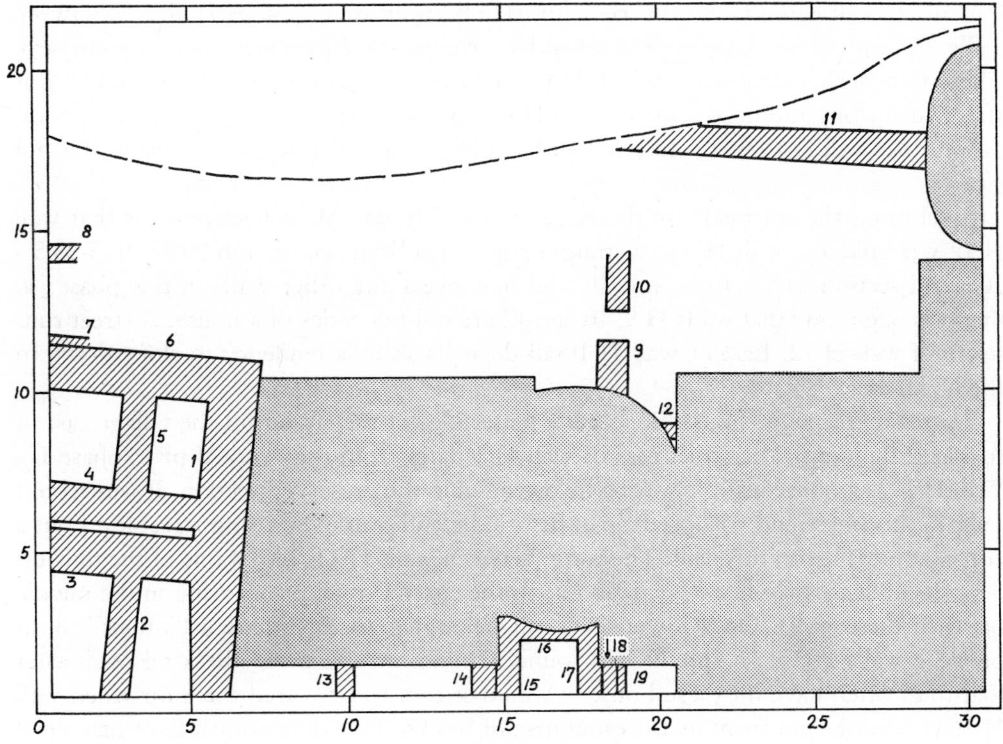

Fig. 13. Plan of phase H

only partly excavated on the north side, but the top showed up clearly in outline by an elevation of a phase J floor which runs over the stump of it. The total space between walls H 1 and 6 was divided into two main blocks, separated by a double wall, each of which had a partition wall running n.-s. The only completely excavated room between walls H 4,5 and 6 had no doorway in the existing wall fragments, which are c. 1 m. high.

Thin wooden beams running parallel to the walls H 4 and 6 were found at the same level of the sleeper beams under the walls, suggesting that there may have been a wooden floor. No traces were found of wooden planking covering these beams. Neither were there any traces of the ordinary type of house floor or any kind of stone pavement, occupation debris or a pottery level in any of the rooms. Eventually some indication of the purpose of this building may be found in an analysis of the material of the large lumps of very soft brown and peat-like fill between fallen bricks found above and under the floor level in these rooms.

Both walls H 7 and 8 were too near to the surface and too much damaged by the mediaeval graves to form a clear plan. They do not belong to one building since H 7 was built after H 8 was destroyed, but both belong to phase H. Wall H 8 was built after the construction of wall H 6.

Wall H 11 (F 8 and G 8) still seems to have been in use in phases H and J. Between walls H 9 and 10 was a passage, marked by a rough stone pavement, into a courtyard. These walls terminate a street which in phase G ran further east. In sub-phase H 1 this street runs along the north side of wall H 6 and under wall H 8. There were no indications that wall H 10 was connected with wall H 11, and the purpose of the wall is not clear.

By clearing the cut made by the large "cistern" (phase M) it became clear that wall H 12 was linked to wall H 9 in a straight angle. The study of section 20.5 / 10.5-28.5 / 10.5 and section 24.5 / 10.5-24.5 / 17 did not reveal any other walls in this phase; so that it is safe to say that walls H 9, 10 and 12 are not two sides of a house. A street runs south of wall H 12. East of wall H 10 all deposits show a tendency to slope down to the north-east.

For the first time it is possible to get a better idea of the lay-out of the village east of the large building. The street east of wall H 1 dates from the original plan (phase E). Wall H 13 is a house wall. It was badly damaged in the preserved section. It was rebuilt once in this phase and collapsed again before the end of it. The rising street level put a constant pressure on this wall. The room between walls H 13, 14 has one of the thickest deposits of successive floors, (c. 0.50 m.) In the latest a small pit was dug in the middle between these walls. On a lower level but belonging to this phase a "kitchen" floor between walls H 15, 16 and 17 was found. This room illustrates the kind of disaster that must often have hit these houses. A mud stream had covered the floor when wall H 16 collapsed right from its lowest course of bricks. This drama must have happened during a heavy winter rainfall, when a stream of mud poured down the street (which we have reason to suspect lies just south of the excavated area) and flooded the lower lying kitchen floor, hitting the wall at the back.

The next floor (phase J,) is 0.80 m. higher than the phase H floor. Wall H 18 dates from phase G and its remains were used in phase H, strengthened by a wall, H 19. East of this is another room. An east-west wall should have shown up in section in the phase M "cistern", but at 21 / 5.5 the "cistern" wall was very badly broken by one of the major cracks through the tell, so that no clear picture could be formed of any stratigraphic links on either side of the crack.

List of deposits

Sub-phase	*Description*	*Field numbers*
H 1	Walls 1, 2, 3	A 430 (= 244), 261, 403
	Walls 4, 5, 6	A 413, 325, 412 (= F 201)
	Beams under wall H 6	A 411
	Walls 9, 10	
	Walls 13, 14, 15	B 179, 180
	Walls 16, 17, 18, 19	B 176, 173, 175 (= 182), 174
	0.60 m. deposits of road levels	

List of deposits (continued)

Sub-phase	*Description*	*Field numbers*
H 1	n. of wall H 6 (3 sub-phases)	A 339, 340, 350, 352, 522, 616, F 205, 210, B 312, 325, 507, E 402, 406, 407
H 2		A 338, 506, 615, B 310, 311, 321, 324
H 3		A 520, 613, B 309, 505, F 202, 416
H 1-3	In 6-9.5/0.5-1.5 this group of road levels is compressed to c. 15 cms. and covered under debris from wall H 13	A 175a
H 2	Debris between walls H 7, 8	F 203, 204, 206, A 521
H 1	Debris e. of walls H 9, 10	D 260
H 2	Courtyard id.	D 249, 257
H 3	Destruction desposits id.	B 317, D 127, 129, 255/6, 251/2
	Destruction walls H 9, 10	B 514, 517, D 254
	Debris near wall H 11	D 259, 306
	Fill room H 4, 5, 6	A 402, 410, 414
	Thick deposit organic matter	A 421
	Fill room 1, 4, 5, 6	A 405, 415/6, 428/9
	Room H 13, 14 floor levels interrupted by 0.10 m. clay deposit from rebuilding wall H 13	B 242, 246; B 244/5
	Floor levels room H 15, 16, 17	B 177
	Mud deposit and destruction	B 178, 176
	Clay deposit e. of wall H 19	B 181

Phase J

In phase J only the southern half of the large building in the s.w. corner still existed, immediately under the mediaeval cemetery. Wall J 4 proves that the northern part had disappeared. This wall runs over wall H 1, and sank deep down into the soft fill of the underlying room, being cut by the stump of wall H 5. The rest of wall J 4, further west, is badly damaged by the cemetery. The same happened to wall J 14; a small section survived between two graves. Walls J 1 and 2 still follow the old course of the phase H building. But instead of the n.-s. division wall of phase H there is now a much thinner wall running e.-w. This wall, J 3, was founded on wooden beams, like the other walls of this building (Pl. IXb). The e. part sank down into a rather soft fill between walls H 1 and 2. This is the last stage of the history of this building in the excavated area. As will be seen (phase K), any later remains were eroded away during the I.A.

The street, e. of wall J 1, was still in use, and from the fact that it was still used after the destruction of the phase J building one may conclude that the building also continued in use in phase K. A curious feature was a stone pavement alongside and e. of wall J 1, stretching out to the middle of the street. This pavement soon disappeared under the ever rising street level (Pl. Xa). There were faint traces of an entrance in wall J 1. Walls J 4 and 14 indicate that the street did not continue beyond that line. Its course further e. is discussed below.

The group of houses in sq. B and C continued to be used and rebuilt. A very strange

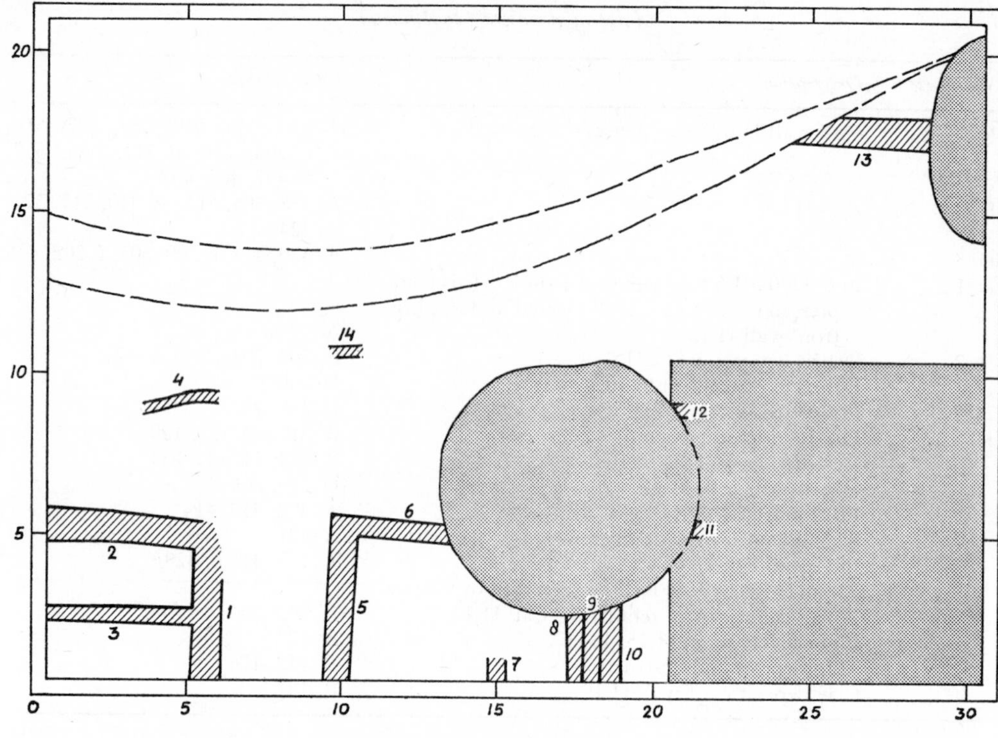

Fig. 14. Plan of phase J

situation was found between walls 8,6 and 5, which during the 1960 season suggested that the "cistern" (phase M) was dug in this phase. Wall J 7 was partly broken down to the floor level and the entire space between walls 8,6,5 was filled with large lumps of earth, often containing a whole succession of floor levels, which could only have been dug up and thrown into the remains of this room. It seems likely, as the "cistern" is definitely later, that an earlier pit existed at the same place, which disappeared completely when the phase M pit was dug. The room was filled with excavated debris to a height of over 1 m. Single lumps measured 60 cms. in length and 20 cms. in height, indicating the use of picks. Under the pressure of the inside accumulation, wall J 5 collapsed and fell over the street. The rebuilding of this wall is attributed to phase K.

Wall H 17 is wall J 9, still being used to support wall J 10 (=H 19) and leaning over to the w. The section, cut by the "cistern", showed that two walls, J 11 and 12, belong to this phase. Wall J 11 formed a room with J 10. A street runs between walls J 2-6 and J 4-14. The stratigraphy between squares B and D was badly damaged by cracks, but it seems that wall J 12 (a rebuilding of wall H 12 but slightly further n.) belongs to a building of which no further remains could be identified with certainty. W. of 22/10.5 layers of clay debris were found, presumably from this building and e. of this point the road levels continue which must link with the street levels between walls J 11 and 12.

The street plan of this phase is therefore as follows: A s.-n. street links with an e.-w. street which at the e. side comes out in a square. It is likely that this square is close to a gate since all the street levels dip down towards the n.e. (cf. phase K tower.)

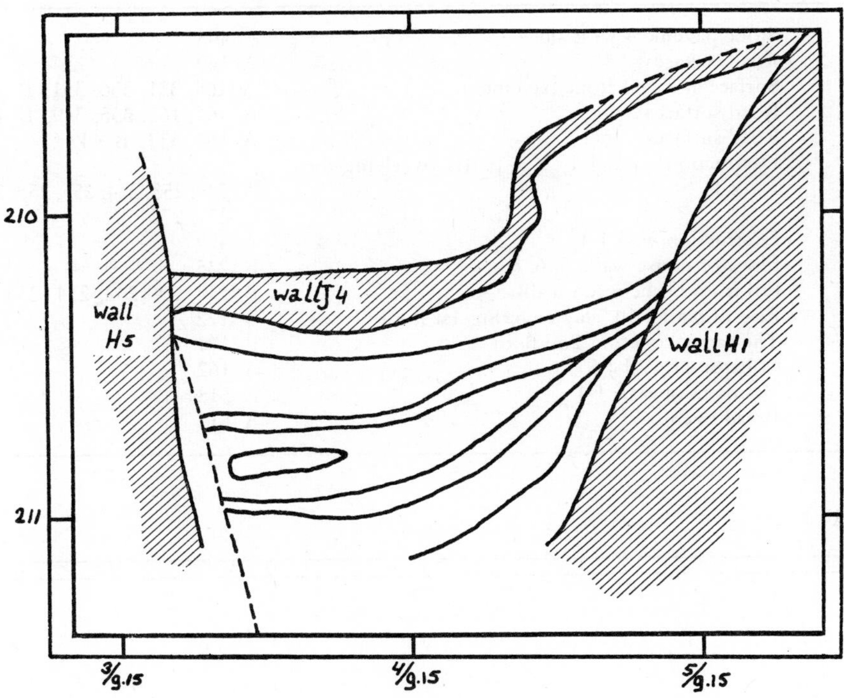

Fig. 15. Wall J 4 in section

List of deposits

Sub-phase	*Description*	*Field numbers*
	Walls 1, 2, 3	
	Walls 4, 14	
	Walls 5, 6, 8	
	Walls 9, 10	
	Wall 13	
J 1	Clay and street levels reaching the cemetery level at 20/10.50	D 240
J 2	Remains of a building, wall J 12 and faint traces of a n.-s. wall in section 21.75-22.5/10.5	D 230, 231
J 3	Destruction of this building and clay debris around it	D 234, 235, 249, 250, 246, 229 B 305, 315, 316, 322, 458, E 405
J 4	Road surfaces running over this destruction level	D 232, 233, 301, B 454, 455
J 5	Collapsed walls over street	D 238, B 453, 521, 522
	The road in square A:	
J 1	Debris and road surfaces	A 170, 174, 406

List of deposits (continued)

Sub-phase	*Description*	*Field numbers*
	Stone pavement west side	A 408
J 2	Road surfaces	A 169
J 3	Surface and 2nd stone pavement	A 168, 331, 336, 351, B 448
J 4	Road surfaces	A 164, 165, 335, 349, B 447
J 5	Road surfaces	A 163, 337, B 449
	Destruction walls J 1, 2, 3, partly overlying the road	A 249, 253, 254, 255, 258, 259, 260, 271, 272
	Destruction wall J 4	A 419
J 1	Floor of house walls 5, 6, 8	B 235
	Fill from pit between walls 5, 6, 8	B 218, 230-232, 234, 236-240
	East of wall J 10, clay covering 1st floor	B 172
	The same, covering 2nd floor	B 171
J 5	Collapse of wall J 5	A 162
	Debris n. of wall J 4	A 518
J 1	Bread oven	A 517

Phase K

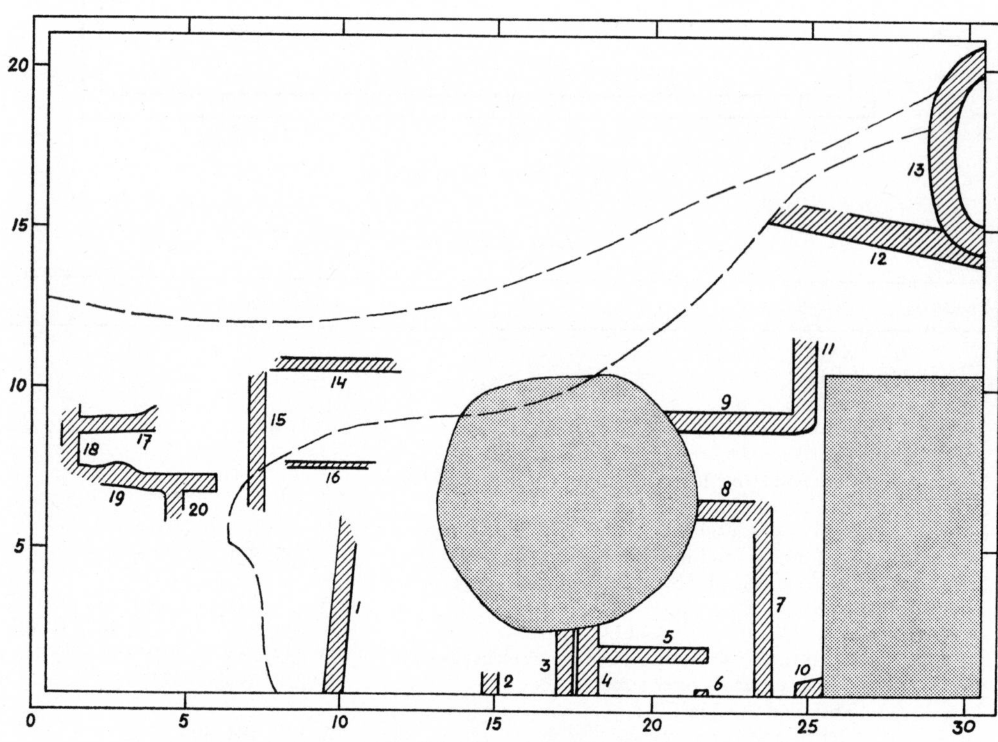

Fig. 16. Plan of phase K

The contour line of the tell surface of phase K shows two disturbances. In the n.e. part (square D 100) of the excavated area a major interruption, noticeable from phase H onward, is explained by the existence of a "round tower", which belongs to phase K. (Pl. Xb)

As it had to be built on the edge of a slope, a flat surface like a terrace had to be dug into the mound for firm foundation. The preserved part of the tower is largely its original foundations, as it lies lower than the other phase K deposits. In the 1960 season it was thought that the tower was built into wall J 13, but in fact the circular foundation trench cut through this wall by accident. From phase H onwards all the road levels slope down towards the n.e. and this may well indicate that the entrance to the village was somewhat farther east. In that case one can assume that the tower is one of two towers guarding the entrance. Wall K 12, which indeed stands on a much higher absolute level than the lowest bricks of the tower, is then a defence wall with the tower protruding in its entirety from the wall. (Wall K 13.) (Pl. Xb)

The second interruption of the contour line is found in the s.w. corner of the excavated area (squares A 100,400). Here already periods II and III (between Iron I and II) levels have been washed away by erosion, followed by accumulation of mixed wash material from higher levels of the tell. To begin with it was very difficult to understand this situation as the whole area was perforated by the mediaeval cemetery. Moreover the period III accumulation, if it ever extended as far as square A 100, had eroded away before the cemetery was made. Period III deposits are found e. of the excavated area, (square H, which is not published here, as it only contains period III material). The diagram fig. 17 shows the process of accumulation and denudation between periods II and III.

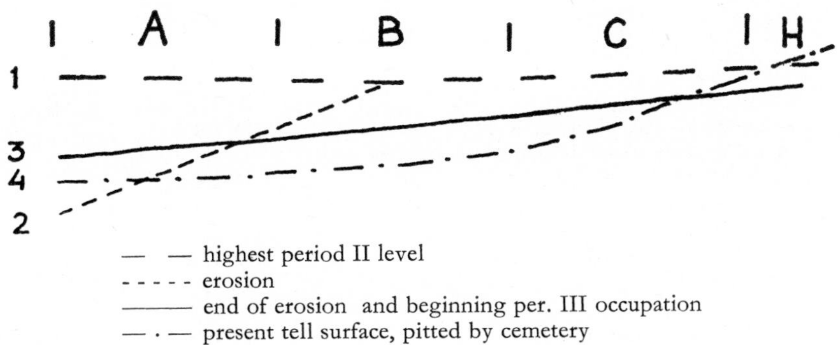

Fig. 17. Schematic drawing of the process of accumulation and denudation between periods II and III

Wall K 1 (wall J 5 rebuilt) still served as a retaining wall for the heap of rubble piled up on the e. side. Very little was left of wall K 2, which formed a room with wall K3, a rebuilding of wall J 8. Walls K 4,5,6 formed a room with an entrance to the e., and seem to form part of a larger house with a wall, K 7, running n.-s., and an e.-w. wall, K 8, further n. At 24/1 is another doorway with a wall, K 10, to the east. In the vertical section 25,5/0.5-10.5 no traces were found of an e.-w. wall farther n. of wall K 10.

The tell deposits in squares C 400 and 300 were in a very bad state from the earthquake cracks.

Traces of the other building remains were all very much obliterated by the cemetery, and in the s.e. corner much disturbance was caused by refuse pits which were dug in period III.

Wall K 12 was extremely fragmentary, it is not certain that it was a defence wall. As, however, the road runs immediately s. of this wall, and the tower was certainly dug into the then existing slope of the mound, there is no reason to suppose that there was a building north of this wall, and so one may assume that it was free standing.

The other wall combinations, walls 9,11; 14,15,16; 17,18,19,20, all belong to this phase and can be interpreted as houses. From the old street plan only the "square" near the hypothetical gate remains. Here the accumulation of road levels is very thick and slopes down to the n.e. West of wall K 1 traces of road levels were found running horizontally and therefore the total deposit is much thinner. The link between this road and the "square" is not clear. The thick deposit of road surfaces in square D near the tower made it possible to distinguish 11 sub-phases. The other deposits are either from the beginning or from the end of phase K.

List of deposits

Sub-phase	*Description*	*Field numbers*
K	Walls 1, 3	A 154, B 173
	Walls 4, 5, 6	B 183, 375, 171
	Walls 7, 9	C 355, 372
	Walls 9, 10, 11	C 424, 373, 428
	Walls 12, 13	
	Walls 14, 15, 16	B 457, A 317, B 318
	Walls 17, 18, 19, 20	A 327, 326, 323, 332
K 1	Foundation trench tower K 13	D 138
	Clay deposits from building-activities of walls K 12, 13	D 253
K 2	Road levels	D 248, A 162s
	Stone pavement	A 330
K 3	Clay deposits and road levels	D 242, 245
K 4	Road levels	D 237, 241, 244, C 427 A 145, 152, 160
K 5	Clay deposits and road levels	D 126, 227, 228, 236, 243, C 361, 423, A 147, 159
	Ash deposit	C 362
K 6	Thick ash deposit, clay and road surfaces	D 125, 226, C 359, 421, 422 A 144, 158, 318
K 7	Road levels (thick deposits of reed)	D 119, 124, 221, 226, C 358
K 8	Road levels	D 123, 223, C 363, 372-374, 420, A 141, 142, 151
K 9	The same	D 122, 224, 225, A 129
	6 large stones in the road	A 125

List of deposits (continued)

Sub-phase	*Description*	*Field numbers*
K 10	Surfaces with much ash	D 214, 215, 217
K 11	Clay debris and surface running over the ruined tower	D 211, 139, A 150
	Road between the end of wall K 1 and wall K 16	B 427, 445, 446
K 1	Floor s. of wall K 19	A 334
	Floor inside walls 14, 15, 16	A 347, 348
	No phase K desposits between walls K 1, 2 over the phase J rubble	
	Fill s. of wall K 5 and floors	B 157, 169, 170, C 371
	Clay fill e. of wall K 7	C 167, 169, 365, 367, 368, 369
	Bread oven s. of wall K 8	C 364
	Burnt destruction debris e. of wall 7	C 370
	In square C 200 excavation reached only the top levels of phase K	
	Wash levels sloping steeply n.	C 256, 257, 260, 261

Phase L

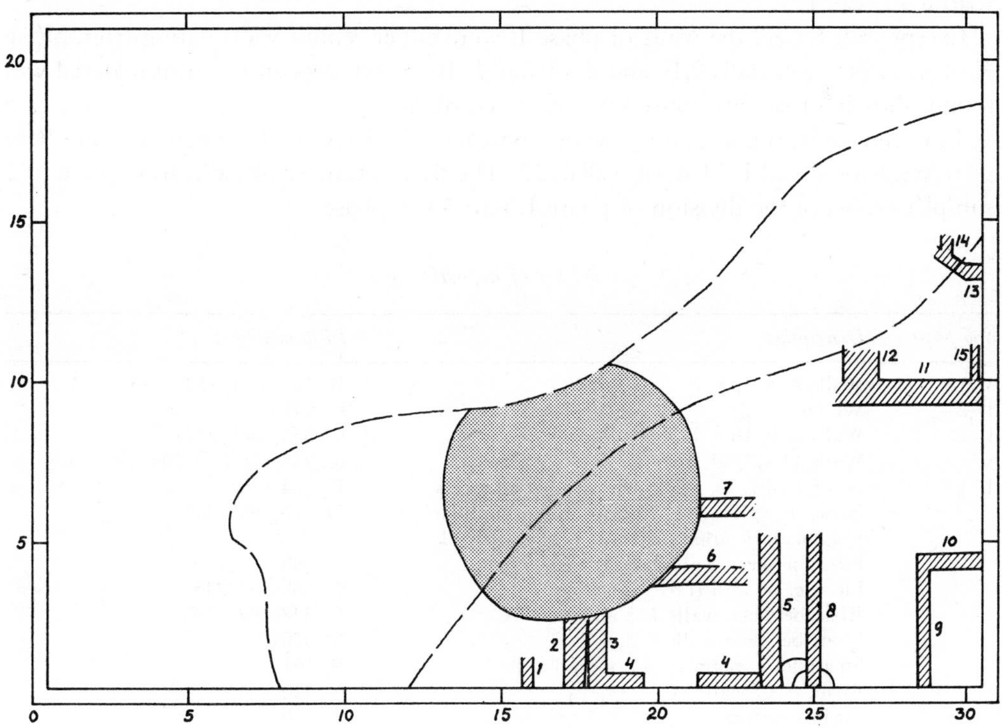

Fig. 18. Plan of phase L

The remains of phase L are very much disturbed by the period III pits. Another disturbing factor was the erosion discussed in the description of phase K. The third disturbance found over the whole area is the cemetery.

The very fragmentary wall L 1 must have belonged to a house w. of it. Wall L 2 is a rebuilding of wall K 3 and wall L 3 is the restored wall K 4. Wall L 4 is almost certainly a rebuilding of a wall that belonged to phase K, but on a line further s. This wall runs lengthwise in the s. section of the excavated area, and a street probably runs immediately to the south of it. A doorway in this wall was blocked and replaced by a new one farther east and at the same time 25 cms. higher than the previous one. This indicates an accumulation of road levels on the south side. Wall L 5 is wall K 7. Walls L 3,4,5,7 form a good example of an ordinary house, showing the position of the entrance, the renewal of the doorway following the rise of the street level, and a later addition of a wall L 6, in sub-phase L 3, which made the house much smaller, as it was placed 2 m. further s. Wall L 7 is wall K 8 but slightly further s. A narrow lane was found between walls L 5 and L 8, running n.-s. Walls L 8 and L 9 formed a room, as did walls L 9 and L 10. It is uncertain whether the space between walls L 10 and L 11 formed a room or a courtyard, as the area was largely disturbed by later pits and graves. Walls L 11, 12,13 formed another room. There were traces of a doorway in wall L 11. West of wall L 12 ran a road, which continued between walls L 5 and L 8, and formed an angle with the road n. of wall L 7.

Except wall L 6 all the walls of phase L were either rebuilt walls dating from phase K or new. Between walls 9,10 and n. of wall L 10 a thick deposit of burnt material was found, showing that this house was destroyed by fire.

Two thin walls, running north were found at 30-31/10 (walls L 15 and 16), and there were traces of a wall L 14 n. of wall L 13. The destruction of phase L took place in 2 sub-phases; hence the division of phase L into 3 sub-phases.

List of deposits

Sub-phase	*Description*	*Field numbers*
L 1	Walls 2, 3, 4, 5, 7	B 173, 183, 153, C 355, 341
L 2	Wall 6	C 341a
L 1	Walls 8, 9, 10	C 334, 244, 244a
	Walls 11, 12, 15, 16	C 249, D 212, 206
L 1	N. of wall L 13, thick deposit of road levels	D 104
	Between walls L 11, 13 floor and accumulation	D 210, 208, 209
	Fragmentary stone platform s. of wall L 11	
	Floor between walls L 9, 10	D 168s
	Floor e. of wall L 8	D 169s, C 245
	Road between walls L 5 and 8	C 348, 356, 357
	Floor between walls L 3, 4, 5, 7	C 370s
	Small floor fragment w. of wall L 1	B 161
	Road, n. of wall L 7	C 420
	Pit in s. section	C 170
	Traces of two walls in square A, one on the line	

List of deposits (continued)

Sub-phase	*Description*	*Field numbers*
	of wall K 1 plus debris	A 126, 137
	Debris between and w. of walls L 15, 16	D 203, 206
L 2	Most of the phase L walls were destroyed in this sub-phase	
	Road levels n. and w. of wall L 13	D 104 (upper part)
	Debris between walls L 11, 13	D 205, 207, C 515
	S. of wall L 11, debris	C 161, 166, 253, 258, 259, 263
	Debris s. of wall L 10	C 158, 159, 160, 166
	Debris between walls L 8, 9	C 162, 163, 164
	Debris between walls L 3, 5, 7, collapse of wall L 7	C 353, B 166, 167
	W. of wall L 2, second floor and debris	B 161, 158
	Road n. of wall L 7	C 419
L 3	Wall L 6, and second door in wall 4	
	Floor in room walls L 3, 4, 5, 6	C 353
	Second floor	C 352
	Debris end of the period	C 351, B 145, 164, 165
	E. of wall 5 new accumulation of burnt debris, partly by erosion	C 154, 155, 157, 165, 240, 241, 242, 246, 247, 255, 506, 513
	Tumble of stones	C 247
	Fine erosion material, burnt	C 152, 153
	Covering wall L 10, washed clay	C 138, 150
	Clay wash in s.e. corner	C 153
	S. of wall 11, pit	C 148, 243
	Debris covering walls L 11, 13	C 513, 511, 523, 524, D 213
	Second layer of debris	C 230, 236, 238, 520
	Third level of (burnt) debris	C 227, 237
	Fourth level, burnt wash	C 505
	Thick deposit of debris w. of walls L 1, 2	B 143
	Debris covering walls L 5, 6, 8	C 147, 340, 412
	Pit, dug into wall L 4	C 345

Phase M

The pottery from phase M has not been used in the following pottery study. It is possible that there was a period after phase L in which the tell was hardly occupied. There are various indications for this supposition. There is an accumulation of washed material over the phase L buildings. Phase M shows a new lay-out of the village, but this could also be the case if a large part of phase L were destroyed on any one occasion. More important is, however, the fact that the large "cistern" which is attributed to phase M, contains some pottery shapes, which do not belong to the village repertoire, nor to that of period III. There must have been a much shorter gap in time between phases L and M (plus N) than there is between phases M-N and the new occupation of period III. The bulk of the phase M pottery comes from the "cistern", as the period III pits and the cemetery have largely destroyed the surface of phase M, and the plan of phase N has been entirely reconstructed from wall fragments found between pits and

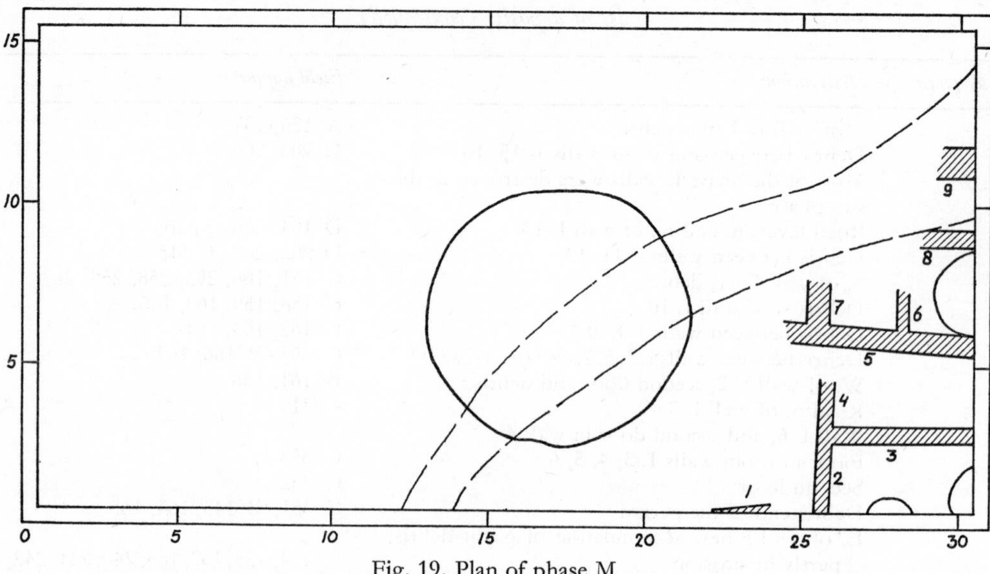

Fig. 19. Plan of phase M

graves. The publication of the pottery from these phases will follow after the excavation has been extended.

The only wall of phase L which still stood in phase M is wall M 1, not used as a house wall, but as part of a catchment area for water, a plaster floor to the n. of it running up against this wall. This is the only plastered floor found in the E.I.A. deposits. On the same absolute level further n. another plastered floor was found, which is a terrassed floor belonging to period III. This floor shows that a considerable amount of erosion took place between periods II and III.

The most striking and peculiar feature of phase M is the large "cistern", to which the plastered floor led the rainwater. This floor actually formed the rim of the pit along the s.e. side, sloping down into the pit. The diameter of this pit is slightly over 8 m. and its depth has not yet been established. It had destroyed underlying deposits at least down to phase G. The purpose of this pit or "cistern" is not clear. Nowhere were there any indications that it was plastered below the rim. It is also certain that no staircase went down into it. Had that been the case it could be supposed that it was dug in a desperate attempt of the villagers to reach ground water level during a siege. If it was meant to collect rainwater, as the "catchment floor" would suggest, it was equally a failure, even had there been a plaster lining. (Pl. XIb)

From the stratigraphy it is clear that the pit had a very short existence and in fact already served as a refuse pit during phase M. All the pottery fragments found in the pit are covered with iron oxide incrustation, suggesting that broken pots were thrown into thick layers of vegetable material that gradually filled the pit. In the next phase (N) a thick clay deposit was put down over the top on which a house was built (Pl. XII). This clay "lid" subsequently sank more than a metre into the soft fill, breaking off around the edge of the pit. The problem of interpretation remains and is not elucidated by the fact that it was not the first pit of its kind, cf. phase J. The phase J pit must have been less wide, and the phase M pit took up more space. From the fact that the pit was already used as a refuse pit during phase M we can conclude that, whatever its original purpose, it soon lost this function.

All the walls of the phase were very fragmentarily preserved in this area. (see above). Walls M 2,3 formed a room. N. of wall M 3 was an open space, blocked by wall M 4. This courtyard shows an earthquake crack which dates from phase M or N. N. of wall M 3 and s. of wall M 5 (Pl. XIa) were found two stone benches, built against these walls, facing each other. Two n.-s. walls were built n. of wall M 5 and the floor space between them was covered by a stone platform.

As all possible links between walls M 6,7,8,9 were destroyed by the graves, no interpretation can be given until excavation further e. has revealed more of the plan of this phase.

Note. After this manuscript was finished the contents of the cistern were studied. Comparison with the phase M material, which definitely belongs to the village, and with material from phase N, has clearly shown that the cistern cannot belong to either of these phases, but to an intermediate period. We have to assume that whether phase M was followed by one or more phases of village occupation, erosion followed after the village was definitely abandoned. Then people dug a pit and made a "catchment floor" running up against the stump of a wall which they found standing, and after that the tell was again abandoned, now for a considerable length of time. This interpretation is based on the study of the pottery only. It is difficult to see why in the second period of erosion the rim of the pit did not erode away completely, unless, as we have reason to believe, buildings belonging to the village (period II) were standing on a much higher level east of the excavated area. In this case the lower parts which were more or less horizontal would be covered by eroded material before erosion started to denude these lower levels. The pottery of the cistern will be published after the excavation of phase N and subsequent phases has been finished.

PART TWO

STUDY OF THE POTTERY

CHAPTER THREE

PRELIMINARY REMARKS

The presentation of this study of the pottery differs in some respects from present day publications of Palestinian pottery. Chapter 8 contains the stratigraphical study of the pottery in the phases of the tell. This part is familiar to Palestinian archaeologists, though some drawings are more detailed than is always usual, but the description of the individual sherds in Chapters 6 and 7 however, breaks new ground in presenting the typological study based not on style criteria but on an analysis of the techniques of pottery making used in Deir ʿAllā.

The dilemma has been to know how much of an introduction was needed to explain this approach. For pre-historians and anthropologists who are acquainted with pre-wheel pottery either from a practical field study, or from the vast literature on the subject, or from both, this chapter is superfluous. But, bearing in mind that Iron Age Palestine officially falls into the historic period, and that many archaeologists concerned with its interpretation have enjoyed no special training in pre-historic or anthropological disciplines, it seemed better to bore a few readers than to confuse the majority. Therefore a general outline of the principles of pottery making has been included.

The presentation of Palestinian pottery is now more or less standardized both in the way it is described and drawn. All sorts of technical terms are used to describe it such as "well levigated" and "self slip", which are primarily potter's terms but which have often acquired an archaeological meaning in which the precision of the original term has become blurred and in some cases meaningless.

Distinction is always made in publications between "wheel made" and "hand made." From this the archaeologist visualizes on the one hand a symmetrical vessel, perhaps with a sophisticated form, often bearing so-called "wheel marks"; and on the other hand he conjures up the picture of an irregularly made vessel, a more or less advanced form of something made by art students before they have progressed to wheel made pottery classes, something bearing more individuality than a wheel made vessel, but less technical skill. To a potter reading such a description no such images arise. Instead a whole series of questions come to him: when he reads "wheel made" he asks himself if that phrase covers vessels thrown on a wheel or turned on a wheel; when he reads "hand made," he wants to know if the vessel was modelled and if so how—by dragging clay upwards from a ring? paddle and anvil worked? piece built with coils in rings or in spirals or with patches? moulded in one or more convex or concave moulds? or a combination of these practices? Once he realizes that the terms "well fired," "well levigated" and "self slip" are all bestowed by the cataloguer after an examination of the vessel unaided by more than his or her sharp eyes, intelligence and experience, he will doubt very much the usefulness of these epithets, as they are all, more or less, undetectable with the naked eye.

It could be argued that this discrepancy between the archaeologist's and the potter's use of certain terms is of little importance. Every profession uses the same words with different meanings. The literary critic, the theologian, the psychologist and the philosopher all make use of the word "myth," each with a special meaning. This may be confusing for the general public, within each profession it is not so. This argument is soon scotched and serious doubts are raised about the misuse of the potter's terminology when the archaeologist realizes that the various elements which go into describing a vessel as a whole do not form a unity which can be interpreted in terms of typology, chronology or pottery classification. That this is so should become amply clear from the following study. Here is an example of a meaningless aspect of pottery analysis based on imprecise knowledge of the potter's work.

Almost every archaeological description of a vessel now contains a note on the "grits" in the clay from which the vessel was formed. All of us are familiar with phrases such as "many fine white grits," "some black and red grits"; scarcely any of us would neglect to record them. But on closer examination, what useful information do these phrases confer? For the amount of temper used was never standardized and if one is to be certain of its size it must be measured in thin section. It is sometimes hard to say whether impurities were deliberately added by the potter, or whether he had simply not bothered to extract them before use. It is impossible to establish accurately of what the temper consists unless a petrographic miscroscope is used.

Thus the knowledge of the number, size and type of grit in a vessel is only of any use to an archaeologist once the temper has been skillfully analysed and compared with hundreds of other sherds and vessels from the same and other sites in connection with the pottery techniques in use in the period concerned. Then, and only then, can reference to the temper of a vessel perhaps tell the archaeologist something useful. For instance it can give indications about the fashioning, firing and use of a vessel and it may be possible to infer from it that the materials for a vessel came from a certain area or the vessel itself from a certain pottery.

In the same way the colour of a vessel is always given. The element of uncertainty in colour differentiation can largely be eliminated by the use of the Munsell Soil Colour Charts, but not every reader of an excavation report has such a chart and even if they did the fact that a vessel is a certain colour does not in itself add much information except as a basis of recognition. Many excavators still resort to the chancey description of colours as their recorders see them, which results in well known circumlocutions such as "pinkish buff" and "pale greenish white" and the like. Clumsy though these descriptions are, if they cover the diversity of shades that occur in so many vessels, they can be more useful than the choice of one scientific shade taken as representative of the vessel as a whole. For the colouring of a vessel is not only an indication of the mixture of organic and inorganic elements in the clay from which it is formed but also an indication of the temperature at which the vessel was fired, the type of kiln used, the fuel, where and how the pot was stacked in the kiln and on occasion the type of soil in which the sherd or vessel lay during the centuries before it was excavated. Moreover a vessel may become discoloured by being re-fired in a burnt destruction level in a settlement. Why self slip can rarely be detected without the aid of thin section has clearly been demonstrated by A. O. Shepard. There is reason to suppose that "selfslip" in Palestinian pottery is in fact often "bloom."[1]

These anomalies are also present in connection with the distinction made between "hard" and "soft" wares. All these factors point up the fact that certain features in a vessel are achieved only as the result of a definite treatment of the raw material by the potter, a treatment which has more to do with his professional craftsmanship than his artistic or aesthetic gifts. If in a certain period the majority of the pottery consists of hard, ringing ware, it indicates that the potter had resource to a certain type of raw material, method of preparing and firing the vessels once made, which produce this type of ware. If, however, among softer vessels, all of the same type, some appear to be harder, and of better quality, this minority is generally accidental.

Their occurrence was probably outside the control or even the concern of the potter. Until the archaeologist knows fairly systematically what the potter did to achieve his end products, these exceptions will always pose problems: do the softer wares indicate a trial period when the potter was experimenting? are they therefore earlier than the harder examples of the same type? or were they made by an inferior potter? and are they local imitations and the harder wares imports from another district? On the other hand the basic question of plastic or lean clay is hardly ever mentioned.

Summing up then, it can be said that, at its most optimal, information gathered about the manufacture of pottery can be used to form a more objective typology than one based on stylistic criteria. At the moment a type series is generally based on rim and body shapes alone, and the degree of refinement used in such a series seems to rest on the purely individual decision of the archaeologist drawing it up.

How then was this study conducted?

Once the basic fact was established that the clay at Deir ʿAllā was prepared in such a way that it could not be used for throwing on a wheel, it was a matter of finding fragments of vessels which still bore the traces of the potter's fingers and tools in order to reconstruct what he had done, and then to compare it with known techniques, other than that of throwing on a fast wheel.

Starting from a wide range of possible practices, it became more and more clear from the increasing amount of material evidence that the overall picture of the Deir ʿAllā techniques is a fairly simple one and forms an intelligible unity. Once one becomes used to the fact that not all Iron Age pottery which superficially looks "wheel made" is in fact thrown on a wheel, but is finished on a turning base after it has been built up by hand, there is nothing strange in Deir ʿAllā techniques.[2] Everything these potters

[1] Shepard 1961 (p. 193); Kelso 1943 (p. 59-68)

[2] Rieth 1960 (p. 78, 84); Leach 1951 (p. 66)

did has been done throughout the history of potting at different times and in different parts of the world. Their techniques can be rediscovered in parts of the world to-day, and were in use in Western Europe long after the Middle Ages.

Not every potsherd or vessel shows clear signs of what the potter did when making it. In general it is only the last treatment given to a pot before it was put aside to dry that remains visible. This involved smoothing the walls of the vessel, and if it was thoroughly done, all other traces of tools or handling were eliminated from the surface. This was luckily not always so, but a very large number of fragments were necessary for this sort of inquiry, about 10,000 sherds have been examined already. There were, however, still some types which occured infrequently at Deir ʿAllā, and from lack of material the study could not be completed. Within each type there were also always some examples which were practically featureless; it will not be surprising if a few of these rims turn out to have been wrongly attributed. However, on the whole a convincing picture of the potter's activities has emerged which demonstrates both a logical sequence of pottery development and the consequent development of very differently shaped vessels from one and the same manufacturing pattern. Thus although, for instance, the rim of the cooking pot and the rim of the storage jar in the first Iron Age period seem to bear no resemblance one to another, it turns out that technically they are very closely related and firmly belong together. Therefore they also fit into the same level of technical development.

Similar observations can be made for instance in the case of the Deir ʿAllā cooking pot, type 1 and type 2. These types are not always distinguished in other publications, but it is clear that they developed independently at different places. But whereas type 1 was introduced at Deir ʿAllā in phase A and continued in use till phase L, type 2 only appears in phase E when the village was founded. However, the curious fact is that type 2 is a straight descendant, technically speaking, of the Late Bronze Age cooking pot, type 2, which is only found in the last phase of the sanctuary. Thus it seems likely that its development took place somewhere else in Trans-Jordan only to return with the villagers some fifty years later in its modified form. From then on it is noticeable that there is a tendency for the type 1 cooking pot to be assimilated, as far as the rim is concerned, to the new 'fashion' of type 2 while still being manufactured in the old way.

These and similar examples help in the interpretation of the history of the inhabitants as well as the interpretation of the chronology. This is particularly so for pre-historic periods, but is also true for those historic periods, such as the transitional period between the L.B. and the Iron Age, when literary evidence for the considerable population movements in the Near East are at best meagre.

A potter trekking with his tribe from the Anatolian mountains where copper and other metals were plentiful and smiths skilled, would have a very different repertoire of goods with a different tradition of manufacturing his vessels than a nomadic potter from the semi-desert area of the outer Hauran, or the commercial potter of the coastal plain of Canaan. They all had a different clientele, different sources of material, and were subjected to different external cultural influences. Once they moved from their homeland, the whole economy and basic way of life of the tribe might alter—nomadic herdsmen might in less than a generation turn into full or semi-pastoralists settled in a village—and the potter's skills, traditional forms and techniques would have to be accommodated to the available raw materials, and be adapted to new needs. This could form an impetus towards finer and better wares, or it could lead to a regression or to the abandonment of some forms. New circumstances demand new vessels. For instance, a nomadic desert potter is unlikely to manufacture large storage jars when water can be so much more easily transported in skins by beasts of burden. However, once a village settles around a water hole or along a stream, and water can be stored in houses, a vessel large enough but not too heavy for a woman to carry, must be constructed. It has always been recognized that supply and demand play their important role in the potter's market as elsewhere, but it is often assumed that fashion or whim chiefly dictated the rise or fall of this or that pottery form, whereas necessity in the form of raw materials coupled with the potter's conservatism or adaptability must be just as important. It is very likely that sophisticated and primitive forms of pottery making were being engaged in at the same chronological period in places no very great distance from each other. An analytical study of the potter's techniques can in this way tell us something about the antecedents of the potter, and thus indirectly something about the history of his tribe or city state.[1]

Although some may reject this approach to the making of a typology because it involves a great deal of work with no guarantee of new information, others will—in the author's opinion, rightly—consider that the study published here does not go far enough. They will be critical that as yet few sherds have been systematically sampled and tested for the analysis of their temper, clay composition, firing temperature etc. Well aware of these shortcomings, the author can only excuse them by stating that under the conditions in which this report was drawn up he was forced into choosing between following these enthralling by-ways, which would have presented many problems of specialist personnel and equipment, or restricting the study to one aspect of Palestinian ceramics, which, though long referred to in publications, has not yet been sufficiently worked out: the technique of pottery building. The pottery is therefore primarily described in terms of manufacturing techniques. Some general observations concerning the chemical features of pottery making have been made, but as they have been made without many of the tests generally in use, some may indeed be defective. On the other hand, these observations have been made by a working potter of many years experience and months of experimentation. All the descriptions in Chapters 7 and 8 refer to the general descriptions in Chapters 4 to 6, and are to be taken as illustrations of the range of possibilities of variations in colour, temper etc. within a certain type.

This way of publishing the pottery seems preferable to the conventional way even within these acknowledged limitations. Because of its novelty, terminology and techniques have been explained as fully as possible. Technical terms have been used in

---

[1] Matson 1966 (p. 161).

accordance with potters' usage, which is not always the same as archaeologists' usage. A short list of terms has been drawn up in order to make it quite clear what is meant. It is based on A. O. Shepard's "Ceramics for the archaeologist" and B. Leach's "A potter's handbook"; both books contain a very useful vocabulary.

It is useful to read some detailed accounts of pot making in societies which are little influenced by the fast wheel. These are available in many languages, and about many parts of the world, though for the purpose of following what happened to Deir ʿAllā Iron Age pottery, the above mentioned volume by Shepard is sufficiently full even though it deals exclusively with American pre-wheel pottery. In this study frequent reference is made to the article by J. L. Kelso and J. Palin Thorly in T.B.M. Vol. III, Ch. IV. This is a study nearer home and, though it is mainly concerned with wheel thrown pottery, is of great importance for earlier material too. Extensive use has also been made of Leach's book because, apart from the wealth of technical detail of pottery making the world over that is given, the potter himself is brought into the fore-front of the picture.

Many films have also been made of the potter's craft in so-called primitive societies, which are extremely interesting and illuminating. These are generally obtainable on loan from ethnological museums or anthropological institutes. With Anna Shepard,[1] our readers are asked when evaluating the place of ceramics in archaeology "to judge if the specialist has viewed his subject in perspective, recognized the limitations of his approach, accepting valid criticisms of his methods and examining carefully the general assumptions on which his deductions are based".

---

[1] *Op. cit.*, p. 334.

CHAPTER FOUR

A SYSTEMATIC APPROACH TO THE STUDY OF THE IRON AGE POTTERY

BY

J. KALSBEEK

In order to evaluate critically the work of a modern potter who uses a fast turning wheel, one has to take into consideration three general aspects of the craft:

a) the quality of the raw material which he uses,

b) the tools at his disposal,

c) the technical skill of the thrower.

Where any of the requirements fall below a certain standard, the result will be obvious in the finished product, and can be studied from it.

When discussing ancient pottery which may or may not have been made on a fast turning wheel, one has to look for evidence of all these three aspects in the excavated pottery.

The Raw Material

The raw material, used for making pottery, is usually termed clay. Although clay in the geological sense of the term is generally the basic substance used by potters, there is such a wide variety of differently composed "clays", that the term is rather vague. What matters to the thrower, however, is obviously not the chemical composition of the raw material but its practical possibilities. The clay may contain components that give it special qualities or that render it impossible for use on a fast wheel. In the latter case preliminary preparation of the clay is necessary before it can be used on such a wheel. There are various ways of purifying clays, such as slipping, grinding, rotting, or mixing with certain other components in order to eliminate unwanted reactions. It will always depend on the technical skill and inventiveness of the thrower whether he succeeds in overcoming the difficulties of any given raw material. His requirements in this respect vary with the different tasks facing him.

These requirements are, for instance, different in the case of mass production, or a real art product or where pottery for special purposes is made, such as cooking pots.

These facts alone make it difficult to judge the degree of the technical skill of ancient potters from their pottery found in the soil.

Clay, as it is taken from the clay beds, may be rather impure. This need not necessarily be of great importance where it is used for the making of simple household wares. A careful examination of a sherd will reveal when impure clay was used (anorganic impurities).

The use of an impure clay does not necessarily point to lack of skill of the thrower, but may be due—at least partly—to shortage of water. In this case one can expect to find the more simple and less effective methods of cleaning. Besides, an important aspect here is time-honoured method and tradition, probably even influenced to a certain extent by religious traditions.

Next to the impurity of the clay comes the question of clays being either too rich (plastic) or too lean (lack of plasticity). This depends on the chemical components of the raw material. A simple test can be done on natural clay found near an excavated site, to find out about the plasticity of the material. After mixing some clay with water until it is kneadable, a roll is made, 15 cms. long and 1 cm. in diameter. One lifts the roll holding one end between the fingers, while the other end can swing freely. If the clay roll breaks off, the clay is not plastic. If the roll does not break, and if it is possible to wind the free end like a snail's shell, without causing the clay to crack, it is a very good plastic or unctuous clay. A lean clay cannot be improved by adding more water.

Methods of Improving the Clay

Impure clay can be cleaned by pulverizing it in a bath and mixing the clay thoroughly with water. In this bath stones and sand will settle first. Before the clay settles the water is poured into another basin, in which the clay slowly settles, after which the water is removed. This is the most thorough way of doing it, and is also the most laborious. It is called slipping.

Less effective is cleaning clay while it is dry. The clay is pulverized and put through a sieve, or the larger impurities like stones and wood are even taken out by hand. Yet another method is to mix the clay with water until it becomes kneadable. Then the clay is rolled over a flat surface such as a stone and beaten flat with the aid of a stick. The coarser elements are then removed by hand.

Only when the finest quality clay is required are attempts made to remove organic materials such as remains of roots and other vegetable matter. This is done by storing the clay for a long period, in which the clay is kept damp and regularly turned over. The vegetable remains are thus exposed to the air and decay.

As found, clays are usually not too lean for use. Lean clay can only be improved by adding a plastic clay and by slipping. Leanness is usually due to the presence of impurities; therefore clay becomes more plastic by being purified.

Often, however, the potter's difficulty is that his clay is too plastic. In order to improve his material the potter has to add reducing substances. A great number of possibilities is at his disposal.

The components to be added to the clay may be coarse or fine, depending on special requirements of utility, porosity, temperature of firing; therefore a potter determines the degree of plasticity in his clay in relationship to the wares he wants to produce and his technical ability. It is useful to discuss here the advantages and disadvantages of plastic and lean clay. The advantage of a plastic clay is first and foremost its capacity of being formed into a required shape without cracking or splitting while still being pliable. The second advantage is that it keeps its shape while drying. The water used to make the clay kneadable is evenly distributed through the clay, keeping the clay at the same time firm and flexible. This clay lends itself well to being rolled out into sheets for special purposes. It is ideal for throwing on a fast-turning wheel.

The disadvantages are:

a) the high percentage of shrinkage while drying and being fired, which may cause cracks in the ware,

b) the necessity of controlling the process of drying and firing, which has to be done in a slow tempo,

c) that two separately made parts of a pot come off easily where they join each other, either during the firing or afterwards,

d) that during firing the ware will not stand a sudden drop or rise of temperature, and therefore requires a well-built kiln.

The advantages of lean clay or clay which is specially made so, are:

a) little shrinkage with the correspondingly small chance of cracks while drying, or deformation of the shape,

b) that it dries quickly and loses the water easily,

c) that jointed parts (like necks, handles and spouts) do not break off,

d) that the leaner the clay the better it stands sudden changes in temperature while being fired.

The disadvantages of a lean clay are:

a) it breaks easily while being shaped,

b) it loses the water with which it is mixed so easily that it becomes less kneadable,

c) it is difficult to smooth the surface of the pot after it has been built.

From this it is clear that though the potter must treat his raw material according to the technique he uses in different vessels, the possibilities of the thrower are limited by the preliminary treatment of the clay.

Temper

Clay can be treated with grits of different kind and size, in order to render it leaner, and the resulting mixture is called temper. A grit mixture of large particles has the advantage of being more easily ground off the rock from which the grit is made, by simply rubbing two small rocks together. There is no need to mix the grit thoroughly through the clay, and the moulded clay keeps its shape more easily than in the case where fine grits are used, which is important when building large vessels. It helps to make for a strong adhesive quality of the clay when building pots from coils, and drying and firing the pots then require less skill.

The disadvantages are:

a) The clay is not fit for throwing on a fast wheel, nor can the surface be smoothed on the wheel.

b) Clay and grit do not fuse during the firing, with the result that cracks form owing to shrinkage, along which the pot will eventually break.

A fine (powdered) grit has important advantages:

a) Throwing on a fast wheel is usually possible (with thick walls as a result) or turning after the pot has been built up to finish off the surface.

b) Separately made parts of the pot stick together easily.

The disadvantages are:

a) The mixing of the clay with the grit has to be very thoroughly done, the grinding of the grit needs a mortar and takes time, and it sometimes needs sieving.

b) It is less adhesive than clay with rough grits.

c) It is less fit for building large vessels.

d) It needs careful supervision while drying.

Grit has either to be prepared or is used as found. Quartz, sandstone, sherds, shells, straw, lime all need grinding. Sand (whether rough or fine), chaff or dung can be used as found.

When the throwing of a vessel is done on a fast wheel a fine grit is required. In the process of firing however, the kind of material used as grit plays an important role. Here three different kinds can be distinguished: *a* quartz and other rock, grog, *b* limestone and *c* vegetable matter.

Quartz, coarse sand, fine and silver-sand. If sand is not available and quartz grit is wanted, it has to be pounded from rock. Using quartz has however the great disadvantage that high temperatures are needed to produce a well fired product. It needs great quantities of fuel and well-built kilns with no draught, leakage etc.

The equal distribution of the temperature inside the kiln is also important here, otherwise the wares that are stacked near the fire become fired at a temperature above melting point, while the rest are still below the temperature that is required to fire them properly.

Other kinds of rock also usually need a high temperature in order to fuse grit and clay.

Limestone, which is easy to grind and very prolific in Palestine was very often used as temper.

Most mistakes made when firing a kiln can be observed on pots treated with lime grits, or those derived from rock, shells, etc.

While being fired to temperatures between 250° and 1000° lime grit absorbs oxygen and water and expands in the process, thus forming an "explosive" element in the clay. In order to prevent the pot from being reduced to dust, the kiln has to be fired at a high temperature for only a short time. This gives a well fired surface, both outside and inside the pot, but leaves the core black. This never produces a well fired, strong vessel but it has one great advantage: Mixing clay with lime grit reduces the maximum firing temperature considerably. The pot becomes hard in a comparatively short space of time, which is important if there is a shortage of fuel. Also the construction of the kiln needs less skill. If the lime grit consists of fine powder or dust it is possible to avoid all firing mistakes and the core will have the same colour as the outside of the wall.

Organic temper has similar advantages. Dung was used as temper in I.A. pottery from Deir ʿAllā, and although this is usually completely burnt, it leaves impressions in the shape of the various seeds, grasses etc. in the clay and many tiny holes. This type of pottery needs little special care in firing, the heat is equally distributed in the clay and firing can be short. Clearly the pot will be even more porous than usual, but high temperatures do not harm the pot as they do when lime grit is used.

Shrinkage

While drying out before being fired in the kiln, the pot not only shrinks, but its shape also changes. A pot will shrink more along its widest circumference between neck and base than where it is narrower. Wide bowls and jars become more slender in appearance. Measured from a horizontal line the angle of the shoulder will become larger, which makes the vessel higher and more slender. This process continues during the firing of the pot. So, if a rim is still practically horizontal after firing, there are two possible explanations: either the rim was made of lean clay (not on a fast wheel) or the wheel on which the vessel was thrown was kept in a really horizontal position. The latter is impossible where a larger part of the pot is concerned, because it will collapse under its own weight during the process of drying, as the clay used for throwing has to be very wet; therefore, these horizontal parts are usually found only on pots that have not been thrown on the wheel. As the plastic clays, used for throwing on the fast wheel shrink much more than lean clays used for making in moulds, the often met phrase "the body is hand made and the rim wheel made" in the sense of *thrown on the wheel*, is impossible. While drying, the rim would break off the body. In such cases the same lean clay is used but certain parts were finished while the pot was turned by hand (cf. the cooking pot p. 118) on a turn-table.

The process of drying should be gradual so as to prevent the pot from cracking. Pots made of plastic clay need more supervision and care while drying than others. If much sand has been mixed with the clay, the water will evaporate quickly, as is the case where lime grit or organic materials are used.

Cracks occur easily where the wall of the vessel is of an unequal thickness. Thin walls dry quicker and become hard much sooner than a thick base which will go on shrinking after the rest is already dry, thus causing cracks where the thinner and the thicker parts meet. The link between body and base is the most vulnerable part of the pot in this respect. Walls of pots thrown on the wheel often become thicker near the base to carry the weight of the pot while drying out. If part of the base is thinner than the lowest part of the wall of the vessel, the base is likely to crack. This crack cannot be mended, because clay put into the crack will also shrink when drying out. While still half dry a crack can be mended by smearing out the clay round the crack, or by adding water to the clay and smearing it out. Occasionally one finds bases mended with calcium.

If a pot stands on its base while drying, the base will dry much more slowly than the rest of the pot; therefore the pot is often put upside down or in a closed room, to slow down the process of drying. The pot is put in the kiln when leather-hard, which does not mean that it is really dry; therefore during firing in the kiln the pot can still crack if there is an uneven distribution of the heat. This usually affects wide bowls. In cases where the grit is not evenly distributed through the clay, cracks may occur during firing. In these cases the clay shrinks less where the highest concentration of grit is. If a pot has been smoothed with a wet cloth or leather after it became leather-hard, the surface will show many cracks. Parts of a pot that have been separately made, like spouts and handles, will come off while drying if the thickness and make prevent them from drying at the same rate as the rest of the pot.

Tiny Holes in the Fabric of the Pot

Tiny holes are invariably found in the walls of the pot where vegetable material has been used to make the clay leaner. This material has been burnt away during the process of firing. Both in the break and at the surface these holes can be seen. Often the opening at the surface is smaller than the hole itself. The vegetable matter however leaves clear impressions in the clay that make it possible to identify the material used.

Other tiny holes occur, when lime particles have disappeared through chemical action in the long period in which the sherd was buried in the soil. These holes usually occur in the surface of the sherd.

Holes under the surface are found where parts of the pot were fitted together by hand. These holes are usually oblong and do not cause the surface to bulge. A bulging surface may indicate an airlock caused by insufficient kneading of the clay before it was used. Unless the bulge was caused by the burning out of an organic impurity, it is a sure indication that the pot was wheel made. In plastic clays with a fine evenly divided grit these bulges have a typical shape. This drawn-out shape can also occur with coarser grits. Usually however clay with coarser grits lets the air escape easier and no bulge exists.

Sometimes one finds narrow grooves on the surface of the pot like scratches. These are caused by coarse grits on the surface, which were transported during the throwing of the pot on the wheel. While being moved these grits tend to bury themselves in the surface, and the grooves deepen in the opposite direction to the direction in which the pot was turned. One often finds the particle of grit at the deep end.

A different groove exists if the vessel was reshaped after becoming leather hard. In this case coarse grits at the surface, often found when the pot was hand made, also tend to move. The impression is different, that is, deeper where the grit started to move. As the clay was already hard, the grit tends to become separated from the wall of the pot.

In this case the deepest end of the groove indicates the direction in which the pot was turned and it runs out at the surface the other end.

Scratches made with a hard instrument on the surface of a wet pot will always push up clay on the sides. If the surface has been smoothed after the scratch was made, the opening of the scratch along the surface will become narrower. If the scratch is made with a hard instrument in a hard or baked surface, the clay will not be pushed up, but the edges will be crumbly.

Perforation through the wall of the pot or through the base can be made in the wet or leather-hard pot. If this were done with a solid object, the clay around the hole would crack. Usually a hollow object is used for this purpose. A hollow stalk is ideal and the hole will show the shape of the object used; therefore the stalk used may have a D shape. Often some surplus of clay can be found at the surface opposite the one from which the piercing began.

Break Lines and Flaws from Shrinking

There is a strong connection between the way a pot is built, the shrinkage during drying and firing, and the way a pot breaks or the shape of sherds. From loss of moisture a clay body shrinks when it is put out to dry. To what extent the clay shrinks depends on the amount of water it contains. Clay used on a fast wheel is very wet and loses a great deal of volume during the process of drying. Pots built up by hand are of comparatively dry clay and will shrink much less. Another element to reckon with is the material used for rendering the clay more lean. Some of these materials take in more water than others. A plastic clay takes in more water than a lean clay, and the former also contains more chemically-combined water. Hence wheel-made pottery will shrink much more during drying and firing than hand-made, both from being worked wet and being made from plastic clay. The process of drying has to be done gradually to avoid strain from shrinkage. Strain in certain parts of the pot will diminish its strength. Firing will have to be done very evenly. During firing chemical changes take place in the clay, organic material disappears and the object goes on shrinking. The higher the temperature goes up, the more the pot shrinks.

The first place to break is where separately made parts are joined. Pots made in spirals will show the same pattern when breaking, but the vertical break will be independent from it. An irregular break pattern is found with bowls made from one sheet of clay in a mould. If a pot has been made on the wheel, either as a whole or partly, the break pattern will show this. While turning, the clay is stretched in the direction counter to the direction of the wheel. Breaks starting from the top of the rim form a sharp angle with the rim and run counter to the direction of turning from the rim downwards. This is not the case when the object is hand-made. In cases of combined techniques, partly turned and partly cast, the pattern of the break will vary with the variously made parts.

This can be seen most clearly with vessels with wide rims. The fracture of wheel-made pottery shows some characteristic features. While turning the clay is stretched, and the clay near the surface stretches more than clay in the core. The fracture of a vertical break will tend to be convex at the side in which the pot was turned (the core sticks out beyond the sides). On the opposite side of the sherd, away from the direction of turning, the fracture will tend to be hollow (the core is deeper than the sides).

In the case of folded rims the break on the inside will run in the opposite direction to the break on the outside. On the inside the break runs counter to the direction of turning, but on the outside it runs with it. In fact this would be the same direction if the rim were folded back again in its original position.

Tools used for Building and Throwing Pottery

1. Scraper. This can be a bone, a large shell fragment or potsherd shaped to fit the purpose, or a pottery scraper specially baked for this use or made from some other material.

Traces of the use of a scraper can be clearly seen on the wall of pots. These traces provide very useful information concerning the way in which the pot was made. The traces are different when the tool was applied while the clay was still wet or when the pot was leather hard.

2. Thin string or wire, used to cut the pot from the base on which it was made. Provided the impression of the string-cut has not been smoothed away afterwards, the pattern can tell us whether the pot was cut loose from a wheel or from a non-turning base.

3. A pin or knife with sharp edge. These tools are used to shape rims while the pot is being turned and for incised decorations. The steadiness and direction of the impressions made with these tools can inform us about the speed with which the vessel was turned and whether the pot swayed while being turned.

4. Rags. During or after turning a rag can be used to smooth the surface of the pot. The rag can be a fragment of textile, leather or a spongy substance, or a kind of brush made of vegetable material like straw, dried grass etc.

5. Polishing tools of various kinds are used to smooth the surface of the leather hard pot. A spatula made of wood, bone or metal, shells and pebbles.

During throwing the potter needs a bowl with water, which stands near the wheel. Any broken fragment of a pot that holds water will do, or even the hard skin of a gourd.

The larger the smoothed part of the surface of a finished pot is, the more the surface traces of the techniques applied vanish, which is of course the general purpose of this last treatment before the pot is fired. However it greatly hampers the study of techniques, as many characteristic features are eradicated from the surface in this way.

In order to prevent the pot from collapsing while drying, wrappings or rope can be used for support. In the case of large jars there is always the danger of cracking caused by the weight of the upper part on the base, or the weight of the lower part on the rim if the pot is dried upside down. Especially where a rather lean clay is used, the danger is always present. These rope impressions can often be clearly seen.

CHAPTER FIVE

SURVEY OF MANUFACTURING DIFFERENT PARTS OF A POT

BY

J. KALSBEEK

Rims

Whichever way it is made, the potter will always try to finish off the rim of a pot as evenly as possible. If the pot is thrown on the wheel and the grit is very fine, the easiest way is to cut the rim with a sharp point. In other cases however, this may be impossible. The use of coarser grit, for instance, does not allow this way of cutting the rim. In that case it is easier to turn over a small part of the rim. The end of this folded over part of the rim will still show the unequal height of the original shape as a wavy line along the neck. The circumference of the fold is slightly higher or lower in different parts. This folding of the rim is only possible when the pot is placed on a turning base, and therefore one does not find these folded rims on pots made by hand without the help of an easily revolving base. Since however in cases where the pot is not turned, the thickness of the rim is of minor importance, it is easy to build up neck and rim to the required height and to smooth the top with a hard object. This often results in an unequal thickness of the rim and usually the rim is not perfectly horizontal. The pressure on the rim in this case may result in deforming the pot or the sinking of the shoulder. If the rim inclines slightly, the pressure is distributed more evenly over neck and shoulder, so as to prevent damage to the shape. The neck can be adapted to this type of rim by being made thicker near the rim than it is near the shoulder. There will always be a gradual transition between the two rim types.

A pot can be entirely or partly hand made, while the rim is finished by turning. The pot is placed on a base which can be turned smoothly. Speed is not required. The hand-built rim is smoothed with a rag or leather while the pot is turning. The body of the pot is turned with one hand and the smoothing done simultaneously with the other. During this process the rim tends to become wider in section, especially since the hand-formed rim seldom starts off with a rim of the equal thickness as the coil ends often overlap. In this process it is easier to keep a partly thickened rim level than to try to eliminate the unequal thickness of the rim by pushing the clay further up to make an even thickness all round. While the top of the rim is kept level all the surplus clay is pushed upwards thus forming an irregular thickness. The surplus clay of the rim is then pushed down again while the top of the rim is kept straight. This can be done with the thumb of one hand while the forefinger of the same hand presses against the inside just below the rim to keep the shape. This pushing down along the outside of the rim is usually done with a spatula or sherd.

While the fingers of one hand support the inside of the rim, the other hand works with the spatula. In this case the pot does not turn round in one go, or is turned by a helper. The result is a rim, which is fairly level on top and with a pointed and frayed lower end which often stands a bit off the neck (in section like a fish hook). This fringe can be smoothed with a finger while the pot is turned. In this case the lower part of the rim joins the neck but the sharp edge will be pushed slightly upwards. A variation is the edge pushed upwards and at the same time against the wall.

In cases where the rim was shaped with the finger and not with an instrument, the rim will take on a slightly hollow profile. Where a spatula was used, the tendency is towards a convex profile. When a rag or leather was used the top of the rim tends to be inverted. In order to fasten the folded part of the rim to the neck better, the sharp side of a spatula pressed against the middle of the rim was sometimes used. These rims have a groove running all round them. This indicates that the pot stood on a turning base.

If the sharp edge has completely disappeared and is rounded off towards the inside, then the fingers of one hand supported the inside while the thumb was placed against the sharp edge and the clay was pressed down with the other hand. The surplus clay was taken away with a spatula.

Rims that are folded double on the outside indicate either that a more kneadable clay was used, or that the lean clay was in a more kneadable state than usual. It can often be seen in section that the rim was folded double. The top of the rim from which the "seam" runs down is as thick as the wall. Sometimes one finds that the folded-over part only joins the wall at the lower end, leaving a cavity, or that there is a tiny hole just where the fold occurs.

If some spare clay was reserved at the top of the rim before this was folded double, then the lower part of the rim will bulge. If after that the top of the rim was rounded, the impression is given that a profile was used to shape the rim. Sometimes the folded rim is pushed up again, which results in a ridge on the outside and a long-drawn rim above it.

These rims have not been shaped with the aid of a profile. If only a fragment of the rim is available this becomes clear as soon as the grit used to temper the clay with, is examined. It is too coarse not to be shifted over and through the surface should a hard object be used to shape the rim. As the pot has been built up by hand in a slow turning movement, the rim is always uneven at the top, which again does not permit the use of a hard tool. A hard tool designed to make a certain profile on the rim can only be applied when the grit is added to the clay as powder. In the case of a large fragment or a complete rim, minor changes of the shape at different parts of the rim are immediately noticeable. A plastic clay permits the following treatment of the rim. The top is rolled down on the outside by an evenly distributed pressure from the top. The roll along the rim can be flattened, giving a triple fold.

The rim-shapes discussed above can be made in a different way if both the clay and the wheel are of a high quality. In this case one does not find the "seam" in the section of the rim. The rim is made even by cutting the superfluous clay away while the pot turns on the wheel, after which the rim is pressed into the required shape.

A groove running along the top of the rim is made by first pressing the rim down, which widens the top of the rim, and then bringing the rim back to its original width. The flat rim is often found on large jars and bowls. A flat rim can be extended on one or on both sides of the rim. Where the rim extends on one side only it can be taken as an extension of the rim.

Before folding the rim the top is made even in the way already described above. Then the rim is folded out to make a right angle with the wall. As the circumference widens considerably when the rim is pushed into a horizontal position, the double thickness disappears again by this process of stretching.

There are three ways of making a flat rim which extends on both sides: a) The top of a rim is folded to form a ring. With the side of a finger the top is flattened while thumb and forefinger of the other hand support the rim from underneath. The result is a T shaped rim. However, the clay must be plastic and the wheel must turn easily. b) The rim is first folded into a horizontal position one way or the other and then back. c) A groove is made along the top of the rim with a hard tool, after which one finger presses aside the two sides that have been split apart, while the thumb and forefinger of the other hand support the rim from underneath. The inturned rim is often found on bowls. The folded part of the rim is usually carefully smoothed out against the wall of the neck to form a whole with it, but in the break one can distinguish the "seam" and often a gap just where the rim was folded. In appearance this rim looks much like the cut rims. Often the rim widens near the top because of having been smoothed down slightly with a finger or tool. With flat saucers the double rim is very typical and is sometimes thickened near the top of the rim.

Sometimes the rim is rolled on the inside. When this fold of the rim is pressed hard against the ball of the thumb, while the fingers support the outside, the wall just underneath the rim often bulges.

The Neck

The neck is the part of the pot that begins where the shoulder curves inwards and ends in the rim. When the pot is not made on a wheel, the neck is built up in a spiral from a coil of clay. Often the neck and rim are made from one coil. If the pot is built on a base which can be turned then this part of the pot is usually the best turned or shaped part. Its position on the vessel and its small circumference with little clay to be pushed up makes it best fitted for being turned or reshaped by turning. Thus one usually finds that the neck is thinner than the rest of the pot. Marks of turning show that wetter and more kneadable clay was used. A sharp angle between the top of the shoulder and the neck may indicate that the neck has been made separately. This will be clearly visible in the break. Traces on the inside of the vessel, showing that the pot was treated with a tool while drying, are often not found inside the neck. This means that the pot was first made up to the neck and after drying the thickness of the wall was readjusted with a scraper, after which the neck was fitted on. When pot and neck were made in one piece there is a regular transition between shoulder and neck, and this is more often found with small vessels than with large ones. To make a large pot in one piece requires great technical skill and a fast wheel. In smaller pots one often sees a strangely twisted pattern near the neck inside. This shows that the neck was first made wider and that afterwards by gentle pressing from the outside, was narrowed. In the case of pots made on a non-turning base one finds the same process. The ridges in the clay caused by pressure will then run perpendicular on the circumference of the neck, and not obliquely in a fan shape, as is the case with turned pots. The former necks are much thicker and squeezed. The height of the neck is important. There are standard heights such as a whole hand, or the width of 3,2 or one finger. Only if the neck has the height of a hand is it possible to work the inside of the pot after it has been built, to scrape for instance the wall to make it thinner, or support the wall when handles are fitted on to it. Traces of these activities can often be found. Where these traces exist, there are two possible explanations: either the neck is wide enough to insert the hand into the pot, or the pot was not yet closed at the bottom, and the inside was dealt with while the upper part was already dry and hard. (see below).

Very wide necks are usually shorter than the width of one finger and the total height of shoulder and neck is often only as high as the width of a man's finger. In those cases the neck is in fact part of the shoulder that has been turned up. The result is that when seen in section the neck is very thin at the top in comparison with the width. A wide and at the same time high neck usually goes with a narrow shoulder which flows smoothly from the body. Otherwise there is a risk that the shoulder will collapse under the weight of the large neck. Also the neck can only be fitted onto the shoulder after the latter has become fairly hard.

Narrow necks are usually the height of the width of the finger of a man's hand. Higher necks more than one finger width are only found where a more advanced technique of turning is known, and a better composition of the clay is present.

The Shoulder

Pots made of bands of clay in spirals usually have a shoulder attached to the body with a sharp angle and a rim attached to the shoulder also with a sharp angle. The more a pot has been made by turning or reshaped by turning, the more fluid the joints will be. The sharp angle between body and shoulder often indicates that the shoulder has been fitted on to a bowl shape which was made in a mould. If the pot has been made by turning, then the upper part of the body is usually turned inwards to get the required width for the shoulder. The widest part of the body is then found just below the shoulder. As the wall has been pressed outside at that point, the shoulder will be thinner near the body than near the neck. If however, the neck was wider to begin with and afterwards narrowed, as discussed above, the shoulder may be thinner near the neck, since it was stretched while the neck was narrowed. A combination of the two possibilities shows a shoulder which is wider in section in the middle than at both ends. Widening the body of the pot near the shoulder often puts too much stress on the wall, which, where non-plastic clay is used, causes the clay to lose its cohesion. Although the clay is smoothed afterwards one can often see the granulation at the surface both in- and outside. In the case of partial turning the height of the shoulder is usually not more than one finger's width. In that case the shoulder can be supported while being made from underneath. This shows in the turn marks. The impression of the knuckles of the finger make a regularly wavy line over the total width of the shoulder. In section this shoulder is concave, slightly sunken, following the line of the supporting fingers. Pots with shoulders made on a wheel will tend to have convex shoulders to prevent any sinking of the shoulder. Turning marks of the fingers run in spirals towards the neck, and the transition from body to shoulder is smooth.

The Body

The body of the pot is that part which stretches from the base to the shoulder. A fast wheel, a plastic clay and good craftmanship are needed to throw a body from one lump of clay. In the case of small vessels the body is often built up in a spiral from coils of clay or coils are added in horizontal layers. Then the pot must be turned to thin out the coils and in this process the coils become overlapping. The wall becomes thinner where it is pressed outwards and this makes turning easier when making a thinner wall than with a vertical wall. Another technique for building up a wall is first to throw the top half from the clay and after this has dried, the lower half is then made by turning the unfinished pot upside down and using the lump of clay on which the first half was left to dry. In this case the wall is usually thicker somewhere near the middle. This technique is also applied with pots with bulging bodies. Here the different direction of turning in the upper and lower part of the pot is an indication. Pots with bodies made from two bowl-shapes show the weld on the inside running right round the circumference of the body. As a rule pots thrown on the wheel will have a wall which is thicker near the base, unless the superfluous clay has been scraped away after the pot was dried. In this case the lower part will show marks of having been worked on the outside with a hard tool while dry. The body of large bowls show two different methods. Either the body is cast in a mould from a sheet of clay, or coils are used.

Bases

The base of the pot is that part which rests on the ground when the pot is standing upright. It is not true that a flat base always indicates that the pot has been made perpendicularly. It is possible to flatten a base by turning after the pot has dried. In this case the base will often be either slightly convex or concave. If the base is also flat inside the pot without a ring to stand on, then the pot has been made upright. A round base always indicates that the pot has not been made standing upright. It is impossible to describe here the different methods that are used by potters to make a base. For the techniques used at Deir ʿAllā in the early Iron Age see chapter seven.

Handles

A very simple way of making a handle is to roll a ball of clay over a flat surface until it becomes pipe-shaped, and then attach it to the pot by both ends. A disadvantage of this method is that the clay often loses too much water when set to dry which causes small cracks on the surface. These cracks will widen as the handle dries out further.

Another method is to make a flat band of clay, which is folded lengthwise or made into a roll. Handles made in this way often have a small hole in the centre of the core.

Skilled throwers have a different way of making handles. A lump of clay is made into a ball between the hands and then shaped as a cone. The base of the cone is taken in one hand and the other end is left hanging free. After having dipped his free hand in water, the thrower then places the cone near the base between thumb and forefinger, and presses the clay downward in gentle movements until the required length is reached. The thick end of the clay roll is then fitted onto the rim of the pot, and the thinner end onto the shoulder or body.

In this way the handle has—in section—the shape of the opening formed by thumb and forefinger of the thrower, which is a more or less oval shape with one pointed end. Another profile is obtained when the thumb is placed on the handle opposite the tips of fore- and middle finger. Thus a flattened almond shaped section is obtained. A flat handle is made by drawing the clay roll between fore- and middle finger. A good plastic clay is needed for this kind of manufacture. A lean clay would break under the strain.

Handles made in this way shrink a great deal during the process of drying. These handles are usually fitted onto the pot after the latter has already been drying for some time, as the drying handle might easily deform or tear the pot. The handle itself changes its shape while drying. Thus the crest of a c-shaped handle will move upwards.

Large handles need more care during the whole process than small handles.

When pots are hand made, the handles are fitted onto the vessel without delay as a dry clay has been used. When a lean clay is used, the handle will always break off with a part of the pot when it breaks. With plastic clays the handle will sometimes break off at the junction.

The place of the handle varies greatly: on top of the rim, on rim and neck, on the shoulder, on the belly or on the base. The position of the handle is usually vertical on jars. Wide vessels may have horizontal handles. Vertical handles are usually fitted onto pots that are partly made in a mould or thrown on the wheel. In the first case the handle is fitted immediately, in the second case only after the pot has been allowed to dry. In the first case the handle can be fitted on without supporting the wall of the pot from the inside (no fingermarks) but in the second case the pot has to be supported and one often finds fingermarks. When the handle protrudes above the rim the pot cannot have been dried upside down, and this is a reason why the handle usually does not protrude above the rim. Handles on necks, shoulders and bodies can have been fitted on while dry or wet, with or without support from the inside. In the case of jars of which the base was closed after the upper part had been thrown, the handle is usually fitted upside down (thick end of the cone below).

Handles fitted onto the base serve to give pots with rounded bases a firm stand, like a ring or legs. These handles have to be fitted in more dry condition and prevent the vessel from being dried upright.

Fitting the handle onto the pot

Both ends of a handle can be fitted onto the wall of the pot at an angle of 90°. In many cases however the upper part of the handle (or the lower part if the handle was fitted on while the pot was held upside down), is fitted on sideways against the wall, in which case the lower part is fitted in the same way, and both ends point in the same direction (downward). One also meets handles the upper part of which are fitted straight onto the rim and the lower part sideways onto neck or shoulder. While pressing and adjusting the handle to make a firm link, the thrower often leaves many fingermarks in the clay. Sometimes small rolls of clay are added to make a larger junction surface, in which case sherds reveal conical lumps of clay where the handle broke off the pot. This can have a crater-shape if the added clay still adheres to the wall of the pot.

Differently shaped handles are sometimes found on large vessels to facilitate lifting. Flat bowls have part of the rim widened instead of handles to form an easy grip. Half dumb-bell shaped handles fitted onto bowls just under the rim are made as follows: a roll of clay is made between the hands and then held in the fist with both ends of the roll sticking out. The ends are then pressed in with the fingers of the other hand, thus making the dumb-bell shape. It is then cut into two halves lengthwise, and each half fitted onto the bowl opposite one another. These handles are usually made with some care.

Sometimes handles and other protrusions on vessels are fitted in such a way that they facilitate stacking on top of each other in the kiln.

CHAPTER SIX

GENERAL SURVEY OF THE TECHNIQUES OF POT BUILDING FOUND AT DEIR 'ALLĀ

The analysis of the potter's techniques in use in the Early Iron Age at Deir 'Allā has shown that pots were made by hand either in a mould or on some form of a hand wheel, and sometimes by a combination of these two basic tools.

The Use of the Mould

Types of pottery: cooking pots and large shallow bowls.

The mould

Neither the exact shape of the moulds in use, nor the material from which they were made can be determined precisely. The reason for this lack of evidence is that the bases were always scraped to take away surplus clay. As a result of this scraping all the impressions which might give an indication of the material of the mould were erased. There is one exception. Many bowls of type 17 show impressions of rush matting on the outside just below the rim down to the point where scraping begins. This has not been observed on bases of cooking pots. Both a piece of matting pressed down in a hole in the ground and a bowl shaped pottery mould could be used as a hand wheel if a coil of clay was added to the clay in the mould in a turning movement to make a rim.

Whatever material the mould was made of, it did not have the exact shape of the base of the pots as the potters wanted them, for scraping was always done afterwards. Nor did the moulds have a depression for a base ring.

The process was as follows:

A lean and fairly dry clay was beaten or pressed to form a large sheet of a roughly circular shape. The sheet was then pressed down into the mould. Then a rim could be made from the fringe of the clay sheet by turning and wet smoothing. At the same time the whole surface of the sheet in the mould was wet smoothed. Often a coil of clay of the same substance was added to the clay sheet in the mould and turned up to become a neck and rim. This coil could be fitted at almost right angles to the clay sheet—carination—(cooking pots) or more or less in a vertical position (bowls). In the case of burnished bowls, burnishing followed immediately, with the vessel still in the mould. As soon as the rim was dry enough, the pot was taken out of the mould and put upside down. The clay on the base was then not yet too dry to be worked with a scraping tool, and a ring was added (bowls) made in various ways. Sometimes the ring was eased out of the clay that was scraped away from the base.

The early cooking pots usually have extremely well-made bases with an even thickness, such as cooking pots require. The bases of the bowls often show much variation of thickness and the cut-out ring on the base was usually neither in the centre nor parallel to the rim and had to be re-shaped.

The construction of rims cf. pp. 118ff., pp. 157ff.

The construction of ring-bases cf. pp 102ff.

Evidence used for the analysis:

The break of the base is featureless, i.e. no signs of stress in the clay. The rim and neck break in right angles, which is typical for slow turning while the clay is pressed upward. The composition of the clay shows that it was lean and fairly dry. The joint of sheet and coil can often be seen in section. The surface treatment points to wet smoothing inside and on the rim outside, done before the clay had been allowed to dry: the rough grit is pushed down below the surface. The base was fashioned by scraping after the pot had dried: the grit is transported over the surface but not pressed down into it. Bowls burnished on the outside show a very different reaction to burnishing on the wet smoothed part and the dry scraped part below. So much so that the latter often shows a slightly undulating surface caused by the burnishing tool on the hard surface. Some bowls still bear impressions of the mould just below the rim. None of the typical features of coil-made bases are found.

Coiling

Coiling is a very common practice of potters all over the world and whenever a potter in Western Europe has to make a really large jar he turns to coiling, since a plastic clay could not carry the weight during throwing. Hence he uses a lean clay.

Types: deep bowls, jars, jugs, cooking pot type 3.

The wheel

Strictly speaking coiling does not need a turning base. It can be done—and is done in parts of the world—by walking round the vessel. The Deir ʿAllā pots show traces of turning, or at least, a turning base was known to the potters. This turning base can be very primitive or more developed, but it always has two distinctive features: one has to keep turning it or it will stop immediately; it does not have enough momentum to bring centrifugal force into the clay. Throwing needs a wheel which is heavy enough and turns easily enough to give the centrifugal force on which the art of throwing is based. Unfortunately no evidence has been found on the pottery so far examined to allow for any conclusion concerning the type of wheel used in the Early Iron Age at Deir ʿAllā. Here we call it a hand wheel. It is certainly possible that this wheel was well developed, that it could spin with some speed and also was fairly heavy. There is a distinct improvement in turning noticeable in the development in the successive phases of the stratigraphy.

The method

Coiling begins with a wide clay base to which coils are added. In Deir ʿAllā the first coil was never the lowest part of the wall, as it probably was by the end of the L.B.A. The first coil laid became part of the body somewhere above the base, at least one coil away from it. The coils are fitted on top of each other. Coiling in spirals has not been found. What has been found is that in the case of irregularly made coils an extra bit of clay was added to bring the circumference all round up to the same level. The coils are thinned out by pressing the clay upward and at the same time formed to the width required. The process then goes on, in the case of jars, to shape the shoulder, neck and rim. The bowls, according to their size, may require only one, two or three coils. Jars would probably normally be built of six to eight coils. After shaping the upper part of the vessel in this way, the outside surface of jars, and both the inside and outside surface of the bowls was smoothed with a wet cloth or piece of leather. The unfinished pot was then cut away from its clay base, just above this base, and put aside to dry. In this type of clay the water would not only evaporate, but also sink down to the lower part, which therefore dried more slowly than the rest. As soon as the clay was hard enough to retain its shape under some strain, the pot was put on the hand wheel upside down and a new coil was added. The potter worked exactly as though he were making a shoulder and a rim. In the early stages we find that turning stopped when the opening in the "shoulder" was about as narrow as a neck. The pot was then simply closed with two slabs of clay, one from the outside, and one from the inside. The next step in development was that a "neck" was added onto the "shoulder", and this "neck" was pressed in during turning. This in its turn was later replaced by coiling and shaping in the direction of the "shoulder" until the opening was so small that the potter could only insert one finger. He then pulled the remaining clay up and shut the hole by pushing it down again. In the case of smaller bowls the coils may have been cut off just below the base, and the base finished by dry scraping. Otherwise the base was finished on the outside by wet smoothing.

Construction of the rims cf. pp. 127ff, pp. 161ff.
Construction of the bases cf. pp. 102ff.

Evidence used for the analysis:

The clay is made lean by the use of coarse temper, often badly mixed with the clay. Typical patterns of stretching in fairly dry clay occur frequently. The break pattern is vertical and horizontal. Jars often show the number of coils used in the break pattern As a rule there is a spot near the base in the wall which is twice as thick as the rest at the same height: this is the overlap of the last coil which would be very hard to smooth away. The three methods of closing a pot at the base show clearly on the inside of jars. This also shows that the pot was finished upside down. The bases are wet smoothed on the outside. The inside is often smoothed with a tool (jars).

TURNING WITHOUT COILING

Throwing pottery from a lump as a device for mass production is common modern practice. Turning pottery from a large cone of clay on a hand wheel was practised as early as the 20th century B.C.

Types: small bowls, lamps, small juglets, industrial pots.

The method

A large cone shaped mass of clay is put on a hand wheel. The clay has to be kept wet, as the type of clay used at Deir ʿAllā with its coarse temper dried very quickly. The top of the cone is flattened in a turning movement, and a rim is shaped in the case of bowls and lamps, a tube in the case of juglets. This tube is narrowed at the top to form neck and rim. The pot is then cut loose from the lump well below the already finished part. After the upper part had dried the solid clay lump at the base could still be re-shaped by scraping.

The bowls have a flat base modelled by scraping. The lamps have a slightly convex base and the method of scraping is different; the rim of the lamp had to be given its proper shape before it dried and the lamp was cut loose. If put upside down, the lamp would rest on only three points of the circumference of the rim. The potter therefore kept the lamp in his left hand while fashioning the base with a tool. In the case of the small juglet, the potter, wanting to avoid the danger of just cutting through the wall of the juglet instead of through the lump below, often took no risks and cut three to four cms. lower than was strictly necessary. In contrast to the late L.B. dipper juglets the Deir ʿAllā Iron Age ones were not shaved but scraped and rounded, and usually finished by wet smoothing.

Construction of the rim cf. pp. 140 ff, p. 105.

Construction of the bases cf. pp. 104 ff.

Evidence used for the analysis:

A break through the base often shows vertical shrinkage which is how the lump would shrink but not a coil. (The "lump" is a clay roll which is made of clay well beaten—to drive the air out—and formed into a thick roll stood on one end. Hence the pattern of shrinkage.) The typical marks of cutting from a lump of thrown clay are never found here. Instead dry scraping is practised. Circular movement of dry scraping on the bowls point to the use of a hand wheel. The clay paste in use is a dry clay, not fit for throwing. In none of the cases is the base in the centre of the pot; therefore there is no quick turning. The turning marks in the juglets do not start from the centre of the base but often in the vertical wall. The extreme differences in the thickness of wall and base in many cases point to the use of a lean clay. Otherwise firing would have been impossible.

The Wheel as Used in Deir ʿAllā[1]

In their study of the potter's techniques at Tell Beit Mirsim J. L. Kelso and J. Palin Thorley have convincingly shown that most of the T. Beit Mirsim Str. A pottery was wheel-made, that is *thrown* on the wheel. There were some exceptions, jars, (par. 88) and some bowl types (par. 81) which were not exclusively thrown. Modern Arabic potters in Palestine know how to throw a large water jar from one lump of clay, using a clay which is not very plastic tempered with sand. They throw the upper part of the jar first, leaving a good deal of clay from the lump untouched, then allow the thrown part with the unused clay below to dry, and after the upper part has become dry enough and while the unused clay is still wet enough, they place the jar upside down on a cone shaped clay lump, wrapped in cloth on the wheel, and finish the lower part of the jar while turning until they close the base.

This process resembles the Early Iron Age technique if one substitutes coiling-turning for throwing. It is likely that between the 12th century and the 6th century B.C. the Palestinian potters learned how to throw pottery, as it is clear from published Early Iron Age material from Palestine and from a study of E. I. A. sherds in the Palestine Museum that the techniques described for Deir ʿAllā were in common use throughout the whole of Palestine.

This presents two problems.

The first problem is: if the art of throwing was known to the potters of the M.B. Age, how did it get lost during the Late Bronze Age? The second problem is: how was the art of throwing re-discovered during the Iron Age?

Wheel-made pottery in the sense of thrown pottery is found in the 19th-16th cent. in Palestine. The potters were very skilled throwers, cf. the dipper flasks as an example. The only technical fault was the temper in the clay, which did not allow the pottery to become really hard ware. It could not be fired to the temperatures of modern biscuit wares, because of the large amount of lime in the clay.

A proper study of the decline of throwing can only be based on a study of a large amount of Late Bronze Age pottery. An enquiry into the re-discovery of the art of throwing in the Iron Age demands a study of the following aspects.

a) The preparation of the clay. To what extent were lean clays purified or plastic clays tempered to become the right substance for throwing? It should be stressed that this is a question not only for the ceramic petrographer but also for the archaeologist, who can study the visible traces of techniques left on the surface of vessels and in breaks. One has to reckon with the possibility that in a given repertoire some types were already being thrown, whereas others were still handmade. It is even likely that one may find a phase in which some examples of one type were already being thrown while the others were still made in the old way.

b) The type of wheel used. Practically all our information must come from deduction

[1] Rieth 1960.

of what can be observed on the pottery. It is therefore useful to keep in mind that the wheel used for throwing was only brought to a state of perfection some fifty years ago with the use of ball bearings, and later still, the electric motor. Between the two mats placed on top of each other as a primitive "wheel" and the modern potter's wheel there are uncountable possibilities of making a more or less satisfactory revolving base on which to shape pottery. There is, however, one significant difference between throwing and all other techniques.

Throwing needs both a plastic clay and a wheel which gives a certain amount of centrifugal force to the clay body. Centrifugal force exercised on a lean clay would pull the clay to bits. On the other hand one could "throw" a small pot from a lean clay on a slowly turning base, provided there is somebody who keeps the base turning. The coarser the temper in the clay, the slower the wheel must turn and the more one has to scrape surplus clay away afterwards. Throwing (and the term "wheel-made") should therefore be reserved for pottery made on a wheel which creates a centrifugal force in the clay and from a clay that responds to this force. One can easily visualize what this means if one thinks of a large shallow bowl with a very wide and flat rim being thrown on the wheel. As soon as the wheel stops and with it the centrifugal force, the rim would collapse.

It is clear that the development of the wheel and the preparation of the clay went closely together in the search for improved throwing. Even if the stone implements found in Palestine and termed potters' wheels could turn in the same plane, they are not heavy enough for the purpose of throwing larger pots like storage jars. The wheel, used in the M.B. need not have been a kick wheel: it could have been turned by hand by a helper, but it certainly was large and heavy and needed much care and attention to keep it in running condition. It must have been either entirely or partly made of wood.

c) The art of throwing was the least of the problems of development of skill. Once a potter had mastered the art of throwing as a skill, he could teach his sons in the same way as all craftsmen hand down their crafts through family tradition.

d) The next problem presented by throwing was the drying of the pottery. Thrown pottery needs much more of an even thickness of the wall than pottery made of lean clays. Generally this pottery had to dry in a room protected from strong draughts or direct sunlight so that all the parts of the pot could dry at the same rate.

e) In the same way firing needed much more skill and better built kilns than coarse tempered clay vessels required.

In every respect therefore throwing requires a high standard of precision. With their techniques the Deir ʿAllā potters could be much less careful and still produce pottery good enough for daily use. They did not have to sieve the material used as temper, nor did they have to mix it so thoroughly. As they used a coarse temper, air in the clay could escape much easier than in the case of plastic clays. They could use a simple wheel as long as it would turn round. Drying went quickly and could be done in the open and firing needed less attention and the type of kiln could be much less developed. In other words, working with a drier type of clay was really much simpler in every respect than throwing. The production of thrown pottery may have broken down after the M.B.A. for even such a reason as, for instance, that carpenters started to use inferior quality wood for making the wheels used by the potters. Less care taken while preparing the clay could have been another reason. Therefore in a way it is amazing to find potters in the Early Iron Age struggling to improve their methods. There may have been an economic necessity behind it like the urgent need for quicker production. There is sufficient evidence of another problem which was urgent. The defective method of making bases for larger vessels by the end of the L.B.A. must have caused a great deal of loss during drying and firing and this in itself could have been sufficient reason for potters to try to find a better solution. Of the five points mentioned above it is clear that throwing could not have been invented at one given moment. Rather we have here a slow process in which improvements were made, which almost certainly started with the improvements in clay preparation. For a long time the type of wheel used was not essential in this process. And it is indeed possible that throwing started with narrow types (in which the centrifugal force is always much less of an element than in wide vessels). It was done from a "cone" which in turn made the potters look for a finer kind of temper and a wheel with a flat top which turned in a horizontal plane.

Although we cannot reconstruct the type of wheel used by these potters there are some indications about the mechanical possibilities of the wheel. There is

a) the preparation of the clay,

b) throwers marks on small types of vessels, (not to be confused with the marks of the turner)

c) the shape of the vessels. Throughout the development of some pottery types at Deir ʿAllā there is a gradual change in shapes, notably in the ones made by coiling, that point to a quicker turning of the wheel.

d) from the way pots break one can study the stress in the clay caused by turning and throwing. In coiling the clay is mainly pressed up, also in the process of widening the coils, while in throwing the clay is pushed up and forced in the direction against the movement of the wheel. And finally

e) in the cases of clear thrower's marks on the inside or "wheel burnishing" one could count how many times a wheel turned round before it had to be pushed again. As late as the 16th century A.D. in Western Europe the thrower had to start up his wheel again and again during throwing.

The Potter's Kiln

As we have not found traces of potter's kilns in the excavated area, we can only point to certain facts, observed on the pottery itself, for the reconstruction of these kilns. First some observations made in Kerami at the present day pottery, where kilns are being fired the whole year round, are listed. These are kilns dug into the soil. The top rises only slightly above the surrounding surface. The ground round the kilns is strewn with waste products. In front of the kilns is a deep hole, partly filled with fuel of all kinds (fruit stones, car tires cut to small bits, broken shoes and discarded rags from clothing, plastic waste, masses of animal bones, dried dung etc.). The kiln consists of two chambers, one on top of the other, the lower chamber being the fire chamber. The top chamber can only be reached from above. When this chamber is filled, a boy descends into it and eventually stands on the leather hard pots. This chamber is closed with broken pots and earth when the required temperatures have been reached. The kilns are oxidizing. Stoking is done by an expert man who constantly watches the colour of the fire in the firing chamber and feeds the fire constantly with small quantities of fuel, on which he sits. When firing is finished, there are three zones of colours on the pottery. The lowest layers contain a lot of wasted material as temperatures went up too high. This pottery is warped and has many greenish patches or is completely molten. This green colour is occasionally found on excavated sherds that also show large blisters. This indicates temperatures around 1100°C. The second group which is by far the largest one has an almost white colour. This is pottery where the salts, deposited on the surface while the pots were drying, have fused with the sulfuric elements in the gases of the fuel (bloom). These vessels often have red patches, where they touched each other and where the flames did not touch the surface. Where water jars were stacked upright, the higher ones will tend to have reddish coloured shoulders. The third group is pottery from the top of the kiln, where temperatures were lower, and the colours are reddish. It is very interesting to find that this pottery from the top of the kiln is considered to be of poor quality, (it must be softer ware) and is only bought by the poorest villagers. It is easy to pick up sherds from one firing batch which show all the colour transitions from almost glazed dark green through white to bright red. There are also some pots which from their position in the top have only been "smoked" by the fuel and come out with a greasy black sooty surface. Around these kilns one finds masses of slag, which does not come from the fuel used, but from the broken down kilns, which have to be rebuilt when the clay walls are burnt through and there is a danger of draughts through tiny cracks. It seems that one kiln load always consists of one type of pottery.

The floor of the pottery chamber is made of bricks and is slightly dome shaped. Pottery drainpipes, through which the flames reach the pots, have been built into it vertically at regular intervals.

From this we can see that the production of the potter is affected by the "bottle-neck" of the kiln. Firing the pottery is the most critical moment in the whole process, the capacity of the kiln is limited for each type of pottery, and fuel is a great problem.

Turning to the Iron Age pottery from Deir ʿAllā we find that a large pot can indeed show all the colours found on the pottery from Kerami. Most sherds show surface discolouration from the salts fused with gases from the fuel. Iron Age pottery in the collection from Shechem in the Rijksmuseum van Oudheden in Leiden shows the same feature. And quite often the red patches where pots have touched each other in the kiln are to be seen. The largest vessel found during the excavation which tells much about stacking is a storage jar (Pl. 14 no. 2). Here we find two spots near the base where the pot rested on two pots lower down in the kiln. At one of these spots the pot is also slightly dented. Next we find four spots, equally divided over the circumference just below the shoulder, showing that at least five pots were stacked on the same level. One of these spots is slightly higher than the others. Finally we find two spots on the shoulder, one of which is dented. The surface colour of the pot is that of the bloom (Munsell colours 5Y-7/2). The colour of the spots is as follows: where the pots touched there is "reduced" firing with lack of a free flow of oxygen, colour 2.5YR-5/0 and around this spot a small area of red: 2.5YR-5/4. One of the four spots around the body is caused by a handle touching the wall of our pot. From this can be deduced that the kiln had a floor space of over 1.10 m^2. if the chamber was more or less rectangular, and the height of the chamber must have been at least 1.20 m. This would in fact be a fairly large kiln in which some fifteen storage jars of this type could be fired at one time. From some bowl fragments it can be deduced that they were stacked standing on their sides, vertically. At least this would explain why some bowls are curiously warped and sometimes show a slight crack just where the circumference is slightly flattened, which is also the place of discolouration.

Another example of stacking is a 7th cent. wheel-burnished water decanter from Gezer (Mus. no. B 1929/1,754, field no. V.1367) which shows three red spots at equal distance around the side and one spot on the shoulder. There is a large amount of bloom on the surface of this pot, which shows that burnishing was done before the pot was leather hard. After burnishing, salts were still coming to the surface. Burnishing of a leather hard pot takes the surface salts away. These few facts observed on the pottery point to the fact that systematic sampling is needed to find out more about stacking and the size of the kilns.

All the Deir ʿAllā pottery was fired in oxidizing kilns, where the flames penetrated between the pots. Few fragments of black juglets were found. Distinction must be made between "black" and "blue" pottery, "blue" being the colour which results from proper reduced firing, "black" is the colour when pots are fired or refired in smoke. This can be tested by refiring in oxidizing circumstances.

Shortage of fuel or the high costs of it were and are still a big problem for potters. None of the Deir ʿAllā pots were properly fired, i.e. the colour of the surface is not the same as the colour in the core as it should be. There were two main reasons for this. First economy of the fuel to be used. The second reason is the amount of lime used as temper or present as a component of the clay itself. If these pots were fired until a good red core was obtained, which is not a matter of higher temperatures (as with the surface colours) but of longer firing, the lime would break the pot. As a lean clay, or a clay made lean, was used, the fire could go up in temperature rapidly until the surface was of the required colour, and then the kiln could be allowed to cool off. The result is a sufficiently hard surface and a softer core to the wall. If storage jars were stacked three high in a chamber, then it is fairly certain that the lower ones were harder than the top ones. But clay tempered with lime, whether as powder or in chips, can never become really hard ware.

The colour of the Deir ʿAllā pottery is therefore dependent on its place in the kiln as much as on the composition of the clay paste and temper material, and hardness is limited to the range reached between c. 700° and the maximum of 900°C. Since the pottery chamber was more than 1.5 m^3. in size, it can be assumed that firing was skilfully done.

Hand-Built E.I.A. Pottery in Palestine

Our thesis that the art of throwing was lost during the L.B.A. in Palestine and that the Early Iron Age pottery was not wheel-made can be substantiated both from a study of material in collections and from published material dating from that period. A number of sherds in the collections of the Palestine Museum (Jerusalem, Jordan) was studied by the author.

Beth-Shemesh.—A bowl, marked T 26, P. 3871, which could be classified in the Deir ʿAllā system as bowl type 9b, diam. 20 cms., shows the following characteristics. There is a slight angle between wall and rim. The angle is smoothed with a hard tool on the outside. Above the angle the rim shows turning marks. Below the angle on the inside the bowl is wet smoothed. Organic matter used as a temper does not show the influence of turning. The outside below the rim shows irregular turning marks. The bowl is mould built with a turned rim.

Four bowls from "tomb 1." (Deir ʿAllā type 4). No. 1.473, diam. 14 cms., has a rim which is turned and wet smoothed. The inside of the bowl is wet smoothed, the outside dry scraped. The bowl clearly shows finger marks impressed when taking the bowl, upside down, from a turning base. It almost cracked in two halves while drying. Bowl 1.479, the same type as no. 1.473, shows the same technical features. Part of the rim was cracked from the lower part of the bowl during drying and repaired before firing. "Turning" marks at the base are not circular but oval in dry clay. Bowl no. 1.478, diam. 16 cms., shows irregular traces of scraping on the outside. The base was repaired before firing and strengthened with a slab of clay. Bowl 1. 484, diam. 17 cms. The inside is smoothed in a turning movement anti-clockwise. The outside, however, was smoothed while the turning base was going in the opposite direction.

Beth El.—Pal. Mus. no. 35.4493, a bowl, diam. c. 20 cms., (Deir ʿAllā bowl type 5c), with a flat base. The lower part of the wall and base are dry scraped. A cooking pot (same P.M.no.), marked Dr 510.I 8-20, (Deir ʿAllā type 1), is made in exactly the same way as the Deir ʿAllā type. A large bowl, marked I,8-22, sub 134, (same P.M., no.) with a flaring rim is coil made and the rim is turned. A krater, (P.M. no. 35.4499) marked I Dr. 373, is turned from the neck up. The lower part is either coiled or mould made. All the Early Iron Age sherds showed typical hand-made characteristics.

Beisan.—Bowls show the same characteristic features as the Deir ʿAllā material and a jar base (Deir ʿAllā type 2b) shows the same technical development.

Shechem.—Early Iron Age sherds in the collection of the Rijksmuseum van Oudheidkunde at Leiden, which come from the excavations of E. Sellin at Shechem show that coiling and using a mould was practised in the Early Iron Age at Shechem. The same is the case with Early Iron Age pottery excavated by Sellin and Garstang at Jericho. Hand made Early Iron Age material can be found in quantities on the old dumps at the north side of the tell.

It is not difficult to give examples from the published material. At Afula, (M. Dothan[1]) there are three variants of jar bases in Str. III A-B. The rounded or slightly pointed base, the slightly flattened base and the knobbed base. The base shown on fig. 11, no. 1, 5, 38 and probably 35 are clearly Deir ʿAllā type 2b, the result of a "neck" being added to the highest coil of the jar when upside down. The rounded variant is Deir ʿAllā type 2c, closed by turning, which causes this shape. And from the shape it is infered that fig. 11, 3 is slab closed (Deir ʿAllā type 2a). The Afula potters did the same thing as the Deir ʿAllā potters and from the similarity of rims and handles on the Afula and Deir ʿAllā jars it is concluded that they had the same manufacturing methods.

Small vessels do not rotate as fast as large vessels on a wheel, the revolving time being the same, the circumference and therefore the speed being less. Vessels with a small circumference, like lamps, small bowls, and juglets can be made from a cone although there is coarse temper, long before wide vessels can be thrown. The centrifugal force is also much less important when small vessels are made. The M.B.A. potters from the 17th century B.C. were the most accomplished throwers of dipper juglets and lamps etc.

Lamp bases from that period show that they threw from a cone.[2] The so-called shaved dippers of the 13th century B.C. clearly demonstrate that the art of throwing was lost. Here the potters were struggling with a dry clay and a "knife" to make a dipper juglet.[3] Lamps from the same period are also "knife" shaved at the base. The very thick bases of dipper juglets may well indicate that potters turned them from a cone. Occasionally there is a 13th century lamp with an unworked base, like a lamp from tell Abu Hawam.[4] This is a lamp from Str. III and not necessarily later, since a similar lamp, though not with such a wide rim was found in the early 12th century sanctuary at Deir ʿAllā. Otherwise the technique of 13th century lamps is the same as the Deir ʿAllā ones. A lamp from the 3rd Fosse Temple at Lachish,[5] shows the characteristic shape of a hand fashioned and shaved base, and the photograph shows the marks clearly. When a wheel does not rotate in one plane the deviation can be corrected by using a cone of clay as long as the wheel turns slowly. It is therefore not surprising to find small pots made from a cone in a period when throwing was not practised.

The late L.B. potters are still trying to fit handles onto large storage jars in the tradition of the M.B. (cf. p. 171). But in the 13th and 12th cent. B.C. the potters had to resort to adding an extra roll of clay to the lower link between handle and wall.[6] This is

---

[1] Dothan 1955 (p. 43)
[2] Amiran 1963 (pl. 59, no. 41, from Megiddo)
[3] Hamilton 1934 (p. 47, no. 287-288)
[4] *Op. cit.*, (p. 23, no. 94)
[5] Tufnell 1940 (pl. xlv, no. 203)
[6] Amiran 1963 (pl. 32, compare with pl. 44)

a clear example that a different composition of the clay paste requires a different handling of the material. The Deir ʿAllā potters and their Palestinian colleagues from the 12th and 11th century found the solution to this problem.[1]

It is by no means surprising that the M.B. potters stuck to E.B.A. methods when making cooking pots. Wheel-thrown cooking pots are about the very last type to appear. There are no wheel-made cooking pots in Palestine before the 7th-6th cent.B.C. In the L.B. the rather ugly looking M.B. cooking pot is replaced by a more elegant shape, and it is possible that this new shape was invented after throwing had been abandoned in favour of coil building. The material available from Deir ʿAllā does not yet allow us to come to a conclusion about the question whether this L.B. type was coil-made or cast, but the former possibility is more likely. However, it seems very unlikely that the E.I.A. cooking pot (Deir ʿAllā type 1) is a straight descendant from the L.B. type. It comes from a different tradition. The earliest examples of this type all have a very carefully made base of equal thickness, a result of the method of using the mould, which is not the case with the L.B. type. The E.I.A. cooking pot was made in the same way right through Palestine. The Str. B cooking pot from Tell Beit Mirsim[2] is treated exactly like the Deir ʿAllā var. c. with an incised line.

The conclusion is, therefore, that potters all over Palestine were using the same methods, and the question which remains is whether differences in technical ability can be located and to what extent potters from different regions can be distinguished by their methods.

Rims made of Non-Plastic Clays and the Type Series

As a rule all the rims from the Deir ʿAllā repertoire were made by folding the upper fringe of the last coil inwards and smoothing it against the inside of the "neck." With every type of rim the Deir ʿAllā potters had to deal with the same problems. The last coil, from which the rim was made, was small with an overlap where the coil was twice the usual thickness. By thinning out the coil, the potter did not widen the circumference (there are only a few flaring rims in the repertoire), but he pushed the clay up. Equal thickness all round meant a very uneven fringe at the top. By folding the fringe inwards he could dispose of it and make a fairly level rim. Usually by pressing the fold against the inside he made a slight horizontal groove just below the new top of the rim. Each type in his repertoire had a rim traditional to the type, but the potter could remodel his rim in various ways. He could turn the rim up again and then fold it outwards or press the top of the rim down and give the side a certain profile.

It is clear that the finished rim was not only the product of what the potter had in mind or made in routine, but also of the amount of surplus clay in the coil, the location

[1] *Op. cit.*, (Pl. 77, no. 2)
[2] Albright 1932 (Pl. 24, no. 6)

of the last fold, the question how much the coil was thinned out as, for instance, the occurance of a small pebble in the last coil which would be a reason for the potter to leave the coil the thickness of the pebble, resulting in a small thick rim.

Given a traditionally determined rim pattern, it is fairly certain that on any excavation can be found practically every possible variation of that pattern, provided a large enough portion of a stratum is excavated. The same applies to the shape of the whole vessels. No two vessels are exact copies of each other. There are, however, two factors which make it possible to draw up a type series.

The first element is that the potter, clinging to tradition, would always be inclined to make rims as near to the known pattern as possible. One can see this only when a great mass of rims of the same type from one level is available. This can be explained by the fact that the potter tackled in a routine way every type of problem caused by surplus clay. In certain cases he would make a thicker rim, or turn the rim up again, or give it a slightly different direction, probably more from "feeling" than by intention. A certain standardization of varieties is the result.

The second element is that as time passed, the patterns would slowly change, either from experience or fashion or both. If viewed right through a certain number of successive levels a change of pattern is noticed, prevalence in the development of one variety, and assimilation of the shape of one type to that of another. While drawing up the type series we have therefore first sorted one type into a limited number of variations, then studied the type through the successive levels to see what developments there were, and from the combination of these tendencies working in each period and their development, we have made charts which enabled us to classify the pottery from each level and at the same time register the development in later phases. What is mere guesswork as long as one works on one phase or level only, is corrected and becomes much more convincing when viewed in the perspective of the stratigraphy.

In Deir ʿAllā a gradual development of technical skill takes place, which is expressed in the preparation of the raw material and treatment of the pots and in the development of shapes.

It shows that the traditions in the trade were by no means fixed for ever, that the potters were searching for improvements and to a certain extent experimenting with materials and techniques.

Returning to the type series it was found that although a seemingly infinite number of possible variations does in fact exist, the vast majority of types cluster round a limited number of variations, and that in the majority of cases it is not difficult to distribute the sherds over that number. There remain a number of sherds that must belong to a type but that are almost featureless so that distribution to a variant becomes mere guesswork. This is, however, always a very small minority of the total amount. The variations of each type used in this study cover the vast majority of the sherds found. Certain variations shown in the charts die out soon, whereas others become dominant in the course of time, and they should therefore not be taken as all contemporary. It means that what is generally known as, say, a 9th century type can be found on occasion in an 11th century level, provided the manufacturing technique has not changed too much.

Fig. 29 shows the variations of rim shapes chosen from the study of the I.A. cooking pot type 2. Variant a is not the original type; this is probably variant g, which still occurs occasionally in the I.A. It can easily be seen that variant b is the "prototype" of the 8th century cooking pot common in Palestine, while the other variants then occur only sporadically. A limited number of the "variants of the variants" have also been drawn in the same fig. Many more could have been added, rendering the system more and more complicated. This observation is important. It shows that a variant is only useful as long as it expresses a tendency in the potter's work. Once the tendencies have been established with some certainty it becomes possible to separate what is intended from what is mere accident. This has become another principle for this study: a "unique" rim shape can often be explained by obvious facts such as lack of clay in the last coil to finish the rim properly and the like. It is no use looking for parallels for such mishaps in other excavations though one can be sure that they are found elsewhere. It should be stressed that the differences between the variants are caused by almost imperceptible differences in the position of the fingers that shaped the rims, or by slightly more pressure of one finger, and the like.

Summing up it can be said that the type series is the result of the study of tendencies noticeable in the potter's work in a certain period but seen in the light of subsequent development. The types distinguished obviously belong to the potters inherited traditions, and the variants are the tendencies of development at work.

CHAPTER SEVEN

DESCRIPTION OF THE POTTERY AND TYPOLOGY

THE BASES

The following analysis of the manufacture of the bases is the result of studying all the stratified, and a great number of unstratified, base fragments.

The study of the base proved to be of great interest, as it provides a rare example of potters gradually learning to improve their technique over a period of time.

Apparently during the Late Bronze Age the art of making a good base for a jar or bowl was gradually lost. This can be deduced from the great number of bases of this period which are cracked. These were either filled in with clay by the potter before the vessel was fired or with plaster after firing.[1]

The reason for this gradual decline will be discussed in the volume devoted to the L.B.

The material from the Early Iron Age, particularly in its earliest phase bears witness to the potters' efforts to resolve their problem of how best to close a jar at the base.

Type 1

Instead of throwing or turning the clay, a lump of prepared clay was rolled out and the slab fitted into a bowl-shaped mould, and smoothed out until an even thickness was obtained. It was then usually wet-smoothed and left to dry out. Once dry, with the clay somewhat shrunken, it was easy to tap it out of the mould, so that the outside could be dealt with. The outside was worked when fairly dry in a turning movement; this is generally clearly visible. For further details: cf. p. 118. As the inside is usually smoothed and the outside rough, these bases must have been made in a concave mould rather than over a convex one. Moreover a convex mould would not allow the potter to finish off the pot before taking the base from the mould.

Type 2

The proto-type of type 2 bases was probably made as follows. A pot was built by coiling on a thick clay base, which was placed on a turning base (such as two superimposed mats). After the pot was finished it was cut loose from the base, and the shape

[1] cf. Tufnell 1958 (p. 138)

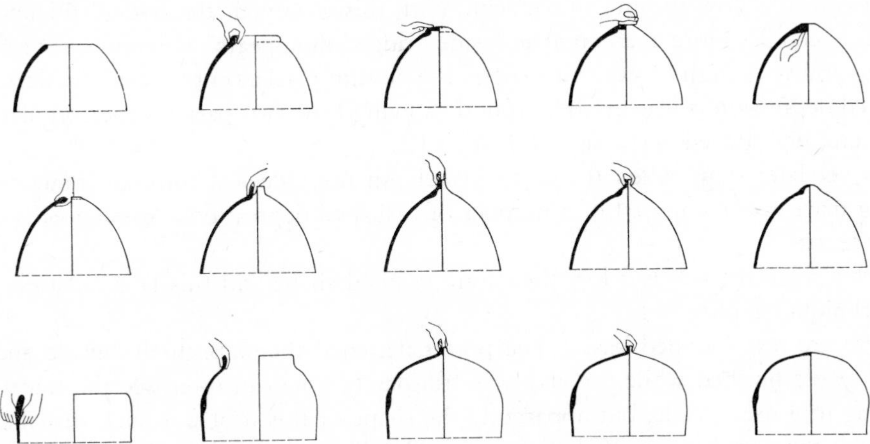

Fig. 20. Bases of jars, construction drawing

was adjusted by cutting away more clay from the outside. This left the vessel with a flat base inside but pointed on the outside. There was a great risk that the thick base would crack when firing.

The E.I. bases that developed from this proto-type were begun in the same way but the vessel was cut free above the clay "base" through the first coil. The coil was still fairly thick and much less dried out than the upper part of the vessel; therefore the potter was still able to work it, add another to it and control the shape and thickness of the base. As the base at this stage was still open the potter tried to make the opening smaller by adding a coil, turning the vessel (upside down), until only a small hole was left. In the earliest stages of the E.I. Age the potter simply added a slab of clay on the outside over the hole and then smoothed it out; and then did the same to the inside. This meant that the finished vessel could not be higher than the potter's arm was long. Therefore one has to assume that vessels which are higher than the length of a man's arm were closed at the base before the upper parts of the pot were built. The inside of many jar necks indeed bear traces of the potter's arm, showing that he worked the inside after the rim was finished. Type 2a, see Plate XIII.

In the earliest stages the inside slab was simply pressed in every direction onto the lowest coils by the potter as well as he could.

The base is rather broad and flat; no scraping tool was used.

In the next stage, potters soon discovered that it was easier to close the pot at the base if the lowest coil was treated in the same way as the neck, that is, turned up. (The pot again being upside down.) In this way the "sleeve" formed by the lowest coil could be closed in a turning movement and a final slab could then be added on the outside for strength. This treatment left the base thickened just above the lowest point and a small cup-shaped depression on the inside. This base is distinctly more pointed than the previous one. Type 2b, see Plate XIII.

The next development was that the base was closed by pushing down the up-turned lowest coil in a slow turning movement. With this treatment the overall thickness of the base becomes more even and the inside "ridge" disappears. This indicates a better turning ability though it was still slow as the closing marks on the inside indicate. An s-shaped depression is usually to be found showing how two parts of the coil met and, as it were, interlocked. Type 2c, see Plate XIII.

In a yet later stage when throwing vessels on the wheel is common practice, the closing mark was composed of a number of S-shaped depressions crossing each other in the centre.

At this stage the jars had lost their long pointed shape and this is compatible with the techniques applied.

There are few rounded bases. The potter flattened them. Both the inside and the outside were finished while the clay was still damp. One can often see the traces of a scraping tool used inside, but apparently the shape of this tool was such that it could not reach the very bottom of the jar, where the distinctive marks give place to finger impressions.

These bases obviously belonged to jars of which the inside would not be seen, and where no special finish of the inside was necessary.

The bases of larger deep bowls and kraters were made in much the same way. The difference for the potter was simply that in these shaped vessels the inside was easily accessible for further fashioning, which was not so with jars. The finishing touches were given as soon as the vessel was made. Often surplus clay had to be taken away. Generally all signs of how the bowl or krater was manufactured have vanished, as they were efficiently wet-smoothed from inside. Sometimes, however, finger marks are still visible where the potter pressed the inside slab against the walls of the vessel, and marks of a damp cloth are also to be seen. It seems that the outside of the base was usually worked after it had dried out for a period. It is worth noting that the flat bases of the larger bowls are often neither circular nor in the true centre of the vessel. This would have been impossible to achieve had they been thrown on a fast wheel.

Small bowls with flat bases and lamps

There is a slight difference in the manufacture of the bases of small bowls and lamps. This difference is closely related to the difference in height of the two sorts of vessels. Lamps are always much lower than bowls with a comparable rim circumference. Both were made out of a single lump of clay. In the case of bowls there is a marked angle formed where the base meets the wall. This is lacking with the lamps where the wall is but an extension of the base. Somewhere between base and rim the surface treatment changed from dry scraping below to wet smoothing above. This applies to bowls and lamps. In both cases the inside was generally wet-smoothed. The single lump of clay was formed in a slow turning movement and after finishing the rim the vessel was put aside to dry, the unfinished base still attached to the remains of the original clay mass. As soon as the walls were fairly dry the outside of the base was shaped.

In the case of the shallow lamp, the vessel had to be held in the hand before the

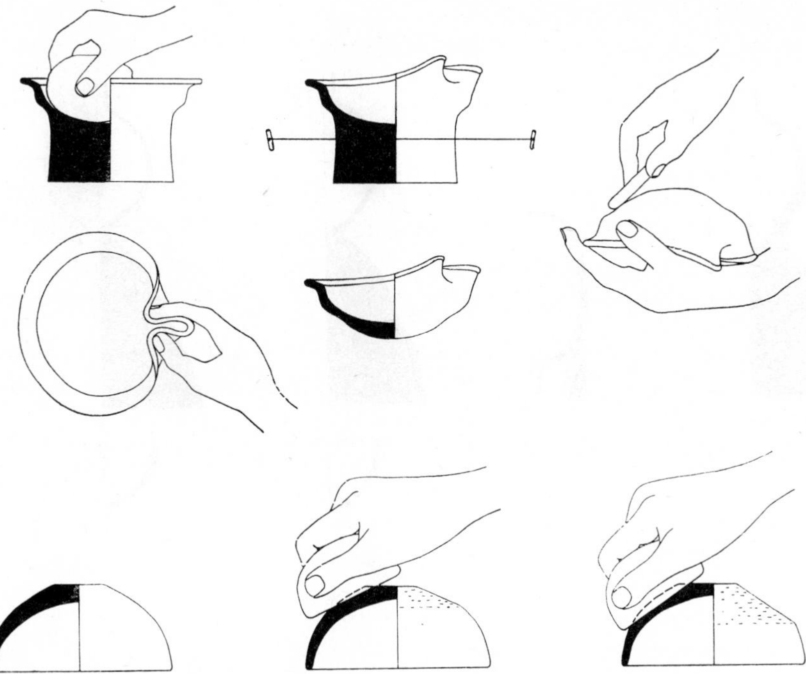

Fig. 21. Bases of small bowls and lamps, construction drawing

surplus clay could be scraped or smeared away. This was the only possible treatment as the rim had to be formed before the clay dried out, yet the whole vessel could not be turned upside down as the rim was no longer a horizontal one and could not bear the weight of the vessel before it was fired. This explains why lamps in the time when they were thrown on the wheel had very heavy, thick bases, cut from a cone. They could not be reshaped before the clay was rather hard. This treatment leaves a slightly concave base. Small bowls could be turned upside down, as the weight was equally distributed over the whole rim. Then a more or less circular base was cut out of the remaining lump of clay. The following further characteristics are to be found: Wet smoothed inside, sometimes with a spiralling mark or completely smooth with no signs of turning.

Below the wet-smoothed outside of the wall, tool marks, made after the clay had become drier, can be seen.

The flat base may be rounded but is more often slightly oval and is not centred true in the vessel.

In the case of lamps there is no marked angle between wall and base.

Bases type 4, *Juglets*

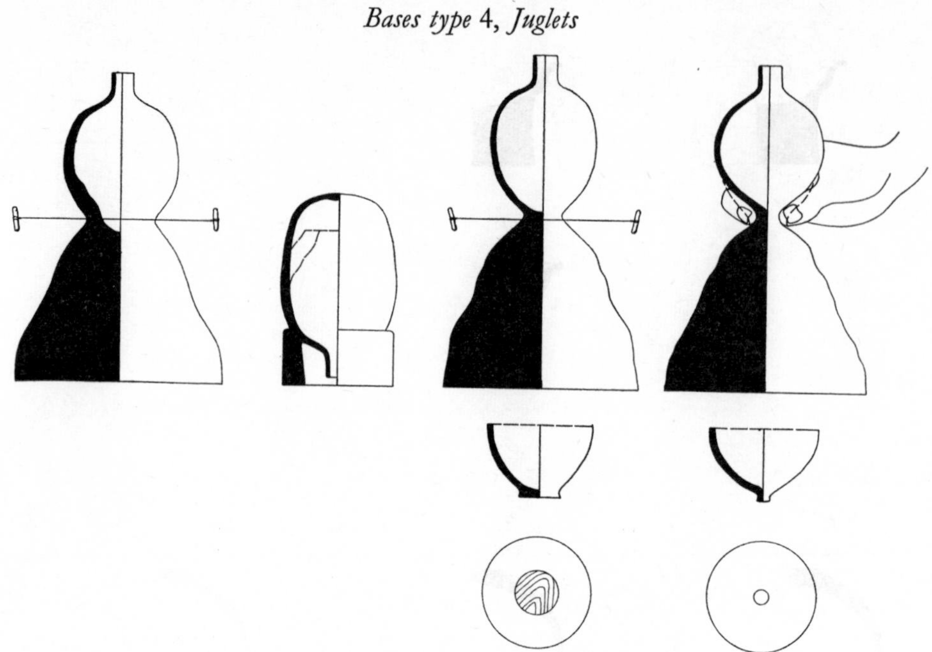

Fig. 22. Juglets, construction drawing.

Juglets and dipper flasks were definitely rare in the Early Iron Age, just as lamps were rare. Statistically their quantity is negligable; therefore it has been impossible to trace the development of these bases properly through the phases. From the stratified and unstratified material it is clear that these juglets were turned up from one lump of clay only, probably from a cone. Bases were finished in various ways.

a) Sometimes the potter cut the vessel loose through its wall, and, holding the pot in one hand closed the base in a turning movement, thus causing the lower end of the wall to fold. Surplus clay was then smeared out or scraped away.

b) The juglet was cut loose below the inside of the base, leaving clear fingermarks inside. The base is then flat inside and rounded outside, and usually wet smoothed.

c) The juglet was cut loose well below the inside of the base, again with fingermarks showing turning inside and a handsmoothed or scraped base outside. These bases are then very heavy.

The important thing is that in the break these bases invariably show vertical lines of shrinkage, which means that it is part of the clay lump as it was prepared for the juglet. (Compare base type 5).

d) In some cases the base is closed while the juglet was standing upside down on the wheel, in which case it was also cut loose first through the wall. In this case the base is not thicker than the wall.

Shaved dippers do not occur in these levels.

Although making a juglet from one lump of clay could be called throwing, the difference between throwing and the treatment of the E.I.A. juglets becomes immediately clear if the 17th cent. M.B. dipper flasks, both the larger and the smaller ones, are compared with the E.I.A. ones which are very primitive indeed. It is possible that the thick based juglet served a special purpose as they were made for a long time.[1]

For statistical evidence cf. the chart fig. 25a. There is, as yet, no explanation for the fact that these juglets were so scarce in Deir ʿAllā.

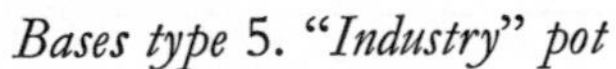

Bases type 5. "*Industry*" *pot*

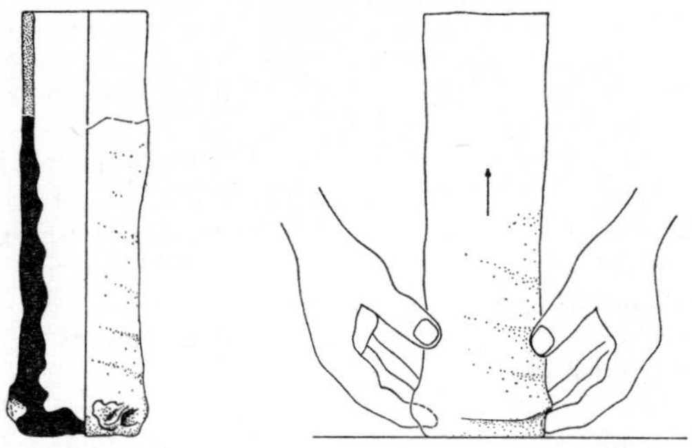

Fig. 23. 'Industry' pot, construction drawing

This base is only important for the analytical study in so far as it was left "unfinished" by the potters and shows all the marks of treatment. As all pottery types used in the household were given a smooth surface, by wet smoothing or scraping the surface after the pot was built, it is likely that this rough pot was used for a special purpose, and used only once. One almost complete example was found, phase F. The pot is straight sided and narrow and has no profiled rim. It occurs only sporadically from phase E on.

The pot was turned up out of one lump of clay and then cut loose from the turning base well below the inside of the base. (For the difference between "throwing" and turning in this case cf. bases type 4 and p. 91.) The clay must have been fairly wet when the pot was made, as very deep finger impressions are invariably found near the base, caused by the fingers of both hands when the pot was lifted to be put aside to dry. Cf. fig. 23. The break lines in the base are vertical. The base belongs to the lump of clay from which the pot was made. This pot cannot be related to any kind of industrial installation in the stratigraphy. As the pot must have been found in small quantities in Palestine too—there is one nearly complete example in the Shechem collection in the Rijksmuseum at Leiden—it seems reasonable to suppose that they were centrally manufactured near some kind of industry such as sugar-making and were used for a liquid to coagulate in. The solid material was then transported to its destination in these containers. (Compare the type of sugar pot used from Crusader times to late in the Middle

[1] Yadin 1958 (pl. xlviii, 4)

Ages of which large dumps can be found in many parts of the Jordan valley). Although this pot was scarce in Deir ʿAllā, it is discussed here for its technical importance. For the statistical evidence cf. chart fig. 25a.

Colour description

no.	*Colour outside*	*Colour inside*
	BASES TYPE 2	
	Phase B. Fig. 48	
1	5Y-7/3 pale yellow (7.5R-6/4 pale red)	10R-5/1 reddish grey
2	10R-6/6 light red	2.5YR-6/4 light reddish brown
3	7.5YR-7/4 pink	7.5YR-6/4 light brown
4	2.5Y-8/2 white	5YR-5/2 reddish grey
5	2.5Y-8/2 white (7.5YR-6/2 pinkish grey)	5YR-6/1 grey
6	2.5Y-8/2 white (5YR-7/2 pinkish grey)	2.5YR-N6 grey
7	5Y-8/2 white	2.5YR-6/4 light reddish brown
8	2.5Y-8/2 white	2.5YR-6/6 light red
9	10YR-7/2 light grey (10R-6/6 light red)	10YR-6/1 grey
10	2. 5Y-8/2 white	10R-5/1 reddish grey
11	10YR-8/2 white (10R-6/6 light red)	7.5YR-8/2 pinkish white
	Phase G. Fig. 63	
1	5YR-7/6 reddish yellow	7.5YR-7/4 pink
2	2.5YR-5/4 reddish brown	2.5YR-6/2 pale red
3	7.5YR-7/2 pinkish grey	2.5YR-6/2 pale red
	BASES TYPE 3	
	Phase B. Fig. 48	
12	7.5YR-6/4 light brown (2.5YR-6/6 light red)	2.5YR-6/4 light reddish brown
13	2.5Y-7/2 light grey (2.5YR-6/6 light red)	2.5YR-6/4 light reddish brown
14	10YR-7/3 very pale brown (5YR-6/4 light reddish brown)	10YR-8/2 white
15	10YR-8/2 white	5YR-7/2 pinkish grey
16	5YR-6/3 light reddish brown (5YR-2/1 black)	5YR-6/4 light reddish brown
17	7.5YR-6/4 light brown	7.5YR-5/4 brown
18	10R-5/3 weak red (7.5YR-6/4 light brown)	2.5YR-6/4 light reddish brown
19	10YR-7/2 light grey	7.5YR-5/2 brown
	Phase G. Fig. 63	
4	7.5YR-6/4 light brown	2.5YR-N5 grey
5	10YR-7/3 very pale brown	10YR-6/3 pale brown

Colour description (continued)

no.	*Colour outside*	*Colour inside*
	BASES TYPE 3 (*Continued*)	
	Phase G. Fig. 63	
6	5YR-6/4 light reddish brown (10R-5/4 weak red)	10R-5/4 weak red
7	10R-6/4 pale red	5YR-7/3 pink
8	2.5YR-6/6 light red	10R-6/8 light red
	BASES TYPE 4	
	Phase B. Fig. 48	
20	10YR-7/2 light grey	5Y-6/1 grey
21	7.5YR-6/4 light brown	7.5YR-N4 dark grey
22	10R-5/4 weak red (5YR-6/2 pinkish grey 2.5YR-N3 very dark grey)	5YR-7/8 reddish yellow (7.5YR-6/4 light brown)
23	10YR-8/2 white (5YR-7/3 pink)	5YR-7/2 pinkish grey
	Phase G. Fig. 63	
9	2.5YR-6/6 light red (2.5YR-6/4 light reddish brown)	2.5YR-6/6 light red
10	5YR-6/4 light reddish brown	2.5YR-6/6 light red
11	10R-6/2 pale red	10R-6/4 pale red
12	7.5YR-6/4 light brown	5YR-7/4 pink
13	10YR-8/1 white	5YR-6/1 grey
	BASES TYPE 5	
	Phase G. Fig. 63	
14	5YR-6/2 pinkish grey (5YR-4/1 dark grey)	2.5YR-6/6 light red
15	2.5Y-8/2 white	10YR-6/1 grey
	BASES TYPE 6	
	Phase B. Fig. 48	
27	10YR-8/2 white	10YR-7/3 very pale brown
28	2.5YR-6/4 light reddish brown	5YR-7/6 reddish yellow (5YR-8/4 pink 2.5YR-N3 very dark grey)
29	2.5Y-8/2 white (10YR-3/1 very dark grey)	2.5Y-8/2 white
30	10YR-7/2 light grey	10YR-8/2 white 7.5YR-8/4 pink
21	2.5Y-7/2 light grey	2.5Y-8/2 white
32	5Y-7/3 pale yellow	10YR-8/3 very pale brown
33	2.5Y-8/2 white	5YR-7/4 pink
34	2.5Y-8/2 white	5YR-7/4 pink
	Phase G. Fig. 63	
16	10R-5/4 weak red	2.5YR-5/4 reddish brown
17	5Y-7/3 pale yellow	5Y-6/3 pale olive

Colour description (continued)

no.	*Colour outside*	*Colour inside*
	BASES TYPE 7	
	Phase B. Fig. 48	
35	2.5Y-7/2 light grey	2.5Y-7/2 light grey
36	10R-6/6 light red	7.5YR-6/4 light brown
37	2.5Y-8/4 pale yellow	10YR-7/3 very pale brown
	Phase G. Fig. 63	
18	10YR-6/1 grey (10YR-6/2 light brownish grey)	7.5YR-6/2 pinkish grey
19	7.5YR-7/4 pink	5YR-6/4 light reddish brown
20	7.5YR-7/2 pinkish grey	10YR-6/1 grey
21	10YR-7/2 light grey	7.5YR-6/2 pinkish grey
22	7.5YR-7/2 light grey (7.5YR-N3 very dark grey)	7.5YR-7/2 light grey (5YR-6/4 light reddish brown 7.5YR-N3 very dark grey)

Phase	*Type 2 large jars* a	b	c	*Type 3 small jars*	*Type 4 dipper flasks*	*Type 5 'industry' pot*	*Type 6 small bowls*	*Type 7 lamps*
A	10	0	7	2	5	0	16	4.8
B	64	11	43	36	11	0	65	2.21
C	30	9	6	36	3	0	33	2.6
D	16	6	11	8	1	0	23	2.4
E	9	2	27	22	4	3	13	1.7
F	1	0	7	0	3	4	6	1.7
G	0	1	9	11	6	4	8	3.15
H	0	0	8	5	2	0	3	2.13
J	0	1	5	4	5	2	9	1.3
K	0	0	6	3	1	0	10	1.7
L	0	0	7	4	0	3	4	1.5

Fig. 25a. Bases types 2 to 7. Statistical chart

(Note. These numbers are only reliable for the earlier phases. In the first two seasons of excavation not all the bases were kept, which concerns mainly phases G-L. The numbers given for phases A-D are reliable. Under type 7 are first given the number of base fragments then the number of lamp rims.)

Comparisons

Note: The analytical and statistical evidence on which this study of the pottery types is based makes it often difficult, if not impossible, to compare these types with drawings of pottery from other sites. The technical aspects are usually not published, or limited to the treatment of the surface of the pot. As the typology is not, strictly speaking, based on a technical analysis of the pottery from other sites, the statistical evidence is again limited to aspects such as burnishing or shape only. Apparently, no statistical evidence of all the main types and their subdivisions from phases or strata dating from the Early Iron Age have yet been published. Yet in the light of these results it seems that reliable statistical evidence is an important element of any comparative study.

Bases 2-7

Bases type 2a, b and c. For comparison with Afula Str. III cf. Ch. 6, the paragraph on handbuilt pottery in Palestine, p. 97. The overlap of the last coil but one near the base can sometimes be found in drawings, cf. Meg. II, P1. 77, 1. Slab closed bases are difficult to recognize from drawings, as they are not necessarily thicker than other bases. Cf. Meg. II, P1. 82, 7, Str. VI; base 2b cf. Meg. II, Pl. 83, 3. Base 2c, the rounded base, is common in the 11th cent.

Bases type 4. Of the various methods of producing the base of small juglets, only the very heavy base can be distinguished in drawings. It is common in the 12th-11th cent. in Palestine, and still found, for instance, in Hazor Str. VIII, (Hazor I, Pl. XLVIII, 4). Cf. Afula op. cit. p. 38.

Bases type 5. No published examples have been found but one nearly complete unstratified vessel is in the Shechem collection of the Rijksmuseum van Oudheden at Leiden. Near Tell es-Sa'idiyeh and other I.A. sites in the Jordan valley these bases can be found on the surface.

Bases type 6 and 7. Flat bases and lamp bases cannot be distinguished from those of the 12th and 11th cent. in Palestine. They are found on all excavated sites. It is however surprising that according to the statistical evidence, lamps were extremely scarce at Deir ʿAllā.

Ring bases

The manufacture of ring bases shows a gradual development from phase A onwards. It is not simply a question of a more or less rounded base to which a roll of clay was added to make a ring base. Fig. 24 shows the shapes and a general typology of ring bases.

General remarks

It is important to notice that pots built on a lump of clay were detached from this clay base by either cutting through the lump or through the wall just above the lump. In the first case the base was closed after cutting, in the second, there was an open hole. One has to assume that there was a fair measure of chance involved in whether the pot came off with an "open" base or was still closed, and if closed, the thickness of the base might vary considerably.

It has already been shown that an "open" base was closed either by fitting one or more slabs of clay into the opening or by adding another coil and closing the pot in a turning movement. It is interesting to note that there is not one example of a type 2b base with a ring added to it, whereas type 2a and c, 3 and 6 all occur with ring bases. The ring bases of the latest L.B. sanctuary level are slightly different from those found in I.A. phase A onwards and they represent an earlier, or technically less developed ring base (fig. 24.1), in so far that the ring part of the base may be termed rudimentary. This is not so in the earliest phases of the I.A. where the same technique is applied but the ring is clearly present. In both cases the latest L.B. sanctuary level and the E.I.A. phases, ring bases are fashioned after the vessel was closed, with a scraping tool to cut away surplus clay if the base had been allowed to dry, or with a wet cloth if the base was finished at one go.

This explains why there are so many differences in the thickness of these bases. Sometimes the central thickness of a base is not more than 2 mm.

The ring was formed by pressing the surplus clay of the base from the centre to the circumference in a turning movement. Scraping across the base was not done as this tends to tear the base. This clay may originally have belonged to the lowest part of the wall of the vessel, or to the closing slab or to both, or to the basic lump of clay from which the pot was made. This is shown in fig. 24 and can frequently be seen in the way bases are broken. However, it is often impossible to detect whether the ring is part of the wall or not. But a clear case is usually to be seen in the break of bases that consist of part of the basic lump of clay from which the vessel was made. The lump will show vertical shrinkage lines that show up in the base. Thick bases of very heavy bowls with thick walls and the base of the "industrial" pot (base type 5) often show this pattern. In all these cases usually no new clay was added to the pot to form a ring. Fresh clay may have been added if a potter noticed in time that the base had become dangerously thin.

A relationship between the angle of the lower part of the wall and the ring on the base has been observed. With rather flat bowls, the ring will tend to "flare", which is natural if one pictures the potter working on the ring with the flat bowl held upside down in his hand. On the other hand, the more vertical the lower part of the wall of deep bowls and jars, the more one finds vertical rings. Systematic measurements of the angles of rings in relation to the angle of the walls have yet to be made.

In all cases of scraped bases a circular mark made by the scraping tool just where the inside of the ring meets the base is very distinctive. It can also be found nearer the centre where the inside of the ring was further shaped by the potter's finger.

Often clay was removed by scraping from the lower parts of the walls near the base. This too influenced the shape of the ring on the base, as part of the clay could be used to make the ring.

No more has been done than to give a general outline of this type of ring base, as a complicated system would emerge if all the possible combinations of ring-base types were distinguished and many bases do not show in the break where their origins lie. Another reason for not going into too detailed a typology is dictated by the principle on which this report is based: that which has happened by chance must be kept separated from that which was intended by the potter. If, for instance, the lower slab of clay, often observed in larger bases, was intended to provide the clay for the ring, this could be classified into a distinctive type. But it cannot be proved. Then again there is the parallelism between the manufacture of rims and rings on the bases, as there are rings which were folded outwards or inwards, or even both, in many cases only in part of the ring. Once again it cannot be proved that these are not accidental features resulting from the simple fact that the clay which was pushed together between the fingers to shape the ring was not equally divided over the whole circumference. Though of more or less equal thickness it would not be the same height.

As the purpose of the ring was to give the pot a firm stand the ring had to be made level, and parts that stood up too much were folded down again.

Caution therefore demands that tendencies of development are noted, and the possibilities of each stage observed. Special attention has been given to rings that are really flat and level, as this seems to be a genuine tendency. Of doubtful tendency value seem

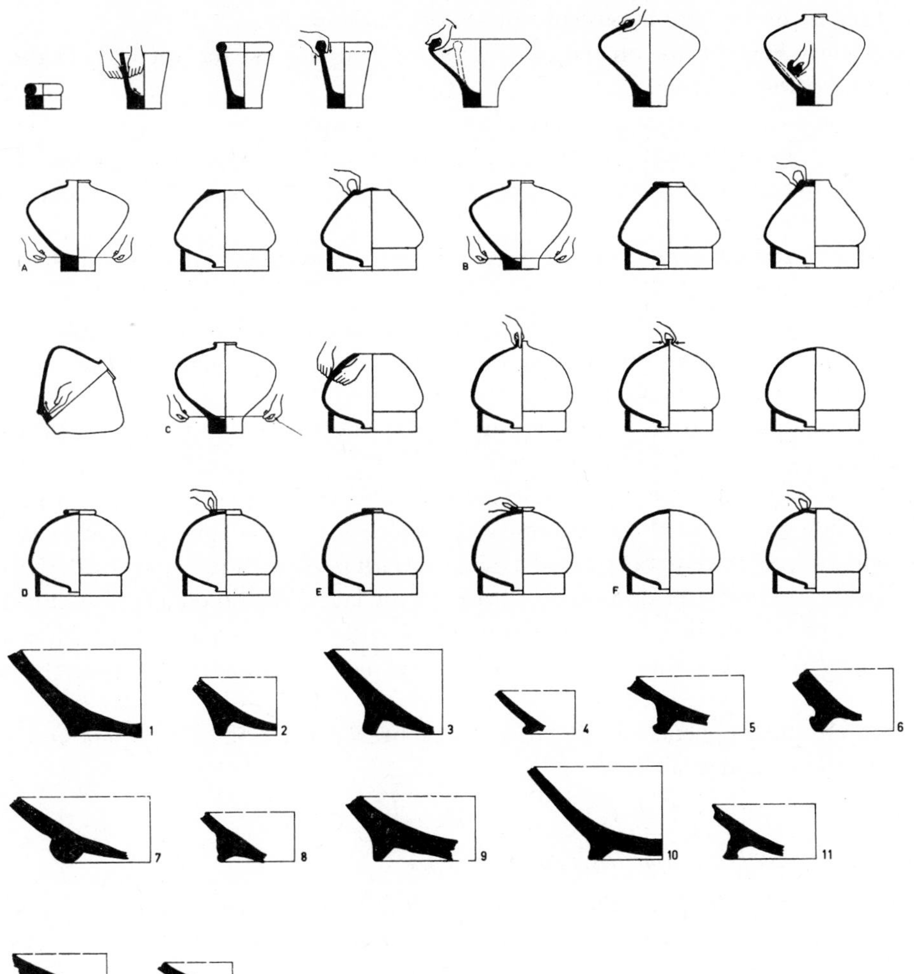

Fig. 24. Ring bases, construction drawing

to be the higher rings which require more clay, as this could simply be dependent on the original thickness of the closed base.

The rings are often neither circular nor sited centrally to the vessel. These features can only be controlled by a potter when throwing on a wheel is practised. Wheel thrown bases are pinched, circular, centred truly and not folded.

1. The common base of the latest L.B. sanctuary level. Note that these bases as a rule show repairs made to cracks which appeared in them. Clay was smeared into them after drying, but before firing.

2. The general principle of all ring bases of this kind is a tool scraped base, wet-smoothed ring with the mark of the tool on the inside (see above) and a different thickness of base and wall.

3. The same as no. 2, but tool marks are nearer the centre of the base.

4. Clay from the base is pushed out almost horizontally.

5. A clear finger mark on the outside of the ring against the wall where the ring was firmly pressed home.

6. Surplus clay of the ring is pushed away to the outside.

7. The base is completely or partially closed by turning. The ring is folded double outwards, but most of the clay is taken from an additional slab of clay added to the outside of the base.

8. Closely related to no. 1 but the ring is more pronounced and shows a small fold outwards.

9. Related to no. 3, but the ring was turned up and folded double inwards.

10. A carefully finished ring with a sharp contour line. The outside of the ring was pushed up to form a double ridge on top of the ring.

11. Corresponds with no. 6 but the surplus clay was pushed up to make a flat top to the ring.

12. Corresponds with no. 7 but here the surplus clay has been folded inwards.

13. A ring consisting of 3 layers of clay in which as the first ring was considered not thick enough, more clay was pushed against it both from the lower part of the wall on the outside and from the base on the inside. (More layers than these could occur. Then the potter had to see that the ring became horizontal, and clay was again pushed away from the top of the ring, thus forming another layer over a section or sections of the ring).

On p. 118 the fragments of ring bases have been divided into large jars and small jars, large bowls and small bowls.
Cf. Fig. 25b.

How to distinguish between jar bases and bowl bases

This can be done only by the manufacturing traits visible in the clay.

A ring base belongs to a *jar* if the base, not the ring, shows:

clear mark of turning inside	certain indication
marks of smoothing the slab inside	certain indication

wet-smoothed outside	uncertain indication
pointed shape inside (angle of inner side of lower wall)	uncertain indication
flame of the kiln touched the outside but not the inside	uncertain indication

Any combination of these characteristics is also valid.

A ring base belongs to a *bowl* if the base, not the ring, shows:

more or less smooth inside (wet-smoothed) and only faint traces of smearing or turning	uncertain indication
dry scraped outside	uncertain indication
saucer shaped inside	uncertain indication
flame of the kiln reached both inside and outside	certain indication

The colour test (mentioned last in both cases) was usually applied after sorting had been done according to other criteria and was usually in agreement with the results already obtained.

The division into large and small refers only to the size of the ring on the base. On the whole there is a surprising uniformity of size. But unless many more complete vessel shapes are found there can be no certainty about the relationship between size of ring, thickness of base and wall and the size of the complete pot.

In order to trace the evolution of shapes four distinguishing features have been highlighted:

a) a high ring – the clay not having been folded back.

b) a ring square in section with a flat and horizontal side. (It was rather surprising that these bases were found to be more worn than other types. In some cases these rings may have got their present shape from always having been placed on a stone surface, and were originally type c. It could also be that for some unknown reason certain vessels—especially bowls—had to stand on a stone base and therefore were made with flat ring bases).

c) a ring triangular in section with the top either left as it is after pushing the clay to the circumference of the base, or folded inwards or outwards in which case the triangle becomes a semi-circle.

d) This is made largely by cutting away the clay, not pushing it up (This is not done in phases A-D.).

Colour description

no.	*Colour outside*	*Colour inside*
	BASES TYPE 8-11	
	Phase B. Fig. 48	
38	2.5Y-7/2 light grey	10YR-7/1 light grey
39	10YR-7/3 very pale brown	2.5YR-6/6 light red
40	10YR-8/2 white (2.5Y-N5 grey)	2.5Y-7/2 light grey
41	2.5YR-5/4 reddish brown	2.5YR-6/6 light red
42	10YR-8/3 very pale brown (7.5YR-8/4 pink)	7.5YR-7/4 pink
43	2.5Y-8/4 pale yellow	7.5YR-7/4 pink
44	10YR-8/3 very pale brown	10YR-7/2 light grey
45	7.5YR-6/4 light brown	5YR-5/2 reddish grey (5YR-2/1 black)
46	2.5Y-7/2 light grey	7.5YR-7/4 pink
47	5YR-7/4 pink (7.5YR-8/2 pinkish white)	2.5YR-6/6 light red
48	10R-5/6 red	2.5YR-6/6 light red
49	2.5Y-7/2 light grey	10YR-7/2 light grey
50	10YR-7/3 very pale brown	5YR-6/3 light reddish brown
51	7.5YR-7/2 pinkish grey	5YR-7/4 pink
52	7.5YR-8/4 pink	2.5YR-6/6 light red
	Phase G. Fig. 63	
29	2.5Y-8/2 pale yellow	10YR-7/2 light grey
30	10YR-8/3 very pale brown	5YR-7/6 reddish yellow
31	10YR-7/3 very pale brown	7.5YR-7/4 pink
32	10YR-7/3 very pale brown	5YR-7/6 reddish yellow
33	5YR-6/4 light reddish brown	5YR-7/6 reddish yellow
34	5YR-7/4 pink	2.5YR-6/6 light red
35	5YR-6/4 light reddish brown	5YR-6/1 grey
36	5YR-7/4 pink	5YR-7/6 reddish yellow
37	2.5YR-6/2 pale red	7.5YR-7/2 pinkish grey
38	5Y-7/2 light grey	5YR-6/3 light reddish brown
39	10YR-8/2 white	10R-6/8 light red
40	10YR-7/3 very pale brown	5YR-5/2 reddish grey
41	10YR-7/2 light grey	10YR-6/2 light brownish grey
42	7.5YR-7/4 pink	5YR-6/3 light reddish brown
43	2.5Y-8/2 white	10YR-7/2 light grey
44	10YR-7/2 light grey	5YR-6/4 light reddish brown (5YR-7/6 reddish yellow 10R-6/4 pale red)
45	2.5YR-6/4 light reddish brown	2.5YR-6/6 light red
46	2.5Y-N8 white	5YR-7/6 reddish yellow
47	7.5YR-7/2 pinkish grey	10R-6/6 light red
48	10R-6/3 pale red (2.5Y-7/2 light grey)	10YR-5/3 brown (7.5YR-3/2 dark brown)
49	10YR-7/2 light grey	5YR-6/4 light reddish brown

Colour description (continued)

no.	Colour outside	Colour inside
	BASES TYPE 8-11 (*Continued*)	
	Phase G. Fig. 63	
50	5YR-8/4 pink	5YR-8/4 pink
51	5Y-7/3 pale yellow	10YR-8/4 very pale brown
52	2.5YR-6/2 pale red	5YR-7/2 pinkish grey
53	2.5YR-5/4 reddish brown	2.5YR-6/4 light reddish brown
54	10R-6/3 pale red	10R-5/6 red
55	10YR-8/3 very pale brown	5YR-7/2 pinkish grey
56	10YR-6/1 grey	10YR-3/1 very dark grey
57	5YR-6/4 light reddish brown	2.5YR-6/6 light red
58	2.5YR-6/2 pale red	2.5YR-6/4 light reddish brown
	PEDESTAL BASES	
	Phase B. Fig. 48	
53	2.5Y-7/2 light grey	2.5Y-7/2 light grey
54	10YR-6/3 pale brown	
55	2.5Y-7/2 light grey	5YR-7/3 pink
56	10YR-7/3 very pale brown	10YR-7/3 very pale brown
57	5YR-7/3 pink	5YR-7/3 pink
58	10YR-7/3 very pale brown	10YR-7/3 very pale brown
59	2.5Y-7/2 light grey	2.5YR-6/4 light reddish brown
60	2.5YR-6/4 light reddish brown (10YR-8/2 white)	5YR-7/3 pink
61	10R-5/2 weak red	10R-5/2 weak red
62	2.5Y-8/2 white	2.5Y-8/2 white
63	10YR-8/2 white	10YR-8/2 white
64	7.5YR-6/4 light brown	7.5YR-6/4 light brown

Other types of bases occurred but are too small in number to be analysed properly. These bases have been published in Ch. 8. High pedestal bases found during excavation have all been kept. Their frequency is as follows:
Phase A: 4; B: 31; C: 21; D: 7; E: 11; F: 6; G: 11; H: 11; J: 11; K: 12; L: 8.

Bases, entirely burnished on the outside:

Phase G: type 4: 1; 10a: 1; 10b: 1; 10d: 1; 11b: 1.

Phase H: type 10d: 5.

Phase J: type 10b: 3; 10d: 1; bowls type 17/18: 5.

Phase K: type 4: 1; 6: 5; 9b: 1; 10a: 4; 10b: 3; bowls 17/18: 11.

Phase L: type 10b: 4;

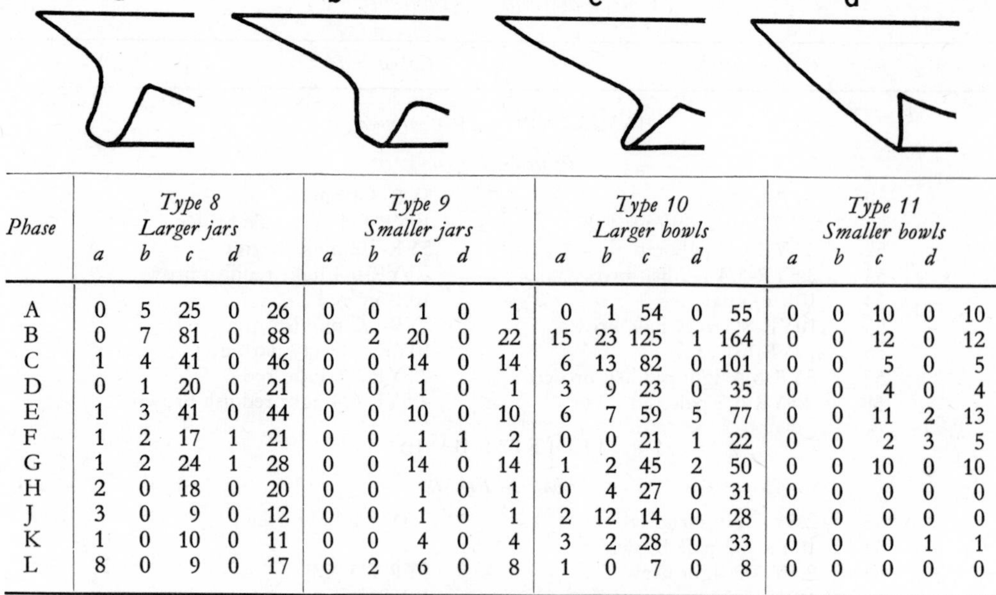

Phase	*Type 8* *Larger jars*					*Type 9* *Smaller jars*					*Type 10* *Larger bowls*					*Type 11* *Smaller bowls*				
	a	*b*	*c*	*d*		*a*	*b*	*c*	*d*		*a*	*b*	*c*	*d*		*a*	*b*	*c*	*d*	
A	0	5	25	0	26	0	0	1	0	1	0	1	54	0	55	0	0	10	0	10
B	0	7	81	0	88	0	2	20	0	22	15	23	125	1	164	0	0	12	0	12
C	1	4	41	0	46	0	0	14	0	14	6	13	82	0	101	0	0	5	0	5
D	0	1	20	0	21	0	0	1	0	1	3	9	23	0	35	0	0	4	0	4
E	1	3	41	0	44	0	0	10	0	10	6	7	59	5	77	0	0	11	2	13
F	1	2	17	1	21	0	0	1	1	2	0	0	21	1	22	0	0	2	3	5
G	1	2	24	1	28	0	0	14	0	14	1	2	45	2	50	0	0	10	0	10
H	2	0	18	0	20	0	0	1	0	1	0	4	27	0	31	0	0	0	0	0
J	3	0	9	0	12	0	0	1	0	1	2	12	14	0	28	0	0	0	0	0
K	1	0	10	0	11	0	0	4	0	4	3	2	28	0	33	0	0	0	1	1
L	8	0	9	0	17	0	2	6	0	8	1	0	7	0	8	0	0	0	0	0

Fig. 25b. Bases, types 8-11, ring bases. Statistical chart

(Note. These numbers are only reliable for phases A-D.)

Cooking Pots

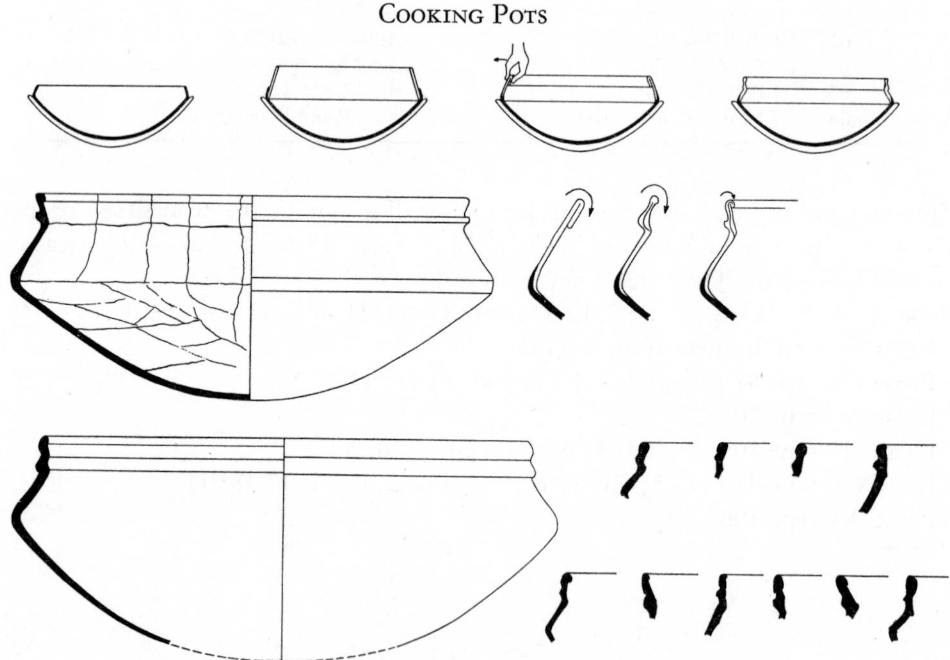

Fig. 26. Late Bronze Age cooking pot type 2, construction drawing

L.B. type 2

This is the only type of cooking pot found in the latest phases of the L.B. sanctuary. It appears that it quite suddenly replaces the well-known L.B. cooking pot type with flaring rim, though until more research has been done on this period it is not possible to be sure.

The type is described here in short because Iron Age cooking pot type 2 is intimately related to it. Immediately after the final destruction of the L.B. sanctuary (first quarter of the 11th century B.C.) this type disappears and is replaced by the I.A. type 1 cooking pot described below. This is the only type in phases A to D. In phase E, type 2 appears beside type 1, and this newcomer is not only made in the same way as the L.B. type 2, but amongst the variations the original L.B. shape is still preserved and remains so until phase M. In the L.B. there are no variations of this type; the I.A. type, however, shows a considerable number of variations and techniques. There are no parallels to be drawn from excavated material in Palestine, which suggests that this development may have taken place east of Deir ʿAllā rather than west. Both types surely stem from the same cultural tradition, and were introduced first at Deir ʿAllā at the end of the L.B. age only to return with the settlement of the I.A. village.

The visual characteristics

The base consists of a wide, fairly shallow bowl, which never shows any signs of turning or of wheel marks. The shoulder is inverted and forms a sharp angle to the bowl. Inside the shoulder there are horizontal tool marks, much narrower than finger marks. The outside is smoothed with some soft material. There is no neck of any height, so that the rim can be said to be attached to the shoulder. This is usually in a vertical or slightly outward leaning position. The rim is profiled with two ridges, and often part of the top of the rim is folded in. The mouth is very wide.
The ware is fairly hard and of a red/brown colour.

The technical characteristics

The bowl-base is made from one sheet of lean clay in a mould. This sheet is uniformally thick. The inside is smoothed with some soft material, and after partial drying, the pot is turned out of the mould and the outside is then worked with a scraper. The shoulder is made of a coil of the same clay and carefully adjusted to the thickness of the bowlbase in a slow turning motion. A tool is now used on the inside and a soft material on the outside. The fringe of clay on top of the thinned out coil is folded inwards and smoothed flat. Then the rim is turned up to a vertical position causing the lower ridge. The second ridge is made by pushing the top of the rim outwards, and before it becomes entirely horizontal, the higher part of the rim is turned inwards again.

The pot is usually very carefully made, with particular concern for an overall equality of thickness both of walls and rim, and for the profiling of the rim.

Occasionally there is a ridge on the inside at the point where the rim joins the shoulder.

The tempering material is basically crystalline calcite.

In contrast to the L.B. cooking pot type 1 with flaring rim, which is found both in large and fairly small sizes, this type belongs to a wide mouthed, very large pot, and does not occur in a small size. The I.A. cooking pots types 1 and 2 are the same size as their proto-type.

I.A. Type 1

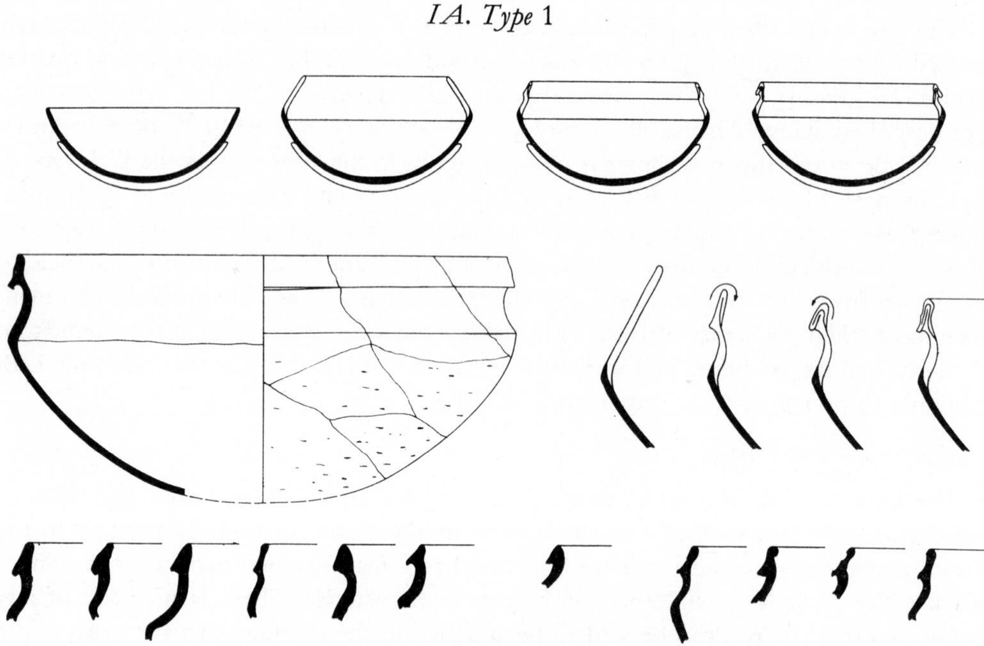

Fig. 27. Cooking pot type 1, construction drawing

Description

The visual characteristics

A very wide mouthed, not very deep pot. The ratio diameter to height is about 1.5-1.

The base, shaped like a shallow bowl, is of an overall equal thickness. There are no traces of throwing or turning on a wheel. The outside is marked by a tool that was used to scrape the surface when the clay was fairly dry. The inside is smoothed with a soft material, perhaps a cloth or a piece of leather. The shoulder is fitted onto the base at an angle that is sometimes sharp and sometimes smoothed with a tool giving a burnishing effect. There are traces of turning on the inside only. The rim either follows the direction of the shoulder or stands vertically in which case the upper part of the shoulder was also bent upwards. There is no profiling. Apart from a few brick-red examples the colour is dark brown to almost black. The break of the base is featureless. The break of the shoulder shows the influence of a slight turning. The shoulder breaks from the body along the carination.

This type is not likely to have handles attached to the rim.

The technical characteristics

The base is made from a lump of lean clay, beaten flat in a saucer-shaped form or mould. The inside of the base is smoothed with a cloth or leather before it is tapped out of the form, and the outside is then worked over with a tool after it has dried further. The shoulder is made by attaching a coil of clay and in a turning movement, adjusting it to the same thickness as the base. The upper part of the flattened coil is turned down on the inside and pressed against the top of the shoulder. The rim is formed by making a second outward fold of the upper part of the coil. This is the cause of the concavity on the inside of the rim; the fold comes down over the bulging part of the outside wall. The top of the rim usually forms a very sharp angle.

Variations

There are very many variations of this type. A statistical count of the number of pots of this type found in the excavated area is only approximate because of the form of the base and the fact that rims were of such uneven thickness and shape that fragments of one and the same rim could, if viewed separately, easily be taken to represent separate vessels. As the total length of a rim on a average vessel of this type was 1.25 m., it is too bold to term every irregularity of form a variation, and the differences listed below should be regarded only as tendencies.

1. The top of the rim may be entirely or partly folded again, usually towards the inside. This occurred where the top of the rim was not yet horizontal. That part which was higher than the rest was pushed down until a horizontal upper part was obtained. The lower end of the fold might be left sticking out over the bulge, or smoothed down over it, or worked flat or even convex with a tool. Sometimes this tool was used to flatten the surface of the rim with a burnishing effect. This explains why the rim of a single pot can show so many individual traits. (fig. 27, var. no. 1-6)

2. In a few cases the rim is only half to three quarters the height of the normal type. This smaller rim shows the same variations as described under 1. (fig. 27, var. no. 7)

3. Right in the middle of the rim a horizontal groove is made with a pointed tool, apparently to make the fold adhere more firmly to its base. A tool with a broad end was used to press the top half of the fold against its base and this seems to develop into the upper part of the rim being pinched between two fingers with, at the same time, the rim being pushed up into a vertical position. The otherwise flat rim is then slightly profiled. The top and the base of the rim are finished in the same way as is described under 1. When the rim is pushed upward, the upper part of the shoulder tends to be bent upwards too. (fig. 27, var. no. 8-11)

4. After the introduction of type 2 in phase E, the new shape is sometimes formed by the techniques of type 1. This variant has been attributed to type 1, as its importance lies in the way a new type is influenced by an earlier. Short of cutting a section through each rim fragment and studying them with a magnifying glass, it is impossible to be absolutely certain that every sherd published under type 2 belongs there. Some may in fact belong to type 1.

Distribution and comparison

a) at Deir ʿAllā

The total number of stratified pots cannot be properly assessed. (see above). The chart, fig. 31, shows the approximate total number, differentiated from phase E onwards. In phases A-D it is the only type; in phase G it is found in the same numbers as type 2. After phase G it becomes rare, but it is still found in phase M.

b) at other sites

It seems highly probable that the cooking pots from Early Iron Age sites in Palestine which resemble Deir ʿAllā types 1 and 2 were manufactured in the same way.

Type 1 is found all over Palestine in the E.I.A. It already occurs in the 14th cent. B.C. It may well be that these 14th cent. pots will have to be regarded as imported from Trans-Jordan or from the southern deserts, and that they are "fossil" types from nomadic incursions. It is not derived from the L.B. cooking pot.

At Afula, Str. III B-A it is the only type. The subdivision made by M. Dothan is at least partly based on the shrinkage of the rim. Meg. Str. VI; cooking bowl type 17 is a much smaller pot and may belong to a different tradition. In Hazor the pot is found in Str. XII-VIII. It seems that in Samaria this type was still found in period VII. Cf. SS III, p. 102. This is surprising since at Deir ʿAllā type 1 is almost entirely replaced by type 2 from phase H on. Comp. tell el-Ghazala, A.A.S.O.R. 25-28, pl. 61, 7 and 12, said to be wheel-made.

Colour description

no.	*Colour outside*	*Colour inside*
	COOKING POTS TYPE 1	
	Phase B. Fig. 49	
1	2.5YR-4/4 reddish brown (10R-3/2 dusky red)	7.5R-5/4 weak red (5YR-3/1 very dark grey)
2	5YR-3/2 dark reddish brown	5YR-4/2 dark reddish grey
3	10R-5/4 weak red	10R-5/4 weak red
4	10R-3/1 dark reddish grey (10R-4/2 weak red)	10R-5/4 weak red (7.5R-N5 grey)
5	5YR-6/4 light reddish brown	2.5YR-6/6 light red
6	2.5YR-5/4 reddish brown (2.5YR-N3 very dark grey)	5YR-6/4 light reddish brown
7	5YR-6/3 light reddish brown	5YR-6/3 light reddish brown
8	5YR-3/2 dark reddish brown	5YR-4/3 reddish brown
9	10R-5/3 weak red	2.5YR-5/4 reddish brown
10	2.5YR-N3 very dark grey (2.5YR-4/2 weak red)	10R-5/4 weak red
11	10R-4/3 weak red	10R-4/3 weak red
12	10R-3/1 dark reddish grey	2.5YR-5/4 reddish brown
13	10R-5/4 weak red	2.5YR-5/4 reddish brown
14	10R-3/1 dark reddish grey	5YR-5/2 reddish grey

Colour description (continued)

no.	*Colour outside*	*Colour inside*
	COOKING POTS TYPE 1 (*continued*)	
	Phase G. Fig. 63	
59	2.5YR-5/4 reddish brown (2.5YR-N3 very dark grey)	10R-4/4 weak red
60	10R-4/4 weak red (2.5YR-N2 black)	2.5YR-4/6 red
61	2.5YR-5/4 reddish brown	10R-4/4 weak red
62	2.5YR-5/4 reddish brown (2.5YR-N2 black)	2.5YR-5/4 reddish brown
63	5YR-5/1 grey	5YR-5/2 reddish grey
64	2.5YR-N3 very dark grey	2.5YR-N3 very dark grey (5YR-5/2 reddish grey)
65	2.5YR-4/4 reddish brown	10R-4/3 weak red
66	10R-4/2 weak red (7.5YR-8/2 pinkish white)	7.5YR-6/2 pinkish grey
67	5YR-2/1 black	10R-6/2 pale red
68	10R-4/3 weak red	10R-4/4 weak red
69	10R-4/4 weak red	10R-4/3 weak red
70	10R-4/4 weak red	10R-4/4 weak red
71	10R-3/1 dark reddish grey	10R-5/4 weak red
72	7.5R-N2 black (10YR-6/2 light brownish grey)	7.5YR-5/2 brown
73	7.5YR-N4 dark grey	5YR-6/4 light reddish brown (2.5YR-N3 very dark grey)
74	2.5YR-5/2 weak red	2.5YR-5/4 reddish brown
75	2.5YR-N2 black (2.5YR-2/2 very dusky red)	2.5YR-4/2 weak red (2.5YR-4/4 reddish brown)
76	2.5YR-2/2 very dusky red (10R-4/3 weak red)	2.5YR-4/4 reddish brown

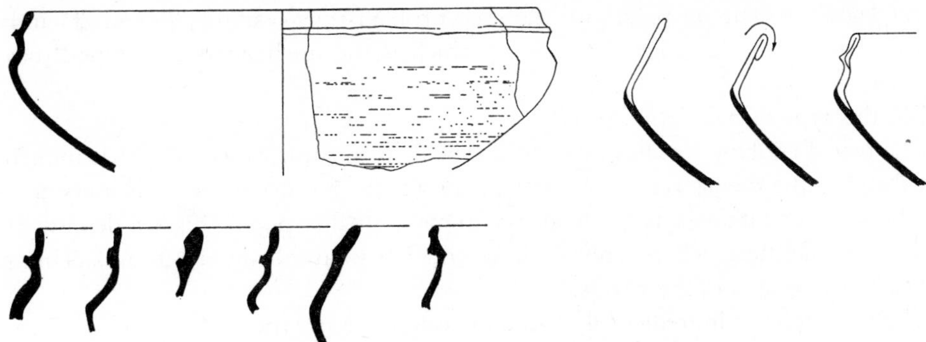

Fig. 28. Cooking pot type 2, construction drawing

I.A. Type 2

Description

The visual characteristics

In its earliest stages this type much resembles type 1, but the rim is always profiled. The base is the same as type 1 but the carination (the link between the "base" and neck) becomes less pronounced (see below).

There is also a tendency to make the shoulder more convex. There are finger marks inside the neck from turning, but not inside or outside the base. Also in contrast to type 1 there are a number of examples of pots much smaller than the average.

The colour is often reddish brown but dark brown to black is still frequent.

The break of the base is featureless. The break of the shoulder shows traces of turning.

A handle sometimes occurs.

The technical characteristics

Apart from the rim the pot is made in the same way as type 1. However, it is clear that more use of the wheel is made for finishing the vessel. After the pot was built, but before the rim was finished, the vessel was turned until the coils forming the shoulder and rim were of the required thickness, and thus the carination tends to disappear. In this way too the shoulder may lose its concave shape.

The rim is simpler than type 1 and directly related to the L.B. type 2, which has been included in this volume of the publication in order to show the tradition from which the I.A. type 2 stems (cf. variation type 2g). Like the L.B. type, the end of the coil is folded inwards only. The top of the rim is often slightly adjusted by pressing it down, with the result that sometimes the clay gets pushed either more to the inside or to the outside.

Sporadically this pot has a handle (probably 2, but this is difficult to determine). These handles occur on pots with the least profiled rims (variants 2a and 2f) and the top is attached to the ridge. Variant 2g which is the unchanged L.B. type 2 has no handles.

For this type of handle, cf. p. 170.

The type 3 cooking pot has influenced type 2, as in some cases type 2 has influenced the shape of the type 1 rim. The handle may well be an instance of this influence and another distinct influence is the tendency to make smaller pots. This is a definite break with early tradition, where only shallow and fairly large pots are found. This may indicate changing cooking habits.

The basic temper ingredient is crystalline calcite, as in type 1.

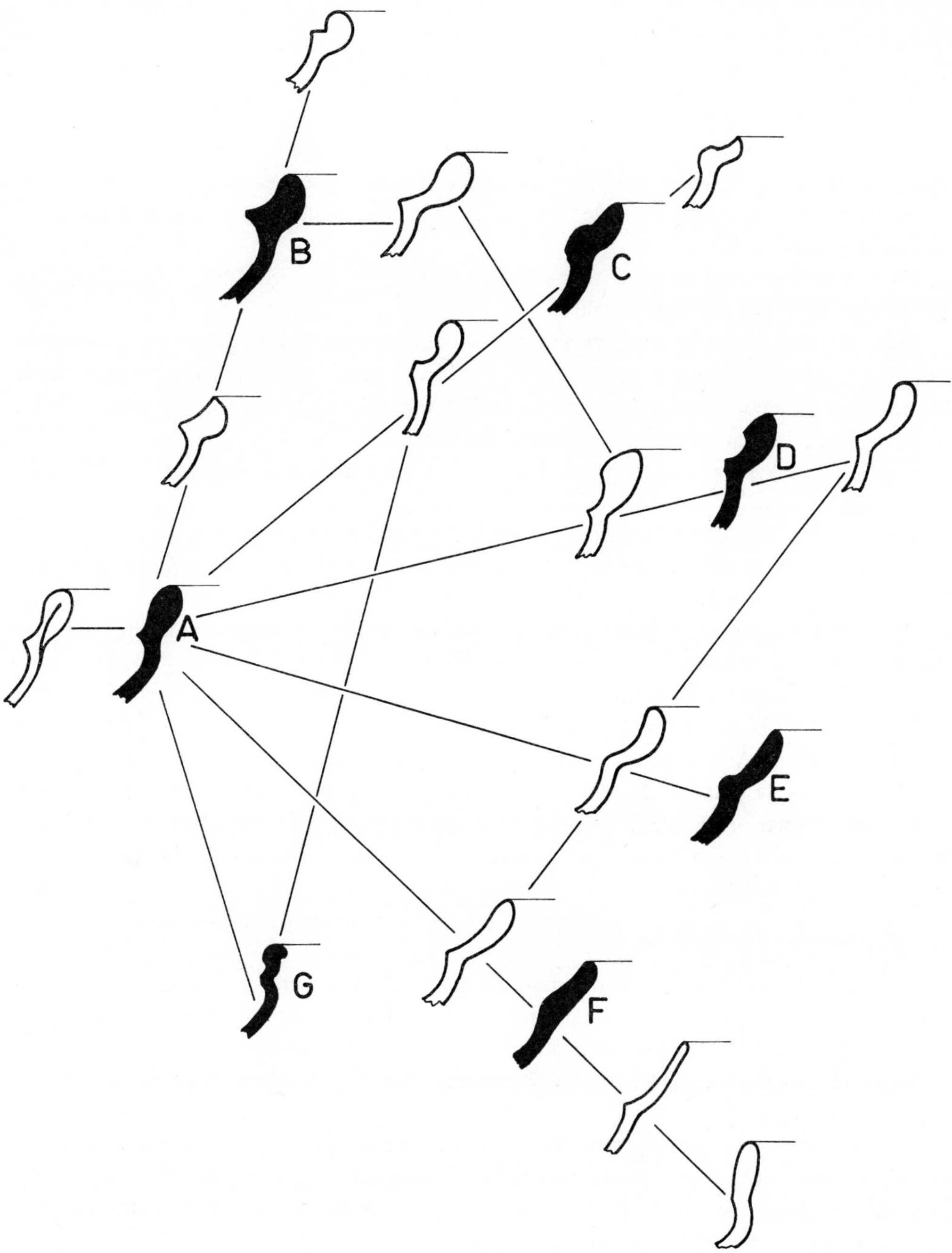

Fig. 29. Cooking pot type 2, the variants

Variations (fig. 29)

The smaller rim, like type 1b, does occur with variants, but very rarely and is not given special treatment here.

The variations of this type as listed below cover most of the possibilities. There are transitional shapes between two or three variations, but it seems that the variants listed do really represent shapes intended by the potter to a much greater extent than those included in type 1.

These variations occur right through the whole period including the "archaic" or proto-type 2g from phase E onwards.

Type 2a This is the most common type and at the same time the least pronounced in any one feature. It almost certainly developed from type 2g (L.B.) and this must have taken place in Trans-Jordan but not in Deir ʿAllā, during the period of phases A-D.

Type 2b-c show a special treatment of the ridge.

Type 2b has a pronounced pointed ridge, resulting from a tendency to bend the top of the rim inwards, with a bulge inside.

Type 2c has a heavy ridge which does not influence the top of the rim.

Type 2d Here a rim which was too straight was hollowed with the finger held horizontally midway on the outside.

Type 2e Here the ridge is preserved but the rim is made thinner and higher without further profiling.

Type 2f The rim is featureless, and indicates careless finishing work by the potter.

Type 2g This is, as has already been stated, the original late L.B. cooking pot, which returned to Deir ʿAllā in period II (I.A.) after being absent during phases A-D. Some development took place in the interval when this type is no longer represented at Deir ʿAllā, but at Deir ʿAllā itself the original shape is preserved until phase M. The only marked difference is that type 2g is treated as the variants 2b-2e. An example is given in phase L. (cf. p. 235)

Further remarks and conclusions

There is clear evidence from the material that this type persisted up till phase M in the way described on p. 124. There is also evidence that turning was practised more and more, not only on the rim but also in order to be able to smooth the inside of the bowl or base. The marks of fingers left by the turning are broader than those on the earlier type (see type 2g).

Together with this development the pot tends to lose its sharp carination, and this is consistent with the practice of quicker turning. Furthermore this type of vessel, which is a wide mouthed pot, shows in the course of time a slight tendency to be made smaller. This is a form of adaptation of the type 3 pot.

Handles remain rare. Not one handle is found on type 2g. It would seem that there is a considerable lapse of time between the first occurrence of this type in Deir ʿAllā in the latest L.B. sanctuary phase, c.1190 B.C., and its reappearance in the I.A. phase E.

It is remarkable that type 2g survives right through the period unchanged. That the development of this type took place elsewhere during phases A-D is shown by the fact that in the L.B. sanctuary only type 2g was found, and this is the only type of cooking pot that quite suddenly and completely replaced the L.B. type 1 vessel.

The original type 2g has not been given the first designation of this type (i.e. type 2a) because it forms only a small minority of all the type 2 cooking pots.

Colour description

no.	*Colour outside*	*Colour inside*
	COOKING POTS TYPE 2	
	Phase G. Fig. 63	
77	2.5YR-4/4 reddish brown (2.5YR-3/2 dusky red)	2.5YR-N3 very dark grey (2.5YR-6/6 light red)
78	2.5YR-5/4 reddish brown	2.5YR-5/4 reddish brown
79	2.5YR-2/2 very dusky red	5YR-6/3 light reddish brown
80	10R-4/2 weak red	10R-5/3 weak red
81	10R-4/3 weak red	10R-4/3 weak red
	Fig. 64.	
1	10R-4/1 dark reddish grey	10R-4/4 weak red
2	10R-5/2 weak red	10R-6/2 pale red
3	10R-3/1 dark reddish grey	2.5YR-5/2 weak red
4	10R-5/4 weak red	10R-5/6 red
5	7.5R-N2 black	10R-4/1 dark reddish grey
6	10R-5/2 weak red	5YR-6/3 light reddish brown

Comparisons, cooking pot type 2

As the shape often resembles that of type 1 it is not yet possible to trace the introduction of this type in Palestine. It does not occur in Afula Str. III A and B. In Hazor it seems present in Str. X, (II, Pl. LI, 12) and is the dominant type in Str. VIII. Handles begin in Palestine in the 3rd quarter of the 11th cent. (cf. Sinclair, Gibea p. 20), but if, as can now be supposed, this type is, like type 1, an "eastern" type, handles may be found earlier in Trans-Jordan. Type 2g was probably found at tell el-Ghazalā by N. Glueck, cf. A.A.S.O.R. 25-28, Pl. 61,4.

I.A. Type 3

The visual characteristics

There are a great variety of sizes. The pot is never so wide as type 1 or 2, but is usually higher and lacks the sharp carination of the other types, though traces of it can still be found. Usually the base and shoulder form a rounded-off angle with "rib" marks at the joint on the outside.

The shoulder is straight, with a tendency to become convex. There are clear, wide

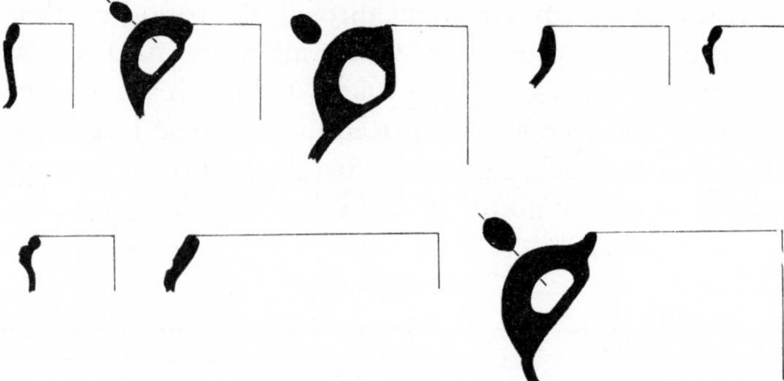

Fig. 30. Cooking pot type 3, construction drawing

turning marks made by fingers on the inside of shoulder and rim, and on fragments of the base. There are no fingermarks left on the outside but there are traces of smoothing the surface left by a tool on the base, and by a wad of soft material on the shoulder and rim. Where the rim is turned up into a vertical position there are traces of the clay having been stretched on the inside. The rim is profiled, but this is never done with the aid of a profiling tool. This is evident from the fact that even on the smaller mouthed pots the height, thickness and shape of the profile on one rim can and do vary.

The colour varies from brick red to very dark grey outside. The rim breaks, in most cases, in rectangular pieces, the shoulder usually in triangular pieces and the break of the base is featureless.

Handles are a normal feature of the pot, spanning the space between the top of the rim or the ridge on the rim to the base of the shoulder.

The ware feels hard and often has a ringing sound.

The technical characteristics

Basically this type pot was built up by hand in much the same way as types 1 and 2. There are, however, some important differences which indicate that this is a distinct type. The most important of these is the clay mixture. Most of these pots have been fired almost to melting point which indicates a lower melting point of the clay rather than a different technique of firing with a higher temperature.

The dark grey colour surface of these pots, outside and sometimes inside, indicate that mineral salts fused with elements of the fuel burning in the kiln. This is not so with the other two types and bears witness to a different composition of the clay. It is also characteristic that calcite grit does not occur in these sherds, whereas it is typical for the other two types. The temper used for this type was a mixture of limestone, quartz, flintstone, a small portion of haematite and some pounded potsherds.

By reducing the maximum firing temperature, the pot acquired a hard surface. In cases where the core is light grey to yellowish grey, instead of brick red to dark grey, it is soft from being over-fired.

Added to these differences, the body of the vessel is more rounded, the rim profile is not the same and the handle is a standard feature. (For the sort of handle, cf. p. 170) An insufficient amount of base fragments make it impossible to say whether these pots were still sometimes made in a mould or whether the whole body was built from coils. It can be demonstrated that at least some bases were still made in moulds, but the smoothing and pressing out of the clay was done with the fingers in a turning movement in some cases.

The coil which was to form the shoulder is sometimes much thicker than the body, but is always shaped by the fingers in the inside and with a cloth on the outside. The fingermarks are interrupted at exactly the point where the rim is turned up. Here on the inside the clay is usually stretched and slightly cracked. This demonstrates two things: the paste was a lean and fairly dry clay when worked on, and the rim was pushed up after its top had been made horizontal by folding the clay inwards and smoothing it flat.

Often after this had been done, the rim, which was then twice as thick as before, was thinned by pressing the clay upwards again in order to give a sufficient surplus of clay for the finishing off of the rim. Generally the rim was pushed into a vertical position, thus causing the horizontal hollowing inside and the ridge outside. The ridge is finished either by being pointed or made collar- or bandshaped. The top of the rim was smoothed out and down, but never (as in type 1) over the ridge. Sometimes the fold does not reach the ridge, but stops 1 or 2 mm. above it, giving the impression that a pointed tool had been used to make the groove. This is, however, not the case.

Variations

It is clear from the analysis of the technique of making this type, given above, that any sub-divisions can only indicate certain prevalent tendencies. The difference between a pointed ridge and a flattened ridge is only a question of turning the pot round once more while pressing a thumb against the point of the ridge.

The difference between variations b and c, is that in b the top of the rim is thickened so as to give the impression that the fold stops half way between the top and the ridge, whereas in c the ridge is flattened. This may have been done with a rib pressed along the outside. The question of whether the outside fold of the rim did or did not practically reach down to the ridge has less bearing on the criteria of sub-division.

Variant d poses some uncertainty in connection with its origins, and thus with its attribution to type 3. The treatment of the rim in this variant is similar to that of type 2, especially type 2a and 2d. The top may be pressed down and out.

The following sub-division does not distinguish between these finishing touches, (cf. phase K) as in all four main variants featureless rims with weak lines are found. (cf. type 2f)

Hardly any unusually long rims are found though there are some short ones.

All shapes found are shown in ch. 8.

a) A more or less pointed ridge is found below the top of the rim. There are some examples where a part of this ridge is smoothed down, thus resembling variant b. This variant a does not resemble type 2b, where the top of the rim tends to become heavier, but is nearer type 2d in shape.

b) The ridge below the rim is smoothed down to become rectangular in section. This is a very common variant and was clearly intended to look different. The difference with type 2c lies in the shape of the ridge.

c) This always has the rectangular ridge but the top of the rim is smoothed down against the upper side of the ridge leaving only a small groove.

d) This type has a small standard size mouth, a very small rim and usually a high neck which is clearly distinguishable from the shoulder by its angle. No complete example of this variant has been found yet. The largest complete section comes from phase H. As there are not many stratified examples, no further sub-division has been made, though it could have been done on the same grounds as in variants a, b and c. To this might be added a completely straight vertical rim.

This variety is not at all common. As the origin of the type 3 cooking pot cannot be explained from influences derived from either type 1 or 2, and the first few examples come from phase F, becoming common in phase G, it is impossible to say whether the type 3, variant d, stems from the same or different origins from the other variants. The high neck and the probability of there being but one handle indicate a different origin.

However, as this variant did not originate at Deir ʿAllā, it is possible to speculate that the high neck developed out of a shorter one. The treatment of the rim, the kind of temper, clay and firing is enough to justify ranking this variant with the other type 3 variants.

Further remarks and conclusions

Some remarks have been made about this vessel as it occurs in phase G. As all cooking pots throughout these periods remain conservative in both shape and material (compare M.B. cooking pots), the introduction of a different clay mixture is a notable fact. This type was not invented at Deir ʿAllā, as can be demonstrated by the already variously shaped rims found here. It is possible that type 3 is the original shape. The definite connection between temper and shape shows that it is a different type of pot. Neither the shape nor the material were used in type 2. The two existed together from phase G onwards, and the only noticeable influence that the one had on the other was that type 2 was sometimes manufactured as a smaller vessel, handles were sometimes applied, and that especially in phase K there is a tendency to apply type 2 rim profiles to type 3. This is the exception rather than the rule.

It was not through a lack of calcite that the type 3 pots were introduced, and this material remained the basic temper in both type 1 and 2. It seems that type 3 was produced more than type 2 during phases H, J and K. It is impossible to say whether the vessels served different purposes, i.e. the larger for solid foods, the smaller for fluids. As the manufacturing techniques differ only slightly (the folding of the rim outward, coiling from the base) and the shape of the rims are also similar, type 3 may well have come from the same cultural background as type 2.

Analysis of tempering material in thin section

Cooking pot type 1.

D 419/32: 1 calcite flakes $1\frac{3}{4}$ mm.
2 lime grains 1 mm.
3 quartz grains (from the clay?) 0.03 mm.

D 700: 1 calcite flakes (pounded) < 1.5 mm.
2 pounded pottery sherds < 2.5 mm.
3 small quartz grains < $\frac{1}{4}$ mm.
lime grains with shell frags. < 3.0 mm.

Analysis of tempering material in thin section

Cooking pot type 2.

(no number) calcite, grain and flake, < 1.5 mm, average 0.6-0.8 mm.
quartz, average 0.1 mm.
muscovite, very little, 0.1 mm.

D 650. 1 calcite flakes < 1 mm.
2 quartz grains, average 0.05 mm.
3 lime grains.
4 flint grains, average $1\frac{1}{4}$ mm.
5 haematite grains

Analysis of tempering material in thin section

Cooking pot type 3.

A 600/36 1 quartz grains < $\frac{3}{4}$ mm.
2 lime grains
3 Fe oxide grains < 2.5 mm.
4 flint flakes < $\frac{3}{4}$ mm.
5 pounded pottery sherds, c 4 mm.

Colour description

no.	*Colour outside*	*Colour inside*
	COOKING POTS TYPE 3	
	Phase G. Fig. 64	
7	10R-5/4 weak red	10R-4/1 dark reddish grey (10R-6/3 pale red)
8	10YR-4/1 dark grey	10YR-7/2 light grey
9	7.5YR-N5 grey	10YR-8/3 very pale brown
10	2.5YR-N5 grey	10R-2/2 very dusky red (10R-6/6 light red)
11	2.5YR-5/2 weak red (2.5YR-N3 very dark grey)	2.5YR-5/4 reddish brown

Colour description (continued)

no.	*Colour outside*	*Colour inside*
	COOKING POTS TYPE 3 *(continued)*	
	Phase G. Fig. 64	
12	10R-6/4 pale red	10R-5/6 red
13	7.5R-N3 very dark grey	7.5R-N4 dark grey
14	10R-6/2 pale red	10R-6/2 pale red
15	7.5R-N4 dark grey	5YR-8/4 pink
16	5YR-5/3 reddish brown	10R-6/3 pale red
17	10R-5/3 weak red	7.5R-N4 dark grey
18	10R-4/1 dark reddish grey	7.5YR-8/4 pink
19	7.5R-4/2 weak red	10R-5/4 weak red
20	7.5R-N6 grey	7.5R-N5 grey

Phase	*Type 1*					*Type 2*								*Type 3*					
	a	*b*	*c*	*d*	*T*	*a*	*b*	*c*	*d*	*e*	*f*	*g*	*T*	*a*	*b*	*c*	*d*	*	*T*
A	34	0	3	0	37														
B	68	29	27	0	124														
C	54	0	22	0	76														
D	21	1	12	0	34														
E	48	2	14	0	64	2	1	4	1	9	7	3	27						
F	18	1	4	0	23	4	2	1	1	5	3	2	18						
G	20	5	19	14	58	13	3	6	0	9	14	9	54	11	10	2	9	0	32
H	2	0	3	3	8	15	3	2	3	3	5	4	35	28	17	3	4	5	57
J	0	0	4	3	7	6	3	0	1	3	6	3	22	28	10	5	5	6	54
K	5	0	4	4	13	7	8	3	7	2	10	10	47	40	46	32	1	16	135
L	2	1	2	0	5	5	9	1	1	4	7	12	39	18	20	15	4	8	65
Total	272	39	114	24	449	52	29	17	14	35	52	43	242	125	103	57	23	35	348

Fig. 31. Cooking pots types 1 to 3, statistical chart

* Handles broken from the rim in such a way that subdividing was impossible. Some of these handles may have belonged to pots, counted under a-d.

The tendency to assimilate the shape of type 1 to 2 begins soon after type 2 is introduced. Note that variant d does not occur in phases A-D. In type 1 var. a is dominant, the ratio a - b - c is appr. 12 - 1 - 3.

In type 2 var. a is the most frequent rim shape, and var. b has not yet acquired its typical 8th cent. shape. The ratio a - b is appr. 5 - 3. It is amazing that var. g, which we suppose is the original shape, comes up again in phases K and L.

In type 3 the ratio a, b, c and d is appr. 5 - 4 - 2 - 1. Var. c seems a slightly later development, belonging mainly to phases K and L. The ratio between types 1, 2 and 3 in the phases G - L is appr.: phase G: 10 - 9 - 5, phase H: 1 - 5 - 8, Phase K: 1 - 4 - 10, and phase L: 1 - 8 - 13.

Deep Bowls

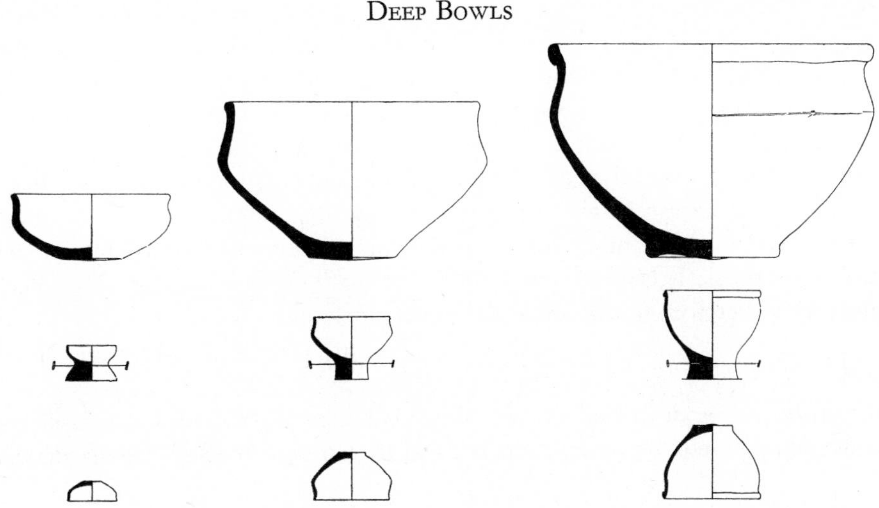

Fig. 32 Deep bowls types 1 to 16, construction drawing

Type 1

Description

The visual characteristics

This is a wide-mouthed bowl. The diameter of the mouth is generally about twice the height of the vessel. The pot has a ring base and rounded body, often with a marked carination at the base of the shoulder. The surface of this shoulder is treated differently technically below the carination, which is dry-smoothed, than above, which is wet-smoothed.

The shoulder is slightly concave.

There is no neck.

The rim is rolled out.

It is a heavy vessel with walls $\frac{3}{4}$-1 cm. thick.

The colour is light grey, tinted slightly greenish, with light red patches. Sometimes the light red colour dominates.

In most cases the colour is the same inside as out.

The technical characteristics

(cf. cooking pot, type 1)

The clay was made lean by adding quartz sand and limestone grit in fine particles but not as powder.

Occasionally large foreign bodies occur, sometimes even as long as the width of the wall.

The bowl was made in three separate parts.

a) the body was made by coiling or in a mould.

b) the shoulder and rim were made from one continuous coil of clay which was turned upwards with a tapering top, which was then folded in. Sometimes the impression of a reed, split lengthwise, can be seen running along the carination showing that the bowl was supported in this way while the coil was being added. The rim was finished off by folding it outwards. The sharp carination in the earlier stages marks the join between the body and the coil. As the rim was either turned upwards or left in its position, the shoulder can be either slightly concave or straight.

c) a ring base is added, made from a small coil of clay and finished by smoothing. This coil is not precisely centred, which indicates that no quick turning on a wheel was employed. It is therefore not of equal height or thickness.

The break

The texture can be described as "self-slip," but then the specification described on p. 69 must be followed. The core is either dark grey or dark reddish-brown, depending on:

a) the length of time during which the pot was fired

b) the amount of reducing caused by the type of kiln used, its size and the way it was stacked.

On the whole there must have been an oxidizing atmosphere in the kilns. This can be deduced by the reddish colour of some pots (probably those stacked near the top of the kiln) and the fact that all the bowls show this reddish-brown colour immediately beneath the surface.

The "self-slip," the greenish-grey colour, is a result of the fusing of sulphuric elements in the fuel used for firing with salts in the clay that rise to the surface of the vessel during the drying out process. It is not a slip added by the potter.

These pots were stacked upside down or on their sides, for the fumes had free access to the inside of the bowls.

Variations

The variations of rim shape listed below are meant merely as a convenient way of surveying the material in order to find out whether there are certain tendencies at work during the course of time. It must be stressed that, as in the case of the cooking pot, type 1, the rim of one and the same bowl can exhibit each of these variations at different places along its diameter. At the same time a difference of $\frac{1}{2}$-1 cm. in height, as well as a different thickness, can be observed. It is therefore not possible to make any statistical observations concerning the total number of bowls found from the number of rim fragments. This can, however, be done from base fragments in so far as they can with certainty be attributed to this type of bowl. Very few complete bowls were found.

The type illustrated above comes from an extension of the excavations not described in this volume.

Variant a) The rim is folded out and the fold is left so that it ends in a right angle against the wall of the pot.

Variant b) The fold is rounded and the flat top of the rim is joined onto the wall making a round profile.

Variant c) The end of the fold is smoothed out against the wall. Cf. further type 2 which is probably a variant of type 1.

Variant d) A rim as short as the second fold and usually showing the lower part of the ridge caused by the first fold.

Colour description

no.	*Colour outside*	*Colour inside*
	DEEP BOWLS TYPE 1	
	Phase B. Fig. 49	
15	10YR-7/3, very pale brown	2.5Y-7/2 light grey
16	10YR-7/3 very pale brown	10YR-8/4 very pale brown
17	7.5YR-7/4 pink	10YR-7/3 very pale brown (7.5YR-7/4 pink)
18	10YR-7/3 very pale brown	2.5YR-6/6 light red (7.5YR-6/4 light brown)
19	2.5Y-8/2 white	2.5Y-8/2 white
20	5Y-6/1 grey	5Y-6/1 grey (2.5Y-N3 very dark grey)
21	10YR-7/3 very pale brown	5YR-6/4 light reddish brown
22	7.5YR-8/4 pink (10YR-7/3 very pale brown)	10YR-7/3 very pale brown
23	10R-5/4 weak red	2.5YR-6/6 light red
24	10YR-7/3 very pale brown	2.5YR-6/6 light red
25	10YR-8/2 white	10YR-8/2 white
26	5Y-8/2 white (5YR-7/4 pink)	5Y-8/2 white
27	10YR-8/3 very pale brown (5YR-7/4 pink)	5YR-7/4 pink
28	10YR-7/3 very pale brown	7.5YR-7/4 pink
29	7.5YR-7/4 pink	7.5YR-7/4 pink
30	10YR-7/2 light grey (7.5YR-7/4 pink)	5YR-7/6 reddish yellow (7.5YR-N3 very dark grey)
31	7.5YR-6/4 light brown	10YR-7/2 light grey
32	5Y-7/2 light grey	5Y-7/2 light grey
33	10YR-8/3 very pale brown	10R-5/4 weak red
	Phase G. Fig. 64	
21	10YR-8/3 very pale brown	10YR-7/3 very pale brown
22	7.5YR-8/2 pinkish white	2.5YR-6/6 light red
23	10YR-7/2 light grey	5YR-7/4 pink
24	5Y-8/2 white	5Y-8/2 white
25	7.5YR-7/4 pink	2.5YR-6/4 light reddish brown
26	2.5YR-5/4 reddish brown	5YR-5/2 reddish grey
27	5YR-7/4 pink	5YR-6/4 light reddish brown

Type 2

It is still uncertain whether this is a separate type. No complete section from base to rim has yet been recovered and it is quite possible that the sherds treated here are really variants of type 1, and do not form a different type. Rim fragments show a tendency to form a transition from type 1 rim to this group, and there are also transitions from one variant to another within this group.

The three variants are based on type 1 variants a, b and c.

Variant a1, b1, c1: show a horizontal depression on the outside of the second fold of the rim.

Variant a2, b2, c2: show a second fold of the top of the rim outside.

Variant a3, b3, c3: have the second fold outside, but the lower part of this fold is also pushed down.

A few cases have been found where the profile takes a different shape. For example, in type 2a where the top of the rim is pressed up but not folded again.

Conclusions

Type 2 is much less frequent than type 1. However, until more complete rims of type 2 are found it is impossible to establish the relation of this type to that of type 1. From phase G onwards there is a tendency for these rims to lose the distinctive features of the profile and to become flat. Because of this, variant c dominates.

In theory there are two more possible variations. Firstly, that only the lower part of the rim (cf. variant a3) is pushed down, but not the top of the rim; and secondly, that more than two secondary folds can be made on the outside of the whole rim or parts of it.

Colour description

no.	*Colour outside*	*Colour inside*
	DEEP BOWLS TYPE 2	
	Phase B. Fig. 49	
34	10YR-8/3 very pale brown	5YR-7/3 pink
35	7.5YR-8/2 pinkish white	7.5YR-7/4 pink
36	10YR-8/4 very pale brown	5YR-7/6 reddish yellow
37	7.5YR-7/4 pink (below carination) (10YR-7/2 light grey (above carination))	7.5YR-7/4 pink
38	10YR-7/3 very pale brown	2.5YR-6/4 light reddish brown
39	2.5YR-6/4 light reddish brown	5YR-7/4 pink
40	5YR-7/6 reddish yellow	5YR-7/6 reddish yellow
	Phase G. Fig. 64	
28	7.5YR-7/4 pink	7.5YR-7/4 pink
29	7.5YR-7/2 pinkish grey	7.5YR-7/2 pinkish grey

Colour description (continued)

no.	*Colour outside*	*Colour inside*
	DEEP BOWLS TYPE 2 (*continued*)	
	Phase G. Fig. 64	
30	10YR-7/2 light grey	10YR-5/3 brown
31	2.5Y-7/2 light grey (2.5YR-6/4 light reddish brown)	5YR-5/2 reddish grey
32	10YR-8/2 white	5YR-6/3 light reddish brown

Type 3

Description

Apart from the rim, this pot seems to have been made in the same way as type 1. Yet this group does clearly form an individual type with its own characteristics.

Technically this vessel is different from type 1 only in that the second fold in the rim is omitted. There are a few cases where the top of the rim is smoothed out and down on an uneven part of the top.

To a greater extent than in type 1 there is a tendency towards a fairly long and almost vertical shoulder, and this is probably due to the absence of the second fold in the rim which accents the carination by downward pressure on the shoulder.

Handles are extremely rare. The paste is the same as that of type 1.

Variations

It is strange that these variations do not run parallel with those of cooking pot type 2. It is possible that this can be explained by the cooking pot in its original state having had a marked outside ridge which this type probably never had and in any case did not develop.

Although the more or less sharp ridge is the natural result of the clay being folded inwards, it is here smoothed away rather than accentuated, as was the case with cooking pots type 2 and 3.

This type is introduced at Deir ʿAllā together with cooking pot type 1 in the earliest I.A. phases, and does not, therefore, run parallel with cooking pot type 2.

The variants

a) This shape is the natural outcome of the basic treatment of this type. The original or proto-type of this form cannot be traced from the Deir ʿAllā material. With a rounded top the rim has a rectangular shape in section, the height being about twice that of the width. The tendency to flatten the top of the rim is not yet noticeable in this type and those rare examples where flattened tops do occur may be accidental. (cf. type 2f. p. 140)

b) This is distinguished from a. by a somewhat pointed top to the rim, which gives it a more or less triangular section shape. Another difference is the obvious hollow inside, directly below the rim.

c) Here the rim has practically lost all its distinguishing features, and only a slight thickening of the pot wall is left. This must have been done deliberately, as it requires more labour than variant a.

d) This differs from c. in that there is a marked angle between the shoulder and rim, and the rim is always vertical. Many rims of variant c. are also vertical but there is a gradual transition to the shoulder. It is possible that in its early stages this variant was accidental. Yet is must have attracted the attention of potters, for in later stages this variant develops into a characteristic shape with a straight "collar" shaped rim, flat top and a short rounded shoulder. This occurs from phase G onwards.

Although c. and d. often appear to be very similar as both have lost their sharp outer ridge, in general it is not difficult to attribute sherds of this type to their correct variant sub-division.

Analysis of tempering material in thin section

Deep bowls type 1.

D 161/31: 1 quartz grains, average 0.5 mm.
2 calcite 0.5 mm.
3 flint $\frac{3}{4}$ mm.
4 Na-Ca velspar $\frac{3}{4}$ mm.
5 haematite grains $\frac{3}{4}$ mm.
6 lime grains 1 mm.

D 343/66: 1 quartz grains max. $\frac{3}{4}$ mm. average $\frac{1}{2}$ mm.
2 flint flakes average $\frac{3}{4}$ mm.
3 lime grains average $\frac{3}{4}$ mm.
4 haematite grains $\frac{1}{2}$ mm.

D 424/23: 1 quartz grains average $\frac{1}{4}$ mm.
quartz flakes 0.03 mm. (probably from the clay.)
2 lime grains max. $5\frac{1}{2}$ mm. average $\frac{1}{2}$ mm.
3 flint flakes 1 mm.
4 haematite grains $< 1\frac{1}{4}$ mm.

D 424/17: 1 quartz grains $\frac{3}{4}$ mm.
id. 0.03 mm. (from the clay?)
2 lime grains average $\frac{3}{4}$ mm., max. 2 mm.
3 haematite flakes $< 1\frac{1}{4}$ mm.
4 flint flakes $\frac{1}{2}$ mm.

E 382/2: 1 quartz grains $< \frac{3}{4}$ mm.
2 lime grains $< 2\frac{1}{2}$ mm.
3 Fe oxide grains $< \frac{3}{4}$ mm.
4 flint flakes $< \frac{3}{4}$ mm.

Colour description

no.	*Colour outside*	*Colour inside*
	DEEP BOWLS TYPE 3	
	Phase B. Fig. 49	
41	10R-5/6 red (10YR-8/1 white)	10YR-5/2 greyish brown
42	2.5YR-6/6 light red	2.5YR-6/4 light reddish brown
43	7.5YR-8/4 pink	7.5YR-7/2 pinkish grey
44	10YR-8/4 very pale brown	7.5YR-6/4 light brown
45	10YR-8/3 very pale brown	10YR-8/4 very pale brown
46	10YR-8/4 very pale brown	10YR-8/2 white (7.5YR-7/4 pink)
47	10YR-8/3 very pale brown	10YR-8/3 very pale brown (2.5YR-6/4 light reddish brown)
48	10YR-7/3 very pale brown	10YR-7/3 very pale brown
49	5YR-6/4 light reddish brown	5YR-6/4 light reddish brown
50	7.5YR-7/4 pink	5YR-7/6 reddish yellow
51	7.5YR-7/4 pink	7.5YR-7/4 pink
52	10YR-7/3 very pale brown	5YR-7/4 pink
53	10YR-7/2 light grey	10YR-7/2 light grey
54	10YR-8/3 very pale brown	10YR-8/3 very pale brown
55	10YR-7/3 very pale brown	2.5Y-8/2 white
	Phase G. Fig. 64	
33	10YR-7/2 light grey (5YR-7/3 pink)	5YR-6/3 light reddish brown
34	10R-6/6 light red (10R-3/1 dark reddish grey)	10R-6/6 light red
35	7.5YR-7/2 pinkish grey	10YR-7/2 light grey
36	2.5Y-7/2 light grey	2.5Y-N5 grey
37	5YR-7/6 reddish yellow	5YR-7/6 reddish yellow
38	5YR-6/2 pinkish grey (10R-6/6 light red 2.5Y-8/2 white)	2.5Y-8/2 white
39	7.5YR-6/4 light brown	7.5YR-6/4 light brown
40	10R-5/4 weak red	10R-5/4 weak red
41	10YR-7/1 light grey	2.5Y-N4/ dark grey
42	2.5Y-6/2 light brownish grey	10YR-7/2 light grey
43	7.5YR-7/4 pink	7.5YR-8/2 pinkish white (5YR-7/6 reddish yellow)
44	10YR-8/2 white	7.5YR-7/4 pink
45	2.5YR-6/2 pale red	10R-6/6 light red

Comparisons

Type 1 can sometimes be distinguished from type 3 in publications, but type 3 usually cannot be distinguished from type 1c in drawings.

It is found in Megiddo, for instance, Tomb 221B, (Tombs, Pl. 71,3,5 - 16. E.I.) Meg. II, bowls 276, Pl. 69,11 and 317, Pl. 69, 12, Str. VIIA. Afula op. cit. Str. IIIB, fig. 17,15.

Phase	*Type 1*				*Type 2**							*Type 3*					
	a	*b*	*c*	*T*	*a*	*b*	*c*	*d*	*e*	*f*	*T*	*a*	*b*	*c*	*d*	*T*	*T*
A	11	8	7	26	0	0	0	1	0	0	1	29	20	16	14	79	106
B	37	30	50	117	4	2	0	10	8	5	29	30	42	19	15	106	252
C	19	6	30	55	2	3	2	4	5	1	17	27	36	11	9	83	155
D	4	5	6	15	0	0	0	1	1	0	2	16	8	5	5	34	51
E	16	7	24	47	0	1	0	4	4	2	11	41	22	11	2	76	134
F	4	3	4	11	0	0	0	0	2	0	2	14	18	6	5	43	56
G	10	1	7	18	2	0	0	3	2	1	8	24	7	1	29	61	87
H	1	0	2	3	2	0	1	4	0	0	7	11	1	4	22	38	48
J	1	0	0	1	0	0	0	4	0	0	4	6	2	0	18	26	31
K	1	3	2	6	1	0	0	2	0	0	3	6	4	0	29	49	58
L	0	0	0	0	0	0	0	0	0	0	0	7	2	0	38	47	47
Total	104	63	132	299	11	6	3	33	22	9	84	211	162	73	186	642	1025

Fig. 33. Deep bowls types 1 to 3, statistical chart

* Type 2a-f consists of the variations a1,a2 etc. 2a=a1; 2b=a2; 2c=b2; 2d=c1; 2e=c2; 2f=c3.

Kh. Sheikh Mohammed, A.A.S.O.R. 25 - 28, Pl. 25,2,5,6,7, said to be M.B. II, but almost certainly this type.

According to the statistical evidence type 1 ends in the 12th cent. and type 11 continues through the 11th cent.

Thin Walled Bowls Type 4.

On the whole these bowls are not so small as the thinness of the wall would suggest. Var. a has some small examples and var. g is invariably small. It is likely that these bowls have the thinnest possible wall for this type of clay mixture. Also the fact that there is no profiling (except a slight thickening of the top of the wall in var. d) separates these bowls from types 5 - 12. There is naturally a fairly gradual transition to walls of normal thickness. The doubtful cases have been attributed to type 5. It is possible that the thinness of the wall allowed the potter to cut away the surplus clay from the rim, which, as has been demonstrated, cannot be done with thicker walls. These bowls with a thin upper wall can have rather thick bases and this is explained by the manufacturing processes, fig. 21.

Variants

a) The upper part of the wall is rounded and the end is either vertical or more often slightly curving inwards. The wall is usually shorter than walls of the c-f group. One sixth of the total amount (unburnished) belongs to this group, both in phases A-D and E-L. It is not known whether these bowls sometimes had ring bases, but it seems unlikely in view of the thin wall which had to be firm enough to enable the potter to handle the bowl upside down. This applies to the whole of group type 4.

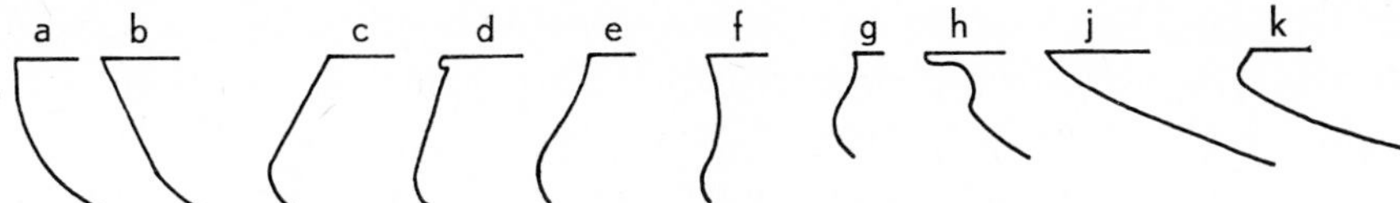

Fig. 34. Bowls type 4, rim variants

Type 4

Phase	*a*	*b*	*c*	*d*	*e*	*f*	*g*	*h*	*j*	*k*	
A	4,1	3,0	3,0	9,0	8,0	25,0	11,0	2,1	1,0	0,0	66 2
B	35,3	7,3	12,1	23,0	23,4	34,7	19,0	33,0	3,0	,1	189 18
C	7,5	7,1	10,2	16,1	7,0	11,0	10,0	6,0	2,0	,1	76 9
D	12,0	4,0	2,0	2,0	1,0	5,0	3,0	6,0	0,0	,0	35 0
E	13,1	1,0	4,1	10,0	3,0	13,1	4,0	8,0	4,0	,0	60 3
F	2,4	0,3	0,1	2,0	4,0	0,1	2,0	4,0	2,0	,0	16 9
G	4,2	8,4	1,1	10,0	2,0	5,7	3,0	4,0	4,1	,0	41 15
H	6,2	2,5	0,1	6,2	0,0	3,5	2,0	3,0	0,0	,0	22 15
J	10,2	2,6	0,0	4,1	1,0	6,0	1,0	2,0	4,0	,0	30 9
K	2,4	4,8	3,0	3,2	2,0	13,2	1,0	0,1	4,1	,0	32 18
L	5,0	8,13	1,5	8,0	2,0	2,0	2,0	1,1	2,0	,0	31 19
Total	100	46	36	93	53	117	58	69	26		598
Phase A-D	58	21	27	50	39	75	43	47	6		336
E-L	42	25	9	43	14	42	15	22	20		232
Burnished:											
Total	24	43	12	6	4	23	0	3	2		117

Fig. 35. Bowls type 4, statistical chart

b) A fairly high and straight wall, bent outwards. Here there often is a marked angle between the lower and upper part of the wall. Only one in twelve/thirteen belongs to this type.

c) A fairly high and straight wall, bent inwards. Usually there is a marked angle between the upper and lower part of the wall. Var. c forms one in sixteen of the total group and is much less frequent than var. d.

d) The only difference from var. c is that there is a slight thickening of the top of the rim on the outside. This feature has not been found on any of the other variants. Perhaps this tiny fold was sometimes found on var. c rims in order to level the rim, but no transitional shapes have been found on either c or d bowl rims. Out of a total of 129 fragments this transition should have been found if it existed, and this justifies the division into two variants. It is exclusive to var. d.

e) The distinctive feature is that this bowl has a concave wall which has however a straight and vertical upper end. This gives the vessel a characteristic shape. It is not frequent, one in ten, and the main concentration is in the early phases A-D. This shape is hardly found with types 5-12.

f) Usually there is a slightly in-curved wall but sometimes the wall is straight and vertical. It can easily be distinguished from var. b and c. It appears to have been the most frequent variant, one in five, and it occurs fairly constantly through all the phases in the same proportion.

g) This is a small bowl with a s-shaped wall profile. It is not frequent, one in ten, and it occurs less in later phases. It does not occur in the group types 5-12.

h) This saucer shape with a clearly marked rim is not frequent. It is related to the lamps, but it is not certain that the fragments all belonged to lamps. The type may have existed as a bowl as well.

j) A shallow saucer with a straight rim. The same uncertainty as mentioned in connection with variant h applies to this variant. There is also a chance that some of the fragments come from a "cup and saucer" vessel of which only two fragments have been identified with certainty. It is not common (approximately one piece in twenty-two) but many more fragments come from phases E-L than from A-D.

k) This curious shape occurs very seldom. It is a saucer with a short upturned rim and as the fragments found are very small, it seems possible that they were the "rim", i.e. bottom edge, of pedestal bases. When found as a rim of a larger bowl one is inclined to think that the potters did not have quite enough clay to finish the bowl properly. Statistically this variant has no significance.

Analysis of tempering material in thin section

Bowls type 4.

D 161/22: 1 quartz grains $\frac{1}{2}$-$\frac{3}{4}$ mm.
id. (from the clay) 0.03 mm.
2 lime grains $\frac{1}{2}$-1$\frac{1}{2}$ mm.
3 flint flakes and grains $\frac{3}{4}$ mm.
4 haematite flakes $\frac{1}{2}$-1$\frac{1}{2}$ mm.

Colour description

no.	*Colour outside*	*Colour inside*
	BOWLS TYPE 4	
	Phase B. Fig. 49	
	TYPE 4a	
56	2.5YR-6/4 light reddish brown (10YR-7/3 very pale brown)	2.5YR-6/6 light red
57	10R-4/4 weak red - 4/6 red	10R-4/6 red
58	10YR-7/2 light grey (5YR-7/6 reddish yellow)	5YR-7/4 pink
59	10YR-7/3 very pale brown (7.5YR-7/4 pink)	5YR-7/6 reddish yellow
60	7.5YR-N3 very dark grey (decor. 7.5R-3/4 dusky red)	5YR-7/4 pink
61	7.5YR-6/2 pinkish grey (decor. 7.5R-3/2 dusky red)	2.5YR-6/4 light reddish brown
62	7.5YR-7/4 pink	7.5YR-7/4 pink
63	7.5YR-N3 very dark grey	7.5YR-N3 very dark grey
	TYPE 4b	
64	5Y-7/3 pale yellow (7.5YR-7/2 pinkish grey)	5YR-6/4 light reddish brown
65	5YR-7/4 pink	5YR-7/6 reddish yellow
66	7.5YR-7/6 reddish yellow	7.5YR-7/4 pink
	TYPE 4c	
67	7.5YR-7/4 pink	2.5YR-6/4 light reddish brown
68	7.5YR-7/2 pinkish grey	5YR-7/6 reddish yellow
69	10YR-7/3 very pale brown	10YR-7/2 light grey
70	5YR-7/4 pink	5YR-7/4 pink
	TYPE 4d	
71	10YR-8/3 very pale brown	7.5YR-7/4 pink
72	5YR-7/6 reddish yellow	5YR-7/6 reddish yellow
73	10YR-8/1 white	10YR-8/1 white
74	10YR-8/3 very pale brown	10YR-8/3 very pale brown
75	2.5Y-8/2 white	2.5YR-6/4 light reddish brown
76	10YR-8/4 very pale brown	7.5YR-7/4 pink
77	2.5Y-8/2 white	2.5Y-8/2 white
	TYPE 4e	
82	10YR-7/2 light grey	10YR-7/3 very pale brown
83	10YR-8/4 very pale brown	10YR-8/4 very pale brown
84	10YR-8/4 very pale brown	10YR-8/4 very pale brown
85	10YR-8/2 white	10YR-8/2 white
86	10YR-8/4 very pale brown	10YR-8/4 very pale brown
87	2.5Y-8/2 white (10R-6/6 light red)	2.5Y-8/2 white
	TYPE 4f	
88	7.5YR-8/4 pink	10R-6/6 light red
89	10YR-8/1 white	2.5YR-6/6 light red
90	10R-6/6 light red	10R-6/6 light red

Colour description (continued)

no.	*Colour outside*	*Colour inside*
	BOWLS TYPE 4 (*continued*)	
	Phase B. Fig. 49	
	TYPE 4f	
91	5YR-7/6 reddish yellow	5YR-7/6 reddish yellow
92	7.5YR-8/4 pink	2.5YR-6/4 light reddish brown
	TYPE 4g	
78	10YR-8/3 very pale brown	10YR-8/3 very pale brown
79	10YR-8/1 white	10YR-8/1 white
80	2.5Y-7/2 light grey	10R-5/2 weak red
81	10R-6/6 light red	10R-6/6 light red
	Fig. 50	
	TYPE 4h	
1	10YR-8/2 white (dec. 7.5R-3/2 dusky red)	10YR-8/2 white
2	2.5Y-8/2 white	2.5Y-7/2 light grey
3	5YR-7/4 pink	5YR-7/4 pink
4	2.5YR-8/2 white	2.5YR-8/2 white
5	2.5YR-6/4 light reddish brown	2.5YR-6/4 light reddish brown
6	2.5Y-8/2 white	2.5Y-8/2 white
7	10R-5/4 weak red	10R-6/6 light red
8	10YR-5/1 grey	2.5YR-N4 dark grey
9	10YR-7/3 very pale brown	2.5YR-5/2 weak red
10	10R-6/6 light red	10R-6/6 light red
11	5YR-7/6 reddish yellow	5YR-7/6 reddish yellow
12	5YR-7/4 pink	5YR-7/4 pink
13	10YR-7/2 white	10YR-6/4 light yellowish brown
	Phase G. Fig. 64	
46	7.5YR-8/4 pink	7.5YR-8/4 pink
47	5YR-7/3 pink	5YR-7/4 pink
48	7.5YR-7/4 pink	7.5YR-7/4 pink
49	10YR-8/3 very pale brown	7.5YR-8/2 pinkish white
50	10YR-7/2 light grey	10YR-7/1 light grey
51	5YR-7/4 pink	7.5YR-8/4 pink
52	10R-6/4 pale red	10R-6/4 pale red

Comparisons

These bowls, which average 10% of the six main types at Deir ʿAllā through all the phases, and are c. two-fifths of bowls 4-16, seem to be much more common in Trans-Jordan than in Palestine. There the thin walled bowls are characteristic for E.I.II. They can be compared with bowls 304-308 from Megiddo, Str. VII A.

Type 4. *Local burnished and burnished "import" wares*

There is an uncertainty about the attribution of burnished rim fragments to type 4. Probably already in phase E, and certainly from phase G on, a new kind of bowl with rim shapes that resemble the rim of type 4 occur. These bowls are always burnished. Chart fig. 35 shows that from phase H on, there are more burnished than unburnished bowls of var. b. The flaring straight rim is common among the new type and it may well be that some of the examples listed under var. b belong, in fact, to the new type.

More or less complete examples found in the stratigraphy have been shown in Ch. 8, after bowls type 17-18. They have not been classified, as there is not enough stratified material available yet. It is likely that when analysed they will show a different clay composition from the Deir ʿAllā repertoire or else that the clay was prepared with much more care. The shapes are different too. Sometimes a slip was used, which is not found on any of the Deir ʿAllā types and, as far as is known, they are always burnished. The walls can be much thinner than those of type 4. There are no comparable bowls from this repertoire known from excavations in Palestine, and it must be supposed that the origin lies east or north-east of Deir ʿAllā. In the text in Ch. 8 they are classed as imports. Some fragments which have the new shapes look as though they were imitations made by the Deir ʿAllā potters. Most of the material comes from unstratified top levels and wash levels of the tell, which renders a proper study based on statistical evidence impossible. Rim fragments, classified according to the type 4 variants, which belong to this new group are:

Phase G: a,2; b,6; f,2.
Phase H: a,10; b, 22.
Phase J: b, 20.
Phase K: a, 2; b, 23; f, 8; g, 1; h, 1; j, 3.
Phase L: b, 26; f, 8; j, 2.

In view of the uncertainty of burnished type 4 bowls these bowls are not included in the study of the practice of burnishing in Deir ʿAllā.

Bowls
Types 5-16

All the bowls have been divided into three major types: the deep bowls (types 1-3), the 'open' bowls, (types 4-16) and the large shallow bowls (types 17-18). This division is based on three different manufacturing techniques.

The first group is made from a fixed number of coils and the base is closed after the rest has been finished.

The second group is made by coiling from a clay base, and the number of coils can vary.

The third group is made in moulds.

The second group is the most difficult type of pot to divide into types. Provided that there is a great deal of pottery, all the shapes that together form a smooth transition in size and rim shape from one "type" to the next one will occur. As a result, every division into types is unsatisfactory; many examples which could be classed together can also be distributed over two or more types and *vice versa*. The typology which has resulted from this study clearly demonstrates this point.

The visual characteristics

For the shape of the rims see below. These bowls are wet smoothed on the inside and over the rim outside. The lower part on the outside may or may not be dry scraped, and there is either a flat base or a ring base.

The technical characteristics (cf. fig. 36)

These bowls were either entirely shaped from one lump of clay, by turning a rim and cutting the bowl through the clay base, or after the lower part was shaped one or more coils were added and turned, depending on the size of vessel the potter had in mind.

The study of how many coils were used in making each bowl ought to be a help in obtaining a better typology, as this would perhaps give us the standard measures, and even the probable purpose of the bowls. This study requires a great number of complete bowl sections, which were not available. The study is perforce based on the upper part of the body and the rim shape. The resulting 'system' is shown in fig. 36 and 34.

Fig. 36 shows how the rim was finished by the Deir ʿAllā potters, and fig. 34 shows the shape of the upper part of the wall. These two elements in various combinations cover all the shapes found in the Early Iron Age. Fig. 34 shows all the shapes found in the type 4 bowl group; these are thin walled bowls (which can be much thicker near the base) without a profiled rim. The variations of wall shape are marked a-k, and this division is combined with the rim shapes of bowls with a thicker wall and a profiled rim, shown in fig. 36 and marked there 5-12. For the nos. 13-16, see below.

This system forms a net which catches all the possible combinations without aiming at a fixed system of types. It is meant to show us what tendencies were at work throughout the whole period and whether some shapes dominated over others. Cf. the statistical chart. It also gives a fair idea of what was accidental and what was done on purpose. It should always be kept in mind that a flat horizontal rim was not necessarily horizontal when put away to dry; nor were the shapes of the walls the same before they were dry. Both before and during firing, shrinkage can have altered the position of the upper part of the wall, and at one period the clay may have shrunken more than at another. Thus bowls, separated in this system, may have looked exactly the same before firing. Apart from this, until many more complete rims are available it is impossible to be certain that bowl rims with a slight (secondary) fold inwards or outwards had this profile all along the rim. The interpretation of the statistical chart (cf. fig. 37) may well be much simpler than it looks at first sight. The repertoire of this group of bowls should be divided according to the number of coils used, the type of bases and a selection of the

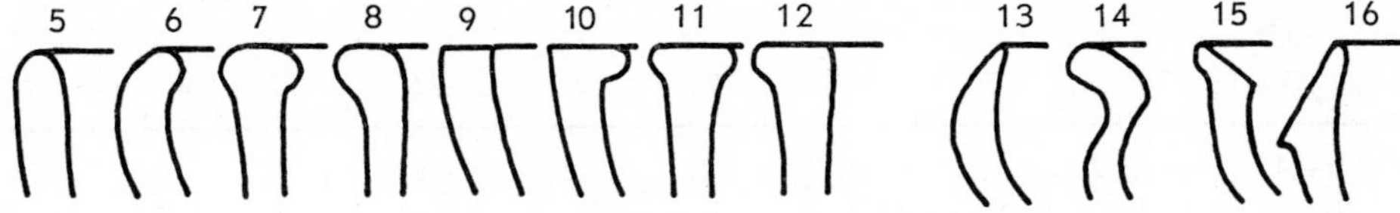

Fig. 36. Bowls types 5 to 16, rim shapes

Phase	*Type* *5*	*6*	*7*	*8*	*9*	*10*	*11*	*12*	*13*	*14*	*15*	*16*
A	a– 6, b– 5, c– 1, f– 8, h– 1,	a– 1, b– 1,	b–1 , c– 1,	a– 3, g– 1,	a– 2, b– 2, c– 2, f– 5, h– 1, j– 3,	, ,	f– 2,	b– 1, f– 3,	7	11	4	14
B	a–16, 3 b– 9, 1 c– 6, f– 5, j– 1,	a– 4,	a–2 , 1	a– 2,	a–25, 2 b– 1, c– 2, f– , 1 j– 5, 1	a–12, b– 1,1 f– 1,2 j– 1,	a– 6, 1 b– 1, f– 3,	a– 6, f– 5 j– 1,	10	13	19	13
C	a–24, 1 b– 4, 3 c– 1, e– 2, f–11, 1 h– 4, j– 1,	a– 6, 1 b– 5,	a– 1,	a– 4, 1	a–12, 2 b– 5, c– 1, e– 1, f– 2, h– 1, j– 1,	a– 4,	f– 2,	b– 2, c– 1, f– 1,	6	9	19	13
D	a–14, b–1 , c– 1, e– 2,	a– 2,	a– 1, f– , 1	a– 5,	a– 4, 3 c– 1, 1 f– 1,	a– 4,	a– 2, f– , 1		5		3	1
E	a–16, 3 b– 1, c– 1, 3 d– 1, 1 f– 4, h– 1,	a– 1,	a– 1,	f– 5,	a–10, b– 1, c– 1, g– 1, k– 1,	a– 6,3 f– ,2	f– 1,	a– 2, b– 1, f– 1,	8	2	6	9
F	a–10, 3 f– 2, j– 1, k– 1,	f– 1,	j– , 1	a– 4, f– 2,	a– 3, 2 b– 1, 1 j– 1,	a– 3,	a– 1,	a– 3,	1		1	
G	a–14,14 b– 5, 6 c– 2, 3 e– 6, f– 8, 1 g– , 1 h– 2, j– 2, k– 1, 1	a– 5, 2 b– 1, c– 1, e– 5, f– 3,	a– , 1	a– 4, 2 f– 6, j– 1,	a– 5, 1 c– , 1		a– 3, c– 2,	a– 4, 1	1	1	3	2

Phase	*Type* *5*	*6*	*7*	*8*	*9*	*10*	*11*	*12*	*13*	*14*	*15*	*16*
H	a– 4, 4 b– 3, 4 e– 1, f– , 2 g– 2, j– 2,	a– 2, 2 j– 1,	a– , 2 f– , 1	a– 3, 1 b– , 1 f– , 1	a– 2, 1	a– 1,	a– 1,	a– 1, f– 1,			2	4
J	a– 4, 4 b– 3, 5 c– 1, e– 1, f– 4, 5 h– 1, j– 1,	a– 1, 3 b– , 2	a– 3, 3	a– 2, 2 b– 3, d– 4,	a– 1, 2 b– 1, 1 f– 1, j– 1,	a– , 1 b– , 1 f– 1, k– 1,	a– 2,	a– 1, f– 1,	1		2	3
K	a– 4,12 b– 1, 7 c– , 1 f– 3, 3	a– , 4 b– , 2 f– 1, k– 1,	a– , 2 f– , 2	a– , 1 b– , 1 f– , 5	a– 1, 1 b– 1, 2 c– 1, f– , 2 h– 1, j– 1, k– 1,	a– 4, 1 b– , 3 f– 1,	b– 2, 1 f– , 1	a– 2, b– , 2 f– 1, 1 g– , 1	4	1	2	1
L	a– 2, 2 b– 2, 7 c– 1, f– , 1 j– 1, k– 1,	b– 1, 6 f– , 1	a– 3, b– , 1	a– 3, b– 1, 2 f– 2,	a– , 1 b– 1, 1	a– 1, 7 b– 1, 9 h– 1,	a– , 2 b– 2, 3 j– 1,	b– 1, 2	6		3	1

Fig. 37. Bowls types 5 to 16. Statistical chart

(note: in phase K 4 thin walled bowls with a flat rim have been included, 1 unburnished and 3 burnished; in phase L 8 burnished have been included).

possible combinations of the a-k group and the 5-12 group. As long as this cannot be done it seems preferable to trace the various tendencies as closely as possible.

The group of bowls marked 13-16 were originally distributed over this system but were later grouped together when it became clear that they were intended as different shapes. This happened with the thin-walled bowls type 4 also.

The types 5-8 with rounded rim tops and the types 9-12 with flat rim tops do not show the fixed rate such as has been found for the main types (cooking pots 1-2, cooking pots 3, deep bowls 1-3, bowls 4, bowls 5-16, jars 1 and jars 2) with a maximum deviation of 3% (cf. Ch. 9). The rates in the phases are: A, 29-21 (approximately 4-3); B, 50-78 (2-3); C, 70-35 (2-1); D, 27-17 (3-2); E, 38-30 (4-3); F, 25-15 (5-3); G, 97-17 (11-2); H, 36-7 (5-1); J, 52-15 (10-3); K, 50-31 (5-3); L, 37-26 (4-3).

We can be fairly certain that the distinction between flat-topped rims and rounded rims is not valid for a distinction of real types, and that the flat rim, which on the whole is in the minority is more or less accidental. Phase B shows a peak in the flat-topped rims and in phases G and H the round topped rims form the vast majority. It is impossible to say whether this was a matter of fashion or just a habit of some individual potters. It cannot be used as a dating criterion. That a flat topped rim tends to cause further profiling, (types 10-12) can be seen by comparison of the total of type 5 with the group 6-8 and type 9 with the group 10-12.

The ratio is here for all phases together: 345:166 and 140:159.

It can easily be understood that while making a rim flat the potter often pushed clay down on the sides of the rim, thus making the profile. From this can be concluded that on the whole there was a tendency to leave a rim with its top just round or flat (types 5 and 9:485 against types 6-8 and 10-12:325). When the flat-top type 9 is taken as profiled the numbers are 345:465.

The treatment of the wall of these bowls

The shapes of the upper part of the wall of these bowls have been divided according to the system of determinition applied to bowls type 4. (For a description see p. 140). The resulting chart (fig. 37) shows that in doing this the types 5-12 have been broken up into many tiny groups, and that these groups taken separately do not have any real statistical value as the numbers have become too small. This can be seen by application of the statistical rule that the margin of uncertainty of any given number is twice the root of that number. However the following groups can be compared: bowls with a rounded, often incurving, wall (a, c and e), bowls with a straight wall with an angle of more than 90° to the base (b), and bowls with a vertical wall which is sometimes practically straight but usually slightly concave (f). Cf. the chart fig. 38. It is clear that taken over all the phases shape a is by far the most common type and if combined with c and e there are 469 for this group, 144 for b and 123 for f which is roughly 4:1$\frac{1}{4}$:1. If taken per phase the picture is much less certain. It seems that from phase G on b is steadily

	Wall shape					
Phase	*a*	*c*	*e*	*total*	*b*	*f*
A	12	4	0	16	10	18
B	80	8	0	88	14	17
C	56	3	3	62	19	15
D	35	3	2	40	1	3
E	42	5	0	47	3	7
F	29	0	0	29	2	5
G	56	9	11	76	12	18
H	24	0	1	25	8	5
J	27	1	1	29	16	12
K	32	2	0	34	19	20
L	21	2	0	23	40	3
total	414	37	18	469	144	123

Fig. 38. Bowls types 5 to 16, wall shapes, statistical chart

increasing in relation to the others, and this could well indicate a real development of shape, in which the curving wall becomes straight.

Other wall shapes occur fairly persistently throughout all the phases in very small quantities. j may well be the saucer of the 'cup-and-saucer' vessel, and sometimes a fragment of a lamp; like h. k could be explained as a case in which the last coil was just not thick enough to make a proper rim. In fact this feature is found occasionally in every type and this is to be expected. From this system the question of a marked angle just below the rim has been omitted for two reasons:

1. Many rims break just above the angle and therefore the statictical evidence is unreliable.

2. The way of manufacturing this group of bowls simply renders the question of a more or less clear angle accidental, cf. fig. 21. When the angle is not accidental but a feature of the manufacturing process, it cannot be overlooked, cf. cooking pots types 1-2 and deep bowls types 1-3.

Burnishing

Right through the phases a tendency to burnish more bowls is noticeable. In the chart fig. 39 there are two columns for each type, separating the unburnished from the burnished bowls. The totals of burnished and unburnished bowls of the types 4, 5-12 and 13-16 are shown in this chart.

From this chart it becomes convincingly clear that the tendency to burnish is much

Phase	*Type 4*		*Type 5-12*		*Type 13-16*	
	a	b	a	b	a	b
A	66	2	49	0	36	0
B	189	18	129	13	55	0
C	76	9	99	9	28	0
D	35	0	38	6	9	0
E	60	3	56	12	25	0
F	16	9	33	7	2	0
G	41	15	86	34	7	3
H	22	15	23	20	6	2
J	30	9	38	29	6	6
K	32	18	27	54	8	12
L	31	19	26	45	10	5
Total	598	117	604	229	192	28
A-G	483	56	490	81	162	3
H-L	115	61	114	148	30	25

Fig. 39. Bowls types 4 to 16, burnishing, statistical chart
a=unburnished, b=burnished

stronger in phases H-L than in phases A-G, when they are taken as unities. A more detailed analysis would be unreliable, as the amount of sherds found in phase F, for instance, certainly does not permit any independent conclusions. With a total of 51 unburnished sherds the margin of error would statistically be appr. 14 and with a total of 15 burnished sherds the margin of error is about 8. (For a total of 1135 unburnished sherds from phases A-G the margin of error is statistically about 68 and for 140 burnished sherds from the same phases the margin of error is about 24). The same rule of statistical error makes it clear that it cannot be said that before phase G none of the types 13-16 bowls were ever burnished.

The technological reasons for burnishing can only be fully appreciated after a good deal of petrographic analysis has been made. It has already been shown by Kelso-Palin Thorly that the sheen of burnishing disappears when pottery is fired above a certain degree of heat. Burnishing is only succesful when applied to a pot which has dried to a certain extent. Apart from the sheen one has, therefore, to watch for the marks of the burnishing tool, as these betray the intention of the potters. It can sometimes be seen on larger fragments that the upper part of the pot was drier than the lower part during burnishing. This is in agreement with the type of temper used and the manufacturing process, in contrast to wheel thrown pottery, which dries differently. One can also sometimes notice that the inside of the bowl is much less shiny than the outside near the base. The chart, fig. 41, showing burnishing on bowl types 17-18 is interesting from the technical point of view, as it clearly indicates that the potters gave up burnishing the outside. (See below).

Types 13-16

The chart, fig. 37, also contains the statistical evidence of types 13-16. These have been selected from types 5-12 because of their characteristic shapes, although none of them is frequent.

Type 13 seems to belong to the earlier phases rather than to the later ones, although some examples were found in phases K and L. The rim is thickened on the outside and ends in a rounded point.

Type 14 seems to belong to the early phases even more and definitely has a concave rim.

Type 15 has a pointed slightly flaring rim that is flat on the inside. It seems mainly concentrated in the early phases.

Type 16 has a double folded rim, is pointed and flat on the outside. This is almost certainly the rim of the "fruit" stand, a bowl on a high pedestal base, and apart from its characteristic shape it has another distinguishing feature: it is as a rule made of clay tempered with organic matter, in contrast to the vast majority of the other bowls. Organic matter as temper is characteristic of some types of bowls found in the last phase of the L.B. sanctuary, where it is also used for this type. It is possible that here we find a tradition in which the preparation of the clay and the function of the vessel were both ritually determined.

For burnishing see above and the chart fig. 39

Analysis of tempering material in thin section

Bowls type 5

D 162/47: 1 quartz grains ½ mm.
2 lime grains ¼-1 mm.
3 flint flakes ½ mm.
4 haematite flakes ¼-1 mm.

D 164/3: 1 quartz sand
2 shale
3 flint flakes
4 felspar

Colour description

no.	*Colour outside*	*Colour inside*
	BOWLS TYPE 5	
	Phase B. Fig. 50	
14	2.5YR-6/6 light red	2.5YR-6/4 light reddish brown
15	2.5YR-6/4 light reddish brown	5YR-7/6 reddish yellow
16	10YR-8/3 very pale brown	10YR-8/3 very pale brown
17	10R-5/4 weak red	10R-5/4 weak red
18	7.5YR-6/4 light brown (7.5YR-N3 very dark grey)	10YR-8/3 light brown
19	10YR-8/3 very pale brown (10R-6/3 pale red)	10YR-6/2 light brownish grey (10YR-8/1 white 10R-6/3 pale red)
20	10R-5/1 reddish grey (10R-6/2 pale red)	7.5R-6/4 pale red
21	7.5YR-8/2 pinkish white	2.5YR-6/4 light reddish brown
22	2.5YR-6/6 light red (10R-5/3 weak red)	2.5YR-5/4 reddish brown (2.5YR-N3 very dark grey)
23	10R-6/6 light red (5YR-7/4 pink)	10R-6/6 light red
	Phase G. Fig. 64	
53	2.5YR-6/6 light red (10YR-7/2 light grey)	2.5YR-6/6 light red
54	10YR-7/2 light grey	10YR-7/2 light grey
55	10YR-7/1 light grey	2.5Y-N6 grey
56	10YR-8/3 very pale brown	10YR-7/2 light grey
57	10YR-7/2 light grey	10YR-7/2 light grey
58	10YR-7/2 light grey	10YR-7/3 very pale brown
	BOWLS TYPE 6	
	Phase B. Fig. 50	
24	7.5R-5/4 weak red	10R-6/6 light red
25	10YR-7/2 light grey	7.5YR-7/2 pinkish grey

Colour description (continued)

no.	*Colour outside*	*Colour inside*
	BOWLS TYPE 6 (*continued*)	
	Phase G. Fig. 64	
59	10YR-7/2 light grey (2.5Y-N6 grey)	2.5Y-8/2 white
60	10YR-7/2 light grey	10YR-7/2 light grey
61	10YR-8/3 very pale brown (2.5Y-8/2 white)	7.5YR-7/2 pinkish grey
62	7.5YR-6/4 light brown	10YR-7/2 light grey
63	10YR-7/3 very pale brown	5YR-7/4 pink
64	10YR-7/3 very pale brown	5YR-6/2 pinkish grey
65	5YR-7/3 pink	5YR-6/3 light reddish brown
	BOWLS TYPE 7	
	Phase B. Fig. 50	
26	5YR-8/4 pink	5YR-7/4 pink
28	10R-6/6 light red	2.5YR-6/4 light reddish brown
29	5Y-8/2 white	5YR-7/3 pink (10YR-7/2 light grey)
	BOWLS TYPE 8	
	Phase G. Fig. 64	
66	5YR-7/2 pinkish grey	5YR-6/3 light reddish brown
67	5YR-7/4 pink	7.5YR-8/4 pink
68	7.5YR-8/2 pinkish white	5YR-6/3 light reddish brown
69	7.5YR-7/2 pinkish grey	5YR-8/3 pink
70	7.5YR-7/4 pink	7.5YR-7/2 pinkish grey
	BOWLS TYPE 9	
	Phase B. Fig. 50	
30	5YR-7/4 pink (7.5R-N6 grey)	10YR-6/1 grey
31	5YR-6/4 light reddish brown	5YR-7/4 pink
32	10R-5/4 weak red	5YR-6/1 grey
33	7.5YR-7/2 pinkish grey (10YR-8/2 white)	7.5YR-7/4 pink
34	10YR-6/2 light brownish grey	10YR-5/1 grey
35	2.5Y-8/2 white (5YR-7/4 pink)	5YR-6/2 pinkish grey
36	2.5Y-8/2 white	10YR-7/3 very pale brown
37	10R-6/6 light red	2.5YR-6/6 light red
38	5Y-7/3 pale yellow	2.5Y-7/2 light grey
	Phase G. Fig. 64	
71	10R-6/4 pale red	10R-5/4 weak red
72	7.5YR-8/2 pinkish white	5YR-7/3 pink
73	10YR-8/3 very pale brown	10YR-8/3 very pale brown
74	10YR-8/2 white	7.5YR-7/2 pinkish grey
75	7.5YR-7/2 pinkish grey	5YR-7/2 pinkish grey
76	7.5YR-8/2 pinkish white	7.5YR-N7 light grey
77	10R-6/6 light red	10R-5/4 weak red

Colour description (continued)

no.	*Colour outside*	*Colour inside*
	BOWLS TYPE 10	
	Phase B. Fig. 50	
39	7.5YR-7/4 pink	7.5YR-7/4 pink
40	5YR-7/4 pink	2.5YR-6/6 light red
41	5YR-6/1 grey	7.5YR-7/2 pinkish grey
42	7.5YR-7/4 pink	7.5YR-6/4 light brown
43	10R-6/4 pale red (dec. 10R-4/1 dark reddish grey)	2.5YR-6/6 light red
44	10YR-7/3 very pale brown (2.5YR-6/6 light red 2.5YR-N3 very dark grey)	5YR-7/4 pink (5YR-6/2 pinkish grey)
45	10YR-7/3 very pale brown (7.5YR-7/4 pink)	2.5YR-6/6 light red
	BOWLS TYPE 11	
	Phase B. Fig. 50	
46	5Y-7/3 pale yellow	2.5Y-7/2 light grey
47	2.5Y-8/2 white	2.5YR-6/6 light red
48	2.5YR-6/6 light red	2.5YR-6/4 light reddish brown
49	2.5YR-6/4 light reddish brown	2.5YR-6/4 light reddish brown
50	5YR-6/6 reddish yellow	5YR-7/6 reddish yellow
51	7.5YR-7/4 pink	5YR-7/4 pink
52	10YR-7/2 light grey	10YR-7/2 light grey
	BOWLS TYPE 12	
	Phase B. Fig. 50	
53	2.5YR-6/6 light red	2.5YR-6/2 pale red
54	10R-6/6 light red	10R-6/6 light red
55	7.5YR-8/4 pink	7.5YR-8/4 pink
56	10YR-8/4 very pale brown	5YR-7/4 pink
57	7.5YR-8/4 pink	2.5YR-6/6 light red
	Phase G. Fig. 64	
78	5YR-8/4 pink	5YR-8/4 pink
79	10YR-8/2 white	10YR-7/2 light grey
80	10YR-8/3 very pale brown	2.5Y-7/2 light grey
	BOWLS TYPE 13	
	Phase B. Fig. 50	
58	10YR-7/2 light grey	10YR-7/2 light grey
59	10YR-7/3 very pale brown	10YR-8/3 very pale brown
60	2.5Y-8/2 white	2.5Y-8/2 white
	BOWLS TYPE 14	
	Phase B. Fig. 50	
61	2.5YR-6/6 light red	2.5YR-6/4 light reddish brown
62	10YR-7/2 light grey	10YR-8/1 white (10YR-5/1 grey)
63	5YR-7/4 pink	5YR-7/4 pink

Colour description (continued)

no.	*Colour outside*	*Colour inside*
	BOWLS TYPE 14 (*Continued*)	
	Phase B. Fig. 50	
64	5YR-7/4 pink (10YR-8/3 very pale brown)	5YR-7/4 pink (10R-4/4 weak red)
65	10YR-8/2 white (7.5YR-N7 light grey)	10YR-7/1 light grey
66	10YR-8/3 very pale brown	10YR-8/3 very pale brown (7.5YR-8/4 pink)
	BOWLS TYPE 15	
	Phase B. Fig. 50	
67	10YR-7/2 light grey	10YR-8/3 very pale brown
68	10YR-7/2 light grey (2.5YR-6/4 light reddish brown)	7.5YR-7/4 pink
69	7.5YR-7/4 pink (2.5YR-6/6 light red)	5YR-7/4 pink
70	2.5Y-8/2 white	2.5Y-8/2 white
	Phase G. Fig. 64	
81	2.5YR-6/6 light red	2.5YR-6/6 light red
	BOWLS TYPE 16	
	Phase B. Fig. 50	
71	7.5YR-7/4 pink	7.5YR-6/4 light brown
72	10YR-8/3 very pale brown	2.5Y-7/2 light grey
73	2.5Y-8/2 white	2.5Y-7/2 light grey
74	7.5YR-7/4 pink (dec. 10R-3/3 dusky red)	7.5YR-8/4 pink
75	2.5YR-6/4 light reddish brown	5YR-8/4 pink
76	10R-5/6 red	10R-5/6 red
77	10YR-7/3 very pale brown	10YR-7/3 very pale brown
	BURNISHED BOWLS	
	Phase B. Fig. 50	
	TYPE 4	
78	2.5YR-4/6 red	7.5YR-6/2 pinkish grey
79	2.5YR-6/6 light red	2.5YR-6/4 light reddish brown
80	10R-5/4 weak red	10R-5/4 weak red
81	7.5R-5/4 weak red (2.5YR-6/6 light red)	2.5YR-6/6 light red
82	5Y-8/1 white (7.5YR-6/2 pinkish grey)	7.5YR-6/2 pinkish grey
83	7.5YR-6/4 light brown	7.5YR-7/4 pink
84	2.5YR-6/6 light red (2.5YR-6/4 light reddish brown)	2.5YR-6/6 light red
	TYPE 5	
85	7.5YR-6/4 light brown	7.5YR-6/4 light brown
86	7.5YR-8/2 pinkish white (10R-5/4 weak red)	5YR-6/1 light grey

Colour description (continued)

no.	*Colour outside*	*Colour inside*
	BURNISHED BOWLS (*Continued*)	
	Phase B. Fig. 50	
	TYPE 7	
87	7.5YR-7/2 pinkish grey	2.5YR-5/6 red (2.5YR-6/4 light reddish brown)
	TYPE 9	
88	2.5YR-6/6 light red	2.5YR-6/6 light red
	TYPE 10	
89	2.5YR-6/6 light red (2.5YR-5/6 red)	2.5YR-3/2 dusky red (2.5YR-N2 black)
90	2.5YR-6/6 light red	2.5YR-6/6 light red
	TYPE 11	
91	10YR-7/2 light grey	2.5Y-N5 grey
	Phase G. Fig. 64	
	TYPE 4	
82	10R-6/6 light red	10R-6/6 light red
83	10R-6/4 pale red	10R-6/2 pale red
84	10R-5/1 reddish grey (10R-5/4 weak red)	10R-5/4 weak red
	TYPE 5	
85	2.5YR-6/6 light red	2.5YR-6/6 light red
86	2.5YR-6/6 light red (2.5YR-5/2 weak red)	2.5YR-6/4 light reddish brown
87	5YR-6/1 light grey	5YR-4/1 dark grey (5YR-6/3 light reddish brown)
88	10R-5/3 weak red (7.5R-N6 grey)	7.5R-N6 grey
89	5YR-8/2 pinkish white	5YR-7/2 pinkish grey
90	5YR-5/3 reddish brown (2.5YR-6/6 light red)	2.5YR-6/6 light red
91	2.5YR-6/6 light red	7.5R-6/6 light red
92	2.5YR-6/4 light reddish brown	10R-6/4 pale red
93	10R-6/4 pale red	10R-6/4 pale red (5YR-7/3 pink)
	TYPE 7	
94	5YR-7/4 pink (2.5YR-6/6 light red)	2.5YR-6/6 light red
	TYPE 8	
95	7.5YR-7/2 pinkish grey	5YR-7/4 pink
96	10R-5/6 red	10R-6/6 light red
	TYPE 9	
97	10YR-8/3 very pale brown	10YR-7/3 very pale brown
98	7.5YR-7/2 pinkish grey (7.5YR-6/4 light brown)	5YR-7/2 pinkish grey

Colour description (continued)

no.	*Colour outside*	*Colour inside*
	BURNISHED BOWLS (*Continued*)	
	Phase G. Fig. 64	
	TYPE 12	
99	5YR-5/4 reddish brown (10R-3/4 dusky red)	5YR-5/4 reddish brown
	TYPE 13	
100	10R-6/3 pale red	2.5YR-6/6 light red
101	2.5YR-6/6 light red	2.5YR-5/6 red
102	10R-6/1 reddish grey (5YR-6/4 light reddish brown)	5YR-7/2 pinkish grey

Large Shallow Bowls

Types 17-18

These bowls were introduced into the village; not one sherd has been found in phases A-D. Although the shape and the clay paste are different from the cooking pots types 1 and 2, the manufacturing process is not very different. It can be assumed that type 17 was introduced by the villagers and that it already existed outside Deir ʿAllā when they came, but type 18 did not then exist in Deir ʿAllā and its production begins later, in phase J. As this type is found on many I.A. sites east of the Jordan, it is uncertain where it was first made. Its beginning may therefore be slightly earlier than the first occurance at Deir ʿAllā. From the statistical evidence it becomes clear that none of the two types can be much earlier than their appearance at Deir ʿAllā, as the burnishing of these bowls was still in an experimental stage.

Type 17

The visual characteristics

The wall is thick. The diameter is often somewhere between 40-60 cms. The ratio height-width is appr. 1-2. There is a ring base, not really in the centre. The rim is as thick as the wall, is short and usually has a groove on the outside as wide as a forefinger. The rim is vertical or slightly flaring. The inside is burnished, occasionally the outside also, and it is rare that there are no traces of burnishing. Two ledge handles are attached to the rim. The outside usually shows two treatments: the upper part is wet smoothed, the lower part scraped, which can only be observed on unburnished types on the outside.

The technical characteristics. cf. fig. 40

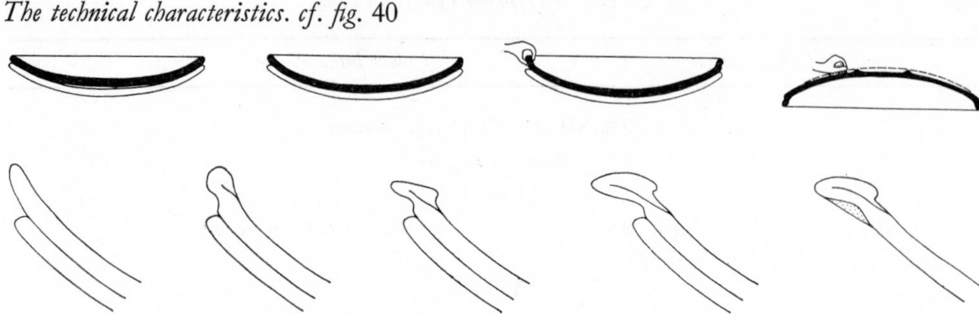

Fig. 40. Bowls types 17 to 18, construction drawing

These bowls were made either in baskets or on mats which were placed in a shallow pit in the ground. On many fragments there are two or three strands of twisted material impressed in the clay at a distance of c. 3 cms., running parallel in concentric circles below the rim on the outside. These must be the impressions of the upper parts of shallow baskets or mats. The clay was worked in a fairly dry state. The base was scraped after the bowl had been taken out of the mould, and from this point usually all the mat impressions apart from deeper ones have been erased. Nearer the base more surplus clay had to be taken away to cut out a ring for the base. This ring was often reshaped after scraping was finished, so that the bowl rim would be more or less horizontal. This correction of the cut ring sometimes involved a partial thinning out of the ring to make it higher or the necessity of pushing it down which made the ring wider at that place.

The rim was made from the thinned out circumference of the circular clay sheet which was pressed into the mould. The rim is always finished with a fold inwards. While pressing the fold inwards, a groove was always made on the outside. The result could be a vertical rim. But the rim could also be flattened, and the clay was then usually pushed outwards—occasionally inwards or to both sides. But it is always a characteristically short and thick rim. It was never pulled up much more than its own thickness.

The handles were added separately as ledge handles and smoothed out against the rim. No examples have been found where the handle was fitted below the rim. The handle appears as a widening of the rim; there were certainly always two handles, opposite each other, and it seems that occasionally there were four handles.

Burnishing of the inside was done while the bowl was still in the mould and followed immediately after the shape was formed, as the clay was already fairly dry when worked and dried quickly. The water oozed down to the outside of the base which could still be scraped after the bowl was already dry enough on the inside to tap out and turn upside down. Often one can see a difference in wetness on bowls that were burnished on both sides, the outside responding better than the inside. It is very interesting to see that in the early phases burnishing was still in an experimental stage, cf. chart fig. 41. At least this must mean that burnishing of this type had only just started, and probably the type was indeed a new feature of the potters' repertoire in the region of Deir 'Allā. The statistical evidence shows that in phase E out of 14 examples 4 were burnished only on the inside, 4 on the outside only, 1 on both sides and 5 were not burnished. In phase G all examples are burnished, 15 on the inside only, 2 on the outside only and 13 on both. In phase J 25 were burnished on the inside only, 2 on the inside and outside, and none on the outside; 1 example is unburnished. Phase K has (types 17-18 together) 64 examples of which 6 are not burnished (all of type 17) and burnishing is exclusively done on the inside. Phase L has only burnishing on the inside. Burnishing on the outside was therefore soon abandoned, which saved much time, as burnishing inside could be done while the bowl was still in the mould.

In the statistics type 17 rims have been divided according to bowl rim types 5-8 (rim treatment). Only 1 example resembles type 15. It shows that in the early stages (phases E-H) the rim was often left without further profiling, (type 5), but later they were as a rule profiled by being pressed down either inwards, or both inwards and outwards, or just outwards.

Phase	*Type 17*					*Burnished*				*Type 18*
	5	6	7	8	15	a	b	c	d	
E	11	3				4	4	1	5	
F	8	4	1	2		0	1	7	5	
G	17	2	5	8		15	2	13	2	
H	9	6	8	11	1	17	4	6	9	
J	3	9	9	4		25	0	2	1	3
K	2	15	15	13		64	0	0	6	24
L	1	6	8	2		39	0	0	1	30
Total	51	45	46	41		164	11	29	29	57

Fig. 41. Bowls types 17 to 18, statistical chart
(a = burn. inside, b = burn. outside, c = burn. inside and outside, d = unburn.)

Type 18

The manufacturing process was the same as type 17. The difference is that this type developed a very wide rim. There is really no gradual transition from type 17 (notably with the rim pushed to the outside, type 8) to type 18, and 17 and 18 could always very easily be separated from each other. It is characteristic that there is a clear, more or less vertical inside edge to the rim. The rim is not really horizontal, as there was a fair amount of shrinkage in this massive rim. It was moreover so heavy that it often had to be supported underneath, and this was done by adding a clay coil in the groove outside, which was smeared out between rim and body. The marks of a knife blade or a similar instrument are then clearly visible. These bowls are only burnished on the inside as they appear when inside burnishing was already the only practice (phases J-K). A typology of these rims has not yet been attempted as they only occur in a stratified context in the last three phases, which is too short a period to make a typology reliable. In Ch. 8 the range of shapes in phases K and L have been shown. It can be assumed that as a rule there were two handles; probably sometimes four. The construction of these bowls has been studied from all the stratified material and a great mass of surface finds and other unstratified examples.

In phase K are 40 type 17 bowls against 24 type 18.

In phase L are 17 type 17 bowls against 30 type 18.

Type 18 is called the "mensif" bowl, by association with the name of the rice and mutton meal which the Arab host offers his guests at a feast.

The size of these bowls amply justifies the name.

Colour description

no.	*Colour outside*	*Colour inside*
	BOWLS TYPE 17	
	Phase G. Fig. 64	
103	2.5YR-6/4 light reddish brown (10R-5/4 weak red)	10R-6/4 pale red (10R-5/4 weak red)
104	7.5YR-6/4 light brown	7.5YR-7/2 pinkish grey
105	2.5YR-6/6 light red	2.5YR-5/4 reddish brown
106	10R-5/1 reddish grey	5YR-6/3 light reddish brown
107	2.5YR-6/6 light red	2.5YR-5/4 reddish brown
108	10YR-7/3 very pale brown	7.5YR-8/2 pinkish white
109	5YR-7/1 light grey	7.5YR-7/2 pinkish grey
110	2.5YR-6/4 light reddish brown	5YR-8/2 pinkish white
	Fig. 65.	
1	10YR-8/2 white (5YR-7/3 pink)	5YR-6/4 light reddish brown (5YR-5/2 reddish grey)
2	5YR-6/1 light grey	5YR-7/4 pink
	KRATERS	
	Phase B. Fig. 51	
48	5YR-7/4 pink	5YR-6/4 light reddish brown
49	2.5YR-6/6 light red	2.5YR-6/4 light reddish brown
50	10YR-7/2 light grey	7.5YR-7/4 pink
51	10YR-7/2 light grey (7.5YR-N3 very dark grey)	7.5YR-6/4 light brown
	Phase G. Fig. 65	
47	2.5YR-6/2 pale red	10R-6/4 pale red
48	10R-4/3 weak red	10R-4/4 weak red
49	10YR-8/3 very pale brown	5YR-7/3 pink
50	10R-5/4 weak red	10R-6/6 light red
51	10R-6/3 pale red	2.5YR-6/6 light red
52	5YR-6/1 grey (2.5Y-8/2 white)	2.5Y-N7 light grey
53	10R-5/6 red	10R-5/4 weak red

Jars

Storage jars, type 1

Very few complete sections of jars were found in the excavated area. This study of the typology of jars is based mainly on the bases, large body fragments and handles, shoulders, necks and especially on rim fragments.

The visual characteristics

For the shape of the storage jars, see below (technical characteristics). The rim is so wide that a hand can be inserted. Often with the early types the neck and rim are not horizontally circular but more or less square. The second number in the chart, fig. 43, gives the number of square necks for each variant and phase. The top of the rim is thickened (with the exception of var. b), and there is a horizontal groove just below the rim inside. As a rule there is a ridge outside below the top of the rim, matching the groove on the inside. Usually the height of neck and rim is the same as the length of a person's fingers. The shoulder is wide, slightly convex and the beginning is often marked by a marked angle between body and shoulder. The top of the handles is always attached at that point. The base is not pointed, but on the early types is often finished on the outside by a slight flattening. Just above the base there is as a rule a thickened spot in the wall, not visible from the outside. Sometimes one finds clear marks of fingers smearing clay inside the base. There are no real turning marks in the early types but there are regular marks of smoothing the inside with fingers or cloth and the outside is always smoothed with some soft material. The pot breaks into right-angular pieces, horizontally and vertically. The inside is darker than the outside, especially near the base. The temper is mainly course lime with an increasing amount of coarse sand in the later types.

The technical characteristics. Cf. fig. 42.

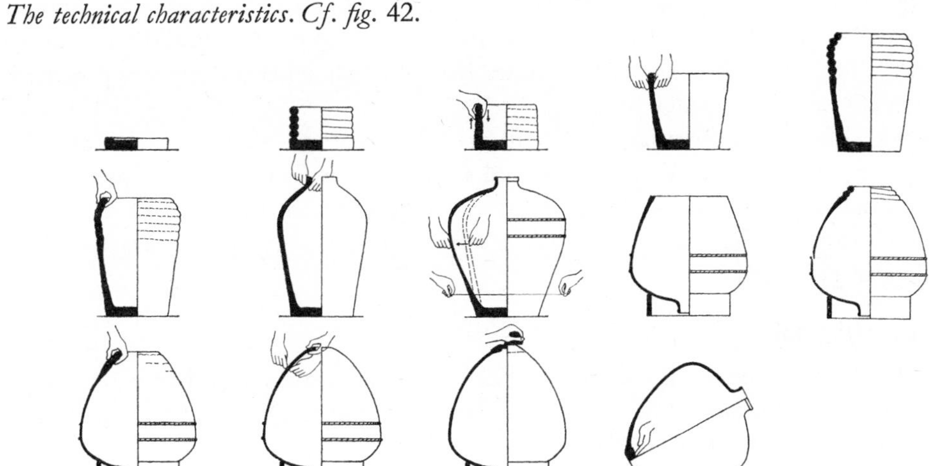

Fig. 42. Jars type 1, construction drawing

Fig. 42 shows the process of manufacturing the large jars. The number of coils shown in the drawings is exaggerated, or applies for the very large jars only. The very large jars were probably not cut from the clay base. The average number of coils may have been 6-8 while the pot was built up on the clay base, and 1-2 more at the base after the pot had been cut loose from the original clay lump. From the material available it seems that in the early stages the pot was cut rather close to the present base. A logical development was that the upper part was made first and the lower half added afterwards. Some later fragments show that the join was nearer the middle of the pot. The two cords shown in the drawing served to keep the shape of the upper part after the coils had been thinned out and while the lower part was made. One can often find slight impressions of one or two strands of twisted material near the widest circumference of the pot. The same was done with wide and deep bowls and some kraters. During the phases A-L the influence of better turning, notably in the bases, but also in the neck and rim can be observed. The development from a slab closed base to a base closed by turning has been discussed already. Base type 2 b shows that at one stage the jar consisted of two identical halves: the body had two openings, one near the neck and one near the base. It is obvious that the pot has to be turned upside down to finish either the upper or lower part. The reason why the base was not finished first was, that if the rim was first made the pot could be put upside down on a cone-shaped lump of clay and then turned. In the construction drawing it is shown resting on the shoulder, which is less likely. As a result of this treatment, however, the shape of the neck and of the lower part of the body show some resemblance, and the only difference is that the pot was intentionally made wider near the neck than in the lower part of the body. This shape was largely influenced by where the potter cut his pot and started to make the second part. As long as this large jar was not properly thrown, the base tended to be broad and rounded. The "pointed" base results from the large amount of surplus clay from the slabs added to close the base, or from a "sleeve" which could be made into either a neck or a base. The next step (base 2c) was to close the base without adding a turned up "neck", but the result was a more rounded base. Once quicker turning was practised, the base became more pointed again.

It is very likely that these jars were still made in the same way in the 8th and 7th cent. B.C. in some parts of Palestine, as well as thrown jars. Clearly this type, and the cooking pots, were the last to be properly thrown, and in many parts of the world where the throwing of smaller vessels is the normal procedure, large jars are still made by coiling in two parts.

The variants (fig. 43)

Type 1 var. a - l all have a rim which is folded twice, first inwards and then outwards. The groove inside the rim is the result of the first fold, but in type 1 b this fold is rudimentary. The rims all belong to the larger jars.

Var. a. This is an early type, usually painted with horizontal bands. The surface treatment is in horizontal and vertical smears. The texture of the clay is rather fine and the colour is a light yellow with reddish patches. The rim is distinctly different from the types c - l. The second fold of the rim of var. a is pushed down and either almost reaches the ridge on the outside or covers it. Var. a is related to var. b and together they could be called a type. Var. b has a much longer life according to the statistical evidence. Var. a is practically exclusively a "nomadic" type.

Var. b is common in phases A - D but does also occur later.

Here the shape of the rim top is triangular, and the ridge on the outside is pushed back, so that the groove on the inside has disappeared too. The texture of this type often resembles that of var. 1a, and sometimes the jar is also decorated in the same way. In phase A its frequency is 1 out of 2, in phase B 6 out of 14, but in phase C it sinks to 1 out of 12, and after that its occurrence is negligible.

Var. c - 1 form one group, type 1c - g being the earlier variants and type 1 h - l the successors.

Type 1 c - g are variants that occur together and are distinguished only by a different finish for the top of the rim.

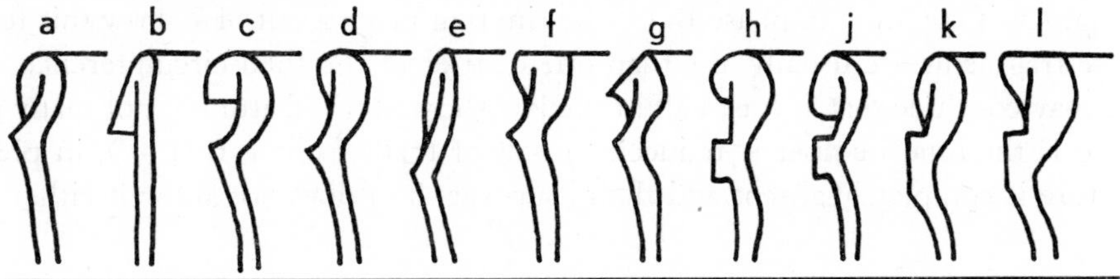

a b c d e f g h j k l

Phase	*Variants Jars type 1*											
	a	*b*	*c*	*d*	*e*	*f*	*g*	*h*	*j*	*k*	*l*	*total*
A	15	53,15	0	8, 2	25, 7	0,	1,	0	0	0	0	102
B	23,1	185,32	40,6	72,22	79,25	10,4	15,	0	0	0	0	424
C	9,	17, 2	11,6	104,25	36,18	10,5	13,6	0	0	0	0	200
D	3,1	3,	4,	39,	9,	5,	3,	0	0	0	0	66
E	2,	9,	13,	66, 6	10, 4	5,1	15,4	0	0	0	0	120
F	0,	5, 1	2,	24, 4	2, 2	1,	9,1	0	0	1	2	46
G	0,	2, 2	28,	96, 3	11,	9,	15,1	0	0	9	2	172
H	0,	1,	11,	42,	2,	5,	4,	4,	0	32	11	112
J	0,	3,	1,	3,	0,	0,	1,	11	3	36	20	78
K	0,	2,	0,	21,[1]	0,	5,[1]	8,	18,	19	59	24	156
L	0,	0,	0,	9,[1]	0,	0,	0,	17,	18	21	17	82
total	52	280	110	484	174	50	84	50	40	158	76	1558
total A-E	52	267	68	289	159	30	47	0	0	0	0	912
F-L	0	13	42	195	15	20	37	50	40	158	76	646

[1]) these shapes are clearly influenced by the new group h - l and can be classed with it.

Fig. 43. Jars type 1, statistical chart
First column: total; second column: "square" rim.

They all have the ridge below the rim. In var. c the top of the rim is folded double after the first fold was made. This is usually a clearly profiled rim. In var. d the second fold is more rounded and smoothed out, either by being pushed up or widened at the top. This is easily the most common variant of this group. Var. e has the rim that has almost lost its features, a regular aspect with all the types of pottery. It is interesting to see that out of 902 examples of var. c - g a total of 174 show this treatment or lack of treatment; it is 1 in 5. Var. f and g are finished by making the top of the rim of var. d flat and horizontal (var. f), or flat and oblique (var. g). The totals of var. f and g do not justify the conclusion of preference of one over the other, and hardly the preference of this treatment over var. c.

The group var. c - g exists beside var. a - b in phase A, occurs with equal frequency in phase B and dominates over var. a - b in phase C by 7 - 1, when it can be said to be the normal type. The change over to var. h - l comes with phase H where var. c - g form only a small majority and in phase J they have practically disappeared.

The square shape of the neck and rim (cf. the second number in the columns of the chart, fig. 43) is common in phase B. Of the rim fragments 2 out of 7 show this feature. As these fragments are usually less than one quarter of the total circumference of the rim we may conclude that at least half of the jars showed this feature, if not many more. In phase E the total number is reduced to half of that of phase B (1 - 7), in phase H this feature is completely absent and the group var. h - l does not show it either.

Analysis of tempering material in thin section

Jars type 1

D 338/28: 1 quartz grains $\frac{1}{4}$-$\frac{3}{4}$ mm.
id c. 0.02 mm. (from the clay?)
2 lime grains $\frac{1}{4}$-$\frac{3}{4}$ mm.
3 haematite 1 mm.
4 flint flakes 1 mm.

Colour description

no.	*Colour outside*	*Colour inside*
	JARS TYPE 1	
	Phase B. Fig. 50	
	TYPE 1a	
92	10R-6/3 pale red (dec: 10R-3/3 dusky red)	5YR-4/1 dark grey
93	2.5Y-8/2 white	10R-6/6 light red
94	5Y-7/2 light grey (10R-6/3 pale red dec: 7.5R-3/2 dusky red)	10R-5/6 red

Colour description (continued)

no.	Colour outside	Colour inside
	JARS TYPE 1 *(continued)*	
	Phase B. Fig. 50	
	TYPE 1a	
95	5YR-7/4 pink (dec: 5YR-5/1 grey 7.5R-3/4 dusky red)	5YR-8/4 pink
	TYPE 1b	
96	2.5Y-7/2 light grey	2.5Y-7/2 light grey
97	2.5Y-7/2 light grey	10YR-7/2 light grey
98	10YR-7/1 light grey (2.5Y-N6 grey)	2.5Y-N4 dark grey (2.5YR-5/6 red)
99	10YR-8/3 very pale brown	7.5YR-7/2 pinkish grey
100	7.5YR-8/2 pinkish white	10R-5/6 red (7.5YR-8/4 pink)
101	5Y-8/2 white	5YR-7/3 pink
102	7.5YR-6/2 pinkish grey (7.5YR-N3 very dark grey)	7.5YR-7/2 pinkish grey
103	7.5YR-6/4 light brown	7.5YR-6/4 light brown
104	5Y-8/2 white	7.5R-6/4 pale red
105	10YR-8/2 white	7.5YR-7/4 pink
	TYPE 1c	
106	5Y-8/2 white	10YR-5/1 grey
107	5YR-7/4 pink	10R-5/4 weak red
108	5Y-8/2 white	5YR-6/2 pinkish grey
109	10YR-7/1 light grey (10YR-5/1 grey)	7.5YR-6/4 light brown
	Fig. 51.	
1	7.5YR-8/2 pinkish white	2.5YR-5/2 weak red
	TYPE 1d	
2	10YR-7/2 light grey	10R-5/6 red
3	2.5YR-6/4 light reddish brown	10R-6/3 pale red
4	5YR-7/4 pink (2.5Y-7/2 light grey)	2.5YR-6/6 light red
5	5YR-7/4 pink	2.5YR-6/6 light red
6	2.5Y-8/2 white	10R-4/2 weak red
	TYPE 1e	
7	10YR-7/2 light grey	10YR-7/2 light grey
8	2.5Y-7/2 light grey	10YR-8/3 very pale brown
9	5YR-6/4 light reddish brown	5YR-6/4 light reddish brown
10	7.5YR-8/4 pink	7.5YR-7/2 pinkish grey
11	2.5YR-6/6 light red	2.5YR-6/6 light red
12	10YR-8/3 very pale brown	7.5YR-5/2 brown
	TYPE 1f	
13	10R-6/4 pale red	10R-5/4 weak red
14	2.5Y-8/2 white	10R-6/1 reddish grey

Colour description (continued)

no.	*Colour outside*	*Colour inside*
	JARS TYPE 1 *(continued)*	
	Phase B. Fig. 50	
	TYPE 1g	
15	2.5YR-6/4 light reddish brown	2.5YR-6/6 light red
16	2.5Y-8/2 white	10YR-6/2 light brownish grey
17	7.5YR-7/2 pinkish grey	10R-6/6 light red
	TYPE 1h	
18	5Y-7/2 light grey	5YR-7/4 pink
	Phase G. Fig. 65	
	TYPE 1b	
3	5YR-7/3 pink (10YR-8/3 very pale brown)	2.5YR-6/6 light red
	TYPE 1c	
4	10YR-8/2 white	5YR-5/1 grey
5	7.5YR-6/4 light brown	2.5YR-6/6 light red
6	10YR-7/3 very pale brown	5YR-5/3 reddish brown
7	2.5Y-8/2 white	10YR-6/1 grey
18	10YR-8/3 very pale brown	5YR-7/3 pink
	TYPE 1d	
8	5YR-7/1 light grey	5YR-7/1 light grey
9	5YR-7/4 pink (10YR-8/3 very pale brown)	5YR-5/3 reddish brown
10	10YR-8/3 very pale brown	2.5Y-8/2 white
11	5YR-7/2 pinkish grey	5YR-6/4 light reddish brown
12	7.5YR-7/2 pinkish grey	7.5YR-7/2 pinkish grey
13	7.5YR-6/2 pinkish grey (5YR-6/4 light reddish brown)	2.5YR-5/6 red
	TYPE 1e	
14	10YR-7/2 light grey	5Y-7/2 light grey
15	10YR-7/2 light grey	7.5YR-6/4 light brown
	TYPE 1f	
16	5YR-7/3 pink	7.5YR-7/4 pink
17	7.5YR-N4 dark grey	7.5YR-N4 dark grey
	TYPE 1g	
19	7.5YR-8/2 pinkish white	5YR-6/4 light reddish brown
20	2.5Y-7/2 light grey	2.5Y-N4 dark grey
21	2.5Y-7/2 light grey (10R-5/4 weak red)	10R-5/6 red
	TYPE 1k	
22	5YR-6/3 light reddish brown	5YR-6/4 light reddish brown
23	5YR-7/2 pinkish grey	5YR-6/2 pinkish grey
24	5YR-6/1 grey	5YR-6/1 grey
25	5YR-6/4 light reddish brown	5YR-6/3 light reddish brown

Colour description (continued)

no.	Colour outside	Colour inside
	JARS TYPE 1 *(continued)*	
	Phase G. Fig. 65	
	TYPE 11	
26	10YR-7/1 light grey	5YR-5/1 grey
27	7.5R-6/4 pale red	10R-6/4 pale red

Jars 1

Comparisons

The rim which is square in horizontal section is not found in Palestine. Type 1a is occasionally found (cf. Meg. Tombs Pl. 72,1). It is doubtful whether 1b is found in Palestine. 1 d - g are common at Afula, Str. III B and A. Cf. op. cit. fig. 11, 11 - 15 (1f), 18 - 22; fig. 16,10 - 13. Megiddo, Jar 141, Vol. II, Pl. 82, (Str. VI); Jar 135, Pl. 73,6 (Str. VI B), 76,4 (Str. VI).

Type 1 h - l does not seem to have been found anywhere as early as at Deir ʿAllā.

Smaller jars, type 2

The excavation did not provide anything like enough material to build up a type series of complete shapes. This statistical study is based on rim shapes.

Characteristic of this group is a fairly tall neck, a small rim, a handle attached to the rim or below the rim onto the neck, and probably an egg-shaped body and a ring base.

Technically these jars were made in much the same way as the larger jars, by coiling. It is probable that the jars were turned up from the clay base and cut loose through the clay lump underneath and then remodelled and a ring added.

The rim shapes can be divided into 5 different groups. Technically, a feature they have in common is that there is only one fold inwards.

Var. a. This is probably a pot with a different origin than the others, as on the whole it responded differently to firing. This may be due to a different clay composition. Usually they are fired red through the entire core, which the others are not. The rim is twice as high as it is thick in section. Out of a total of 153 rim fragments, 9 had a handle attached to the rim. If it is taken into account that the sherds found usually represent not more than one fifth of the total circumference of the rim, the conclusion must be that a handle is not a common feature of these jars; at least not a handle which was attached to the rim. After phase H the type hardly occurs any more. No pinching to make a spout was noticed. There was one decorated example. Only 8 fragments show the square rim shape (cf. jars type 1). This was certainly not common.

Var. b. This is a small rim, triangular in section. The handle is attached to the rim.

40 examples out of a total of 123 fragments had a handle, which means that a handle attached to the rim was a regular feature. No decorated rims were found. 1 fragment was pinched to form a spout.

This variant occurs fairly regularly throughout all the phases and does not show signs of diminishing in the later phases.

Var. c. is a rim with double profile, but it almost certainly has only one fold to the inside. Out of 141 frags. only 5 had a handle attached to the rim, 8 showed a square rim and 4 had a pinched spout, showing that none of these features were characteristic for this variant. This jar occurs fairly constantly through all the phases like var. b.

Var. d. This is a long vertical rim, often flat or slightly rounded at the top, sometimes slightly flaring. Some fragments with a handle show that the handle was attached to the middle of the neck and not to the rim. This type of rim was not rare in the early phases but it becomes the dominant type from phase G on. In phase H it is already more frequent than the other three variants together and this increases in later phases.

Var. e. This is a wide flaring rim, probably a modification of var. d. It was not found in phases A - D, but it is not a frequent type and it may already occur there occasionally.

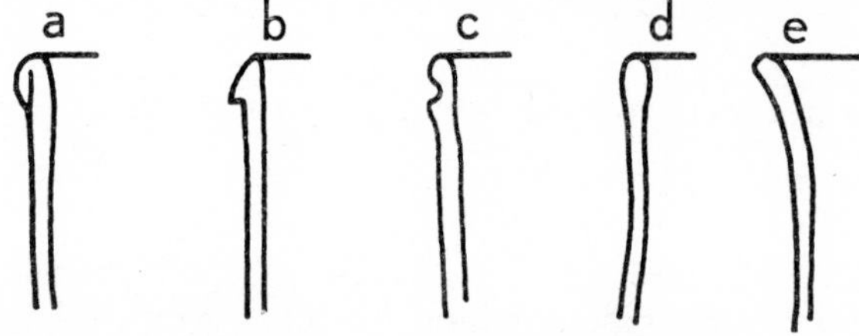

Phase	*a*			*b*			*c*			*d*			*e*	*f*	*total*
A	12	5		3		1	5			2			0	2	24
B	35	0		56	0	23	35	5		16			0	4	146
C	39	2		10	1	1	20	1		13			0	4	86
D	17	5		5	0		5	2		9			0	0	36
E	30		4	9		1	26			20			2	3	90
F	11		5	0			15		1	16			3	0	45
G	11	1		24	2	12	15	1	2	41	0	3	0	24	115
H	7			3			12			26			7	2	57
J	1			4		2	9			27			9	2	52
K	0			5			15		2	36		1	0	0	56
L	2			7			8			28			8	0	53
Total	165			126			165			234			29	41	760

Fig. 44. Jars type 2, statistical chart. A. B, C, and D: first column: total; second column: "square" rim; third column: handle. Column f: Fragments too small for further identification

Analysis of tempering material in thin section

Jars type 2 b

D 405/18: 1 quartz grains ¼-1 mm.
id flakes 0.03 mm (from the clay?)
2 lime grains ¼-1¼ mm.
3 haematite flakes ¼-1¾ mm.
4 flint flakes 0.4 mm.

D 331/38: 1 quartz grains ¼-1 mm. (and 0.03 mm.)
2 lime grains ¼-1 mm.
3 haematite flakes ¼-1½ mm.
4 flint flakes 0.6 mm.

Colour description

no.	*Colour outside*	*Colour inside*
	JARS TYPE 2	
	Phase B. Fig. 51	
	TYPE 2a	
19	10YR-7/2 light grey	10YR-6/1 grey
20	7.5YR-7/4 pink	7.5YR-7/4 pink
21	2.5Y-7/2 light grey	10YR-6/3 pale brown
23	7.5YR-7/4 pink	7.5YR-7/4 pink
24	10YR-6/2 light brownish grey	10YR-6/2 light brownish grey
25	10YR-7/2 light grey	5YR-5/2 reddish grey
	TYPE 2b	
26	2.5YR-6/6 light red (10YR-7/3 very pale brown)	2.5YR-6/6 light red
27	10YR-7/3 very pale brown	7.5YR-6/4 light brown
28	10YR-7/3 very pale brown	7.5YR-7/2 pinkish grey
29	10YR-7/2 light grey	10YR-7/3 very pale brown (7.5YR-7/4 pink)
30	2.5Y-8/2 white	2.5Y-8/2 white
31	2.5YR-6/6 light red	2.5YR-6/6 light red
32	10YR-7/3 very pale brown	2.5Y-7/2 light grey
	TYPE 2c	
33	10YR-8/3 very pale brown	5YR-7/4 pink
34	10YR-8/3 very pale brown	10R-5/4 weak red
35	10YR-7/2 light grey	10YR-6/1 grey
36	7.5YR-7/4 pink	7.5YR-7/4 pink
37	10YR-8/3 very pale brown	10YR-7/3 very pale brown
38	10YR-8/4 very pale brown	10YR-8/4 very pale brown (10R-6/6 light red)
	TYPE 2d	
39	2.5Y-8/2 white	10YR-7/3 very pale brown
40	10YR-7/2 light grey	7.5YR-6/2 pinkish grey

Colour description (continued)

no.	*Colour outside*	*Colour inside*
	Phase B. Fig. 51 (continued)	
	TYPE 2d	
41	10YR-8/2 white	10YR-7/2 light grey
42	2.5Y-7/2 light grey	10YR-7/3 very pale brown (7.5YR-6/4 light brown)
43	7.5YR-6/2 pinkish grey	5YR-6/4 light reddish brown
44	10YR-8/3 very pale brown	7.5YR-7/4 pink
45	5YR-6/4 light reddish brown	5YR-6/4 light reddish brown
46	2.5YR-6/6 light red	2.5YR-6/4 light reddish brown
47	10R-5/4 weak red	10R-5/4 weak red
	Phase G. Fig. 65	
	TYPE 2a	
28	10R-6/4 pale red	5YR-7/4 pink
29	10R-6/3 pale red	10R-5/4 weak red
30	10YR-7/2 light grey	5YR-7/3 pink
31	2.5Y-7/2 light grey	5YR-6/1 grey
	TYPE 2c	
32	7.5YR-8/4 pink	5YR-6/4 light reddish brown
33	5YR-6/3 light reddish brown	5YR-6/2 pinkish grey
34	5YR-6/1 grey	5YR-5/1 grey
35	7.5YR-8/7 pink	7.5YR-7/2 pinkish grey
	TYPE 2d	
36	2.5Y-7/2 light grey	2.5Y-7/2 light grey (5YR-4/1 dark grey)
37	10YR-8/3 very pale brown	10YR-5/1 grey
38	10YR-8/3 very pale brown	10YR-7/2 light grey (5YR-7/3 pink)
39	5YR-7/2 pinkish grey	5YR-7/4 pink
40	7.5YR-7/2 pinkish grey	7.5YR-6/2 pinkish grey
41	2.5Y-7/2 light grey (10R-6/4 pale red)	10R-6/4 pale red (2.5Y-7/2 light grey)

Handles

The shape of the handle and its construction are an important indication of the potter's understanding of the practical properties of the clays he is working with. The Deir ʿAllā repertoire supplies clear evidence of this.

In the Deir ʿAllā repertoire there are two different ways of making lug handles to the jars.

1. The handle is partly made before, and partly during the fitting on to the pot. A fairly wet clay is used, made into a roll and the flat top of the roll is fitted on by being pressed vertically against the wall of the pot, near where the shoulder begins. The roll is then stretched and bent down by pulling it between forefinger and thumb of the right

hand and the end which is now thinner than the upper part is pressed sideways against the wall of the pot, not vertically. The upper part of the handle is fitted at right angles to the pot, the lower part at an angle of roughly 30°. This means that the horizontal part of the handle is short, the vertical part long and in as far as this handle shrinks, it pulls at the long side. As a rule these handles have an extra roll of clay added between wall and handle at the lower part of the handle to give an enlarged area of contact between handle and pot. Quite often handles came off there during firing but were kept in place by this added roll of clay; therefore thus the upper part of the handle breaks with a fragment of the wall attached, the lower part comes away from the wall. The lower part is always smoothed out against the wall with a tool. While shrinking the handle becomes more bow shaped, making the distance between handle and wall smaller. The shape is elegant but less useful than that of type 2. These handles are fitted when the pot is leather-hard. They occur on jars type 1 in the phases A - H.

2. The handle is made from a small sheet of clay which is folded or rolled lengthwise. These handles contain sand as temper, are worked dry and they cannot be pulled or stretched while being fitted onto the pot. They receive their shape before being fitted. Both ends are fitted vertically (at right angles) to the wall. These handles do not shrink. They always break with a part of the wall attached to them. They offer much more room for the hand than the other type and are firmer. This type begins in phase F and is common from phase J onward. From phase K on one often finds that fitting the handle onto the pot was done with support of the fingers on the inside of the wall. This is in agreement with the overall picture of greater skill with wetter pots being worked on and with quicker turning. Clearly these pots were not leather-hard when the handle was fitted on. These handles were technically better than the earlier type.

"Thumb impressions" are mainly found on handles from phases A - H. From phase F onward two wide incised parallel lines running vertically over the upper part of the handle are often found. These lines were made while the clay was not yet leather-hard.

As special attention was paid only to handles during the last two seasons no reliable statistical evidence about them apart from the general remarks made above can be given. Some further observations follow here. A handle which is fitted onto the pot with its side instead of with its end loses much of its "grip space", unless the ends are bent towards each other in a circle. Unless plastic clays are used (throwing) the potter will be inclined to fit his handle at right angles to the pot, and shape the handle in such a way that there is no unequal stress by shrinkage at the ends. In general this can be seen on handles from the M.B.A. onward. The potter would at all costs avoid fitting his handle onto those parts of the pot that were most influenced by shrinkage. On the whole, therefore, handles were fitted with both ends onto the shoulder or onto the body but not from the middle of the shoulder to somewhere on the wall below the shoulder. The handles on jars type 2, the smaller jars with long necks, are fitted with the ends vertically against the jar. In the early phases (A - G) the handle is fitted onto the rim (a profiled rim gives a better grip) and the lower end onto the shoulder. This is practical, as it gives a wide "grip space", and it is also technically sound. The shape of the handle and that of shoulder-neck are such that if there is any shrinkage, it will be equal in both parts: the angle between shoulder and neck and the angle or bend in the upper part of the handle will both tend to become less sharp. Often the handle shrinks and contracts slightly more than the neck-shoulder combination, resulting in the handle's being slightly pushed up above the rim. In the same way, handles on kraters are fitted onto the rim or onto a ridge just below the rim and the lower end onto the link between shoulder and body where the pot is as wide or wider than the rim. In contrast one could compare the handles on large M.B. storage jars. Here the upper part is fitted on at right angles, the lower part is fitted on sideways. But the area of contact between wall and handle is twice as large at the lower part than it is at the upper part.

Handles are therefore very much a test case for the potter's skill and understanding of practical possibilities. It is very interesting to see that in the Chalcolithic age, which was very much an experimental stage of pottery making, far more than the subsequent periods, potters did not much experiment with the position of the handles. Handles were the least successful part of their explorations; they often came loose from the wall. Therefore they made them as small as possible or turned to ledge handles.

Further information about the handles is found in Ch. 5.

Painted Decoration on Pottery

Comparatively little decorated pottery was found in the Early Iron Age levels. Many small and some large fragments of a Philistine pottery type and decoration were found in phases A - D. Analysis of paints, paste and temper material would be required to see if this is a foreign element in the Deir ʿAllā repertoire. The possibility of Philistine or Peoples-of-the-Sea contacts will be dealt with in a later volume (see below).

Every decorated sherd was preserved, but more material is needed before an attempt can be made to classify the material. The main problem in this kind of study is that these stereotyped decorations stem from a long tradition, and cannot properly be explained unless the origins of the tradition are known. This applies to factors like the use of one or two colours in relation to the type of motif, the original surface treatment before the paint was applied, the kind of brush used and the type of paints. These factors are important. If one has a pottery group representing only the middle period of that tradition or the tail end of it, one may find that the method of painting does not match the surface treatment, but one cannot say that this was so originally. Also the decorative patterns may have been kept whereas the shape of the pottery changed. At the best, therefore, only some observations from the material which is available can be made.

A natural approach to this traditional kind of decoration seems to be to try and see it first from the painter-potter's point of view. Usually those parts of the pot are decorated that make painting on a turning pot not too difficult: shoulder, neck, rim, the base (pilgrim flasks) or the inside of the base (bowls). This painted area can be uninterrupted and complete in itself or interrupted by handles or a spout. This gives two possibilities: a continuous line decoration or decoration in panels or fields. If in the course of time a type changes, the potters may continue to use the old decorative pattern and try, for instance, to paint a circular band through the handles.

Similarly the painted * sign on some handles may well find its origin in the palm-tree motif normally painted on the shoulder in panels. This sign is only found on broad handles and not on the round ones, where it is too difficult to be painted quickly.

A continuous set of concentric circles is found on pots without handles. Handles break the set up into two groups of concentric circles, one above and one below the handles.

The surface treatment of pottery which is to be painted is important, and where a tradition of painting arises, the potters must prepare the surface carefully. A dry scraped surface gives a good painting surface, provided the temper is not too coarse. A wet and hand smoothed surface is too uneven for a brush to make a good painting surface. Where quicker turning or throwing is practised painting tends to disappear, or to be done on a fine grained slib surface. Any change in paste composition and surface treatment influences the result of painting. Where sand is introduced as temper material to replace a lime grit, the painted line will get a different quality. A hand smoothed surface will cause the brush to jump over small depressions in the wall by which the band is broken, but too much paint will be squeezed out of the brush where the surface rises, causing the paint to drip. An uneven surface may cause the painter to make his paint thinner in which case the paint is darker on the lower side of the horizontal band than on the upper side. This is an indication that the pot was standing upright or upside down while being painted. All these things can be observed on the material from Deir ʿAllā and point to the fact that a fixed tradition of painting was applied to a changing manufacturing system. It is not so surprising that by the end less pottery was painted than in the earlier phases.

After phase E it seems that the potters tried to improve on their fairly poor results. A darker colour appears and the line becomes stronger than before, which may indicate the use of a brush that was better adapted to the surface of the pots. One can distinguish between mechanical painting (the pot is turned round and the brush does not move) and free decoration. Free decoration seems to stop fairly soon after the end of the L.B.A. or survives only in combination with mechanical painting, such as filling a field between horizontal bands with a criss-cross pattern. This pattern and the horizontal zigzag line both become almost mechanical in so far that in one direction the line is oblique and in the other direction almost vertical: the potter keeps his pot turning. But the turning movement was slow as the horizontal bands show. One or more handles break the painted area into panels and these may have a continuous upper and lower border of horizontal lines, which make the height of the decorated part bigger than the height of the handles. The panels are filled by free decoration and can have vertical border lines or be subdivided by vertical lines. But the panels can also be completely filled with a continuous row of "border lines", vertical straight and wavy lines alternating.

There are horizontal lines the width of the brush (piping), and wider bands made by several strokes of the brush. Real "piping" requires a carefully prepared surface. Compare for instance the surface treatment and painted bands on the imported Mycenaean and Early Iron Age Cypriote wares with the indigenous Palestinian painting of the 12th century B.C. The conclusion is simply that the Deir ʿAllā potters had no idea how to do it properly, nor was this even a problem to them.

An interesting question is whether the original colours have changed in the soil and lost some brightness or not. Using two colours died out very soon. In phase E a few last examples were found of this tradition and these are probably survivals from phase D. It stops definitely after phase E. Piping and wider bands occur through all phases, as do dry-scraped and wet-smoothed surfaces, and groups of circular bands. A continuous set of bands was not found after phase F. Spirals are difficult to trace from small fragments, and could only be demonstrated with certainty in phases E and G. The "Philistinian" semicircles in groups were only found in phases A - D.

From the decorated pottery, published in Ch. 8 it is clear that not much thought was given to the idea of decoration.

From these observations we may conclude that the potters were losing their feeling for decoration, and while changing their methods of manufacturing pottery did not attempt to find an answer to the problems which the changing surface-treatment and clay composition posed to painting. They were also no longer aware of the relation of pot shape and decoration, as it is found in the L.B.A.

No attempt has been made to classify the patterns, for which earlier material should also be studied. But from what has been observed it is clear that these aspects are sufficiently important to be studied when there is a good deal more material available. In Ch. 8 there is a short survey of types of decorations from each phase.

CHAPTER EIGHT

THE POTTERY ACCORDING TO THE PHASES

The following plates are an illustration of the Deir ʿAllā ceramic tradition and how this tradition developed through eleven phases. They form a catalogue of the pottery found during excavation and can be used for dating purposes just as the published material from other excavations is always used. They are, however, primarily an illustration of the type description given in Ch. 7.

As the types have been described extensively, there is no need to describe each individual sherd as is usually done. The findspot is indicated by the level number. Colour, temper, hardness etc. are discussed in Ch. 7. The colour of all the sherds of phases B and G have been described with the aid of the Munsell Soil Colour Charts.[1])

Colour interpretation is not fully considered here. The colour of the core is not noted. A black, dark or light grey core can always be expected with this kind of pottery and the way it was fired.[2]) Systematic sampling and testing is needed to learn more about firing methods.

No mention of the colour found immediately under the surface has been given. This has never been described in publications up to date but it is the colour to be studied for the relation of firing temperatures and clay paste. There should be more uniformity of colour just under the surface, as the surface colours are influenced by the kind of fuel used, and even by agents in the soil. However here the colour description has been restricted to the minimum necessary for recognition by other archaeologists. The colour of the inside of sherds has been added, which can be a help for identification. This colour also reveals whether the atmosphere inside the pot was oxidizing or reducing.

Just mentioning a colour without an attempt to understand its cause renders the description more or less meaningless. However, for the moment, the lists of colours found for each type in the two phases B and G, taken as samples, should be sufficient for the purpose of recognition. Most sherds from the E.I.A. show four colour zones. In the long run an intelligent interpretation in terms of the potters' work will have to be worked out.

Hardness is also mentioned under the heading of type description, with an attempt at interpreting this feature in terms of firing.

Here again hardness can only be used as a means of recognition to a certain degree. If ware is called hard in a publication, it can be taken that the *surface* is hard. But the core is never tested for hardness and standard testing equipment is not used. The

[1]) For the use of these charts cf. Shepard 1961 (p. 107).

[2]) Lachish IV Text p. 138.

relation colour—hardness is not studied. In other words, no intelligent use is being made of this feature, apart from type recognition. To quote A.O. Shepard's remark, (op. cit. p. 113) "a hard nut is one we cannot crack." Cooking pot type 3 has a very hard surface and a very soft core.

Although almost all pottery descriptions include mention of grits, this is done without any standard measure being used, or interpretation of the temper being made. Here no more has been done to remedy this situation than to publish some tests (thin slides) made on some types.

This different approach to the study of the E.I.A. pottery makes comparison with published pottery from other sites rather more difficult since, as a rule, only shapes can be compared and not the construction behind them. It is certain that much hand-made pottery was found in Iron Age Palestine, but what now seems to be a matter of importance is whether different methods were used in different regions. It means that, even if the assumption is justified that development of shape took place all over Palestine at the same rate, potters locally may have stuck to traditional patterns for certain types much longer than elsewhere; moreover the development of a small village like Deir ʿAllā may have been well behind that of a settlement found on the Mediterranean coast. Much more ceramic study will have to be done before a fruitful comparative dating of sites from this period can really be made with any certainty.

All these considerations lead to the conclusion that the material published in this chapter should be primarily taken as an entity in itself. Its usefulness for the purpose of dating material from other sites depends on how thoroughly the potters' work from the sites to be compared is known.

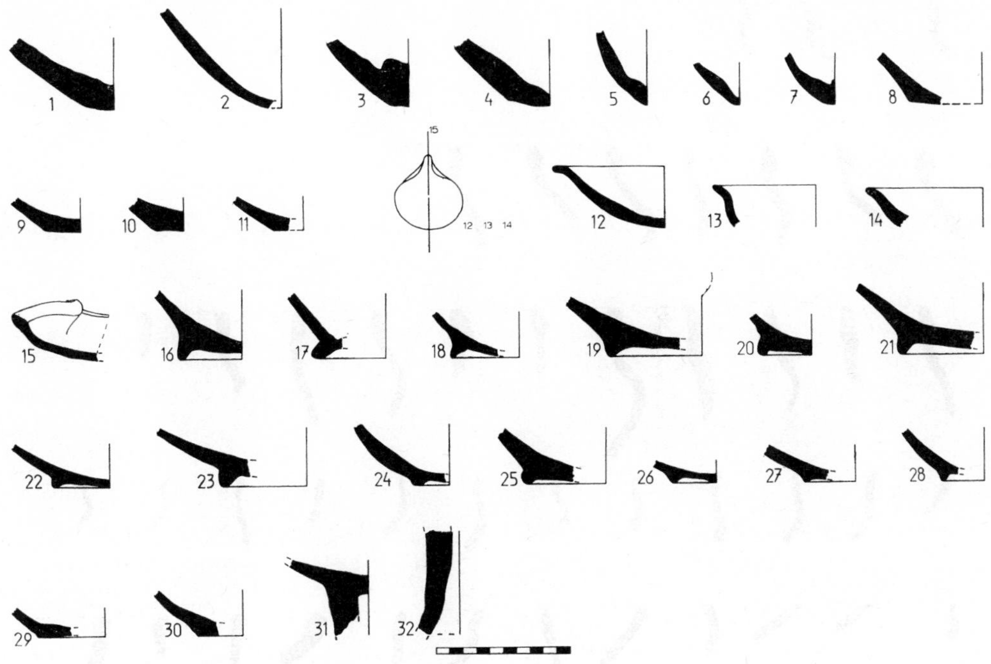

Fig. 45. Phase A

Bases

Type 2a	1 - D 162.4
	2 - E 437.1
	3 - E 378.1
Type 2c	4 - G 218.8
Type 4	5 - D 162.33
	6 - D 158.2
	7 - D 168.1
Type 6	8 - D 168.6
	9 - G 104.20
	10 - D 161.18
	11 - D 162.21
Type 7	12 - D 508.19
	13 - D 164.2
	14 - D 162.26
	15 - L 111.34
Type 8c	16 - D 166.22
	17 - D 162.16
	18 - D 507.18
	19 - D 164.14
Type 9c	20 - E 601.3
Type 10c	21 - E 609.43
	22 - D 162.37
	23 - D 423.1
	24 - F 508.42
	25 - D 168.11
Type 11c	26 - E 610.5
	27 - F 610.1
	28 - E 609.37
	29 - D 165.2
	30 - D 508.3
Pedestal bases	31 - D 165.11
	32 - D 168.15

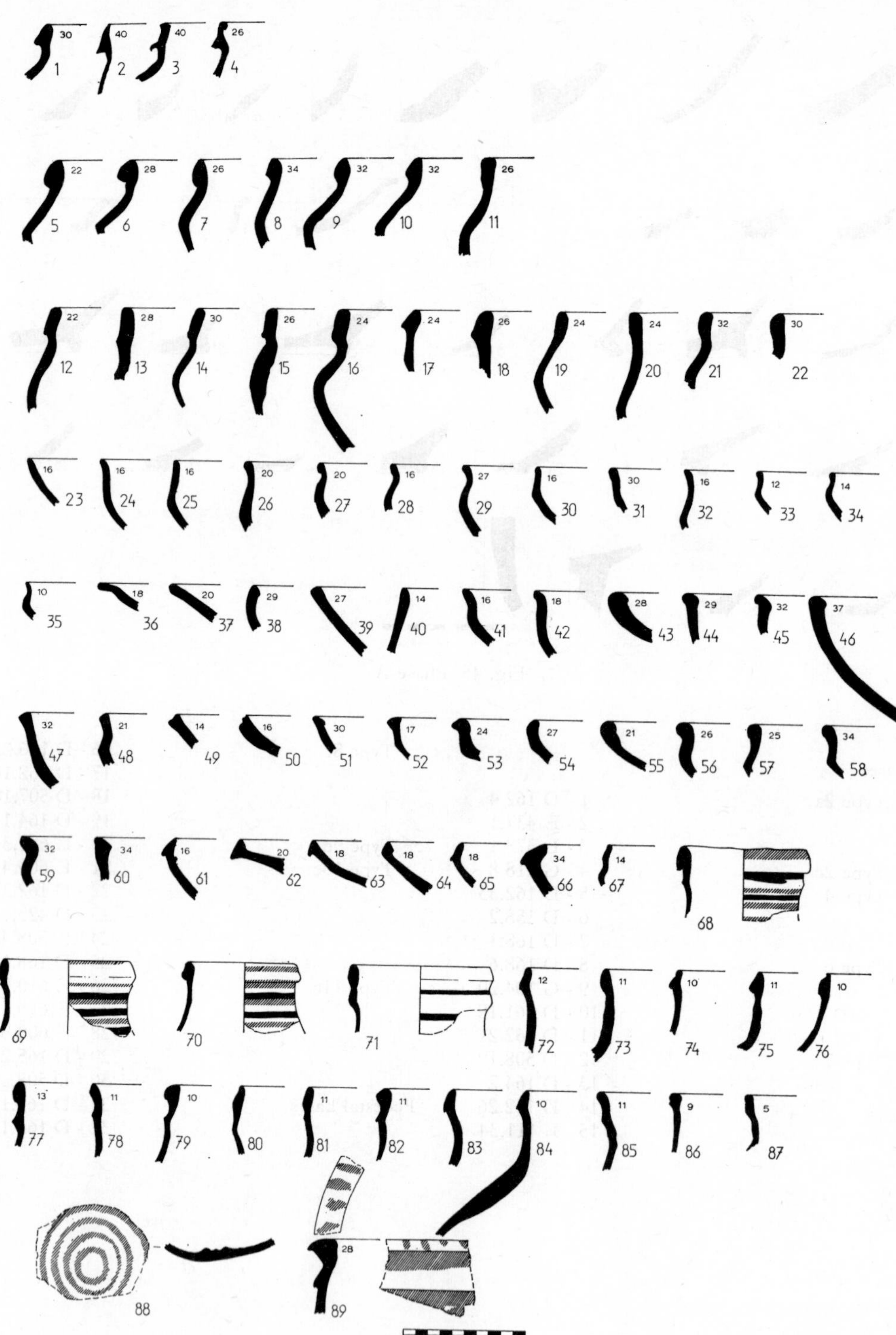

Fig. 46. Phase A

Cooking pots	
Type 1a	1 - G 105
	2 - D 424.36
Type 1c	3 - E 386.9
	4 - D 423.13
Deep bowls	
Type 1a	5 - E 520.77
	6 - G 104.30
	7 - D 425.1
	8 - D 155.1
Type 1b	9 - D 424.8
	10 - E 609.51
Type 2c	11 - E 331.26
Type 3a	12 - F 473.4
	13 - D 342.76
	14 - E 520.16
	15 - F 374.28
	16 - F 474.48
Type 3b	17 - E 339.5
	18 - D 423.6
Type 3c	19 - F 447.15
	20 - F 383.1
	21 - F 340.62
Type 3d	22 - F 508.18
Bowls	
Type 4a	23 - D 425.5
Type 4b	24 - E 609.22
Type 4c	25 - D 423.12
Type 4d	26 - D 424.13
Type 4e	27 - D 423.10
	28 - L 111.35
Type 4f	29 - E 531.8
	30 - D 424.21
	31 - E 609.19
	32 - D 424.5
Type 4g	33 - D 426.10
	34 - D 509
	35 - D 161.35
Type 4h	36 - D 166.6
Type 4j	37 - D 166.19
Type 5a	38 - G 220.15
Type 5b	39 - D 162.1
Type 5c	40 - E 609.24
Type 5f	41 - D 424.24
	42 - D 423.27
Type 6a	43 - D 164.1
Type 8	44 - D 426.12
	45 - D 162.5
Type 9a	46 - D 426.22
Type 9b	47 - D 412.12
Type 9f	48 - D 423.3
Type 9j	49 - E 378.4
	50 - D 415.6
Type 10j	51 - D 163.2
Type 11f	52 - D 405.35
Type 12f	53 - L 204.28
Type 13	54 - D 508.10
	55 - D 405.5
Type 14	56 - D 423.18
	57 - D 424.29
	58 - D 405.13
	59 - D 424.19
Type 15	60 - D 403.4
Type 16	61 - D 508.9
	62 - D 423.24
	63 - D 423.55
	64 - D 161.30
	65 - D 164.16
	66 - D 162.8
Type 4 (burn.)	67 - E 423.64
Jars no diameter means: square rim	
Type 1a	68 - D 504
	69 - D 162.43
	70 - D 507.1
	71 - D 164.6
Type 1b	72 - E 515.40
	73 - E 609.93
	74 - D 168.3
	75 - E 515.33
	76 - F 508.27
Type 1d	77 - D 424.8
	78 - D 424.12
	79 - D 424.15
Type 1e	80 - D 405.33
	81 - D 507.2
Type 1g	82 - D 404.4
Type 2a	83 - D 162.18
	84 - E 515.20
Type 2c	85 - D 162.33
Type 2d	86 - E 347.41
	87 - D 424.9
Decorations	
Fragment of pilgrim flask	88 - D 162.48
Fragment of krater	89 - E 507.10

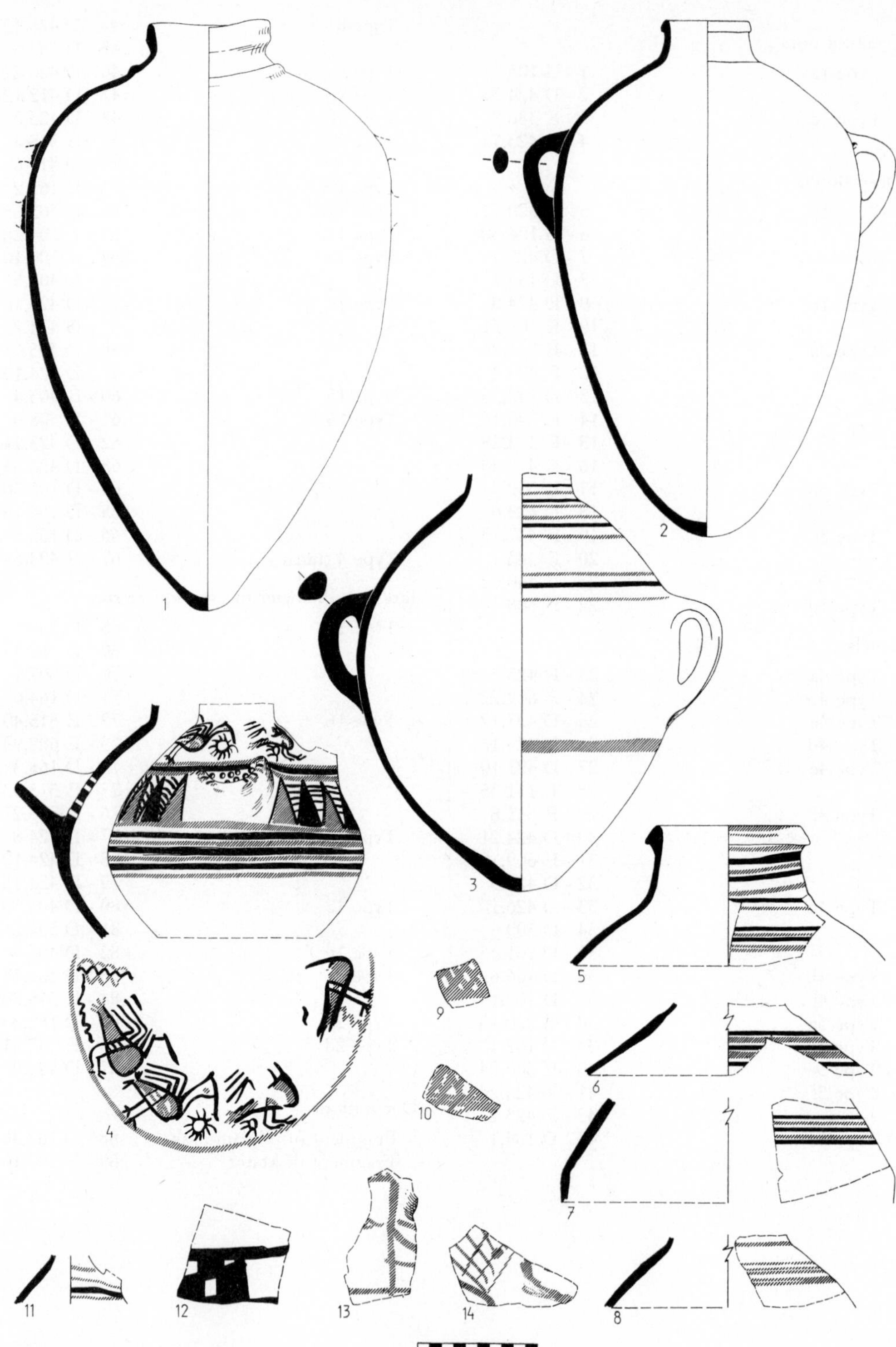

Fig. 47. Phase A

Miscellaneous	
Large storage jar (Plate XIV)	1 - F 506 (r.n. 1188) scale 1 :10
Large storage jar	2 - F 506 (r.n. 1189) scale 1 :10

Decorations	
Jar Type 1a	3 - G 104 (r.n. 1030)
Philistine jug (Plate XIV)	4 - G 104 (r.n. 900)
Jar fragments	5 - D 162.45
	6 - D 160.13
	7 - G 218.23
	8 - D 404.10
Krater fragments	9 - D 162.2
	10 - D 424.1
Small jar fragment	11 - D 423.45
Krater fragments	12 - D 509.5
	13 - C 429.1
	14 - D 509.4

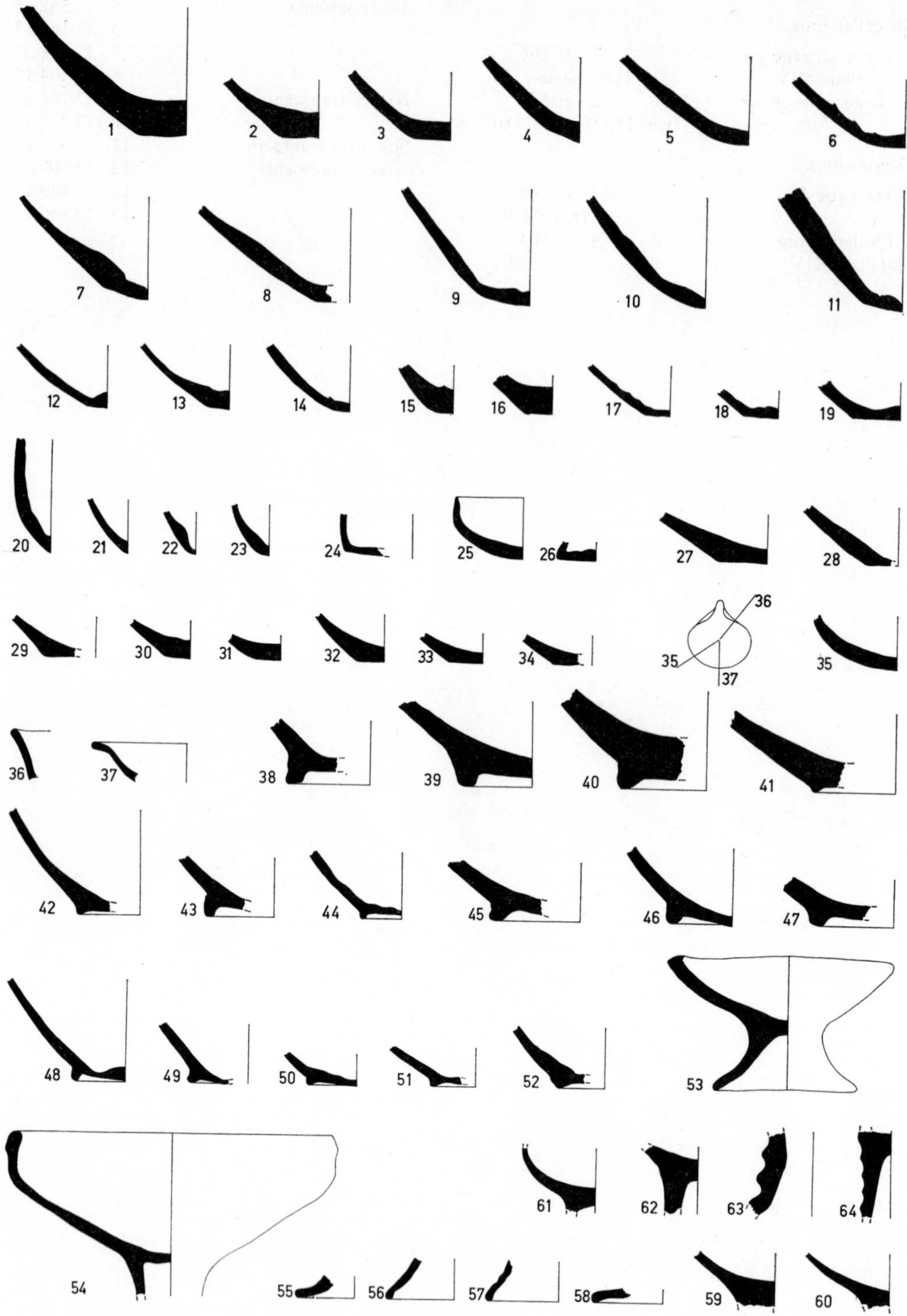

Fig. 48. Phase B

The colours of all sherds of Phase B have been described in Ch. 7

Bases

Type 2a	1 - E 382.4
	2 - D 352.18
	3 - D 419.48
	4 - D 422.14
	5 - E 382.6
	6 - E 425.137
Type 2b	7 - F 374.26
	8 - D 427.1
Type 2c	9 - F 382.15
	10 - F 373.7
	11 - F 381.45
Type 3	12 - D 162.30
	13 - E 351.70
	14 - E 331.45
	15 - E 351.25
	16 - E 382.27
	17 - D 417.9
	18 - F 454.29
	19 - D 153.3
Type 4	20 - F 376.2
	21 - D 156.9
	22 - E 426.129
	23 - E 382.26

2 Pyxis-type bases	24 - E 381.26
	26 - F 390.2
Type 6	25 - F 450.43
	27 - F 462.1
	28 - D 360.3
	29 - G 419.37
	30 - D 345.1
	31 - F 503.6
Type 6	32 - D 360.18
	33 - F 373.8
	34 - F 330.13
Type 7	35 - L 216.2
	36 - E 450.15
	37 - F 507.10
Type 8b	38 - E 381.74
	39 - F 331.15
	40 - E 382.48
	41 - E 350.8
Type 8c	42 - F 450.104
	43 - F 450.89
Type 9c	44 - D 409.11
Type 10b	45 - D 333.35
Type 10c	46 - E 351.18
	47 - D 418.1
Type 11c	48 - E 425.120
	49 - E 602.5
	50 - F 450.67
	51 - F 334.31
	52 - F 340.63

Pedestal bases

Bowl Type 16	53 - D 153 (r.n. 279)
Bowl Type 8a	54 - D 148 (r.n. 211)
	55 - F 369.6
	56 - D 419.22
	57 - E 350.39
	58 - F 334.2
	59 - D 156.12
	60 - E 349.23
	61 - E 338.11
	62 - E 332.21
	63 - E 381.52
	64 - D 155.4

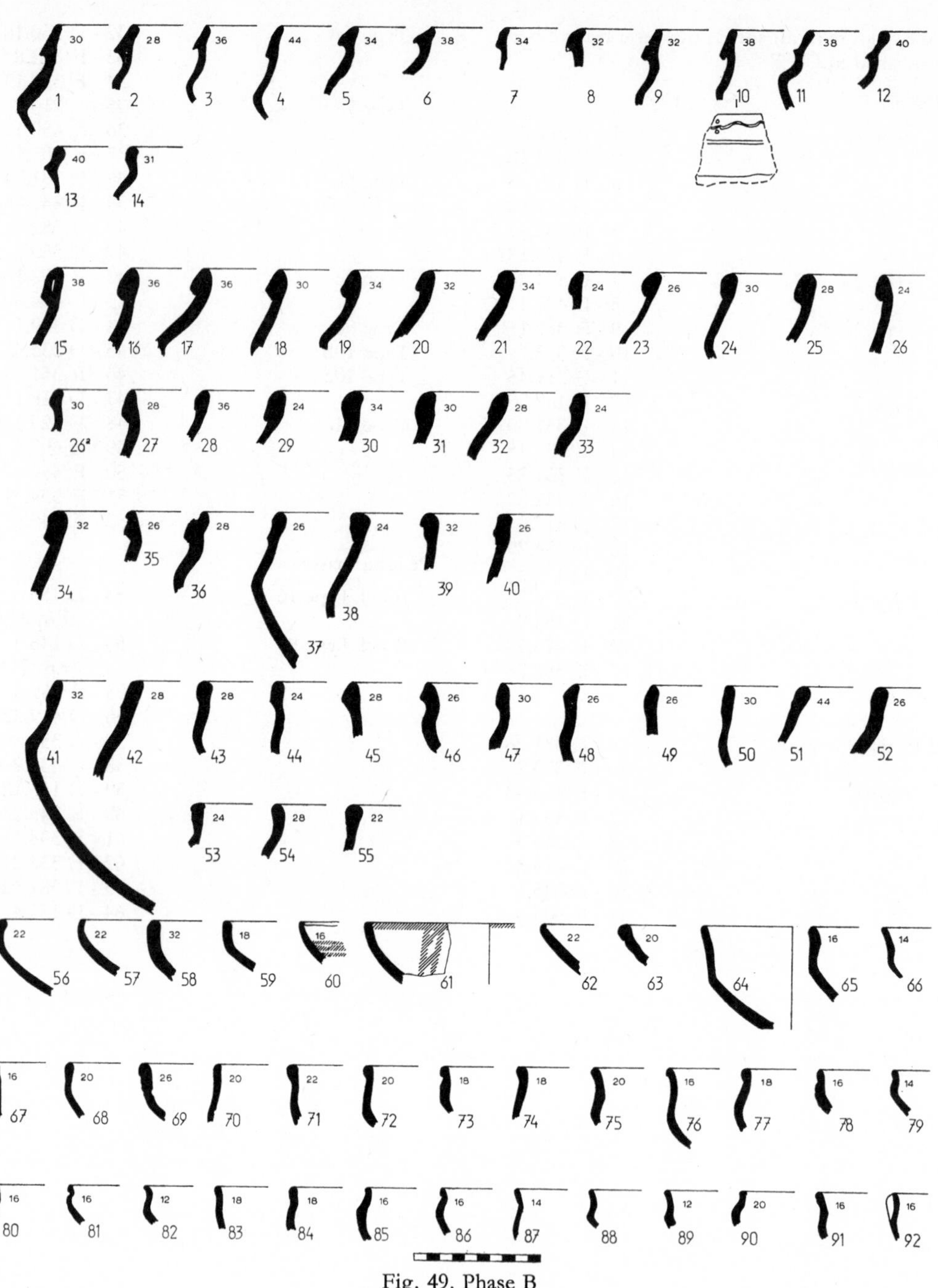

Fig. 49. Phase B

Cooking pots	
Type 1a	1 - E 376.2
	2 - E 446.8
	3 - E 425.133
	4 - E 425.60
Type 1b	5 - D 149.14
	6 - E 102.17
	7 - D 150.5
	8 - E 375.5
Type 1c	9 - F 450.18
	10 - E 348.2
	11 - F 373.10
	12 - F 340.21
	13 -
	14 - F 450.51
Deep bowls	
Type 1a	15 - F 447.52
	16 - E 376.2
	17 - L 107.8
	18 - F 473.14
	19 - D 355.3
	20 - E 340.12
	21 - F 454.89
	22 - F 500.15
Type 1b	23 - F 447.5
	24 - F 454.97
	25 - E 351.1
	26 - F 457.12
	26a - E 381.4
Type 1c	27 - E 446.5
	28 - E 425.58
	29 - E 446.9
	30 - F 344.1
	31 - F 454.102
	32 - D 342.68
	33 - E 419.5
Type 2a	34 - F 390.4
	35 - F 340.53
	36 - E 440.15
Type 2c	37 - E 450.1
	38 - F 503.39
	39 - E 338.43
	40 - F 450.5
Type 3a	41 - D 148
	42 - E 328.37
	43 - D 336.35
	44 - E 446.30
Type 3b	45 - E 381.81
	46 - G 114.33
	47 - E 332.13
	48 - E 331.9
Type 3c	49 - F 334.7
	50 - E 340.80
	51 - D 418.10
	52 - D 151.3
Type 3d	53 - C 325.133
	54 - F 450.121
	55 - D 360.15
Bowls	
Type 4a	56 - F 340.74
	57 - F 474.45
	58 - E 350.56
	59 - F 331.38
	60 - E 431.5
	61 - E 431.17
	62 - D 419.14
	63 - F 454.93
Type 4b	64 - E 425.41
	65 - E 331.16
	66 - F 450.69
Type 4c	67 - E 474.9
	68 - E 343.2
	69 - F 601.8
	70 - E 338.47
Type 4d	71 - E 381.60
	72 - G 118.14
	73 - F 450.28
	74 - D 160.14
	75 - D 160.37
	76 - L 202.3
	77 - F 454.87
Type 4e	82 - E 434.5
	83 - D 156.7
	84 - E 334.103
	85 - D 149.24
	86 - E 338.28
	87 - E 450.8
Type 4f	88 - D 413.21
	89 - D 352.15
	90 - F 454.71
	91 - E 381.6
	92 - F 331.14
Type 4g	78 - D 419.29
	79 - D 146
	80 - E 336.3
	81 - F 454.19

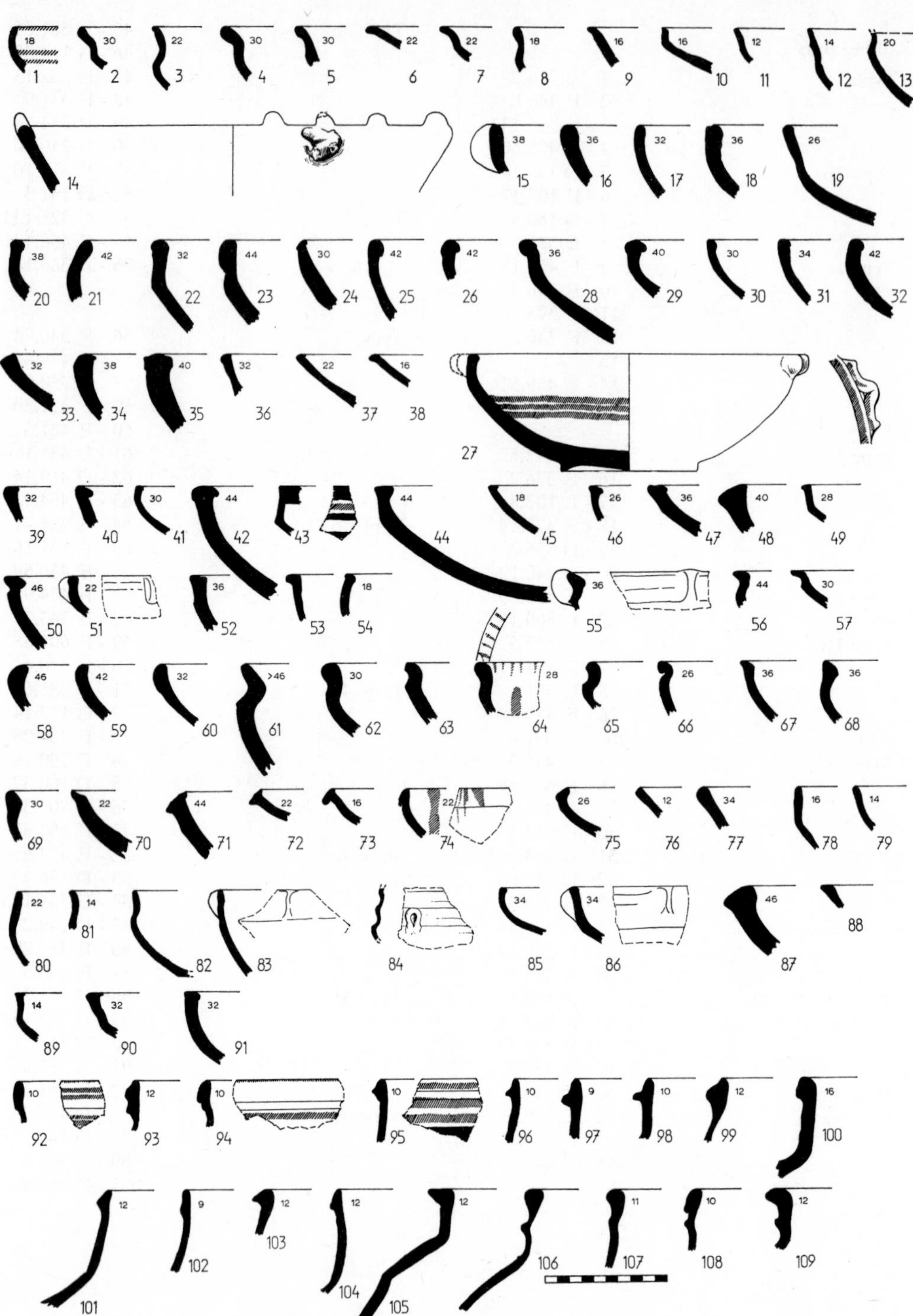

Fig. 50. Phase B

Bowls	
Type 4h	1 - F 454.123
	2 - D 350.1
	3 - F 330.14
	4 - D 154.2
	5 - D 419.47
	6 - E 423.126
	7 - D 148.15
	8 - D 153.16
	9 - E 507.25
	10 - E 425.95
	11 - E 450.23
	12 - F 340.68
	13 - D 153
Type 5	14 - D 419.2
	15 - F 601.2
	16 - E 331.53
	17 - F 452.78
	18 - D 417.4
	19 - F 374.27
	20 - E 425.59
	21 - E 450.13
	22 - F 454.67
	23 - E 330.5
Type 6	24 - E 330.2
	25 - E 329.8
Bowl (Plate XV)	27 - D 148 (r.n. 213)
Type 7	26 - E 425.109
	28 - D 413.26
	29 - E 425.44
Type 9	30 - F 450.122
	31 - E 425.168
	32 - E 445.15
	33 - D 360.19
	34 - F 454.76
	35 - E 425.81
	36 - F 331.11
	37 - D 149.25
	38 - D 419.44
Type 10	39 - F 474.40
	40 - D 421.1
	41 - F 484.1
	42 - F 427.4
	43 - F 503.65
	44 - D 146 (r.n. 190)
	45 - D 418.8
Type 11	46 - D 415.6
	47 - E 450.10
	48 - F 430.3
	49 - E 351.84
	50 - D 421.1
	51 - F 450.112
	52 - F 450.124
Type 12	53 - E 425.157
	54 - F 454.74

	55 - F 370.3
	56 - E 425.9
	57 - E 445.32
Type 13	58 - F 374.20
	59 - E 351.69
	60 - D 414.23
Type 14	61 - D 419.1
	62 - E 445.52
	63 - F 340.75
	64 - E 381.40
	65 - E 381.41
	66 - E 382.12
Type 15	67 - F 454.125
	68 - E 350.35
	69 - E 350.3
	70 - F 503.3
Type 16	71 - E 425.2
	72 - E 381.29
	73 - D 148.3
	74 - F 458.113
	75 - F 474.12
	76 - E 446.17
	77 - D 413.14
Type 4 (burn.)	78 - F 340.20
	79 - D 418.6
	80 - F 340.24
	81 - F 450.132
	82 - E 425.122
	83 - F 450.102
	84 - D 418.7
Type 5 (burn.)	85 - E 423.12
	86 - D 137.3
Type 7 (burn.)	87 - C 372.11
Type 9 (burn.)	88 - D 348.9
Type 10 (burn.)	89 - D 352.11
	90 - F 450.119
Type 11 (burn.)	91 - F 386.3
Jars	
Type 1a	92 - D 146.1
	93 - D 422.30
	94 - D 355.13
	95 - G 201.12
Type 1b	96 - E 340.3
	97 - E 351.68
	98 - E 331.50
	99 - E 338.20
	100 - E 447.2
	101 - D 422.27
	102 - F 340.65
	103 - B 152
	104 - E 376.3
	105 - F 503.37
Type 1c	106 - E 425.121
	107 - F 454.79
	108 - E 332.26
	109 - E 442.110

Fig. 51. Phase B

Jars	
Type 1c *(cont.)*	1 - E 425.131
Type 1d	2 - E 425.90
	3 - F 331.24
	4 - D 503.5
	5 - F 454.98
	6 - D 148.17
Type 1e	7 - F 450.17
	8 - E 338.24
	9 - D 355.24
	10 - B 160
	11 - F 374.6
	12 - F 331.1
Type 1f	13 - E 507.31
	14 - E 446.20
Type 1g	15 - F 450.34
	16 - E 425.39
	17 - F 474.31
Type 1l	18 - F 343.8
Type 2a	19 - F 450.55
	20 - F 386.12
	21 - F 340.33
	23 - F 386.57
	24 - E 338.40
	25 - E 350.49
Type 2b	26 - E 446.29
	27 - E 514.46
	28 - E 351.61
	29 - F 450.105
	30 - E 351.90
	31 - D 335.32
	32 - E 376.1
Type 2c	33 - F 473.11
	34 - E 337.14
	35 - F 450.49
	36 - E 445.48
	37 - D 410.46
	38 - F 334.23
Type 2d	39 - F 330.15
	40 - F 474.18
	41 - E 351.4
	42 - D 346.7
	43 - F 386.4
	44 - D 153.17
	45 - E 446.34
	46 - D 149.27
	47 - F 361.11
Kraters	48 - E 423.15
	49 - E 446.29
	50 - F 454.131
	51 - D 148.2
Decorations	
Philistine decoration	52 - E 418.9
Sherd	53 - E 414.2
Sherd	54 - F 474.8
Neck of jug	55 - D 355.8
Sherd of jug	56 - E 514.12
Sherd of jug	57 - G 210.7
Handle of jar	58 - E 425.55
Handle of jug	59 - E 331.20
Decorated jug fragment	60 - E 450.19
Decorated fragment	61 - L 107.2
Neck of jar	62 - F 454.140
Decorated jug fragment	63 - F 454.118
Neck of jar	64 - F 474.18

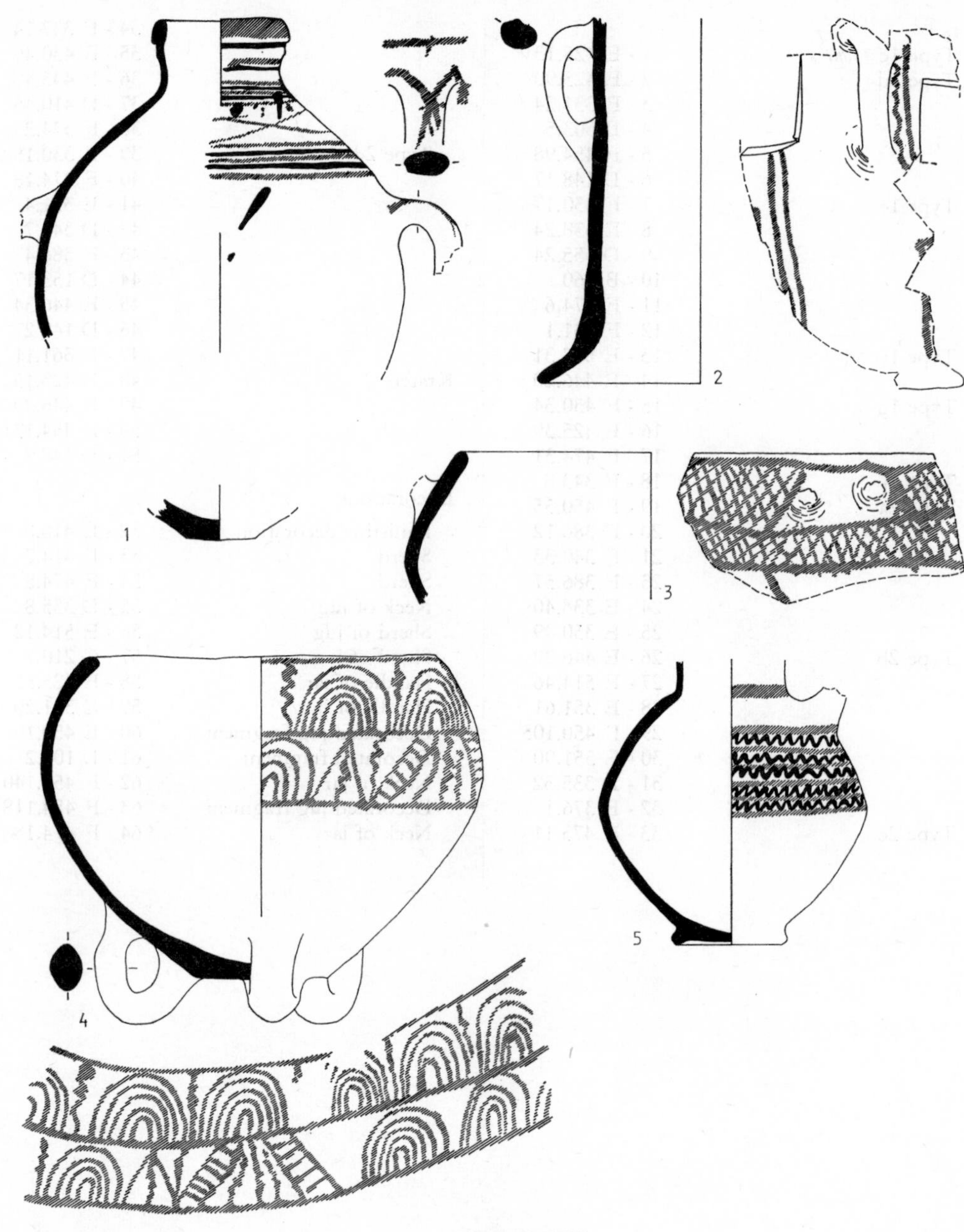

Fig. 52. Phase B

Decorations		Philistine bowl (Plate XIV)	4 - D 503 (r.n. 120)
Decorated jar	1 - D 504 (r.n. 136)	Jug	5 - D 148 (r.n. 323)
Stand	2 - D 152.1		
Bowl	3 - F 454.23		

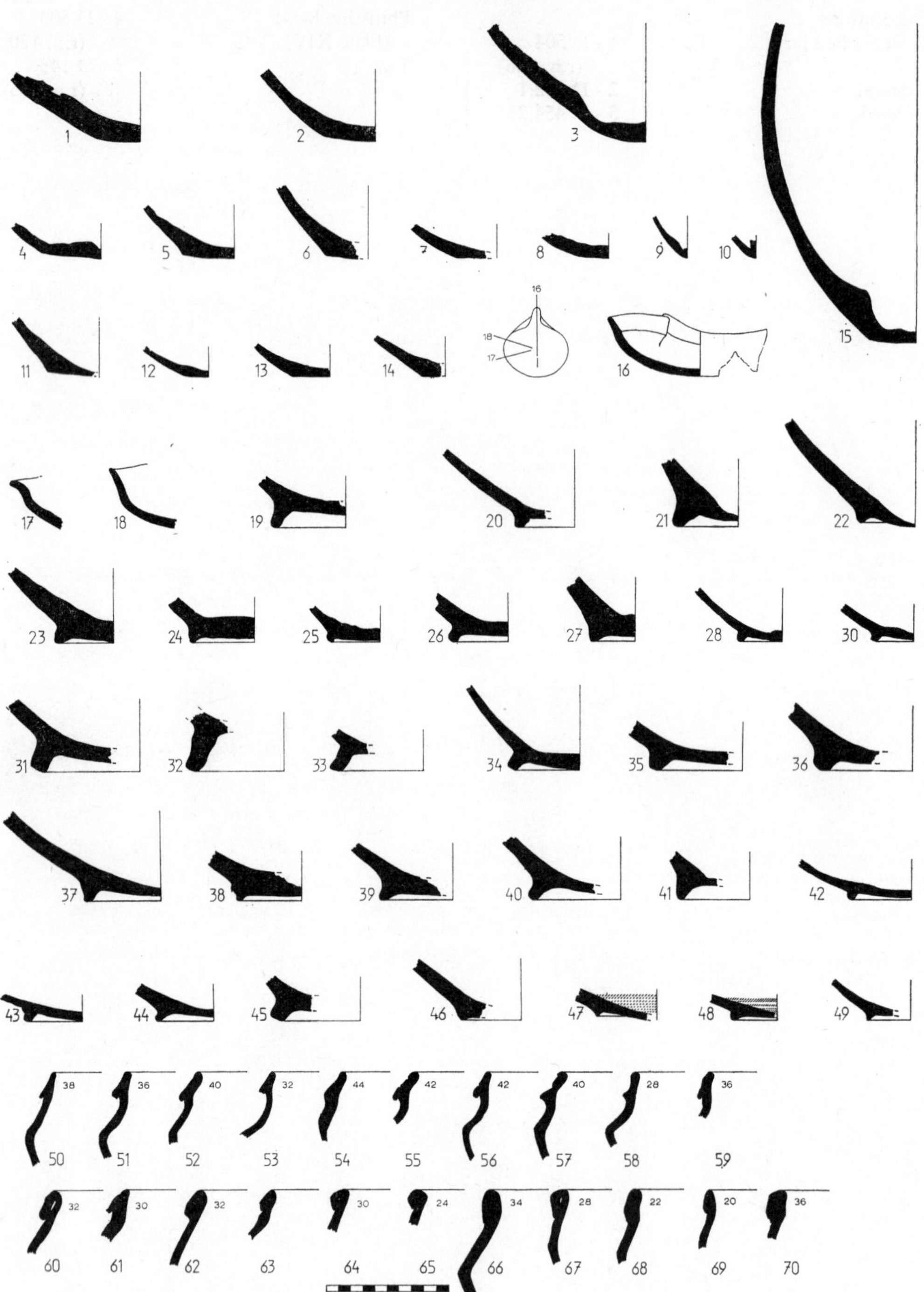

Fig. 53. Phase C

Bases	
Type 2a	1 - D 342.77
	2 - F 452.13
Type 2b	3 - E 322.13
	15 - F 339.40
	4 - D 252.12
Type 3	5 - E 424.7
	6 - F 452.54
	7 - D 298.4
	8 - D 334.1
Type 4	9 - F 452.62
	10 - E 322.27
Type 6	11 - E 418.77
	12 - D 351.60
	13 - E 327.11
	14 - E 326.2
Type 7	16 - F 334.37
	17 - D 349.12
	18 - D 351.28
Type 8a	19 - E 346.10
Type 8b	20 - F 339.59
Type 8c	21 - F 482.5
	22 - D 343.52
	23 - F 339.60
	24 - E 327.70
	25 - D 327.105
	26 - D 147.48
Type 9c	27 - D 340.93
	28 - E 418.11
	30 - D 412.3
Type 10a	31 - D 147.19
	32 - D 349.17
	33 - D 342.19
Type 10b	34 - F 339.15
	35 - D 335.21
	36 - F 329.10
Type 10c	37 - E 418.63
	38 - E 322.4
	39 - F 452.83
	40 - E 424.18
	41 - D 351.41
	42 - F 315.5
	43 - F 337.22
	44 - F 337.30
	45 - F 452.134
	46 - F 355.1
	47 - D 147.17
Type 11c	48 - F 337.6
	49 - D 333.25
Cooking pots	
Type 1a	50 - E 418.12
	51 - F 452.90
	52 - E 322.18
	53 - D 412.31
	54 - E 418.36
Type 2c	55 - E 418.156
	56 - F 339.95
	57 - F 452.143
	58 - F 482.14
	59 - E 418.105
Deep bowls	
Type 1a	60 - E 347.10
	61 - D 353.6
	62 - E 306.3
	63 - F 452.116
Type 2b	64 - F 337.36
	65 - D 333.23
Type 2c	66 - F 347.4
	67 - E 424.13
	68 - D 412.24
	69 - D 349.14
	70 - D 333.2

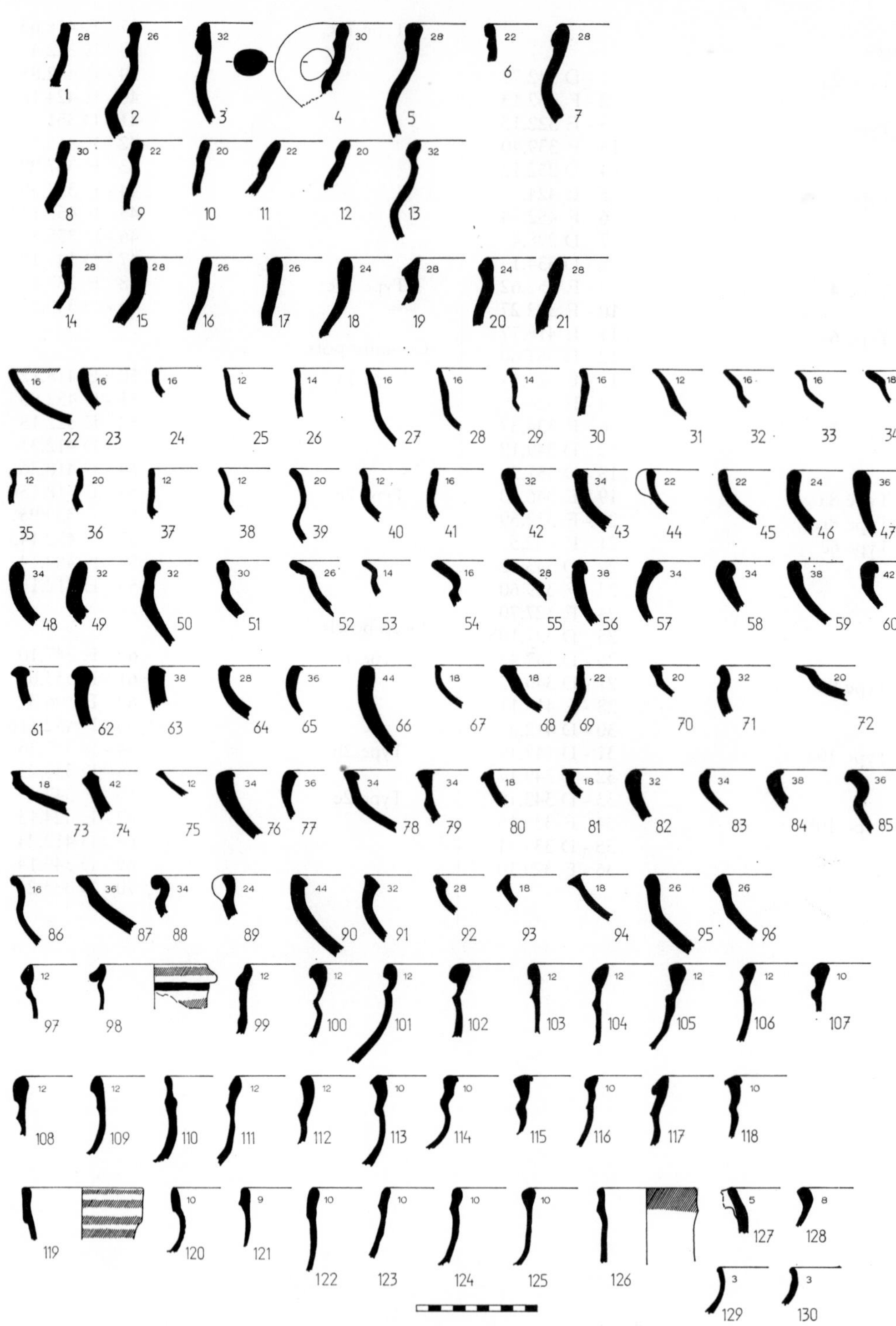

Fig. 54. Phase C

Deep Bowls	
Type 2a	1 - D 412.29
	2 - F 339.8
Type 2b	3 - D 412.33
Type 2c	4 - D 331.35
	5 - E 418.71
	6 - D 349.4
	7 - E 430.1
Type 3a	8 - E 418.94
	9 - E 418.56
	10 - E 418.159
	11 - F 355.30
	12 - D 342.41
Type 3b	13 - E 418.64
	19 - D 147.7
	20 - F 358.3
	21 - E 327.68
Type 3c	16 - D 340.55
	17 - F 339.25
	18 - F 452.136
Type 3d	14 - D 342.85
	15 - D 333.16
Bowls	
Type 4a	22 - D 340.53
	23 - D 342.84
	24 - D 342.45
Type 4b	25 - D 340.44
Type 4c	26 - F 355.10
	27 - F 342.51
Type 4d	28 - F 452.22
	29 - D 351.44
	30 - D 410.1
Type 4e	31 - D 345.32
	32 - E 424.59
Type 4f	33 - D 349.29
	34 - E 418.29
	35 - F 449.10
Type 4g	36 - D 349
	37 - E 418.45
Type 4h	38 - D 412.10
	39 - D 340.51
	40 - D 340.74
Type 4j	41 - E 424.8
Type 5a	42 - D 334.3
	43 - D 342.56
	44 - F 337.47
	45 - F 452.80
	46 - D 343.29
	47 - F 358.6
Type 5b	48 - E 418.39
	49 - E 339.16
Type 5f	50 - F 452.76
	51 - D 285.35
Type 5h	52 - D 340.12
	53 - E 322.14
	54 - E 418.20
Type 5j	55 - D 349.26
Type 6a	56 - D 147.9
	57 - E 418.95
	58 - D 334.99
Type 6b	59 - E 418.5
	60 - E 424.40
Type 7	61 - F 452.177
Type 8	62 - F 452.82
Type 9a	63 - D 353.24
	64 - E 418.29
	65 - E 418.72
	66 - E 325.53
Type 9c	67 - F 355.4
	68 - F 355.1
Type 9e	69 - D 331.20
Type 9f	70 - E 443.55
Type 9h	71 - D 342.21
Type 9j	72 - F 339.46
	73 - D 351.14
	74 - E 418.84
	75 - D 343.58
Type 10a	76 - D 353.13
	77 - E 418.111
Type 11f	78 - D 343.15
	79 - D 340.31
Type 13	82 - D 353.14
	83 - E 418.107
	84 - E 322.16
Type 14	85 - D 332.19
	86 - L 216.1
	87 - D 412.32
	88 - D 327.96
	89 - E 418.173
Type 15	90 - F 337.9
	91 - F 329.7
	92 - F 339.30
Type 16	93 - D 411.3
	94 - D 334.19
Type 5b (burn.)	95 - F 339.92
Type 5f (burn.)	96 - E 424.21
Jars	
Type 1a	97 - E 418.16
	98 - D 340.78
Type 1b	99 - D 331.28
Type 1c	100 - F 337.24
	101 - F 452
	102 - D 327.99
Type 1d	103 - E 418.106
	104 - D 331.8
	105 - E 418.93
	106 - E 418.31
	107 - F 339.61
	108 - F 330.33
Type 1e	109 - D 349.14
	110 - D 340.9
	111 - F 339.91
	112 - E 418.160
Type 1f	113 - D 298.23
	114 - F 424.33
	115 - D 298.2
Type 1g	116 - F 452.114
	117 - F 452.169
	118 - D 501.2
Type 2a	119 - F 452.42
	120 - F 452.71
	121 - F 472.8
	122 - D 410.38
	123 - F 337.34
Type 2c	124 - F 358.16
Type 2d	125 - E 418.109
	126 - F 452.94
	127 - D 340.2
Miscellaneous	
Jars	128 - D 340.14
	129 - D 298.32
	130 - E 418.125

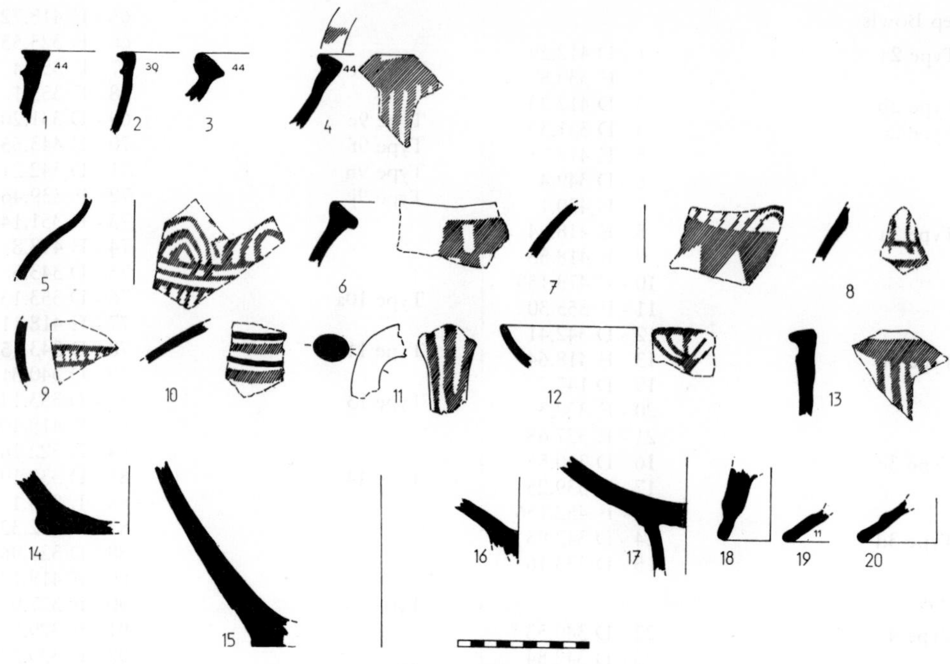

Fig. 55. Phase C

Kraters	1 - D 412.26	Jug fragment	10 - D 147.58
	2 - D 411.19	Handle	11 - D 332.15
	3 - D 343.225	Bowl fragment	12 - E 327.80
	4 - D 412.37	Rim fragment	13 - D 412.37
Decorations		Miscellaneous	14 - D 332.6
			15 - D 411.16
Jug fragment, Philistine	5 - E 418.9	Pedestal bases	16 - D 340
Rim fragment	6 - D 349.15		17 - D 298.24
Jug fragment, Philistine	7 - E 418.21		18 - F 339.24
Sherd	8 - E 327.67		19 - F 452
Sherd	9 - E 452.20		20 - D 349

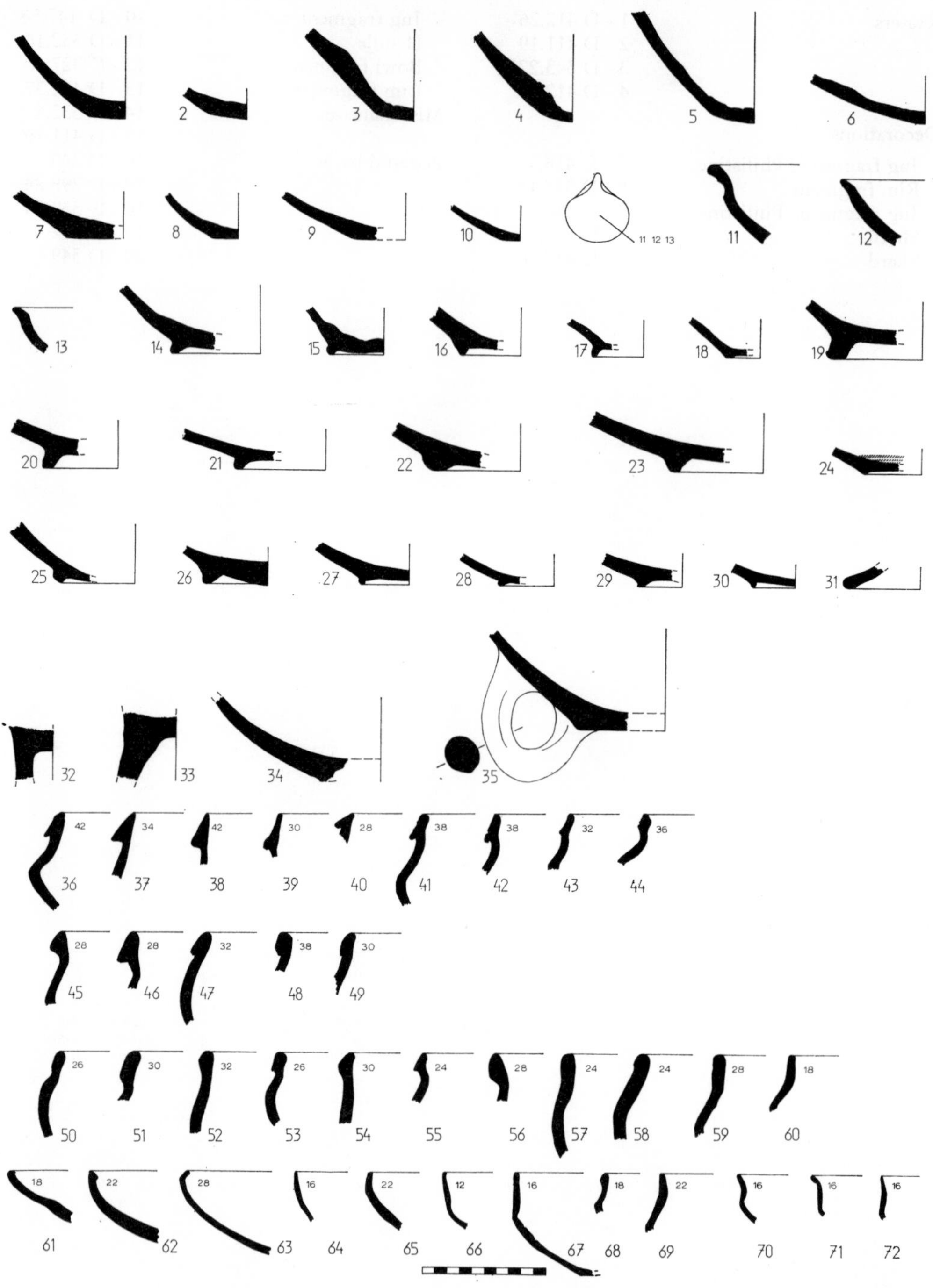

Fig. 56. Phase D

Bases	
Type 2a	1 - D 409.9
	2 - E 325.127
Type 2b	3 - D 327.114
	4 - D 325.153
Type 2c	5 - E 325.81
	6 - D 290.7
Type 6	7 - E 325.69
	8 - E 325.110
	9 - E 417.57
	10 - E 325.80
Type 7	11 - D 290.35
	12 - E 321.9
	13 - D 290.39
Type 8c	14 - E 325.146
	15 - D 327.100
	16 - D 290.10
	17 - D 290.40
Type 9c	18 - E 345.7
Type 10a	19 - D 328.3
	20 - E 419.9
Type 10b	21 - D 290.47
Type 10c	22 - D 290.1
	23 - D 290.19
	24 - E 325.76
	25 - E 325.75
	26 - E 325.21
	27 - E 325.111
	28 - D 281.1
Type 11c	29 - E 325.83
	30 - D 290.23
Pedestal bases	31 - D 329.4
	32 - D 290.44
	33 - E 417.62
Miscellaneous bases	34 - E 417.31
	35 - E 335.11
Cooking pots	
Type 1a	36 - E 325.33

	37 - E 417.10
	38 - E 349.2
	39 - E 321.13
Type 1b	40 - D 327.49
Type 1c	41 - D 327.1
	42 - D 325.10
	43 - D 145.18
	44 - E 325.119
Deep bowls	
Type 1a	45 - E 443.1
	46 - E 325.106
	47 - E 417.38
Type 1b	48 - D 145.26
Type 2e	49 - E 325.104
Type 3a	50 - D 145.15
	51 - D 327.7
	52 - D 409.1
	53 - D 330.35
Type 3b	54 - D 145.24
	55 - D 327.89
	56 - D 145.30
Type 3c	57 - D 282.2
	58 - D 327.36
Type 3d	59 - D 291.54
	60 - D 327.39
Bowls	
Type 4a	61 - F 467.6
	62 - E 417.9
	63 - D 325.18
	64 - C 330.5
	65 - E 417.20
Type 4b	66 - E 335.13
Type 4c	67 - D 327.120
Type 4d	68 - E 325.138
Type 4e	69 - D 327.18
Type 4f	70 - D 409.14
Type 4h	71 - E 325.77
	72 - E 325.40

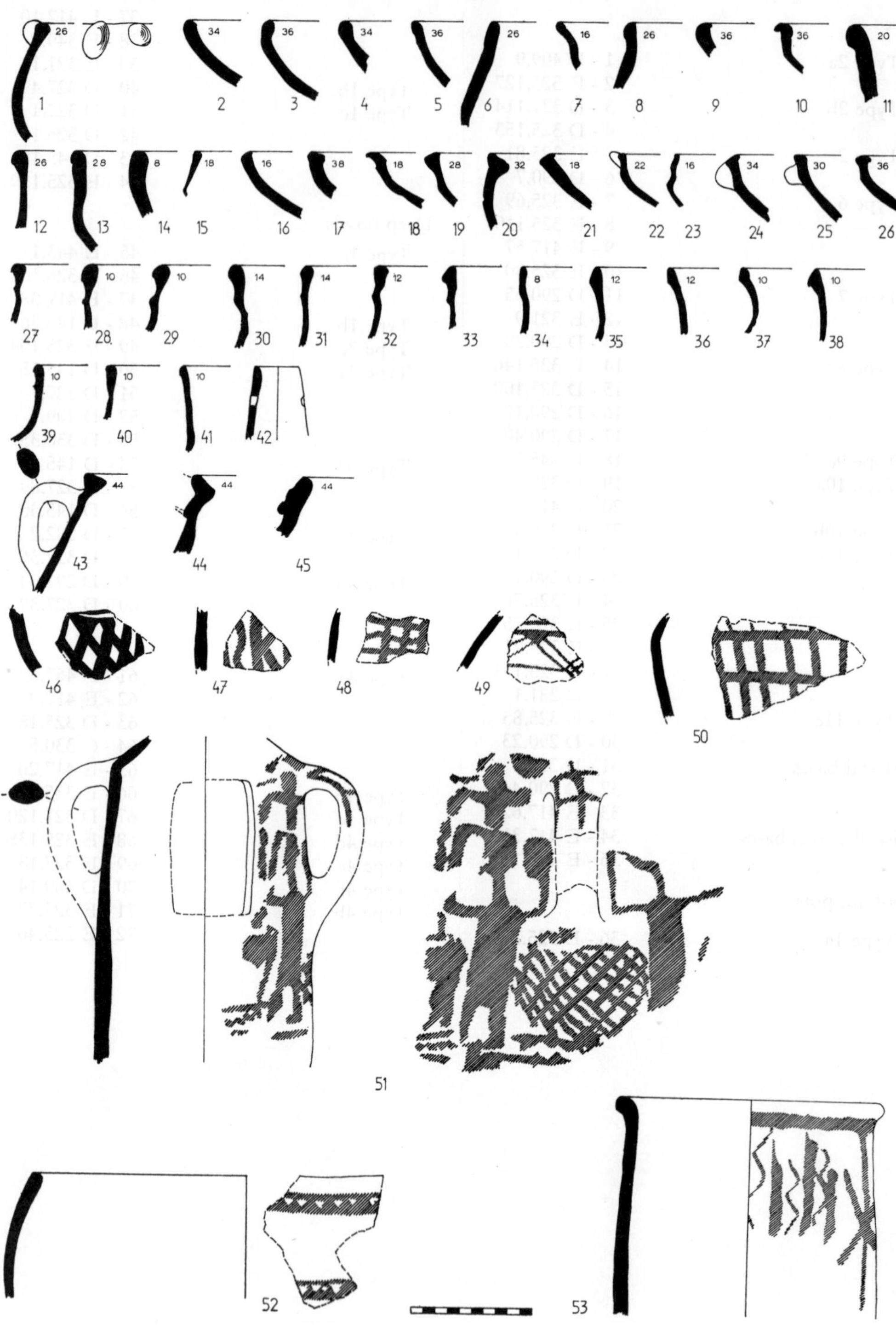

Fig. 57 Phase D

Bowls	
Type 5a	1 - D 145 (r.n. 251)
	2 - E 330.1
	3 - E 417.8
	4 - F 467.3
Type 5b	5 - E 325.89
Type 5c	6 - E 325.123
Type 5e	7 - E 335.21
	8 - E 325.5
Type 6	9 - D 327.119
Type 7	10 - D 330.19
Type 8b	11 - D 409.8
Type 8c	12 - E 325.103
	13 - E 325.114
Type 9a	14 - D 331.25
Type 9c	15 - D 281.13
Type 10	16 - D 290.4
	17 - D 282.7
Type 5h	18 - D 290.36
Type 11	19 - E 325.23
	20 - E 325.64
Type 16	21 - D 145
Type 4a (burn.)	22 - E 419.15
Type 4c (burn.)	23 - D 351.9
Type 7f (burn.)	24 - F 467.8
Type 9a (burn.)	25 - D 290.6
Type 11f (burn.)	26 - E 325.25
Jars	
Type 1d	27 - E 335.18
	28 - D 145.12
	29 - F 355.4
	30 - F 345.10
Type 1e	31 - D 409.16
Type 1f	32 - E 325.52
Type 1g	33 - F 467.10
Type 2a	34 - E 321.29
	35 - F 345.1
	36 - F 450.131
Type 2b	37 - D 290.58
	38 - E 325.65
Type 2c	39 - E 335.1
	40 - E 321.11
	41 - E 417.71
	42 - D 330.27
Kraters	43 - D 327.84
	44 - D 409.13
	45 - D 327.83
Decorations	
Sherds	46 - E 325.44
	47 - D 330.40
	48 - E 417.32
	49 - D 327.50
	50 - F 345.5
Stand (Plate XIV)	51 - D 145 (r.n. 253)
Bowl fragment	52 - F 345.16
Jar fragment	53 - D 145 (r.n. 252)

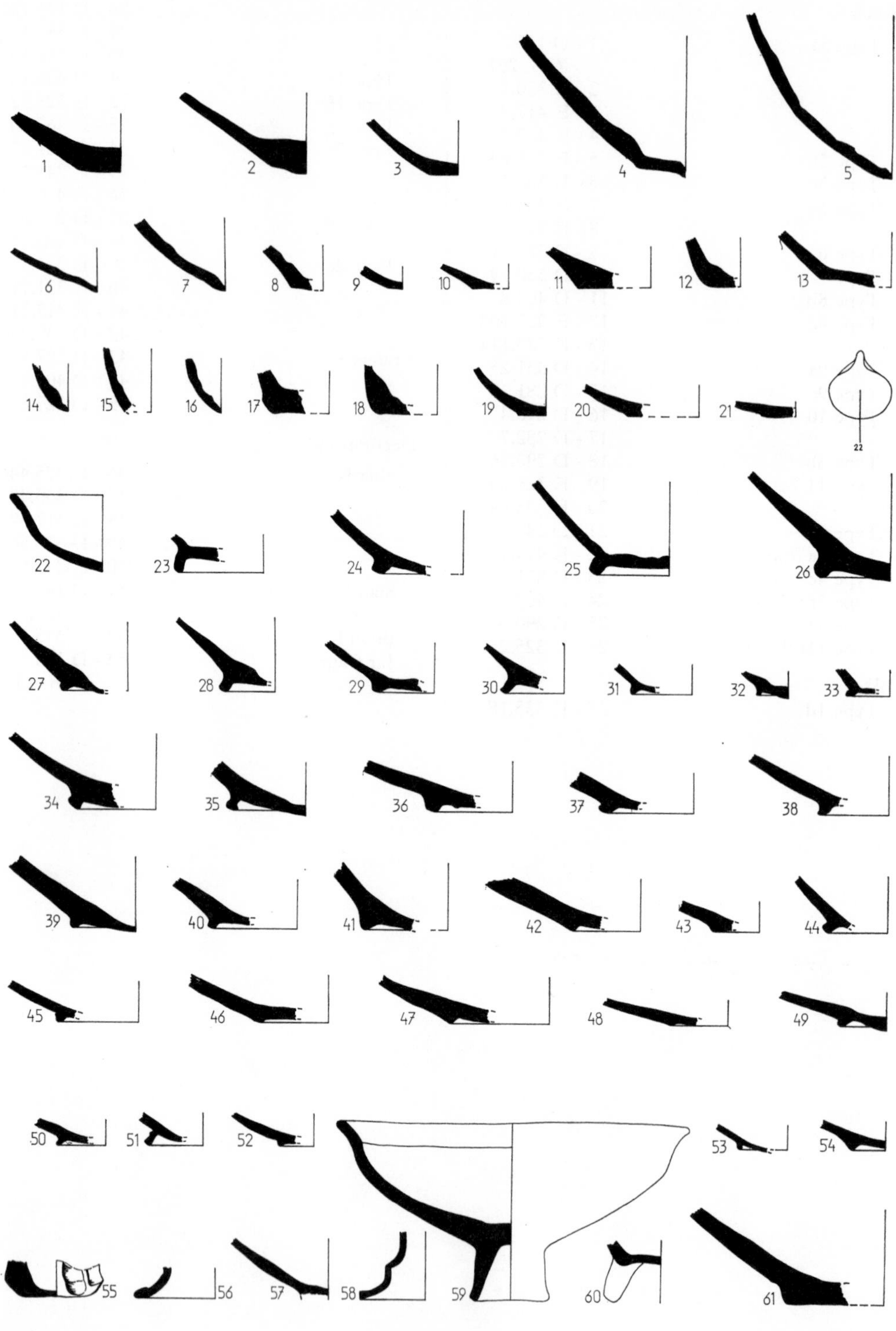

Fig. 58. Phase E

Bases	
Type 2a	1 - D 320.16
	2 - F 328.66
	3 - D 324.7
	4 - E 382.16
Type 2c	5 - E 303.34
	6 - D 142.18
	7 - E 603.78
Type 3	8 - F 325.8
	9 - E 318.61
	10 - D 320.51
	11 - D 320.42
	12 - D 137.20
	13 - E 303.61
Type 4	14 - F 328.80
	15 - E 303.58
	16 - F 384.4
Type 5	17 - D 314.23
	18 - E 303.44
Type 6	19 - E 303.1
	20 - F 444.1
	21 - F 442.23
Type 7	22 - E 303.33
Type 8a	23 - D 316.31
Type 8b	24 - D 314.15
	25 - E 415.27
Type 8c	26 - E 318.33
	27 - D 327.98
	28 - D 137.15
	29 - E 334.43
	30 - D 141.1
Type 9c	31 - E 318.42
	32 - E 303.49
	33 - E 417.42
Type 10a	34 - E 413.29
	35 - D 320.33
Type 10b	36 - E 413.14
	37 - E 413.60
	38 - D 142.14
Type 10c	39 - E 417.54
	40 - D 312.29
	41 - D 320.62
	43 - D 320.8
	44 - E 318.65
	45 - D 337.11
Type 10d	42 - E 382.30
	46 - E 303.43
	47 - E 415.6
	48 - E 303.54
Type 11c	49 - E 416.2
	50 - E 317.303
	51 - E 303.59
	52 - E 317.23
	53 - E 318.53
Type 11d	54 - A 425.1
Miscellaneous	
Base of industry pot	55 - E 415.30
Pedestal bases	56 - E 413.5
	57 - E 318.57
	58 - F 348.29
Pedestal bowl	59 - D 142 (r.n. 133)
	60 - E 413.1
	61 - E 318.35

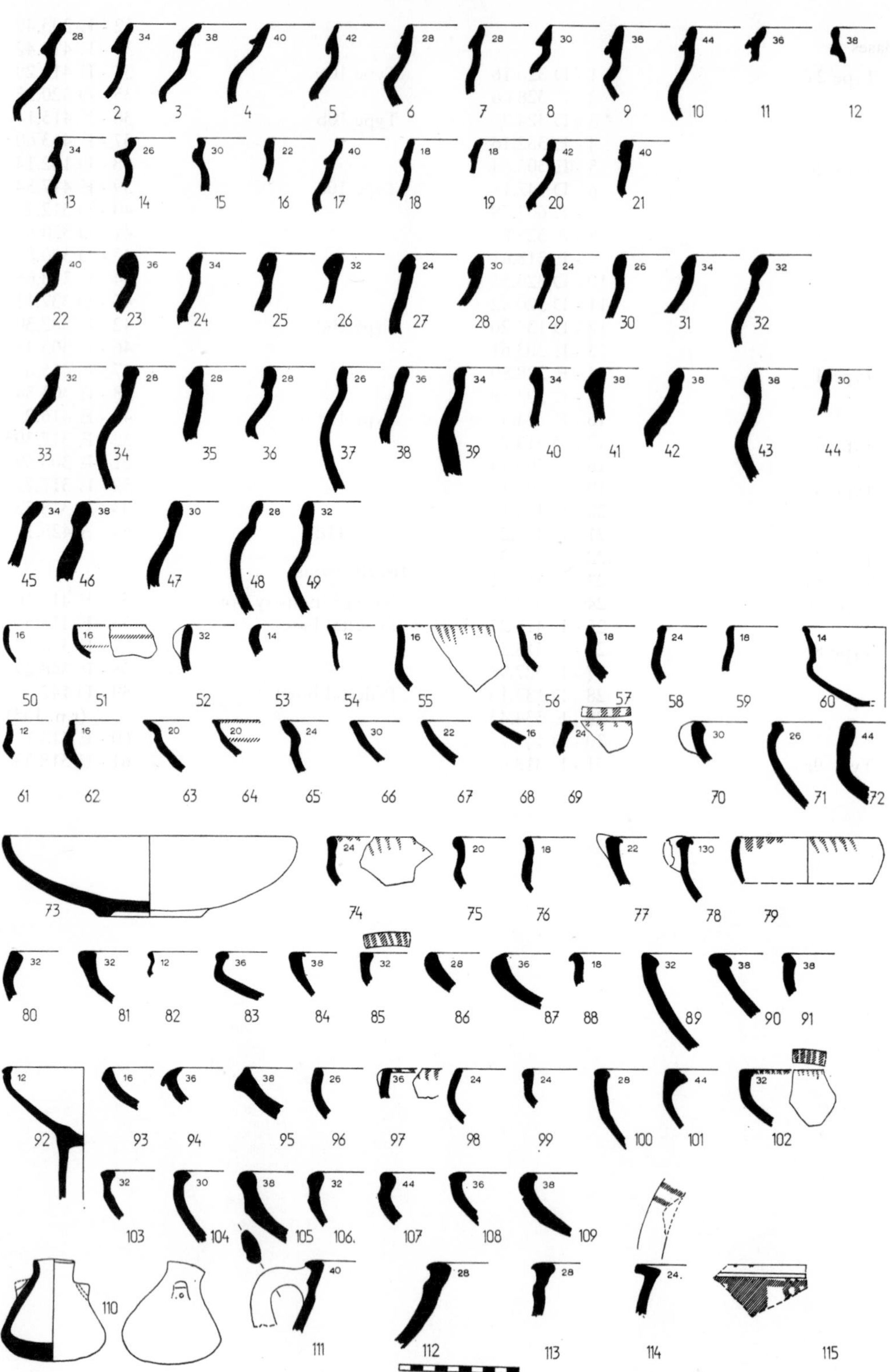

Fig. 59. Phase E

Cooking pots	
Type 1a	1 - E 303.77
	2 - F 328.95
	3 - F 328.40
	4 - E 318.66
	5 - D 320.45
	6 - F 378.19
Type 1b	7 - D 276.22
	8 - E 416.15
Type 1c	9 - F 448.1
	10 - D 316.40
	11 - E 303.45
	12 - D 448.14
Type 2a	13 - F 328.14
Type 2b	14 - A 417.1
Type 2c	15 - E 317.82
Type 2d	16 - E 316.7
Type 2e	17 - F 442.25
	18 - E 303.82
	19 - F 442.15
Type 2g	20 - F 328.47
	21 - D 276.1
Deep bowls	
Type 1a	22 - F 448.11
	23 - F 328.35
	24 - E 317.34
	25 - F 328.52
Type 1b	26 - D 276.45
Type 1c	27 - D 142.17
	28 - F 448.29
	29 - F 318.1
	30 - E 415.33
	31 - E 317.30
	32 - F 328.90
Type 2a	33 - F 328.20
Type 2c	34 - E 325.142
	35 - G 213.1
	36 - F 116
Type 3a	44 - D 276.28
	45 - D 320.41
	46 - F 442.5
	47 - E 317.20
	48 - E 414.6
	49 - D 316.12
Type 3b	40 - E 318.41
	41 - E 317.12
	42 - F 448.14
	43 - E 321.14
Type 3c	38 - E 415.11
	39 - F 433.31
Type 3d	37 - D 313.10
Bowls	
Type 4a	50 - D 316.19
	51 - F 378.17
	52 - E 413.26
	53 - F 378.14
Type 4b	54 - F 111.3
Type 4c	55 - F 442.38
	56 - E 413.84
Type 4d	57 - F 213.41
	58 - F 442.35
Type 4e	59 - D 143.31
Type 4f	60 - F 444.19
	61 - F 348.1
Type 4g	62 - E 318.101
Type 4h	63 - E 317.87
	64 - F 448.30
	65 - D 291.9
Type 4j	66 - F 378.3
	67 - D 142.11
	68 - D 328.4
Type 5a	69 - D 269.12
	70 - E 416.12
	71 - E 318.83
	72 - F 325.2
Bowl	73 - D 276
Type 5c	74 - D 271.2
Type 5d	75 - D 143.26
Type 5f	76 - D 285.82
Type 6	77 - E 415.35
Type 7	78 - F 116
Type 9a	79 - E 318.1
	80 - D 276.25
Type 9b	81 - F 328.1
Type 9g	82 - D 143.28
Type 9k	83 - F 378.5
Type 10	84 - D 143.25
	85 - E 317.32
Type 13	86 - F 448.38
	87 - E 318.73
Type 14	88 - D 276.15
Type 15	89 - D 237.111
	90 - E 383.17
	91 - D 291.17
Type 16	92 - F 328.85
	93 - E 318.6
	94 - F 328.108
	95 - F 326.1
Type 5 (burn.)	96 - E 317.24
	97 - E 314.7
	98 - E 303.56
	99 - D 291.2
Type 10 (burn.)	100 - A 427.1
	101 - E 318.36
	102 - E 415.5
	103 - E 317.75
	104 - E 413.13
Type 17 (burn.)	105 - D 276.8
	106 - F 328.10
	107 - E 303.15
	108 - F 378.6
	109 - F 320.6
Pyxis	110 - F 328 (r.n. 864)
Kraters	111 - E 325.94
	112 - E 303.75
	113 - E 317.66
	114 - E 303.94
Miscellaneous	115 - F 442.19

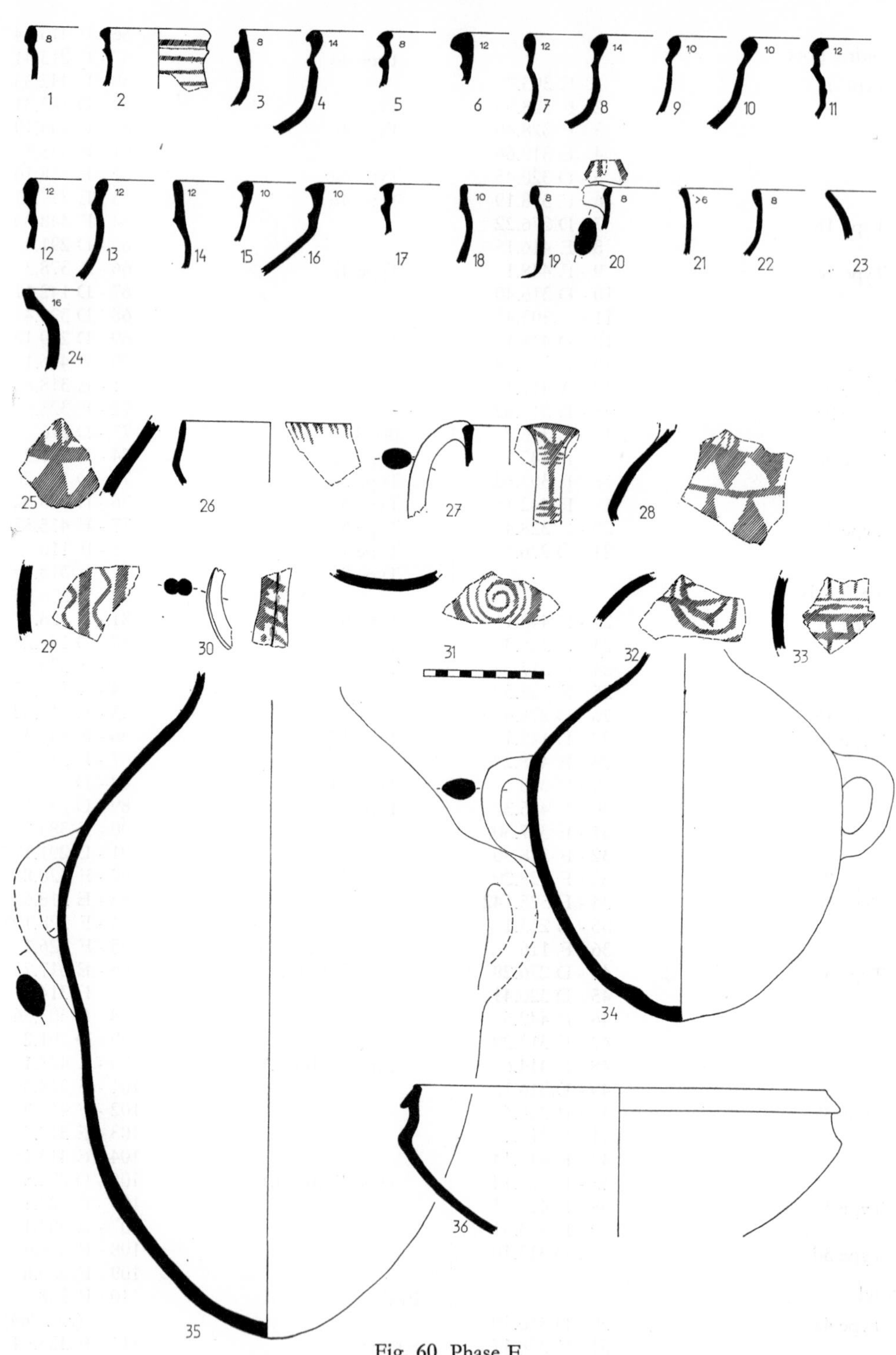

Fig. 60. Phase E

Jars

Type 1a	1 - F 378.4
	2 - E 303.38
Type 1b	3 - F 448.19
Type 1c	4 - E 416.1
	5 - F 442.11
	6 - D 315.5
Type 1d	7 - E 317.106
	8 - F 444.5
	9 - E 413.58
	10 - E 413.54
	11 - F 444.13
	12 - F 328.74
Type 1e	13 - F 328.45
	14 - F 326.10
Type 1f	15 - E 303.78
Type 1g	16 - E 409.5
	17 - E 415.4
Type 2a	18 - F 116
	19 - F 328.89
Type 2b	20 - E 414.10
Type 2d	21 - F 416.19
	22 - E 514.33
Type 2e	23 - F 442.20
	24 - D 143

Decorations

Sherd	25 - F 444.16
Bowl fragment	26 - F 442.38
Handle	27 - E 416.9
Sherd	28 - E 414.2
Sherd	29 - E 413.49
Handle	30 - F 442.46
Pilgrim flask fragment	31 - F 325.11
Jug fragment	32 - F 442.40
Sherd	33 - E 413.48

Miscellaneous

Jug	34 - F 111 (r.n. 1077)
Jug	35 - D 142 (r.n. 166)
Cooking pot, type 1	36 - D 143 (r.n. 191)

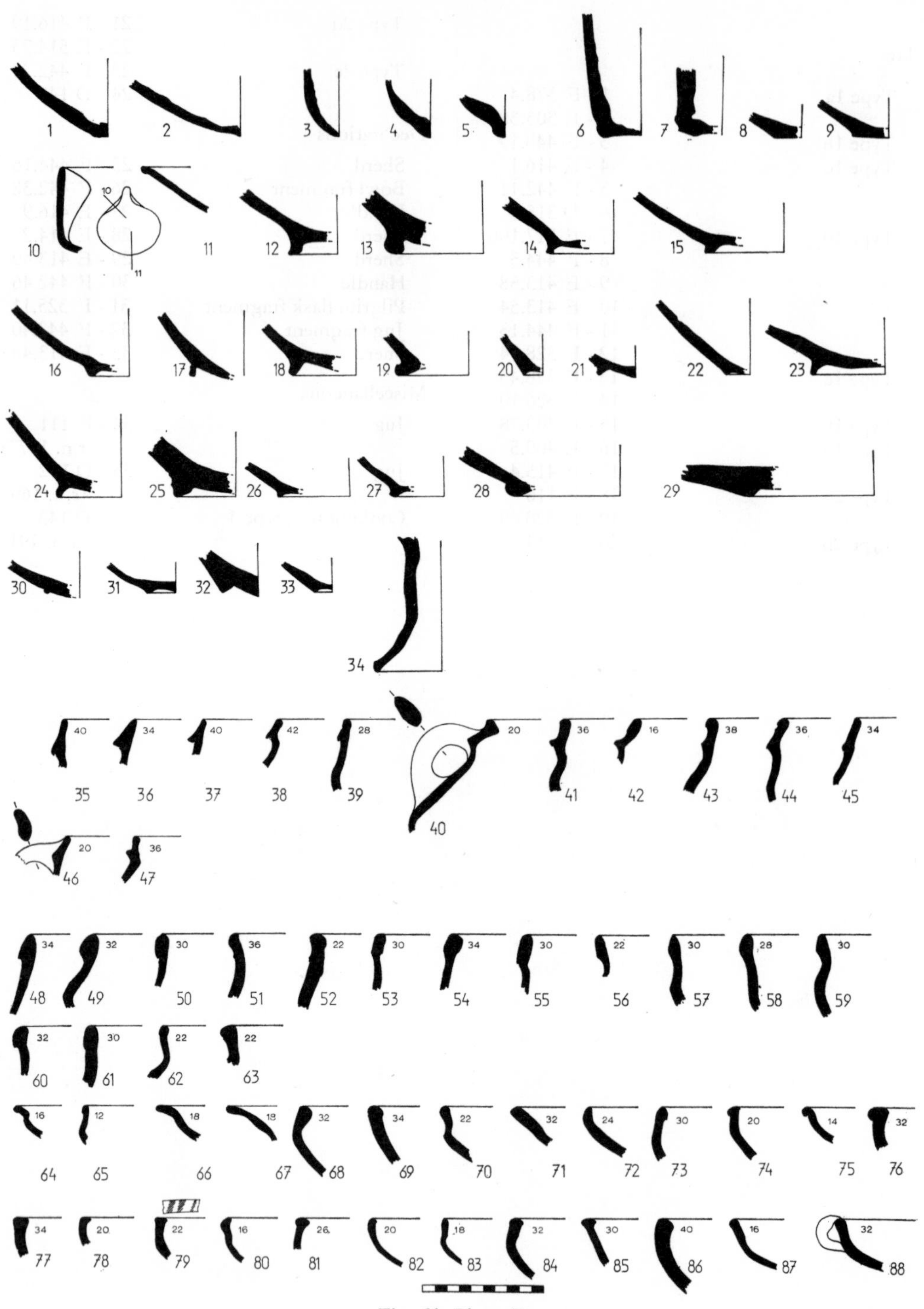

Fig. 61. Phase F

Bases	
Type 2e	1 - D 269.10
	2 - D 133.54
Type 4	3 - D 295.101
	4 - F 102.27
	5 - D 277.21
Type 5	6 - D 358.3
	7 - D 268.26
Type 6	8 - D 313.3
	9 - D 269.1
Type 7	10 - D 268.3
	11 - D 274.32
Type 8a	12 - F 102.5
Type 8b	13 - F 433.18
	14 - F 310.2
Type 8c	15 - D 277.15
	16 - F 102.14
	17 - F 433.19
	18 - D 277.14
	19 - D 287.3
Type 8d	20 - D 287.20
Type 9c	21 - F 102
Type 9d	22 - F 433.10
Type 10c	23 - D 358.4
	24 - D 278.2
	25 - D 313.1
	26 - D 358.17
	27 - F 305.8
	28 - D 277.27
Type 10d	29 - D 295.4
Type 11c	30 - F 102.15
Type 11d	31 - D 260.12
	32 - F 102.8
	33 - F 102.9
Pedestal base	34 - D 277.8
Cooking pots	
Type 1a	35 - D 295.1
	36 - D 133.7
	37 - D 295.112
Type 1b	38 - F 305.12
Type 1c	39 - D 268.2
Type 2a	40 - F 305.1
Type 2e	41 - F 379.1
	42 - D 133.1
Type 2d	43 - F 102.24
Type 2e	44 - F 320.5
	45 - D 295.92
Type 2f	46 - F 305.10
Type 2g	47 - F 321.11
Deep bowls	
Type 1a	48 - D 133.38
Type 1b	49 - E 379.1
Type 1c	50 - D 313.2
	51 - D 287.18
Type 2c	52 - D 287.1
Type 3a	53 - D 320.20
	54 - D 269.9
	55 - D 295.109
	56 - A 623.6
Type 3b	57 - D 295.95
	58 - E 413.69
	59 - E 315.3
	60 - F 222.16
Type 3c	61 - F 433.57
Type 3d	62 - D 133.7
	63 - D 277.49
Bowls	
Type 4g	64 - D 359.11
	65 - D 359.7
Type 4h	66 - D 277.59
Type 4j	67 - D 277.53
Type 5a	68 - F 222.20
	69 - D 295.93
Type 5f	70 - A 623.9
Type 5j	71 - F 379.5
Type 5k	72 - E 351.31
Type 6	73 - D 133.28
Type 8	74 - D 278.7
	75 - F 379.4
	76 - A 623.20
Type 10a	77 - D 269.5
	78 - D 278.10
Type 12	79 - F 433.11
	80 - D 277.5
	81 - D 295.110
Type 4 (burn.)	82 - F 433.15
	83 - F 222.14
Type 5 (burn.)	84 - F 102
	85 - D 274.9
Type 9 (burn.)	86 - F 222.10
Type 17 (burn.)	87 - D 277.51
	88 - F 203.1

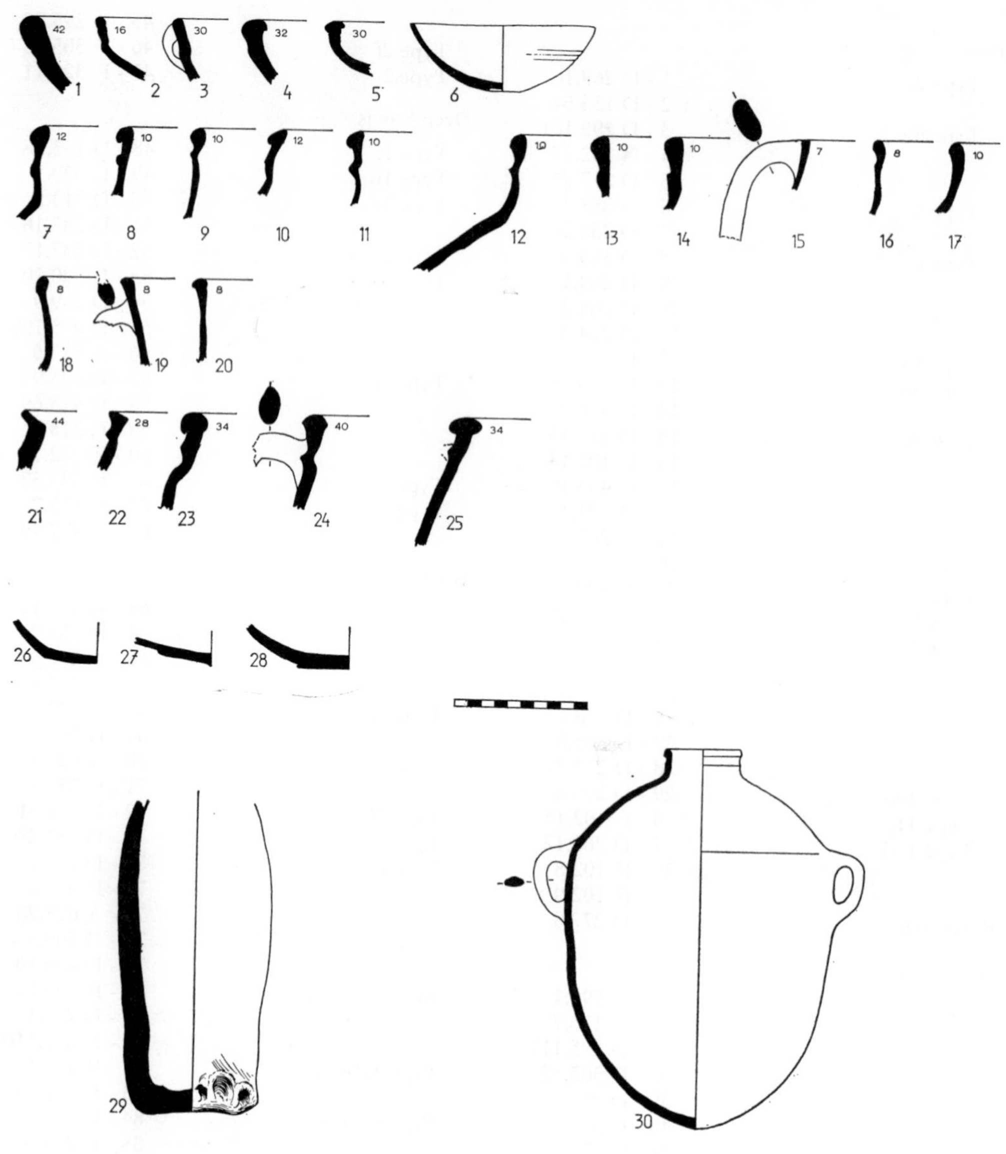

Fig. 62. Phase F

Bowls		Type 2a	15 - D 316.32
Type 17 (burn.) (cont.)	1 - A 618.28	Type 2c	16 - D 323.1
	2 - D 141.8	Type 2d	17 - D 358.2
	3 - D 137.6		18 - D 133.5
	4 - A 623.13		19 - F 310.10
	5 - E 101.33		20 - D 274.8
Bowl, import	6 - D 313 (r.n. 880)	Kraters	21 - D 133.15
			22 - D 268.4
Jars			23 - A 623.5
			24 - B 511.5
Type 1d	7 - F 315.2		25 - D 133.10
	8 - F 101.1	Miscellaneous	26 - D 133.65
	9 - D 358.20		27 - D 277.45
Type 1g	10 - F 433.1		28 - D 133.58
	11 - D 133.4	Industry pot (Plate XV)	29 - F 110 (r.n. 734)
	12 - D 133.35		
Type 1k	13 - D 133.33	Jar, scale 1 : 10 (Plate XIV)	30 - F 453 (r.n. 916)
Type 1l	14 - D 113.9		

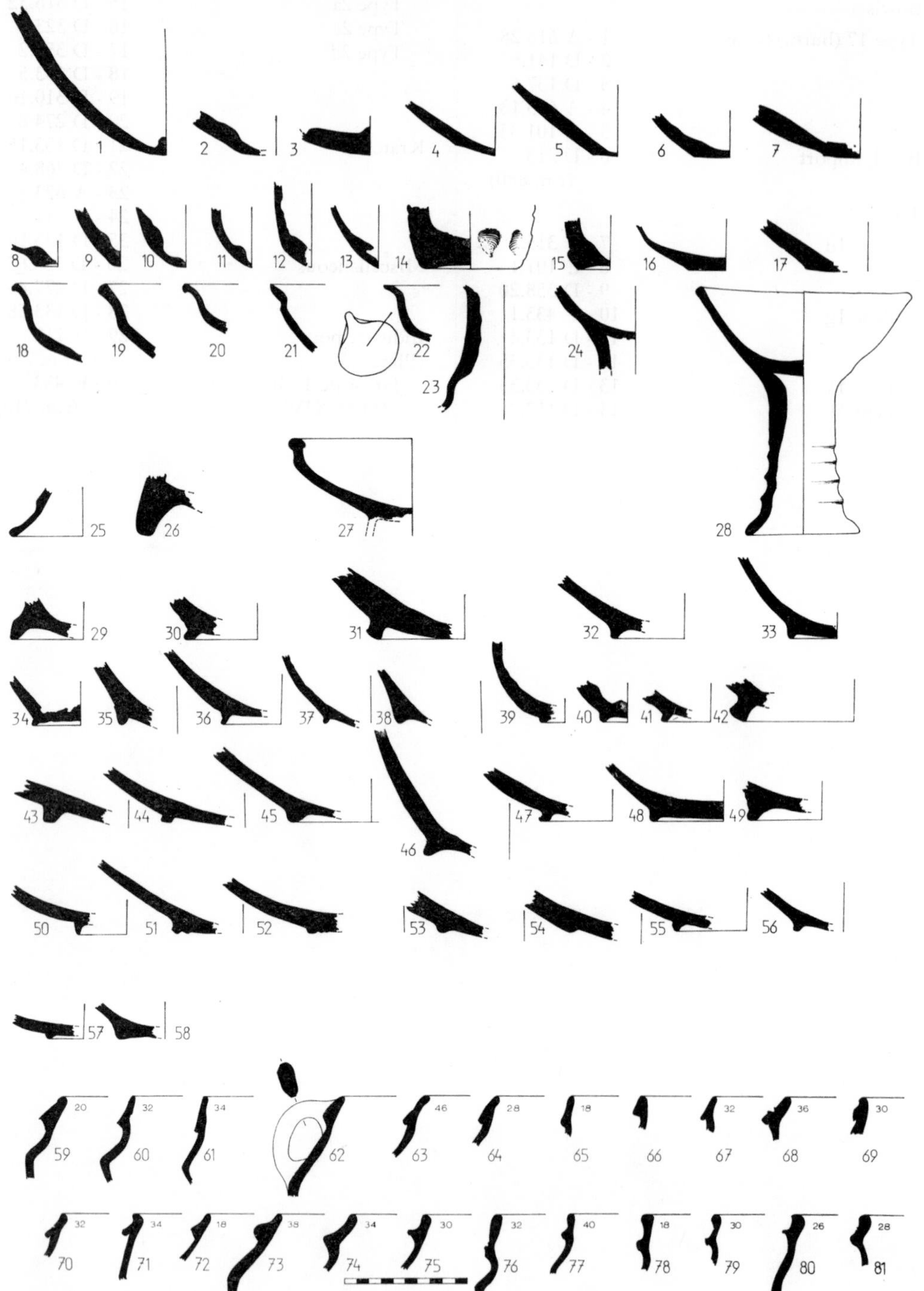

Fig. 63. Phase G

The colours of all sherds of phase G have been described in Ch. 7

Bases	
Type 2c	1 - F 421.3
	2 - F 424.1
	3 - D 271.15
Type 3	4 - F 447.42
	5 - F 447.40
	6 - D 136.9
	7 - F 447.64
	8 - D 261.5
Type 4	9 - B 314.4
	10 - D 265.57
	11 - D 285.124
	12 - E 101.3
	13 - D 280.5
Type 5	14 - A 618.12
	15 - F 106.3
Type 6	16 - D 271.2
	17 - F 447.81
Type 7	18 - A 622.10
	19 - D 265.1
	20 - B 513.14
	21 - D 294.11
	22 - D 265.35
Pedestal bases	23 - A 621.11
	24 - D 263.17
	25 - F 216.1
Miscellaneous base	26 - F 439.12
Part of pedestal bowl	27 - A 618 (r.n. 469)
Pedestal bowl (Plate XIV)	28 - D 261 (r.n. 845)
Type 8a	29 - D 263.66
Type 8b	30 - D 263.16
Type 8c	31 E 201.7
	32 F 447.24
	33 E 101.68
	34 D 262.1
	35 E 447.12
	36 D 265.21
Type 8d	38 D 285.60
Type 9c	37 E 101.42
	39 E 201.26

	40 D 264.5
	41 D 136.21
Type 10a	42 D 285.42
Type 10b	43 D 270.2
	44 D 294.3
Type 10c	45 E 201.23
	46 F 427.2
	47 F 452.127
	48 F 209.6
	49 D 263.68
	50 - E 100.10
	51 - F 212.32
	52 - D 249.9
Type 10d	53 - D 136.22
	54 - D 285.64
Type 11c	55 - F 440.3
	56 - D 265.7
	57 - E 101.34
	58 - F 447.47
Cooking pots	
Type 1a	59 - D 136.4
	60 - D 280.19
	61 - F 418.5
	62 - D 137.1
	63 - F 447.41
	64 - E 447.55
	65 - D 136.3
Type 1b	66 - D 265.16
	67 - D 294.15
	68 - F 234
Type 1c	69 - D 270.6
	70 - F 229
Type 1d	71 - F 478.1
	72 - E 100.7
	73 - A 176
	74 - D 135.13
	75 - D 137.2
	76 - F 447.70
Type 2a	77 - D 273.3
	78 - D 263.45
	79 - A 618.31
Type 2b	80 - D 135.11
	81 - D 132.3

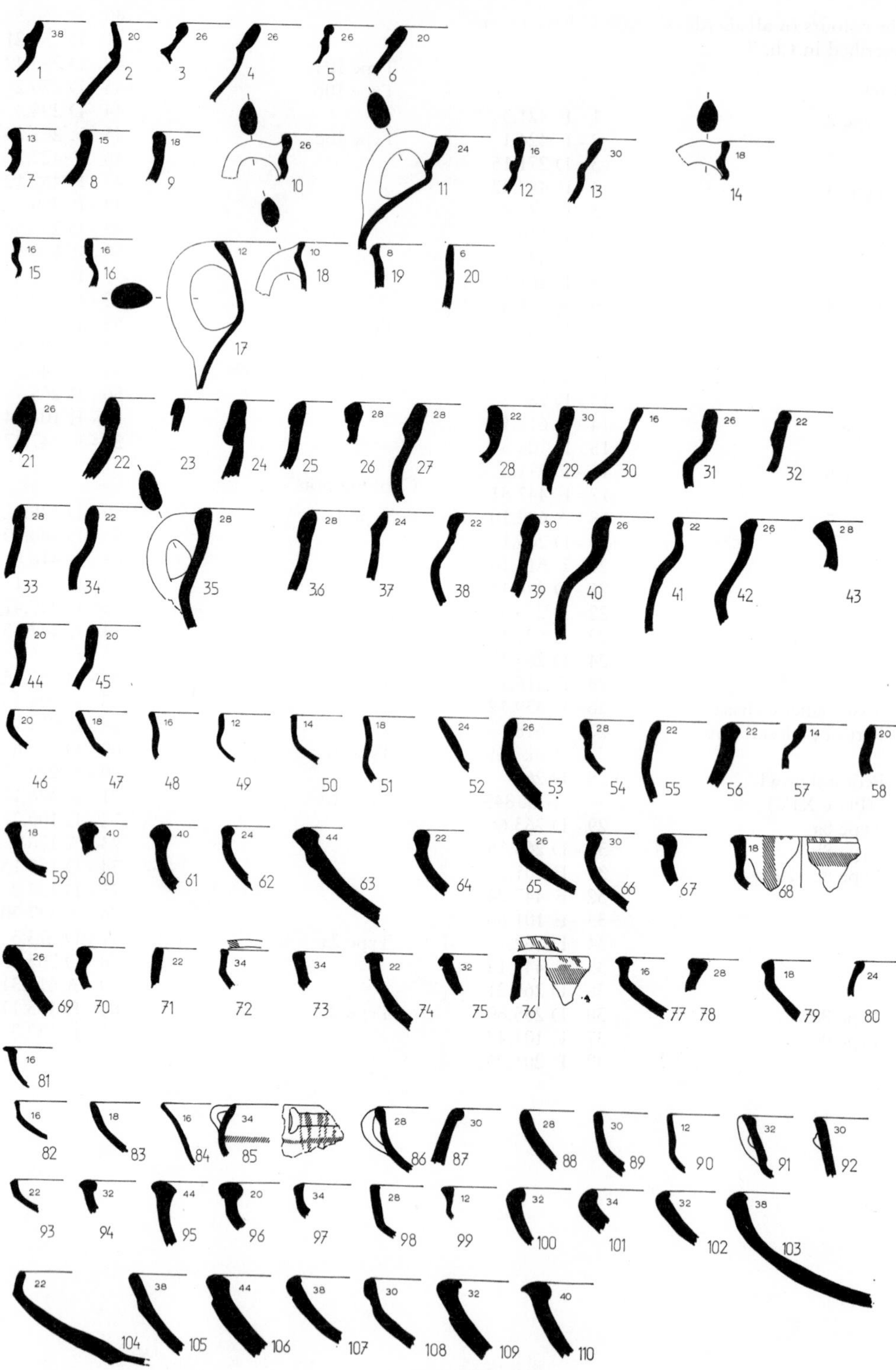

Fig. 64. Phase G

Type	No.
Cooking pots	
Type 2c	1 - F 447.34
Type 2e	2 - F 106.14
	3 - D 285.122
Type 2f	4 - D 261.16
Type 2g	5 - F 447.84
	6 - F 213.23
Type 3a	7 - D 135.4
	8 - B 511.18
	9 - D 135.14
	10 - D 135.10
Type 3b	11 - D 261.32
	12 - D 264.11
	13 - F 213.1
	14 - D 135.6
	15 - D 261.11
Type 3c	16 - D 135.3
Type 3d	17 - F 425.2
	18 - D 135.2
	19 - F 212.2
	20 - B 513.2
Deep bowls	
Type 1a	21 - D 265.44
	22 - F 447.62
	23 - D 262.2
	24 - F 447.63
Type 1c	25 - E 317.78
	26 - F 215.10
	27 - F 213.43
Type 2a	28 - A 617.26
	29 - F 440.2
Type 2c	30 - F 421.5
	31 - F 447.2
	32 - E 101.70
Type 3a	33 - F 232
	34 - D 137.7
	35 - D 135
	36 - F 421.7
Type 3b	37 - D 307.3
	38 - E 418.129
	39 - E 101.15
Type 3d	40 - D 285.131
	41 - D 135
	42 - F 212.21
	43 - B 513.17
	44 - D 285.15
	45 - F 106.9
Bowls	
Type 4a	46 - F 225.3
Type 4b	47 - D 136.18
Type 4d	48 - D 262.40
Type 4e	49 - B 513.4
Type 4f	50 - F 215.20
	51 - F 208.4
Type 4j	52 - D 137.35
Type 5a	53 - E 206.5

Type	No.
Type 5b	54 - D 263.67
Type 5c	55 - D 261.20
Type 5e	56 - F 212.15
Type 5f	57 - D 265.36
	58 - D 135
Type 6b	59 - A 618.32
Type 6c	60 - D 285.88
Type 6f	61 - D 285.42
	62 - E 421.8
Type 6l	63 - D 266.27
	64 - D 265.6
	65 - E 201.25
Type 8a	66 - A 621.9
Type 8f	67 - A 617.30
	68 - D 137.55
	69 - A 618
Type 8j	70 - D 280.16
Type 9a	71 - A 617.33
Type 9f	72 - D 263.11
	73 - D 137.43
Type 11a	74 - D 262.32
	75 - D 270.16
Type 11c	76 - D 285.20
Type 11f	77 -
Type 12a	78 - A 621.30
	79 - D 280.6
	80 - D 286.9
Type 15	81 - D 272.1
Type 4a (burn.)	82 - D 286.2
Type 4b (burn.)	83 - A 618.27
Type 4f (burn.)	84 - D 135
Type 5a (burn.)	85 - D 285.32
	86 - D 265.58
	87 - D 266.20
	88 - F 212.11
Type 5b (burn.)	89 - B 513.12
	90 - E 201.3
	91 - D 135
Type 5c (burn.)	92 - A 621.27
Type 5k (burn.)	93 - F 212.4
Type 7 (burn.)	94 - A 177
Type 8 (burn.)	95 - D 135
	96 - F 421.11
Type 9 (burn.)	97 - D 285.77
	98 - D 261.40
Type 12 (burn.)	99 - D 285.52
Type 13 (burn.)	100 - D 271.11
	101 - D 271.9
	102 - A 618.33
Type 17 (burn.)	103 - F 427.5
	104 - F 216 (r.n. 680)
	105 - E 201.2
	106 - D 137.40
	107 - D 266.19
	108 - F 213.12
	109 - F 213
	110 - A 176.3

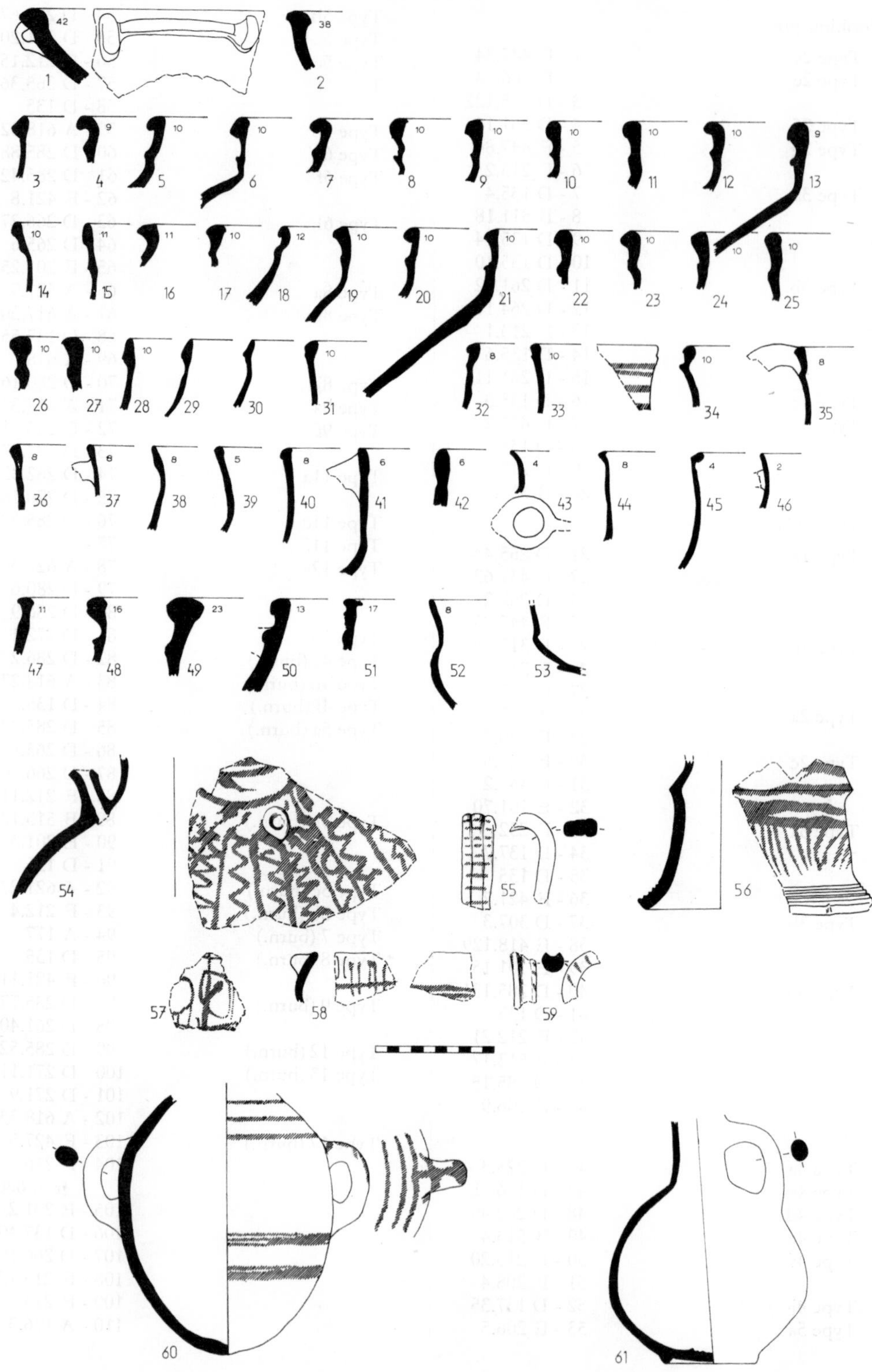

Fig. 65. Phase G

Bowls	
Type 17 (burn.) (cont.)	1 - D 137.20
	2 - D 135
Jars	
Type 1b	3 - D 307.2
Type 1c	4 - D 265.28
	5 - F 425.1
	6 - A 617.7
	7 - E 100.11
	8 - F 106.3
Type 1d	9 - E 410.8
	10 - F 213.10
	11 - D 261.13
	12 - D 262.6
	13 - E 411.5
Type 1e	14 - F 417.65
	15 - E 425.108
Type 1f	16 - D 135
	17 - D 280.7
	18 - D 261.1
Type 1g	19 - D 285.136
	20 -
	21 - E 411.6
Type 1k	22 - F 213.2
	23 - D 135
	24 - D 135
	25 - D 135
Type 1l	26 - F 439.22
	27 - D 265.29
Type 2a	28 - F 447.53
	29 - F 474.157
	30 - F 447.75
	31 F 212.30
Type 2c	32 D 137.24
	33 F 209.1

	34 D 135
	35 F 213.5
Type 2d	36 F 430.1
	37 D 272.15
	38 D 294.1
	39 F 439.19
	40 F 215.2
	41 D 261.37
Miscellaneous	
Jars	42 D 266.32
	43 D 266.33
	44 A 621.8
	45 F 212.28
	46 F 213.82
Kraters	47 F 225.1
	48 F 212.17
	49 D 261.35
	50 E 201.32
	51 E 207.2
Import	52 D 265.77
	53 D 262.19
Decorations	
Jar fragment	54 F 447.16
Handle	55 D 263.15
Pedestal base fragment	56 D 285.91
Sherd	57 A 622.3
Bowl fragment	58 D 285
Handle	59 D 260.21
Jug (Plate XIV)	60 F 216 (r.n. 685)
Miscellaneous	
Jar	61 F 425 (r.n. 848)

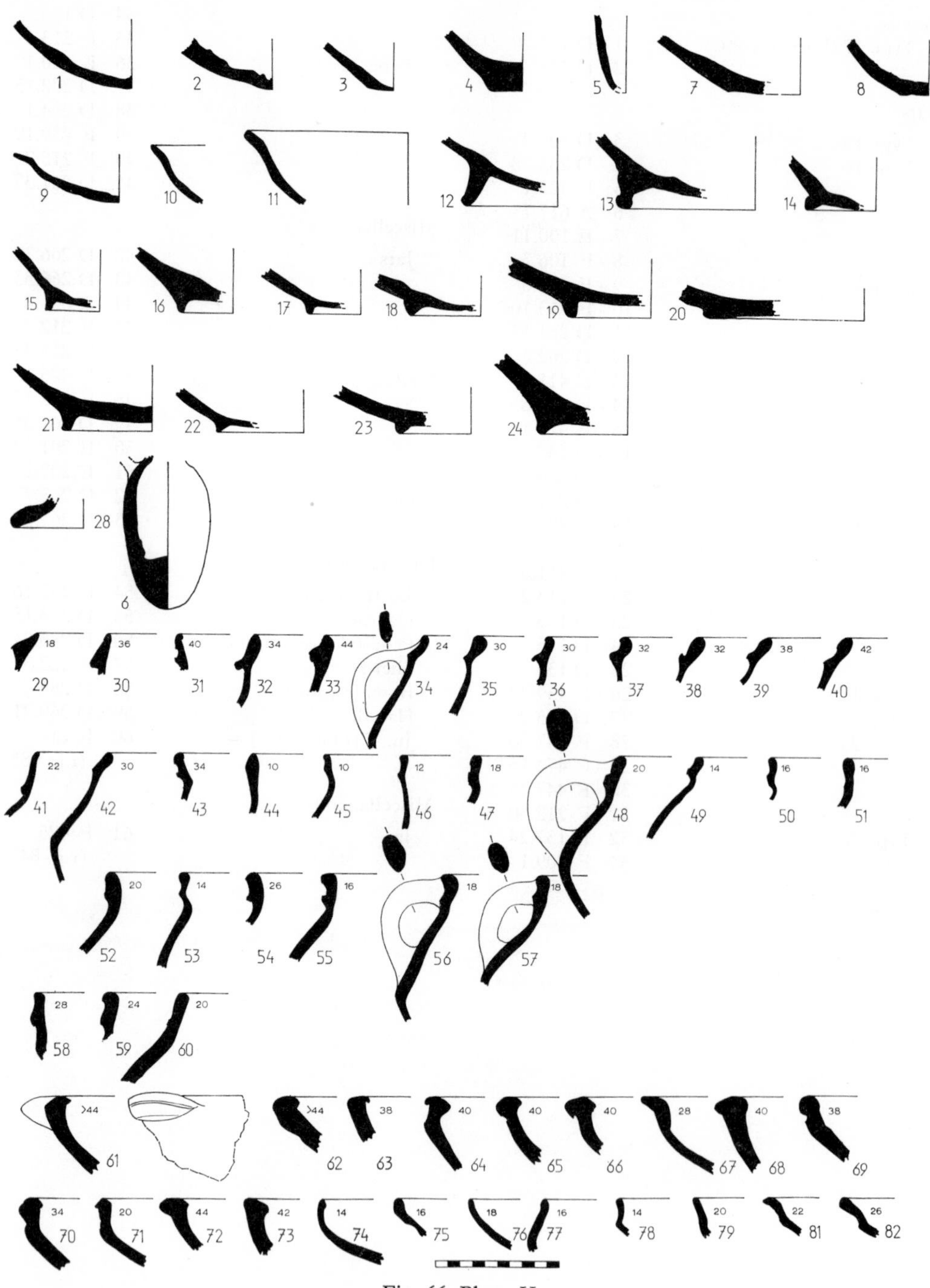

Fig. 66. Phase H

Bases	
Type 2c	1 F 416.20
	2 D 256.62
Type 3	3 D 260.1
	4 D 295.114
Type 4	5 D 257.24
	6 - F 210 (r.n. 722)
Type 6	7 - A 416.30
	8 - G 202.3
Type 7	9 - A 520.3
	10 - F 205.7
	11 - A 350.6
Type 8a	12 - D 258.11
	13 - B 506.23
Type 8c	14 - D 166.50
	15 - E 407.1
	16 - D 260.11
	17 - D 251
	18 - B 218
Type 10b	19 - E 402.18
Type 10c	20 - B 507.10
	21 - F 416.8
	22 - D 257.4
	23 - A 428.11
	24 - D 286.1
Pedestal base	28 - D 258.17
Cooking pots	
Type 1a	29 - F 203
	30 - F 416.11
Type 1c	31 - B 324.1
Type 1d	32 - A 405.6
	33 - D 256.65
Type 2a	34 - A 416.22
	35 - F 206.40
Type 2b	36 - E 416.41
	37 - D 256.32
	38 - F 206.12
Type 2c	39 - E 402.6
Type 2d	40 - B 506.5
Type 2e	41 - B 506.9
Type 2f	42 - B 317.9

Type 2g	43 - A 613.3
Type 3a	51 - A 338.5
	52 - D 256.30
	53 - D 254.4
	54 - B 507.8
	55 - D 257.13
	56 - A 414.10
	57 - F 206.4
Type 3b	49 - A 339.10
	50 - D 256.67
Type 3c	47 - D 129.2
	48 - D 257.69
Type 3d	44 - F 203.4
	45 - B 321.9
	46 - D 256.90
Deep bowls	
Type 2a	58 - D 256.68
Type 2b	59 - F 210.32
Type 2c	60 - F 206.2
Bowls	
Type 17 (burn.)	61 - B 317.5
	62 - B 321.3
	63 - F 206.16
	64 - D 254.23
	65 - A 616.1
	66 - D 256.41
	67 - D 256.73
	68 - D 255.3
	69 - A 613.6
	70 - A 177
	71 - A 616.124
	72 - D 257.6
	73 - D 129
Type 4a	74 - A 416.26
	75 - D 257.43
	76 - B 506.19
Type 4d	77 - B 127
Type 4f	78 - A 416.1
	79 - D 256.19
Type 4h	81 - D 260.16
	82 - F 210.39

Deep bowls types 1 and 3 see Fig. 77, 1-17.

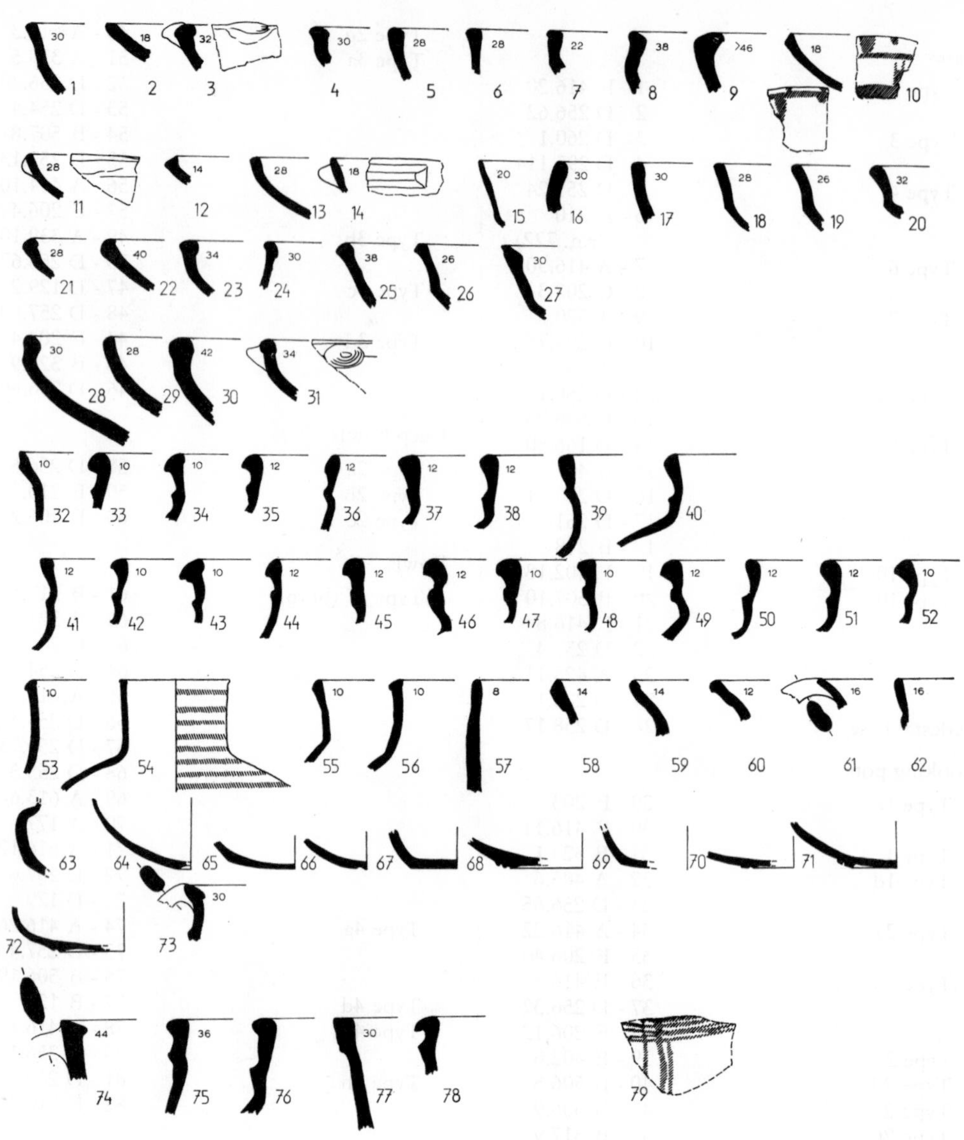

Fig. 67. Phase H

Bowls		
	Type 5b	1 - D 258.13
	Type 5j	2 - D 256.65
	Type 6	3 - A 338.3
	Type 8	4 - B 408
	Type 9a	5 - A 410.14
	Type 11a	6 - D 251.12
	Type 11f	7
	Type 15	8 - D 260.9
	Type 16	9 - A 340.6
		10 - A 410.17
		11 - A 521.5
		12 - D 256.13
	Type 4a (burn.)	13 - A 416.2
		14 - A 350.13
	Type 4b (burn.)	15 -
	Type 5a (burn.)	16 - D 258.9
	Type 5b (burn.)	17 - A 402.2
		18 - D 251.34
	Type 5f (burn.)	19 - D 258.6
		20 - D 256.83
	Type 6a (burn.)	21 - D 258.31
	Type 6j (burn.)	22 - F 210.5
	Type 7a (burn.)	23 - A 350.8
	Type 7f (burn.)	24 - C 161.10
	Type 8b (burn.)	25 - B 311.1
	Type 8f (burn.)	26 - D 255.5
	Type 15 (burn.)	27 - C 415.66
	Type 17 (burn.)	28 - A 428.6
		29 - B 317.3
		30 - B 506.2
		31 - F 210.48
Jars		
	Type 1b	32 - A 522.6
	Type 1c	33 - B 511.19
		34 - B 507.18
		35 - A 522.22
	Type 1d	36 - D 258.39
		37 - D 256.6
		38 - A 416.18
		39 - D 257.18
		40 - D 256.41
	Type 1f	41 - D 256.19
		42 - D 259.52
	Type 1g	43 - F 203.14
		44 - F 202.12
	Type 1h	45 - D 257.61
		46 - D 129
	Type 1k	47 - D 251.15
		48 - C 421.23
		49 - D 129
		50 - B 312.12
	Type 1l	51 - D 257.55
		52 - D 251.15
	Type 2d	53 - F 203.18
		54 - F 206.10
		55 - A 428.12
		56 - B 506.22
		57 - F 202.27
	Type 2e	58 - B 181
		59 - A 520.5
		60 - A 339.4
		61 - D 357.3
Miscellaneous	Import	62 - A 350.10
		63 - D 256
		64 - F 416.10
		65 - B 507.12
		66 - D 256.66
		67 - A 613
		68 - D 256.51
		69 - D 257.36
		70 - D 129
		71 - D 257.22
		72 - D 252.1
		73 - D 256.44
Kraters		74 - B 310.6
		75 - F 210.40
		76 - D 260.13
		77 - E 325.1
		78 - D 254.9
Decoration		
	Sherd	79 - B 312.8

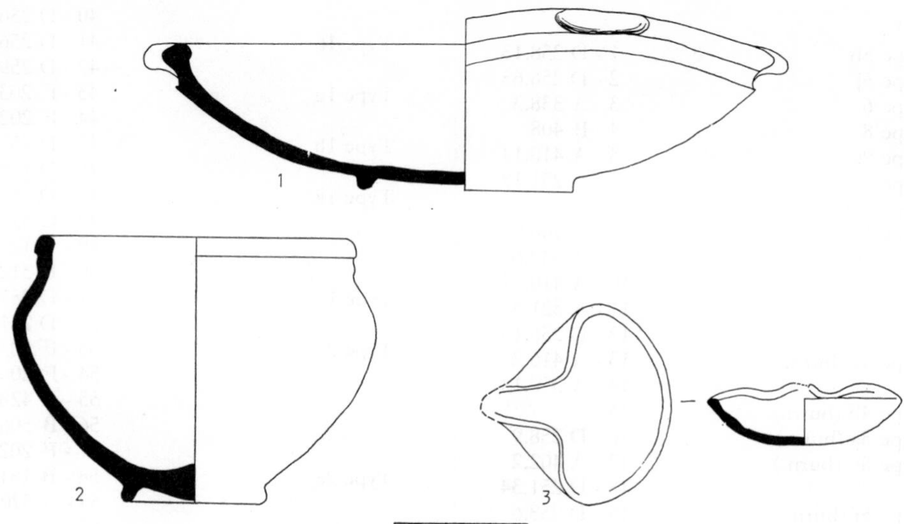

Fig. 68. Phase H

Miscellaneous		Lamp	3 - D 127 (r.n. 51)
Bowl Type 17 (Plate XV)	1 - B 176 (r.n.1087)		
Deep bowl, type 2f (Plate XIV)	2 - B 514 (r.n. 464)		

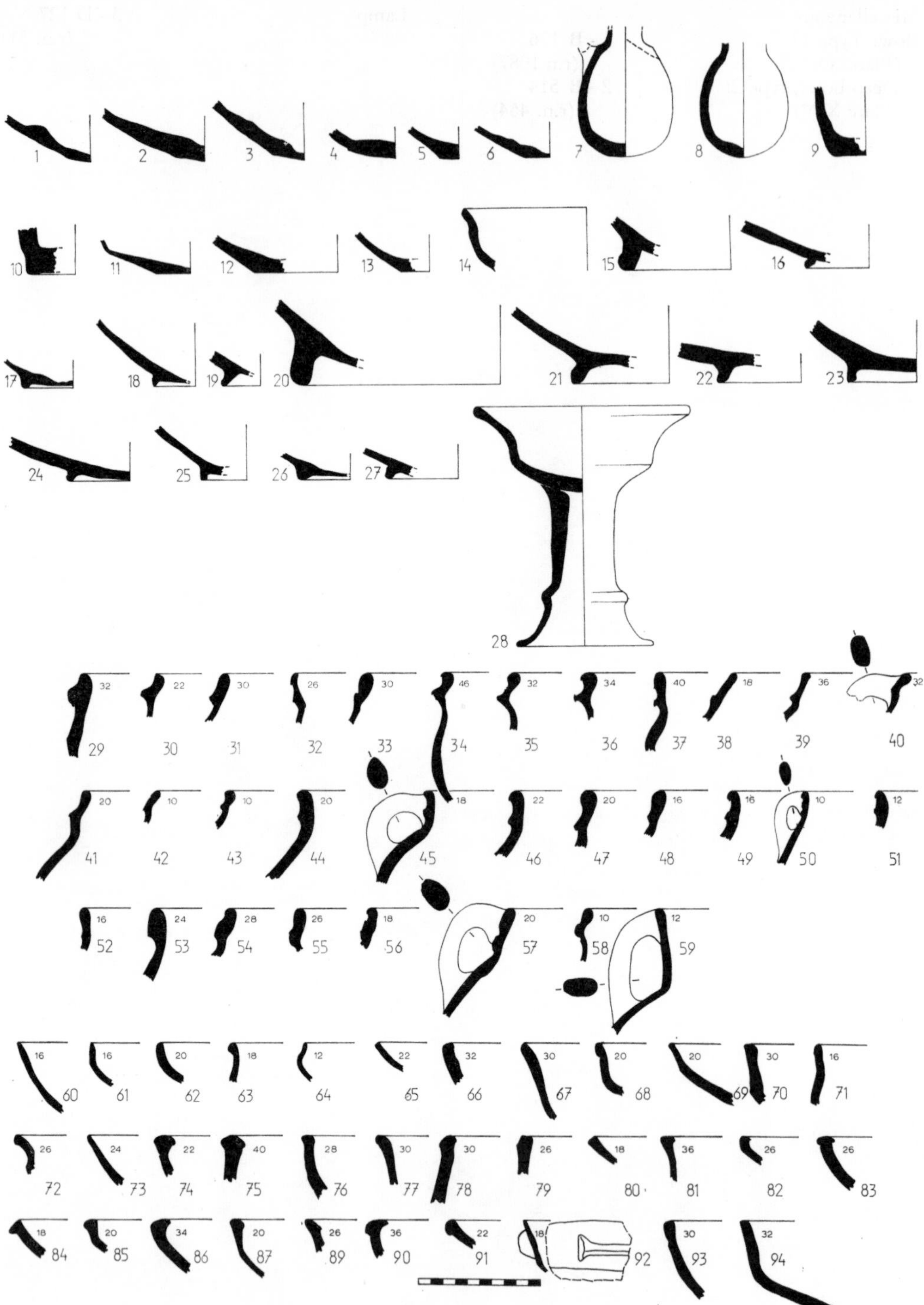

Fig. 69. Phase J

Bases	
Type 2b	1 - B 521.10
Type 2c	2 - B 521 14
	3 - A 272.10
Type 3	4 - B 521.6
	5 - B 218
	6 - B 521.8
Type 4	7 - D 301 (r.n. 569)
	8 - B 218 (r.n. 104)
Type 5	9 - A 174.28
	10 -
Type 6	11 - B 235.21
	12 - A 260.23
	13 - B 235
Type 7	14 - A 335.5
Type 8a	15 - D 301.24
Type 8c	16 - D 249.4
	17 - A 174.14
	18 - B 235.24
	19 - A 249.5
Type 10a	20 - D 249.1
	21 - A 258.3
Type 10b	22 - A 349.12
	23 - A 336.11
Type 10c	24 - D 230.1
	25 - A 169.1
	26 - A 174.23
	27 - D 230.5
Pedestal bowl (Plate XIV)	28 - A 419 (r.n. 525)
Cooking pots	
Type 1d	29 - B 172.6
	30 - D 246.11
	31 - D 134.3
Type 2a	32 - B 521
	33 - D 246.4
Type 2b	34 - D 134.7
	35 - D 134.8
	36 - D 246.13
Type 2d	37 - D 134.6
Type 2e	38 - D 246.36
	39 - B 218
Type 2f	40 - B 453.12
	41 - A 174.16
	42 - D 231.27
Type 2g	43 - B 448.8
Type 3a	44 - A 325.2
	45 - A 336.2
	46 - A 335.6
	47 - B 235.7
	48 - A 168.8
	49 - A 174.9
	50 - F 330.16
	51 - B 171.6
	52 - A 336.15
	53 - B 235.12
Type 3b	54 - B 453.20
	55 - D 233.42
Type 3c	56 - B 453.6
	57 D 249.1
Type 3d	58 B 453.22
	59 F 205.1
Bowls	
Type 4a	60 B 453
	61 B 235.23
	62 A 255.4
Type 4d	63 - B 218
Type 4f	64 - B 521.19
Type 4j	65 - B 218.16
Type 5a	66 - A 349.10
Type 5b	67 - D 301.25
Type 5e	68 - D 235.13
Type 5f	69 - B 218 (r.n. 83)
	70 - B 234.3
	71 - A 259.6
Type 5h	72 - B 218
Type 5j	73 - B 315.31
Type 7a	74 - A 335.37
Type 8a	75 - A 336.12
	76 - D 230.31
Type 8b	77 - A 163.4
Type 8c	78 - A 174.2
Type 9a	79 - B 458.1
Type 9j	80 - B 218
Type 10f	81 - A 258.1
Type 10k	82 - A 337.1
Type 11a	83 - A 272.11
Type 12	84 - B 453.21
	85 - B 218
Type 13	86 - B 447.28
Type 15	88 - D 249.7
	89 - D 246.16
Type 16	90 - A 419.3
	91 - A 336.20
Type 4b (burn.)	92 - A 419
Type 5a (burn.)	93 - A 419.6
Type 5b (burn.)	94 - B 235.9

Deep bowls types 1 and 3 see Fig. 77. 18-28

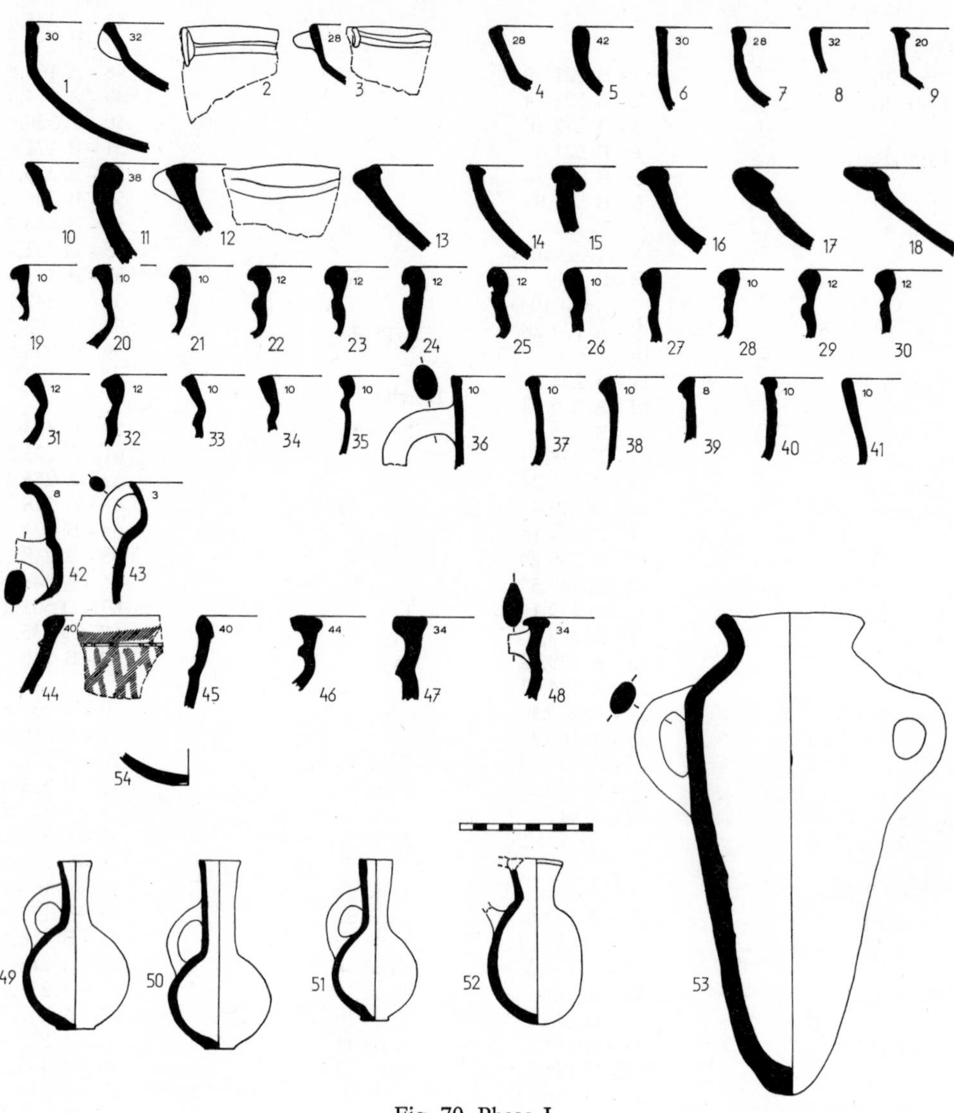

Fig. 70. Phase J

Bowls	
Type 5f (burn.)	1 - B 235.8
	2 - A 419.1
	3 - B 171.3
Type 6b (burn.)	4 - A 164.2
Type 9a (burn.)	5 - D 231.73
Type 9b (burn.)	6 - C 376.8
Type 10a (burn.)	7 - B 315.4
Type 10b (burn.)	8 - B 315.14
Type 15 (burn.)	9 - B 218
	10 - B 218.9
Type 17 (burn.)	11 - B 235
	12 - B 315.2
	13 - A 518.2
	14 - B 218
	15 - D 235.4
	16 - D 134
	17 - B 218.8
	18 - B 218.11
Jars	
Type 1c	19 - A 174.6
Type 1d	20 - B 171.4
Type 1g	21 - D 301.7
Type 1h	22 - B 453.10
	23 - B 315.8
	24 - C 420.32
Type 1j	25 - B 218.4
Type 1k	26 - D 232.5
	27 - A 164.8
	28 - A 272.4
	29 - B 453.9
	30 - B 453.4

Type 1l	31 - B 315.27
	32 - D 235.3
	33 - B 315.31
	34 - B 316.3
Type 2c	35 - A 260.1
Type 2d	36 - A 336.6
	37 - B 218
	38 - B 521.9
	39 - A 174.3
	40 - B 218
	41 - A 168.5
Type 2e	42 - D 301.28
Miscellaneous	
Juglet	43 - D 430.70
Kraters	44 - B 218
	45 - B 169.9
	46 - B 315.8
	47 - B 315.9
	48 - A 260.15
Miscellaneous	
Juglet (Plate XV)	49 - B 305 (r.n 403)
Juglet (Plate XV)	50 - B 305 (r.n. 404)
Juglet (Plate XV)	51 - B 305 (r.n. 409)
Juglet	52 - D 301 (r.n. 623)
Jar	53 - B 218 (r.n. 58)
	54 - C 369.2

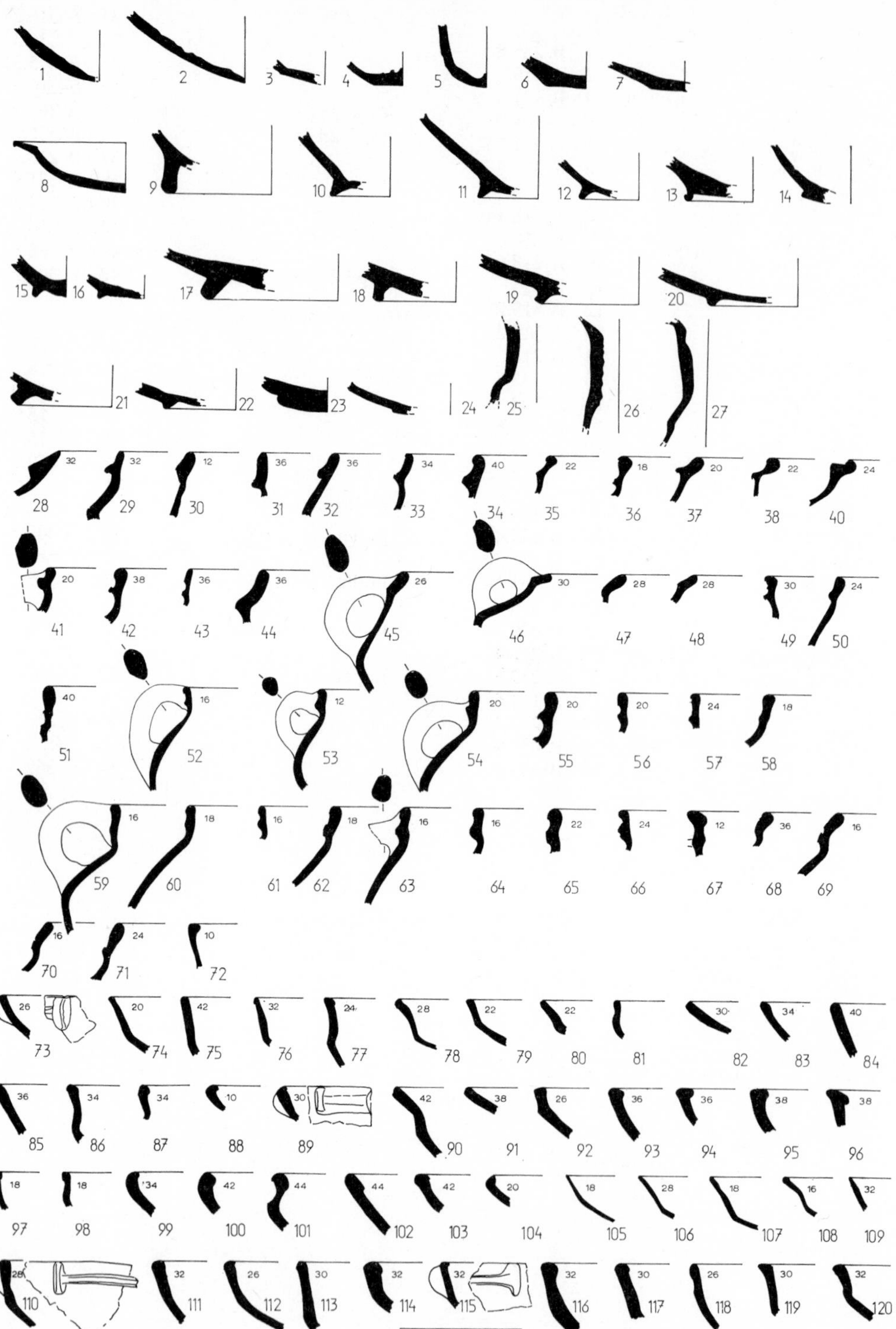

Fig. 71. Phase K

Bases	
Type 2c	1 - C 373.5
	2 - E 403.1
Type 3	3 - B 218
	4 - C 374.15
Type 4	5 - C 330.7
Type 6	6 - B 169.10
	7 - D 125.13
Type 7	8 - C 422.56
Type 8a	9 - C 427.14
Type 8c	10 - A 151.31
	11 - D 126.11
	12 - D 227.8
	13 - A 318.3
Type 9c	14 - C 371.10
	15 - C 257.24
	16 - D 123.40
Type 10a	17 - D 126.26
	18 - C 359.26
Type 10b	19 - C 370.7
Type 10c	20 - D 217.17
	21 - D 124
	22 - B 169.25
	23 - D 227.1
	24 - C 421.42
Pedestal bases	25 - D 124
	26 - B 446.30
	27 - D 237.37
Cooking pots	
Type 1a	28 - D 139.8
	29 - D 237.3
Type 1d	30 - A 151.48
	31 - C 257.5
	32 - C 422.16
Type 2a	33 - C 167.3
	34 - C 421.41
	35 - A 151.11
	36 - A 151.32
Type 2b	37 - D 221.25
	38 - A 318.38
	40 - D 125.42
Type 2c	41 - C 257.34
Type 2d	42 - C 371.40
	43 - C 374.8
Type 2e	44 - C 256.7
Type 2f	45 - B 427
	46 - C 261.1
	47 - B 159.12
	48 - C 422.64
Type 2g	49 - D 247.26
	50 - C 373.18
	51 - B 446.14
Type 3a	52 C 372
	53 C 374.24
	54 C 257.26
	55 C 370.17
	56 C 423.24
	57 B 445.6
	58 B 169.13
	59 D 244.1
	60 B 446.36
	61 B 169.30
Type 3b	62 A 151.29
	63 C 422.1
	64 C 422.3
	65 D 226.4
	66 D 226.7
	67 D 139.3
Type 3c	68 D 139.7
	69 D 227.1
	70 C 359.31
	71 A 158.16
Type 3d	72 C 361.11
Bowls	
Type 4a	73 A 318.42
Type 4b	74 - D 243.17
Type 4c	75 - D 169.58
Type 4d	76 - A 318.48
Type 4f	77 - D 274.16
	78 - A 151.52
	79 - A 125.7
	80 - D 221.19
Type 4g	81 - C 423.19
Type 4j	82 - C 422.42
	83 - D 253.5
Type 5b	84 - D 122.16
Type 5f	85 - B 169.46
	86 - B 170.16
Type 6f	87 - C 422.5
Type 6k	88 - A 158.12
Type 9a	89 - D 224.10
Type 9h	90 - D 139.12
Type 9j	91 - B 170.10
Type 9k	92 - D 286.6
Type 10a	93 - B 169.2
	94 - C 427.7
	95 - C 217.11
Type 11	96 - A 318.59
Type 12a	97 - D 125.32
Type 12g	98 - B 169.50
Type 13	99 - B 427
	100 - B 446.23
Type 14	101 - B 169.6
Type 15	102 - D 221.18
	103 - D 123.11
Type 16	104 - B 169.75
Type 4a (burn.)	105 - D 221.23
Type 4b (burn.)	106 - D 221.15
Type 4f (burn.)	107 - A 141
Type 4h (burn.)	108 - D 214.12
Type 4j (burn.)	109 - D 221.16
Type 5a (burn.)	110 - A 144.6
	111 - D 224.11
Type 5b (burn.)	112 - A 144.2
Type 5f (burn.)	113 - A 147.4
Type 6a (burn.)	114 - A 318.31
	115 - C 427.6
Type 6b (burn.)	116 - D 134
	117 - D 221.28
Type 8a (burn.)	118 - A 152.19
Type 8b (burn.)	119 - C 223.21
Type 8f (burn.)	120 - D 126.110

Deep bowls type 3 see Fig. 77, 29-39

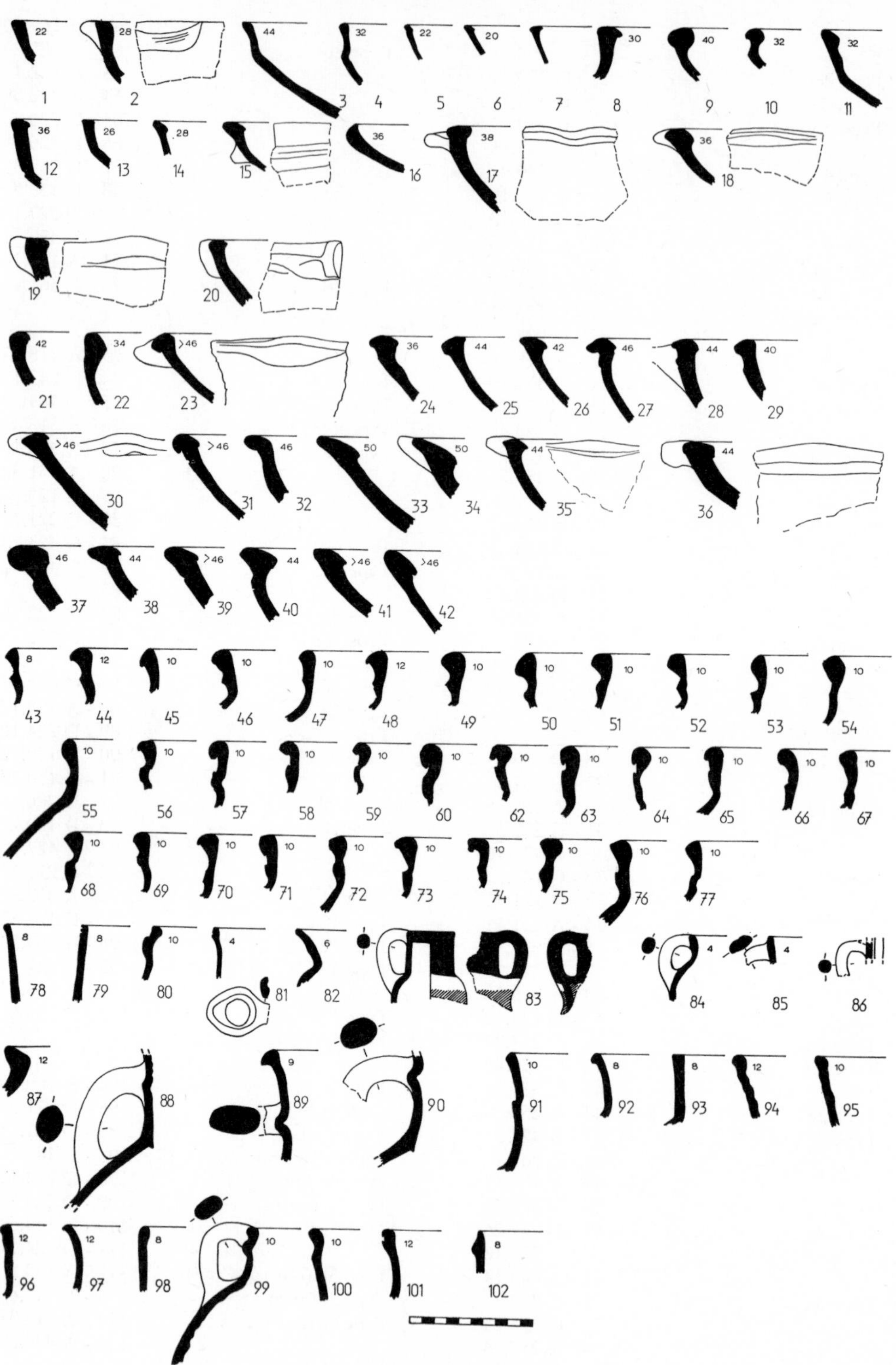

Fig. 72. Phase K

Bowls

Type 9 (burn.)	1 - A 151.60
	2 - D 215.1
	3 - D 124
	4 - D 237.16
Type 10 (burn.)	5 - D 124
	6 - D 125.16
	7 - D 139.15
Type 11 (burn.)	8 - D 224.4
	9 - B 169.26
Type 14 (burn.)	10 - C 257.7
Type 15 (burn.)	11 - D 217.1
	12 - D 217.2
	13 - D 139.18
	14 - D 123.15
	15 - D 119.3
Type 16 (burn.)	16 - C 329.16
Type 17 (burn.)	17 - A 147.8
	18 - A 144.9
	19 - C 422.46
	20 - C 423.3
	21 - B 446.9
	22 - D 237.3
	23 - B 427
	24 - D 227.6
	25 - A 151.21
	26 - D 242.9
	27 - C 421.25
	28 - A 152.9
	29 - A 318.22
	30 - A 155.12
	31 - D 125.34
	32 - D 226.2
Type 18 (burn.)	33 - C 247.17
	34 - D 225.6
	35 - C 421.24
	36 - C 257.41
	37 - D 228.4
	38 - D 227.1
	39 - D 226.5
	40 - C 261.5
	41 - D 123.3
	42 - D 123.7

Jars

Type 1b	43 -
Type 1d	44 - D 126.4
	45 - B 446.20
	46 - D 123.38
	47 - A 160.7
	48 - C 361.78
	49 - C 422.39
	50 - C 422.14
Type 1f	51 - D 241.12
	52 - C 421.16
Type 1g	53 - D 226.11
	54 - C 422.26
	55 - D 244.9
Type 1h	56 - C 359.24
	57 - D 237.5
	58 - D 125.11
	59 - A 151.8
Type 1j	60 -
	62 - D 124
	63 - D 139.2
	64 - D 122.3
Type 1k	65 - D 215.5
	66 -
	67 - D 244.9
	68 - A 160.1
	69 - C 421.9
	70 - D 221.4
Type 1l	71 - C 374.10
	72 - A 144.17
	73 - C 257.38
	74 - D 138
	75 - D 253.18
	76 - B 427
	77 - C 421.32
Type 2b	78 - C 371.28
Type 2c	79 - D 253.4
	80 - C 421.47
	81 - D 123.5
Type 2d	82 - D 125.22
	83 - D 241.20
	84 - D 248.4
	85 - D 243.15
	86 - D 227
	87 - D 226.7
	88 - D 125.1

Miscellaneous

Jars	89 - D 224.15
	90 - D 224.34
	91 - D 125.5
	92 - D 125.31
	93 - D 211
	94 - D 126.12
	95 - C 373.10
	96 - B 169.35
	97 - D 228.14
	98 - A 162.14
	99 - D 244.10
	100 - B 427
	101 - A 151.41
	102 - C 370.74

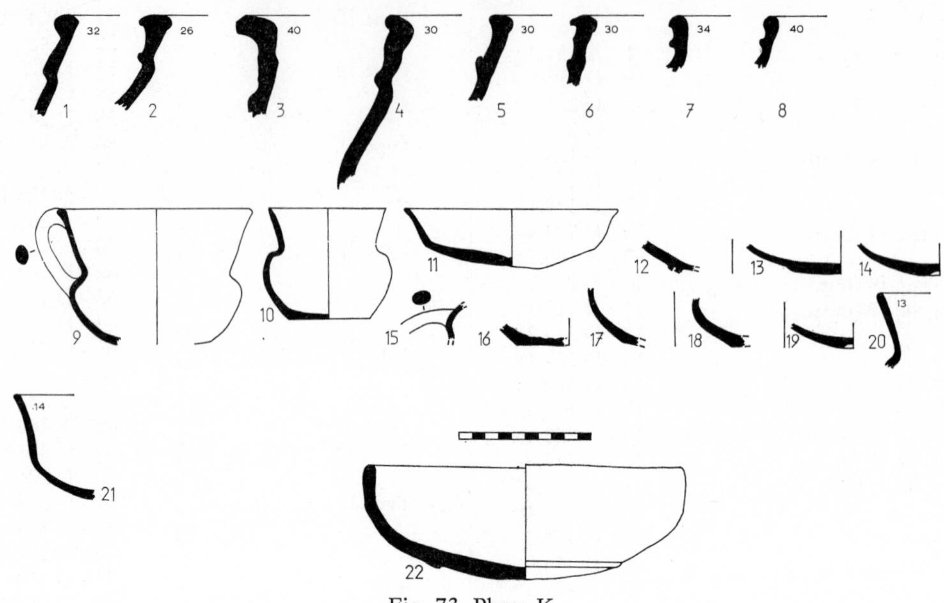

Fig. 73. Phase K

Kraters	1 - C 369.1	Bowl, import (Plate XV)	11 - C 367 (r.n. 538)
	2 - D 227.12		12 - D 253.14
	3 - C 256.4		13 - D 123.33
	4 - C 372.12		14 - D 237.15
	5 - D 124		15 - B 226.10
	6 - B 446.22		16 - D 226.1
	7 - D 122.24		17 - D 139.25
	8 - C 276.7		18 - A 318.5
Miscellaneous			19 - C 422.14
Bowl, import	9 - A 218 (r.n. 55)		20 - D 253.9
		Import	21 - D 126.21
Bowl, import	10 - B 446 (r.n. 400)	Bowl	22 - E 403 (r.n. 863)

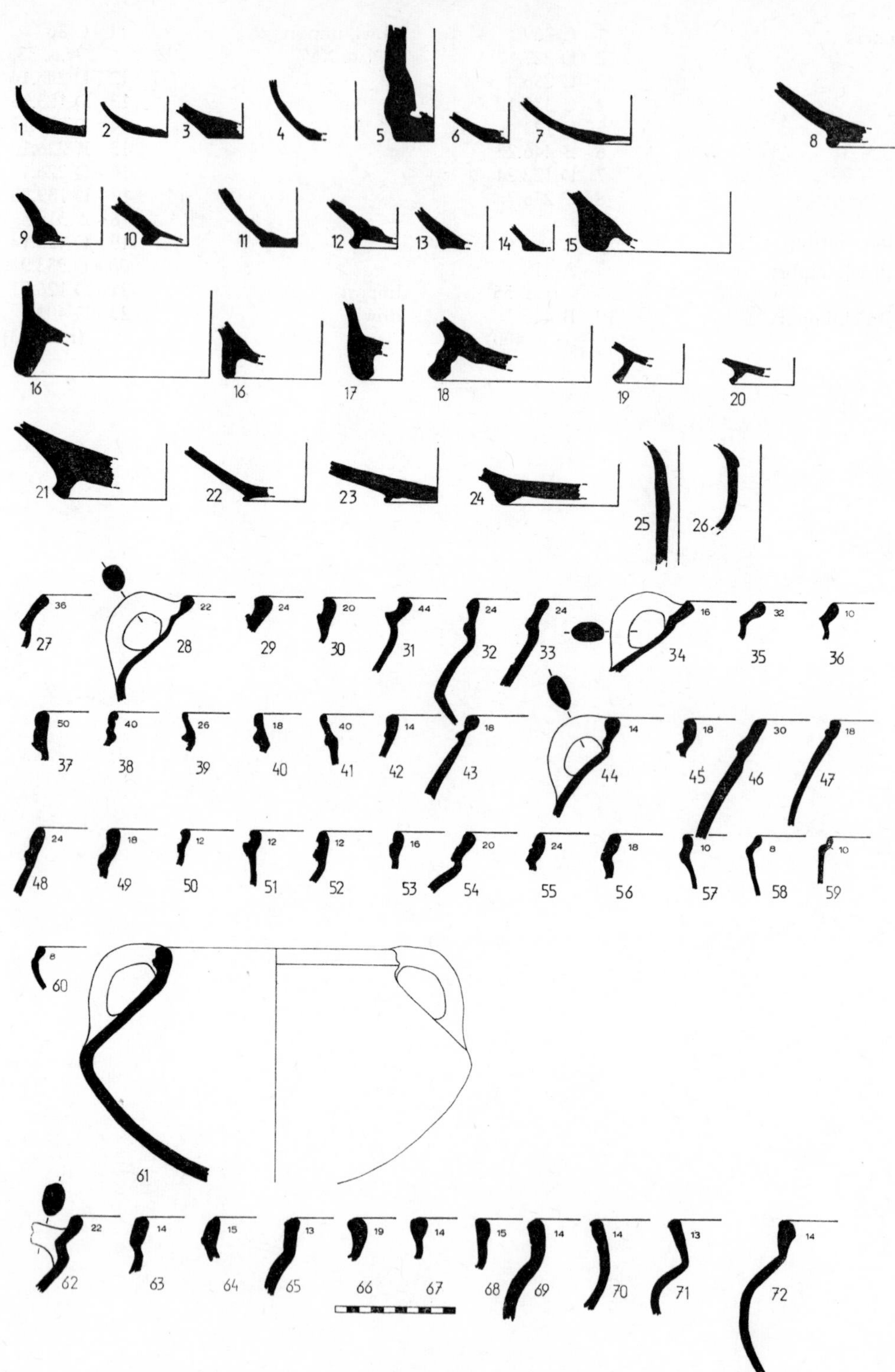

Fig. 74. Phase L

Bases	
Type 3	1 - C 513.5
	2 - C 348.8
	3 - C 150.24
	4 - C 354.5
Type 5	5 - C 255
Type 6	6 - C 237.2
	7 - C 162.3
Type 8c	8 - B 143
	9 - C 168.30
	10 - C 247.26
Type 9c	11 - C 523.18
	12 - C 263.17
	13 - B 169.12
	14 - C 159.5
Type 10a	15 - C 372
	16 - D 217.14
	17 - A 151.37
	18 - C 257.25
	19 - C 351.13
	20 - C 419.4
Type 10c	21 - C 242.10
	22 - B 152
	23 - C 148.2
	24 - C 412.1
Pedestal bases	25 - D 205.18
	26 - C 253.1
Cooking pots	
Type 1a	27 - C 160.7
Type 2a	28 - B 166.6
	29 - D 213.37
	30 - C 160.4
Type 2b	31 - C 513.19
Type 2c	32 - C 513.4
Type 2e	33 - C 168.2
Type 2f	34 - C 236.4
	35 - C 520.5
	36 - C 419.63
	37 - B 165.1
Type 2g	38 - C 227.12
	39 - C 155.1
	40 - C 241.2
	41 - C 241.4
	42 - C 227.8
Type 3a	43 - C 227.19
	44 - C 165
	45 - C 348.13
	46 - B 167.14
	47 - C 520.7
Type 3b	48 - C 513.26
	49 - B 145
	50 - C 523.3
	51 - C 420.20
	52 - B 145
	53 - C 263.25
Type 3c	54 - C 348.30
	55 - C 351.19
	56 - C 419.62
Type 3d	57 - C 419.42
	58 - C 320.1
	59 - C 419.77
	60 - B 158
Type 3a (Plate XIV)	61 - C 242 (r.n. 473)
Deep bowls	
Type 3a	62 - D 126.2
	63 - C 506.8
Type 3b	64 - C 348.41
Type 3d	65 - D 208.2
	66 - C 336.7
	67 - B 145
	68 - B 143
	69 - C 241.12
	70 - C 237.1
	71 - C 513.3
	72 - D 206.16

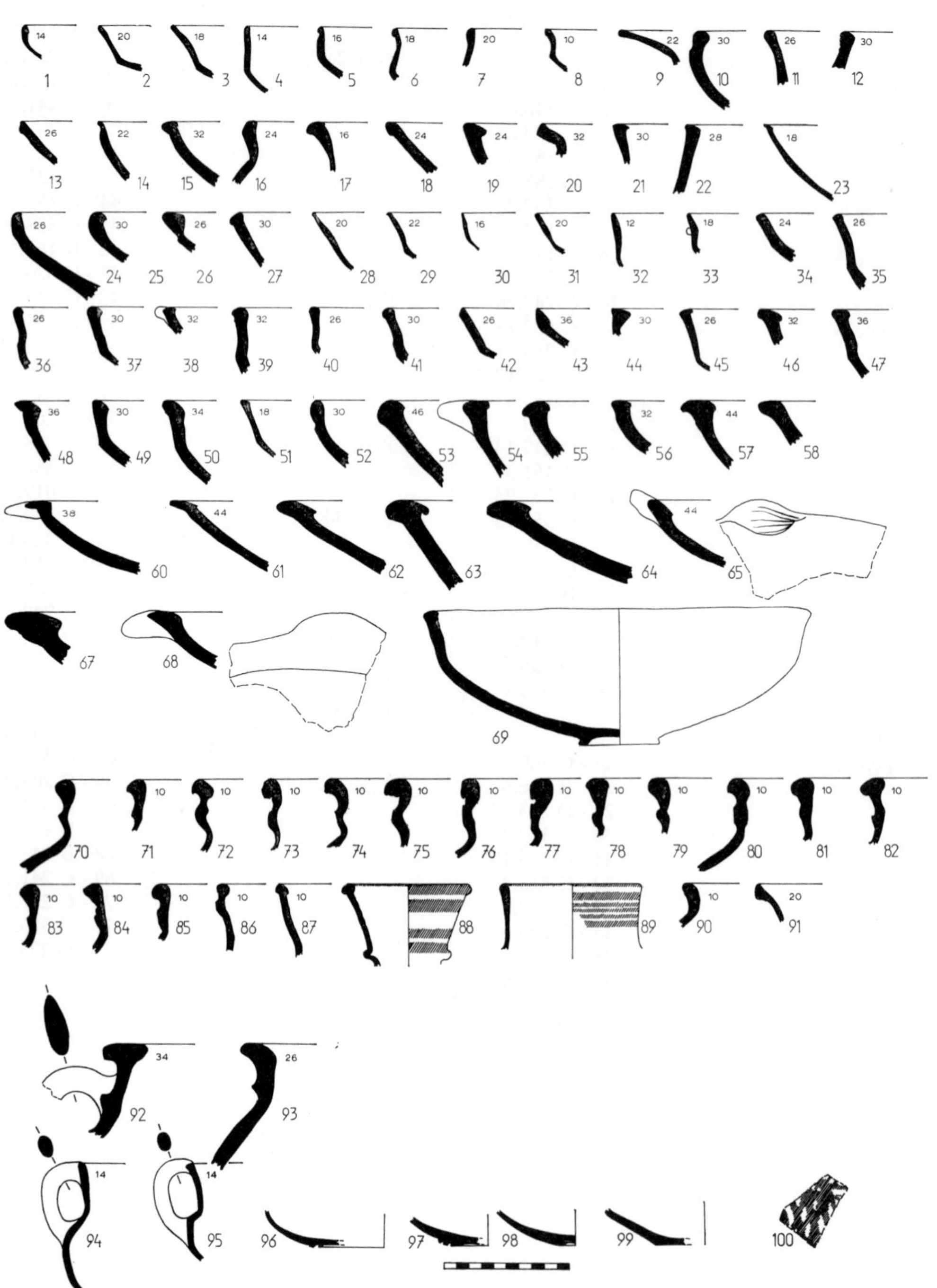

Fig. 75. Phase L

Bowls	
Type 4a	1 - C 513.16
Type 4b	2 - C 419.51
	3 - C 412.2
Type 4c	4 - C 255.23
Type 4d	5 - C 242.9
	6 - C 340.9
Type 4e	7 - C 163.3
Type 4f	8 - C 247.9
Type 4j	9 - C 511.2
Type 5a	10 - C 247.23
Type 5b	11 - C 166.5
Type 5c	12 - D 213.28
Type 5j	13 - C 348
Type 5k	14 - B 158
Type 8a	15 - C 161.1
Type 8f	16 - C 236.2
	17 - D 203.21
Type 8j	18 - D 256.31
Type 10a	19 - C 150.20
Type 10h	20 - C 243.6
Type 11b	21 - C 523.22
Type 12b	22 - C 246.1
Type 12j	23 - C 419.79
Type 13	24 - D 830.20
	25 - C 164.4
Type 15	26 - B 145
Type 16	27 - C 513.14
Type 4b (burn.)	28 - C 412.19
	29 - B 145
	30 - C 166.11
	31 - C 348.19
Type 4c (burn.)	32 - C 340.2
Type 4f (burn.)	33 - C 513.11
Type 5a (burn.)	34 - C 157.2
Type 5b (burn.)	35 - C 513.22
Type 5f (burn.)	36 - C 255.2
Type 6b (burn.)	37 - C 243.5
	38 - D 203.19
Type 7b (burn.)	39 - D 205.25
Type 7f (burn.)	40 - C 420.30
Type 8f (burn.)	41 - B 166.2
Type 9b (burn.)	42 - C 419.73
Type 10a (burn.)	43 - B 143
	44 - B 143
Type 10b (burn.)	45 - D 210.10
Type 11a (burn.)	46 - C 166.4
Type 11b (burn.)	47 - D 213.24
Type 12b (burn.)	48 - C 513.29
Type 15 (burn.)	49 - C 351.16
	50 - C 351.3
	51 - C 147.1
Type 17 (burn.)	52 - B 116.15
	53 - C 419.17
	54 - C 511.2
	55 - C 247.24
	56 - B 145
	57 - D 203.15
	58 - C 419.47
Type 18 (burn.)	60 - C 168
	61 - B 145
	62 - D 203.14
	63 -
	64 - C 166.1
	65 - D 208.1
	67 - B 166.11
	68 - C 412.17
Bowl	
Type 5 (Plate XV)	69 - C 340 (r.n. 131)
Jars	
Type 1d	70 - C 513.28
	71 - A 170.8
Type 1h	72 - C 511.1
	73 - D 118.5
	74 - C 155.4
	75 - B 167.25
Type 1j	76 - D 205.57
	77 - C 357.9
Type 1k	78 - C 513.2
	79 - C 419.57
	80 - C 420
	81 - C 412.18
Type 1l	82 - C 247.11
	83 - D 213.3
	84 - C 523.1
	85 - C 247.15
Type 2c	86 - B 169
Type 2d	87 - B 145
	88 - C 247.14
	89 - D 205.52
Type 2e	90 - B 143
	91 - C 146
Kraters	92 - C 168
	93 - D 204,4
Miscellaneous	
Imports	94 - D 206.9
	95 - C 523.30
	96 - C 348.11
	97 - D 213.6
	98 - C 166.4
	99 - C 245
Decoration	
Sherd	100 - C 227.7

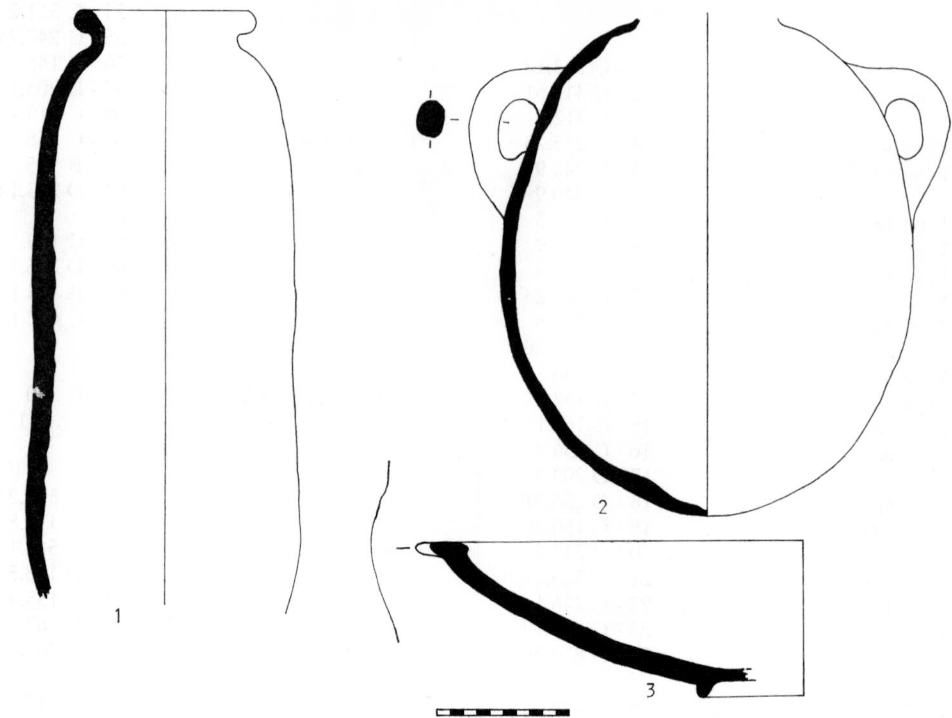

Fig. 76. Phase L

Miscellaneous		Jug	2 - B 167 (r.n. 1088)
Jar	1 - C 242 (r.n. 413)	Bowl type 17	3 - C 340 (r.n. 129)

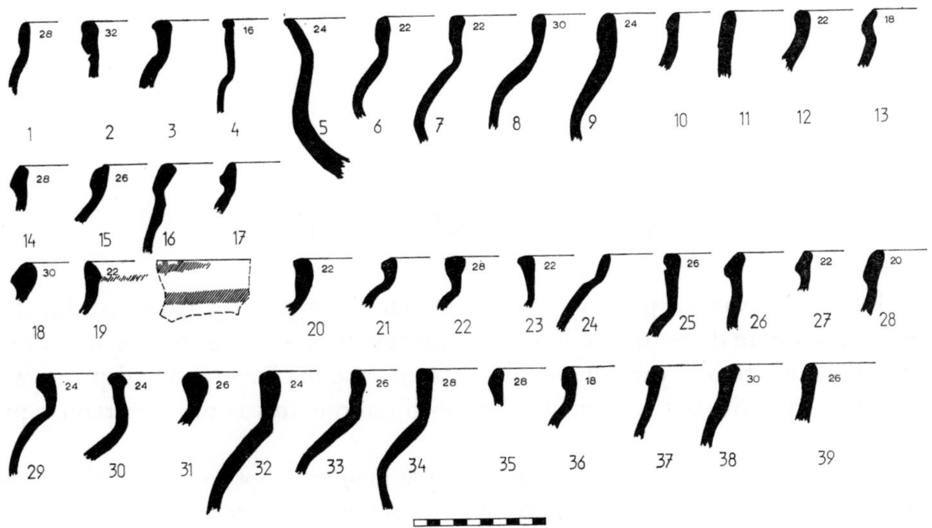

Fig. 77. 1-17, Phase H
18-28, Phase J
29-39, Phase K

Deep bowls	
Type 1c Phase H	1 - B 507.14
	2 - A 414.8
Type 3a	14 - A 522.19
	15 - A 410.22
	16 - F 416.10
	17 - D 260.6
Type 3b	13 - A 340.10
Type 3c	10 - A 339.2
	11 - D 256.43
	12 - A 616.20
Type 3d	3 - A 410.1
	4 - F 203.2
	5 - B 507.3
	6 - F 210.23
	7 - A 419.31
	8 - A 428.8
	9 - A 428.1
Type 1a Phase J	18 - A 258.4
Type 3c	19 - B 272.8
	20 - B 218.15
	21 - B 218
	22 - B 218
	23 - B 235
	24 - B 235
	25 - B 305.5
Type 3a	27 -
	28 - B 316.8
Type 3b	26 - A 174.25
Type 3a Phase K	37 - D 217.10
	38 - D 125.6
	39 - B 170
Type 3d	29 - B 145
	30 - D 239.12
	31 - C 423.2
	32 - D 217.15
	33 - C 359.38
	34 - C 427.116
	35 - B 170.12
	36 - B 427

CHAPTER NINE

DATING AND DATES

The dates of the various pottery types have been discussed. It is clear that this does not provide accurate dates for the individual phases. It is possible to give an estimate of the relative duration of each phase by comparing the thickness of the deposits with the amount of sherds. But without further qualifications this is too uncertain a procedure.

The statistical chart fig. 79 was originally made in an attempt to check the accuracy of the work on the typology as described in the previous chapters. If the division of the main types of pottery according to an analysis of the technical features were right, some pattern should show up in a graph consisting of the percentages of each type in each phase. We fully expected that each type might vary 15-20 points from an average percentage in each phase. The phases M-N had to be omitted from the graph. Phase A may have too many intrusive sherds from the sanctuary that cannot be readily recognized as such and phases M and N are too much disturbed. It should be noted that all the rims found during excavation were kept and that all the rims that could safely be attributed to the phases were used.

Fig. 79 is a chart showing the total amount of sherds found in each phase. Fig. 78 is a chart illustrating the percentages of each type in phases B - L as they are calculated in fig. 79, last column. From this have been omitted the bases, the minor types like lamps and fragments such as handles. As the percentages of each type have been calculated to one decimal the total in % is not exactly 100%, but never more than 0.4% from 100%. While comparing the main types, cooking pot type 3 has been included as this seems to reach its normal frequency after one phase (G), but bowls 17-18 were excluded as they show a slow increase through 4 phases (F-J) and seem to reach their normal frequency only in phase K. For the deep bowls two averages have been given (phases B-F and G-L: see below). The chart is thus mainly made up of the cooking pots 1 - 3, bowls 1 - 3, 4, 5 - 16, jars 1 - 2. The kraters have been added as an illustration of a small group. At the bottom of the chart the average % of the types is noted. The number of calculations is 6 types through 10 phases (=60). The deviation from the average in each case is as follows. Out of 60, 12 are one point or less from the average, 29 are 2 points or less from it, 42 are 2½ point or less from it and 49 are 3 points or less from it. 5 are 3 - 4 points away and 4 are more than 4 points from it. This means, for instance, that the chances are 5 to 6 that one finds 7.9% - 13.9% cooking pots in each phase, 7% - 13% bowls 4, 19.2% - 25.2% jars 1 etc. This holds good for phases D and F with less than 300 sherds, C, G and K with over 700 and B with nearly 1400.

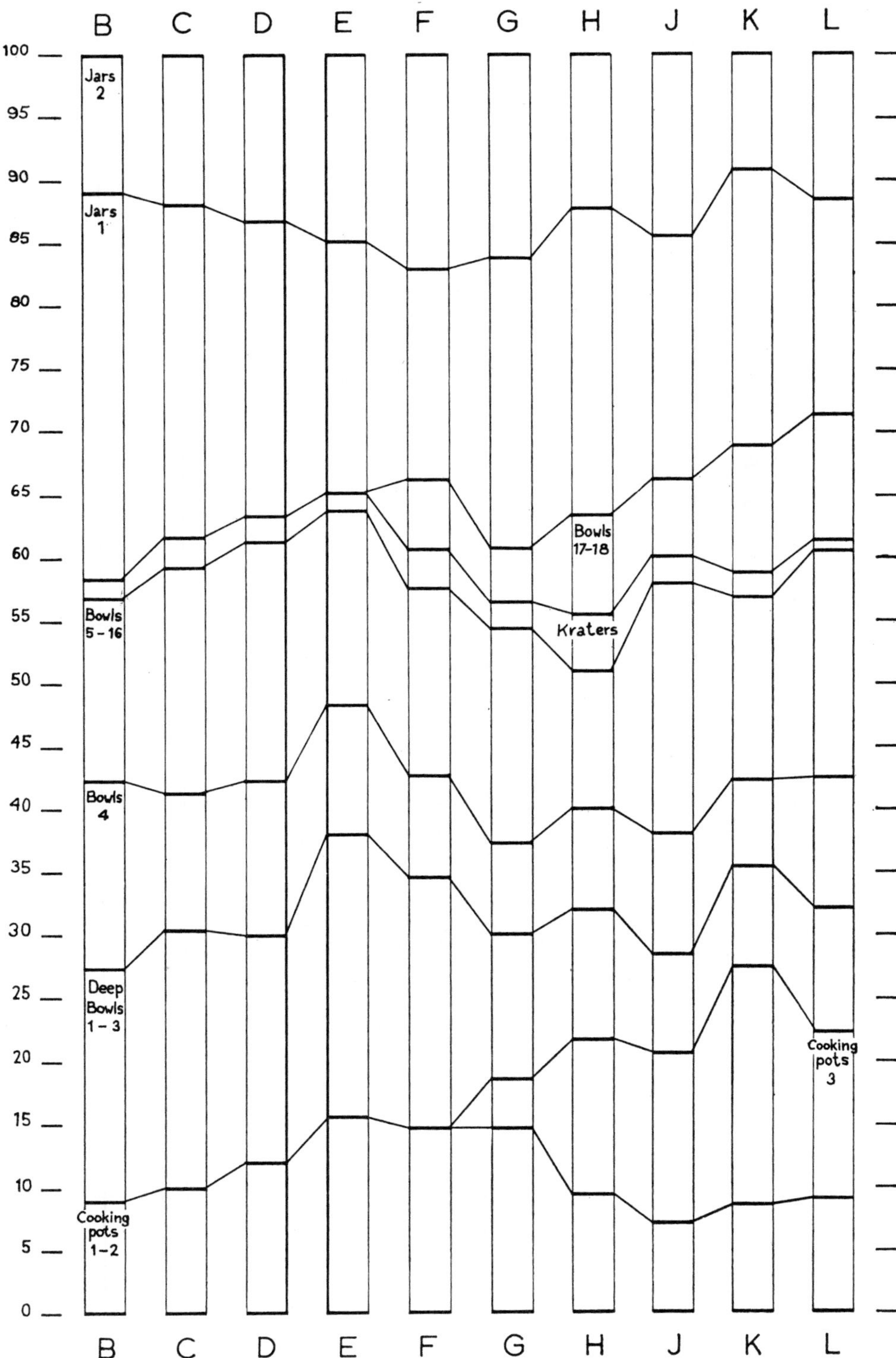

Fig. 78. Chart illustrating the percentages of the main types through phases B-L

Fig. 79. Statistical chart of the main types of phases A-L

Phase	*Cooking pots*		*Deep Bowls 1-3*	*Bowls 4*	*Bowls 5-16*	*Kraters*	*Bowls 17-18*	*Jars 1*	*Jars 2*	*Totals*
	1-2	*3*								
A	37-8.7%	0	106-25.3%	66-16%	85-20%	2-0.4%	0	102-24.1%	24-5.6%	424-6.5%
B	124-9%	0	252-18.3%	207-15%	197-14.3%	24-1.7%	0	424-30.8%	146-10.6%	1374-21%
C	76-10%	0	155-20.4%	85-11.2%	136-17.9%	21-2.7%	0	200-26.3%	86-11.3%	759-11.6%
D	34-12%	0	51-18%	35-12.4%	53-18.8%	7-2.4%	0	66-23.4%	36-12.7%	282-4.3%
E	81-15.2%	0	134-22.3%	63-10.5%	93-15.5%	9-1.5%	0	120-20%	90-15%	600-9.2%
F	41-14.7%	0	56-20%	25-8.9%	42-15%	9-3%	15-5.4%	46-16.5%	45-16.1%	279-4.2%
G	112-14.8%	32-4.2%	87-11.5%	56-7.4%	130-17.2%	17-2.2%	32-4.2%	172-22.8%	115-15.3%	753-11.5%
H	43-9.3%	57-12.3%	48-10.4%	37-8%	51-11%	21-4.5%	35-7.5%	112-24.3%	57-12.4%	461-7%
J	29-7.2%	54-13.5%	31-7.7%	39-9.7%	79-19.7%	13-3.2%	25-6.2%	78-19.5%	52-13%	400-6.1%
K	60-8.5%	135-19.1%	58-8.2%	50-7.1%	101-14.3%	20-2.8%	69-9.8%	156-22.1%	56-7.9%	705-10%
L	44-9.2%	65-13.5%	47-9.8%	50-10.4%	86-18%	5-1%	47-9.8%	82-17.1%	53-11%	479-7.3%
Aver-age:	10.9%		B-F: 19.8% G-L: 9.5%	10%	16.1%	—	—	22.2%	12.5%	6516-98.7%

The conclusion derived from this fact is that the potters had a fairly regular manufacturing programme. (The study deals with the destroyed products of this programme, but the breakage pattern was less regular as will be argued below). Throughout phases B - L there may be occasionally a much higher or lower amount of a certain type than the average would indicate, yet on the whole the pattern is consistent.

The potters certainly adjusted their "production programme" to the demands of their customers. They knew this demand from long experience. This does not mean that there was always enough pottery on the market (except perhaps in towns), nor that the potter would immediately start making a type that had run out. It is much more likely that, although they would indeed replenish their stock regularly, if by chance there were no cooking pots left they simply could not interrupt the production of the type they were working on just to produce a few extra cooking pots. It is much more likely that the customers had to wait until the lot the potters were working on was properly finished and fired. This means then that for weeks there would be no cooking pots for sale and that people had to do without them or try and fetch one from the next village. In other words, the pots could break at random, but the replacement was held up by the production procedures. Obviously no more pots could break, than had been produced.

It is important to try to reconstruct the limitations which restricted the potter from a more flexible production programme. For one thing he could not suddenly produce much more than the amount he was used to. The claybed may have been extensive enough for a much larger production, but the clay still had to be fetched by a man and a donkey. So too had the water and the fuel for the kiln. Material used as a temper had to be prepared. Clay had to be broken up, mixed with water and the temper material and then left to dry to a certain consistency. Once sufficiently wet it had to be divided and made into clay rolls and the air had to be beaten out of them. The clay rolls were made the size to be used for one type of pot. No more rolls would be made than the kiln or kilns could take. Kilns could not be used constantly but had to be rebuilt regularly. Drying, firing the kilns and cooling them off all had their fixed time schedule. From this it is clear that where pottery making is done by hand the process of making a hundred bowls can be timed step by step, and if the process has suddenly to be stepped up this can not be done by economizing on the time table. It can only be done by adding a greater labour force to the potters' personnel and working longer hours. In a primitive society this does not normally happen.

The potters would not produce more than was in regular demand and would certainly not flood the market. They might, in fact, constantly produce slightly too few vessels. For our purpose whether this was so or not is immaterial. The point is that it is in the nature of this kind of production to be steadily putting out a fixed quantity of products, and that these products were for a 100% utilized by the community and eventually discarded. It is not the discarding but the production that sets the pace. The annual production of a pottery must have been fairly constant.

There must also somehow be a fairly regular element in the whole process of breakage. Our percentages do not indicate that every household, for instance, had one cooking pot and one bowl type 4 against two storage jars type 1. It rather indicates that some types broke much more quickly than others, either because of the way they were used or as the result of constructional weakness.

This, for instance, may well be the case with jars type 1. As everybody knows, the type of crockery which looks fragile is usually handled with more care than rather sturdy looking pottery. The cooking pots were probably hardly ever taken from the three stones on which they stood above the fire, (supposing that that is how they were used), or taken out of the hollow in the floor, (if heating was done with hot stones submerged in the broth), so that they usually broke only when the base was burned through.

This is the reason why so few cooking-pot bases of types 1 and 2 were found. Besides this it should be noted that soft wares do not have a long life span and it is therefore not so surprising that there is an average duration for each type. The chart cannot be used for a reconstruction of a complete standard kitchen outfit. But the production does reflect the pattern of breakage in so far that the types were made in different but fixed quantities.

The Evidence for Dating

The division into phases is done according to changes in the plan in the excavated area. Theoretically it is possible that a phase lasted for only one year or less. On the other hand it is unlikely that a phase lasted longer than c. 25 years owing to the accumulation on the roads and the nature of the building materials. The first question then is: does the evidence found in the pottery statistics enable us to fix relatively the duration of each phase? Phase B contained 21% of the total amount of sherds found in phases A - L and phase C contained 11.6% of that amount. Does this mean that phase B lasted twice as long as phase C? Phase D with slightly less than 300 sherds and 4.3% of the total follows very closely the average of each type (deviations from the average are: cooking pots 1.1, deep bowls 1 - 3 1.8, bowls 4 2.8, bowls 5 - 16 2.7, jars 1 1.2 and jars 2 0.2). These 282 sherds closely reflect the potters' production and timetable. Twice the amount would mean that potters had produced twice as much pottery and therefore worked twice as long. The relative duration of phases A - D should therefore be something like 6.5:21:11.6:4.3. How far can this be substantiated by other evidence?

During his visit to Deir ʿAllā in 1964 Prof. Dr. H. T. Waterbolk of the Biologisch-Archaeologisch Instituut of Groningen University spent much time in studying the courtyard levels described in Ch. 1. Examining them in the main east-west baulks over the total width of the excavated area, he concluded that there were c. 40 deposits running continuously over the whole area. He suggested that this might indicate a regular and possibly annual deposit. If the interpretation of this type of courtyard level in phases A - D and the street levels in phases E - M is right, it is indeed an annual deposit (cf. p. 28). From the section drawings it is clear that the division of these 40 odd deposits is not far from that of the pottery quantities over these phases.

There are also some C 14 dates from Groningen. Grn. no. 4553 (D ʿA, D 816) is charcoal from one of the roof beams from the latest L.B. sanctuary, the destruction of which coïncides with the beginning of phase A. The result is 1180 B.C. ± 60.

Grn. no. 4749 (D.ʿA, D 276) comes from an ash deposit which marks the end of phase D. The result is 1190 B.C. ±50.

These two dates indicate a short period of time for phases A - D. The next date, Grn. no. 4554 (D.ʿA, D 331) comes from a small ash level in phase J and is calculated at 1050 B.C. ±40.

The next dating criterion is the evidence of pottery dating from other sites.

Evidence from Imported Material

Only one very small sherd of Cypriot origin was found and the attribution to phase K is uncertain, as it was found on the edge of an Arabic grave.

The only other imported material which is important for dating purposes is the "Philistine" type material. Some typical shapes and decorated sherds have been found. These are exclusively found in the phases A - D. If one had to assume that this pottery reached Deir ʿAllā from Philistine centres of manufacture in the south west of Palestine, and that it belongs to the distribution pattern as it is known up till now, then phase A could not be dated earlier than c. 1150 B.C. Philistine pottery has not, as yet, been found east of the central mountain ridge of Palestine, and apparently did not even reach Beth Shan. As it is comparatively scarce at Deir ʿAllā, its presence can be explained by trade. However, phases A - D are interpreted as industrial phases, typified by the melting and casting operations by an itinerant tribe of smiths. The "Philistine" pottery disappears from the scene with them; therefore it is quite possible that a) this material does not come from the south west of Palestine but from places where these smiths met other metal workers when obtaining their raw material, and b) these contacts may date from an earlier phase of the "trek" of the Peoples of the Sea. The meeting place could just as well have been Egypt as along the coast of the Lebanon. Until these relationships can be traced properly too much weight should not be put on the evidence of this pottery for dating purposes. At the moment it seems rather as though it disappears at Deir ʿAllā just at the time it is beginning to penetrate into Palestine.

When taken as a whole, the Deir ʿAllā repertoire comes close to the Afula repertoire, Str. III, apart from the typical Trans-Jordanian types. From the technical aspect of 10th cent. Palestinian pottery, this seems on the whole to show a further development which was not yet reached in Deir ʿAllā phase L. Some 10th century shapes are found in the "cistern" which follows phase M. As it is by no means certain that the Trans-Jordanian 10th cent. evolution of techniques and shapes ran closely parallel to the Palestinian evolution, what little evidence there is from Deir ʿAllā itself must be considered reliable. One instance is that the outer ridge on the necks of 10th cent.

jugs in Palestine is usually found half way up and not immediately under the rim, as it is in the 12th - 11th cent. There are few exceptions. Cf. flasks 15 and 16, Meg. II, Pl. 86, no. 1 and 2. It is common in Meg. Str. V, Hazor Str. X, cf. Lachish Tomb 521, type 364. It is not found in Afula Str. III, T.B. Mirsim Str. B 2. This development follows after phase M in Deir ʿAllā. The variety of rim shapes of cooking pot type 2 fits better in the 11th cent. Jars 1 c-g are replaced from phase G - H by jars 1 h-l, but this does not seem to be the case in Palestine, where the earlier variants go on much longer. Phase L could date from the last quarter of the 11th cent. B.C.

Evidence from Local Palestinian and Trans-Jordanian Wares

There are here several difficulties. The first one is that distinctions made in this study, for instance, between cooking pots type 1 and 2, deep bowls 1 and 3 are often not found in other publications. Types which in a publication look very much the same may have been made in a different way and cannot properly be compared until this has been established. In other words, the factor of technical development of the art of pot making should be taken into consideration and the question should be answered whether the potters in the different areas of Palestine and Trans-Jordan had reached the same technical stage at the same time. This is especially so for the rather more "isolated" areas like the Zerqa region. Theoretically it is certainly possible that the Deir ʿAllā potters were about a generation behind in development, or on the other hand more advanced in some aspects than their contemporaries elsewhere.

It has been demonstrated that throughout the periods of occupation on Tell Deir ʿAllā a considerable development in technical skill and forms took place. Moreover this development has been pin-pointed from step to step in the successive phases. The more important aspects of this development are listed here. Slab-closed and "cup"-shaped jar bases (type 1a and b) are common in phases A - E as well as type 1c, but after that 1a and 1b disappear quickly and 1c becomes the normal type. Cooking pot type 1 occurs from A to L, but diminishes quickly in numbers with the introduction of type 2 in phase E. From phase H on type 2 is the normal type (type 3 seems to have been a Trans-Jordanian type). Deep bowls types 1 and 3 occur in equal proportions in phases A - C, but in phases D - E type 1 diminishes in numbers and practically disappears after phase G. The tendency to burnish bowls increases from phase H onward. Type 4 bowls continue after phase E but becomes less frequent than in phases A - D. Jar type 1a does not occur after phases D - E. Type 1b continues in very small quantities. It is the most common type in phase B and not types 1c-g. Type 1d is after that the dominating type until phase G. The transition to types 1h-l comes in phases G - H and in phase K 1c-g are practically non existent.

Comparing this village pottery with, for instance, the ceramic repertoire from Afula Str. III A, dated c. 1150 - 1025, Beth Shan level VI, dated c. 1150 - 1000, Megiddo VI, dated c. 1150 - 1100, Tell Abu Hawam IV B, dated 1150 - 1000 and Tell Beit Mirsim, Stratum B 2, dated c. 1150-1000, one is forced to compress the development shown above into a picture which has lost its dimension of time. One has to reckon with the fact that phase E material stems from a development which took place elsewhere, that the phase D development was interrupted at Deir ʿAllā but continued elsewhere, that the phase L stage of development likewise continued in the same slow process as before and that pottery development took place in an equally slow but distinctive way in the towns mentioned above in so far as they were again inhabited after the disasters that destroyed them. Certain types were introduced at Deir ʿAllā that must have already existed at earlier stages elsewhere.

It is only from the burnishing experiments on bowl types 17 - 18 that one could probably deduce that these bowls were a fairly new invention, although this will remain uncertain until excavations elsewhere show a similar development in burnishing; therefore in order to fix a date from comparative study it must be known whether certain types that belong to a certain stratum, did in fact occur all the time, whether they belong only to the end or probably to the beginning and whether they were newly introduced. If one has to assume that the published pottery or the main bulk of it, belongs to the very end of that stratum, then frequency tables are essential. The frequency formula which is drawn up for the main types of the Deir ʿAllā repertoire is based on a minimum of three hundred diagnostic sherds per level. Within the six main groups of types there are considerable changes in the frequency of variations which are also based on the same minimum of three hundred sherds per level. This number then should be sufficient to make it possible to extract those types that had in fact already ceased to be made by the end of the occupation of a stratum or those that were just emerging.

Assuming then that phases E - L cover about one century and fall between c. 1150 and 1050, the formula for subdividing this period into seven phases of occupation would seem to be as reliable as any attempt to date the important phases E or G by comparative dating with other sites. It should be stressed that there is no reason to doubt that the dates mentioned above in connection with the destruction of various towns are wrong. However, it is to be hoped that the conclusions arrived at in connection with the problems of dating the phases of occupation at Deir ʿAllā have made it clear that a division of types based on an analysis of the technical aspects of the potter's work, together with statistical evidence concerning the frequency of these types, opens up the possibility of building up a much more finely divided time scale for dating.

As the Deir ʿAllā ceramic repertoire contains a number of types not found in Cis-Jordan, this repertoire can be said to be related to, but not identical with, the repertoires hitherto known, and therefore a slightly different development in the time scale must also be taken into account.

APPENDIX

Some Potter's Terms

Biscuit — Unglazed fired ware.

Blisters — Bubbles formed in the body of pots during firing due to rapid liberation of gases.

Bloom — see *scum*.

Body — The clay of which the pot is made. Also called *paste*.

Burnishing — involves rubbing down the surface of a green-hard shape with a smooth, hard, round faced tool.

Clay — Certain earths and crushed rocks when combined with water form sufficiently cohesive bodies to be made into shapes, which when hardened by fire become pottery. Clay is formed by the decomposition of felspars.

Coiling — A method of building up the walls of pots with ropes of clay. Often made on a turn table or tournette.

Collaring — Reducing the size of the opening of a pot as it spins on a wheel by compressing the clay with both hands.

Engobes — Another word for *slips*.

Fat clays — Highly plastic clays as opposed to lean, aplastic clays.

Felspar — An opaque white rectangular crystal found in granite which melts between 1200° and 1300° C. It is extensively used for bodies and glazes. When it loses its alkaline content through decomposition it becomes china clay and is thus the origin of most potter's clays.

Ferric and ferrous oxides — Red ferric oxide (Fe_2O_3) is almost infusible in an oxidized atmosphere, but both it and black magnetic iron oxide (Fe_3O_4) turn to the ferrous state in a reduced atmosphere. The iron oxides are the most important for providing the potter with red, yellow, brown, black, green and blue according to combination of atmosphere and temperature.

Firing — The burning or stoking of a kiln.

Flues — The passage ways for flames in kilns either between chamber and chamber, or chamber and chimney.

Flux — Any substance that promotes fusion.

Green hard — see *leather hard*.

Grog — Powdered, burnt fireclay of varying degrees of fineness, usually made from old sherds, crucibles etc.

Kneading — The process of mixing plastic clay to a homogeneous texture by hand or foot.

Lean clay — Non-plastic, short clay as opposed to long or fat, plastic clay.

Leather hard — Partially dried clay wares; texture is tough and aplastic. Also *green hard.*

Levigation — The method of refining clay by carrying it in a current of water which deposits the finer particles at successive removes from source.

Marls — Clays which contain a considerable proportion of lime.

Oxidation — The firing of a kiln in such a manner that combustion is complete and in consequence the burning gases are amply supplied with oxygen which causes metals in clay to give their oxide colours.

Reduction — in contradistinction to oxidation is a condition of burning gases in a kiln in which combustion is incomplete or smoky, the carbon present having the effect of reducing the oxides to their respective metal forms.

Rib — A tool made of wood or metal for smoothing the outer surface of a pot whilst it is being thrown or turned.

Scum — is caused before, during or after firing by soluble salts contained in the body migrating to the surface. Also *bloom.*

Shrinkage — During the process of drying, clays vary in their contraction up to a maximum of about 25%.

Silica — is one of the most important elements in ceramics; it serves as a refractory, an opening material in clays and as a flux according to circumstances.

Slips — Liquid clay.

Temper — Any material added to clay to reduce plasticity; also called a *filler* or opening material.

Throwing — The process of shaping cylindrical forms by hand with plastic clay upon a potter's wheel. Also *shaving.*

Tournette — Turn table from stone, matting etc. on which ring or coil built pots are made; hand rotated.

Turning — Shaving or paring leather hard clay from the walls or feet of pots.

Warping — of pots both whilst drying and in the kiln takes place from approximately the same cause; unequal heating and consequent shrinkage.

Wheel-throwing — is the making of pottery from a single lump of clay on a turn table that can rotate continuously over a fairly long period of time, the centrifugal force acting on the clay being utilized by the potter to form the vessel.

PLATES
II - XV

a) Tell Deir ʿAllā, looking n.

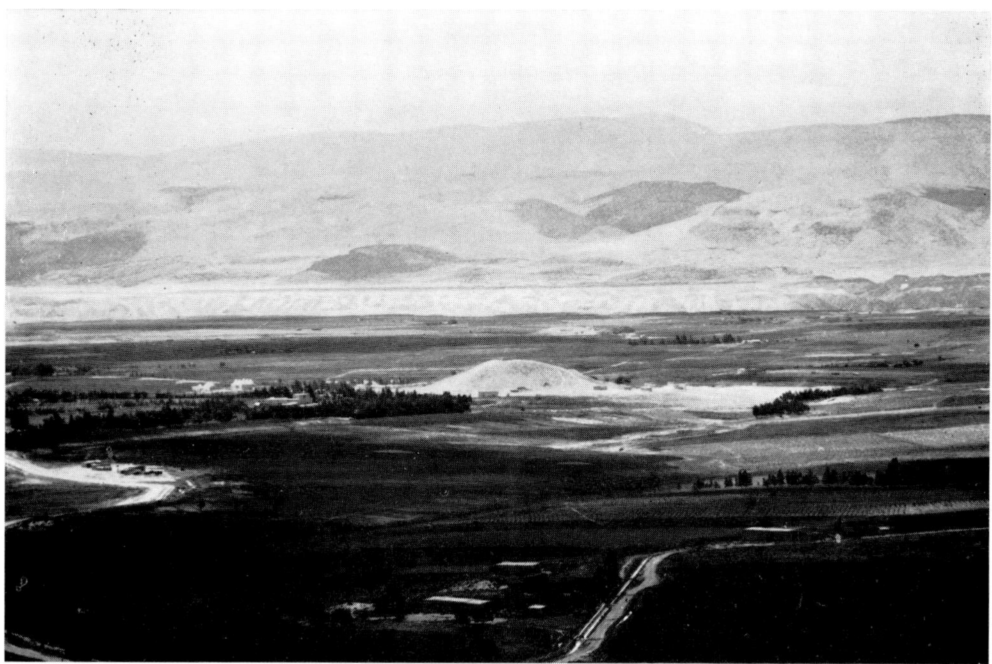

b) Tell Deir ʿAllā, looking w.

a) Tell Deir ʿAllā, looking s. (1960)

b) Tell Deir ʿAllā, looking e.

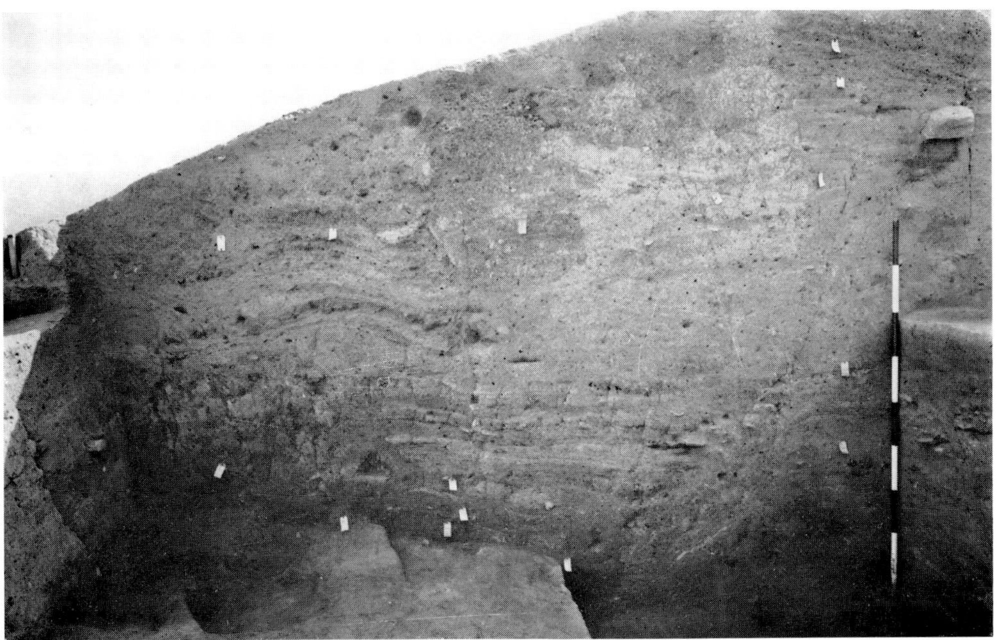

a) Photograph of section 5.50/15.50-20, with earthquake crack, dated to phase C

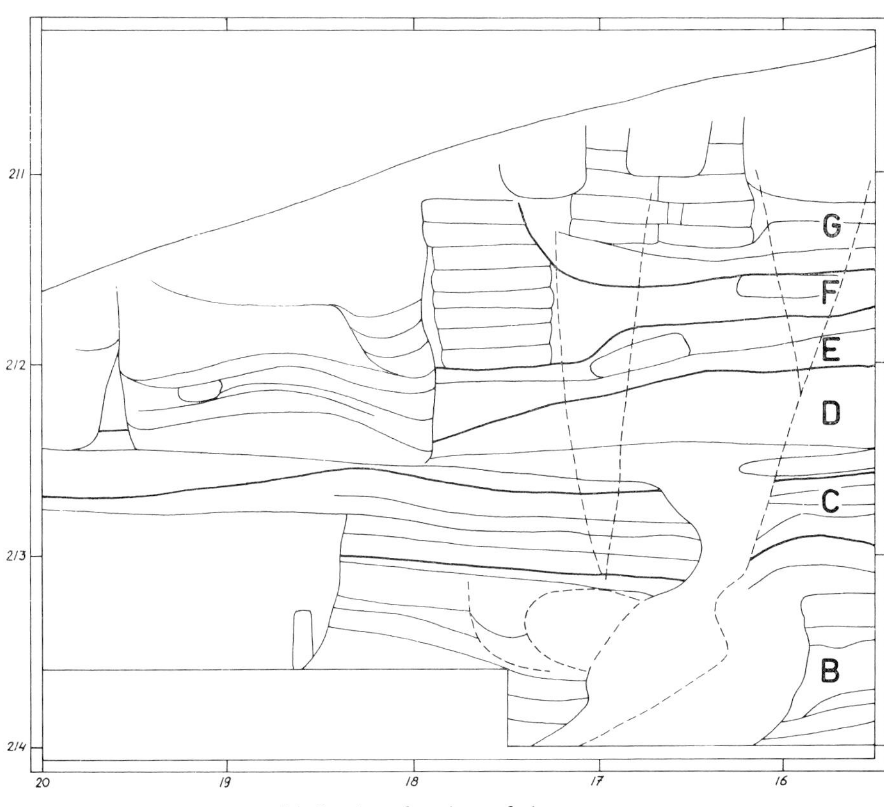

b) Section drawing of the same

a) A typical section through phases A-D courtyard deposits. Section to the left cf. fig. 3. The black burnt deposit clearly shows the disruptions by the shifting of the earth. In the centre: collapsed sides of a pit. Looking s.

b) Trench D, looking s. Foreground phase A courtyards. Burnt floor of B 1 furnace. Top left the round tower, (wall K 13), cut through wall F (G) 8. Below the round tower remains of wall E 7 and phase D courtyards

a) Phase A stone pavement (E 619), immediately on top of the ruins of the unfinished rebuilding of the L.B. sanctuary, looking s.e. To the left ash deposits from D 908, sunken into a pit

b) Phase A accumulation over the red burnt L. B. ruins. Thick ash deposit (D 908), interrupted by pits and cracks

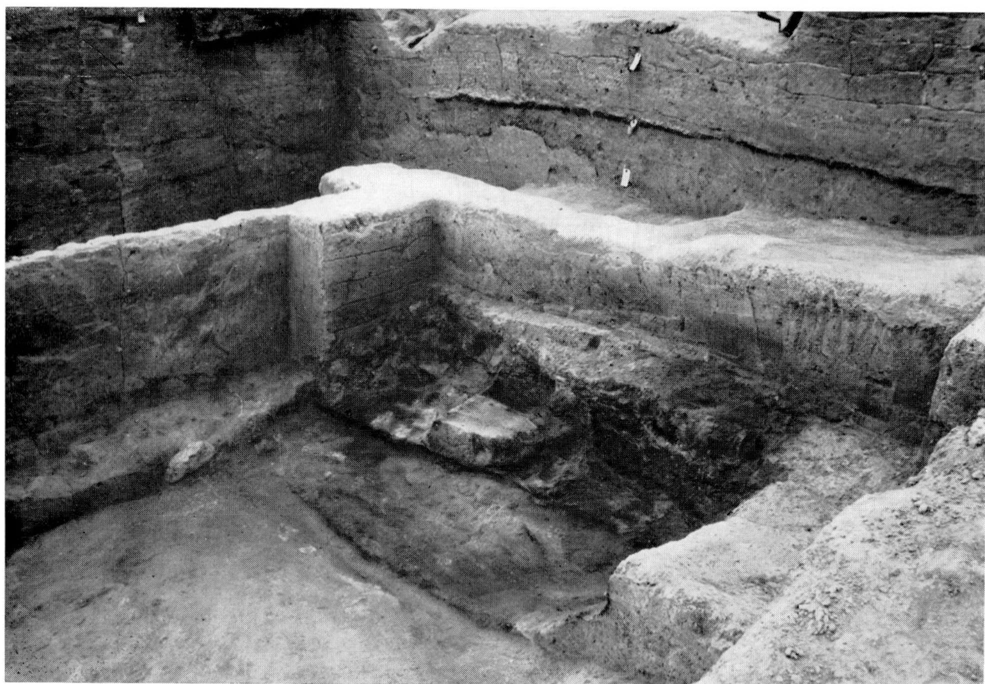

a) Phase B furnaces and walls B5 and 4, looking s.e. Three furnace floors run up against wall B 5

b) Phase F bread ovens in section, with thick ash deposits on the right. Cf. fig. 82, 0.50/16-18

a) Phase G bread ovens between walls G 3 and 4, looking s.

b) Foreground Wall F (G) 8, and walls F 7-6, looking w. N. of wall F 6 the stone fill. Wall G 9 is seen in section built over the stone fill of the phase F building

a) Wall F 8 in section, showing the reed 'foundation' and cracks running through it

b) Wall J 3 and wooden beam underneath. On the left wall J 1

a) Phase J road levels, looking s. and stone pavement running along wall J 1

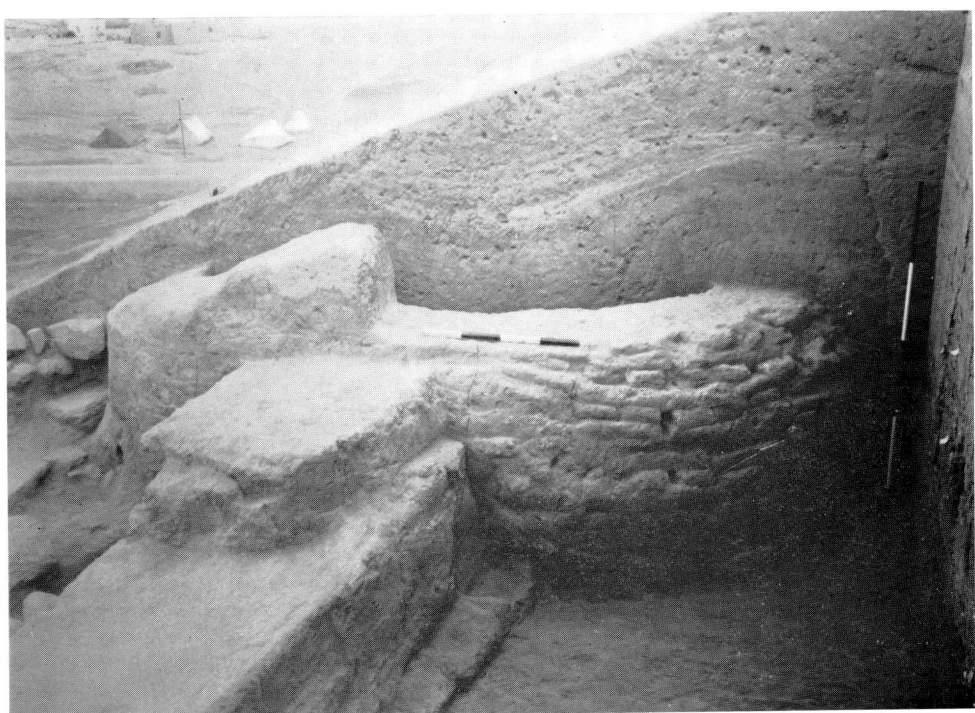

b) Phase K, wall K 13, the round tower dug into the ruins of wall F 8

a) Phase M, wall M 5

b) Phase M cistern, showing the circular pattern of the compressed fill in horizontal section

Fill of phase M cistern near the surface. In the centre, a wall of a house built on a clay deposit over the cistern with stone floor. In the burnt debris of this house, a mediaeval grave

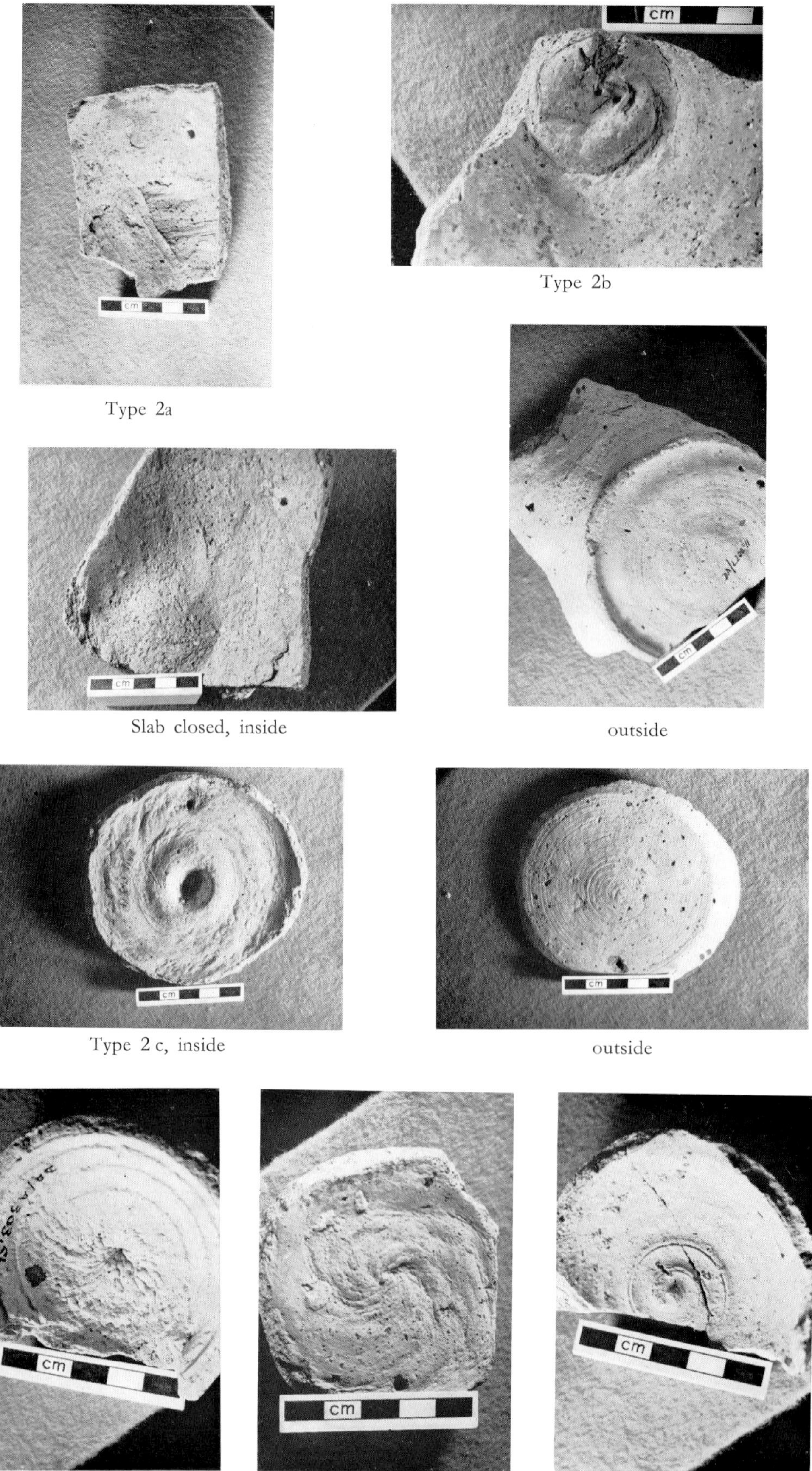

Type 2a

Type 2b

Slab closed, inside

outside

Type 2 c, inside

outside

Pinched

Interlocking

Thrown

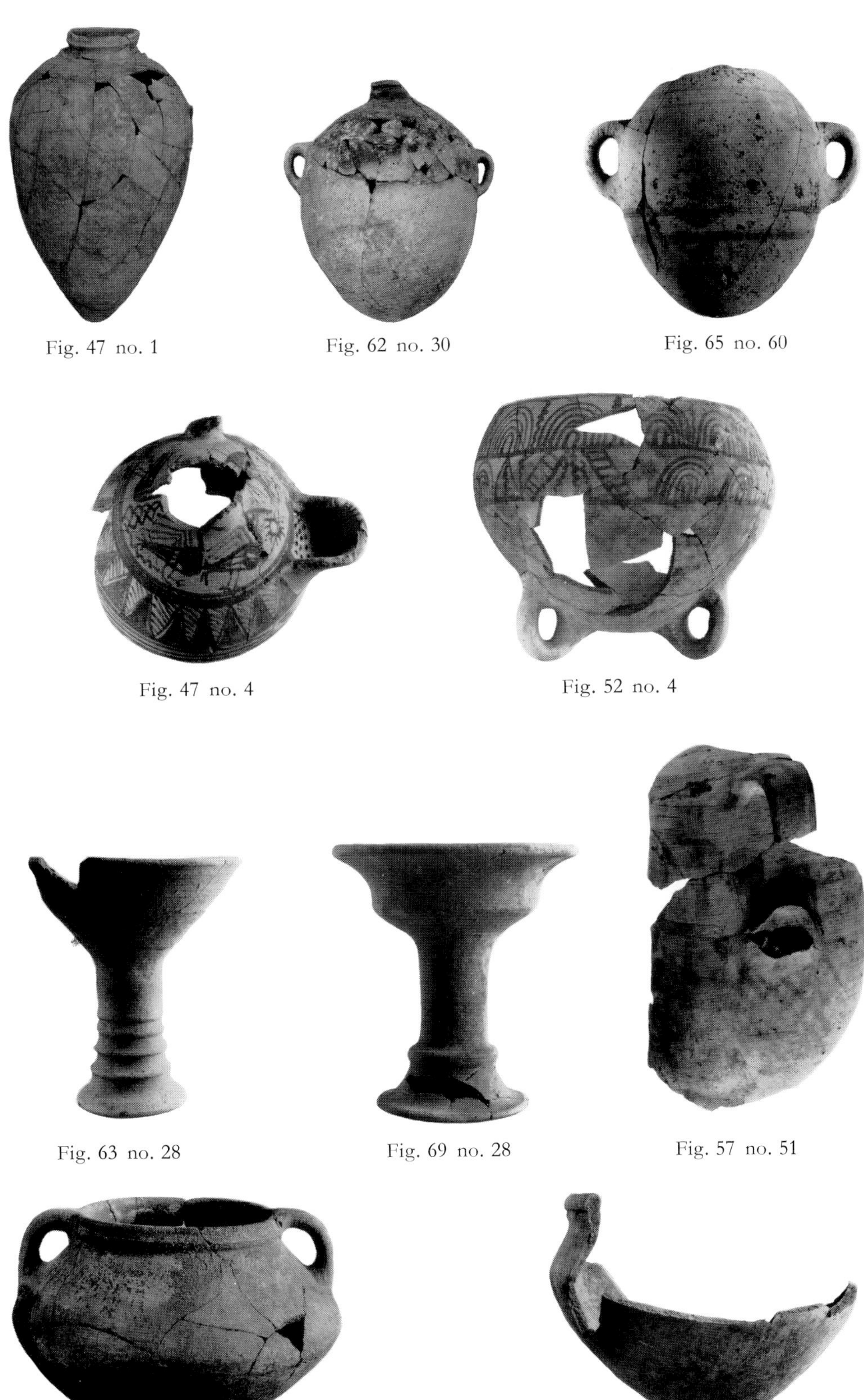

Fig. 47 no. 1

Fig. 62 no. 30

Fig. 65 no. 60

Fig. 47 no. 4

Fig. 52 no. 4

Fig. 63 no. 28

Fig. 69 no. 28

Fig. 57 no. 51

Fig. 74 no. 61

Fig. 68 no. 2

Fig. 50 no. 27

Fig. 75 no. 69

Fig. 73 no. 11

mensif dish, unstratified

unstratified, "import"

Fig. 68 no. 1

Fig. 62 no. 29

Fig. 70 no. 49

Fig. 70 no. 50

Fig. 70 no. 51

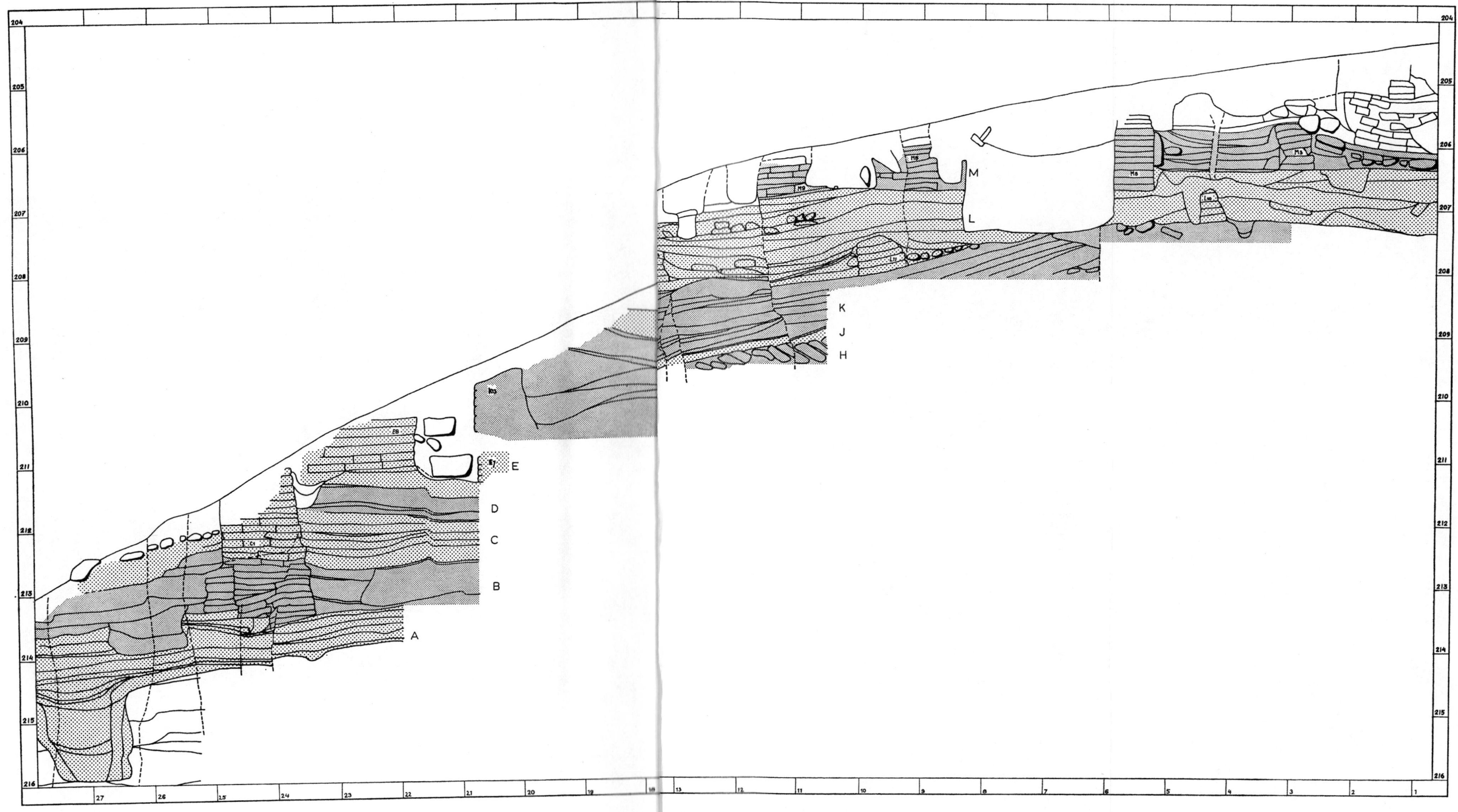

FRANKEN, *Excavations at Tell Deir 'Allā*

ated area.